TRANSGRESSIVE TALES

SERIES IN FAIRY-TALE STUDIES

General Editor
Donald Haase, Wayne State University

Advisory Editors
Cristina Bacchilega, University of Hawai`i, Mānoa
Stephen Benson, University of East Anglia
Nancy L. Canepa, Dartmouth College
Isabel Cardigos, University of Algarve
Anne E. Duggan, Wayne State University
Janet Langlois, Wayne State University
Ulrich Marzolph, University of Göttingen
Carolina Fernández Rodríguez, University of Oviedo
John Stephens, Macquarie University
Maria Tatar, Harvard University
Holly Tucker, Vanderbilt University
Jack Zipes, University of Minnesota

A complete listing of the books in this series
can be found online at wsupress.wayne.edu

TRANSGRESSIVE TALES

Queering the Grimms

EDITED BY KAY TURNER

AND PAULINE GREENHILL

Wayne State University Press

Detroit

16 15 14 13 12   5 4 3 2 1

Library of Congress Cataloging-in-Publication Data

Transgressive tales : queering the Grimms / edited by Kay Turner
and Pauline Greenhill.
p. cm. — (Series in fairy-tale studies)
Includes bibliographical references and index.
ISBN 978-0-8143-3481-2 (pbk. : alk. paper) — ISBN 978-0-8143-
3810-0 (e-book)
1. Kinder- und Hausmärchen. 2. Grimm, Wilhelm, 1786–1859—
Criticism and interpretation. 3. Grimm, Jacob, 1785–1863—Criticism
and interpretation. 4. Queer theory. 5. Homosexuality in literature.
6. Fairy tales—Germany—History and criticism. I. Turner, Kay,
1948– II. Greenhill, Pauline.
GR166.T67 2012
398.20943—dc23
2012012523

Published with the assistance of a fund established by Thelma Gray
James of Wayne State University for the publication of folklore and
English studies.

All illustrations by Bettina Hutschek © 2012

Designed by Ashley Muehlbauer
Typeset by Maya Rhodes
Composed in Scala, ScalaSans, and Fidelia Script

CONTENTS

Queering the Tales

Beyond the Grimms

PREFACE

The *Transgressive Tales* project began in 1998 when Pauline Greenhill, along with her University of Manitoba women's studies colleague Janice Ristock, invited Kay Turner to teach a course on feminist and queer theory and folklore in the summer semester at the University of Winnipeg. Kay devoted a portion of that most enjoyable task to feminist interpretations of the fairy tale. In the process, she became at first intrigued, then somewhat obsessed, with queer possibilities in the Grimm brothers' *Children's and Household Tales*, such as "Frau Trude" (ATU 334), "Mother Holle" (ATU 480), and "The Three Spinners/Spinsters" (ATU 501). In particular, the class period for which she assigned reading another Winnipeg scholar Kay Stone's "The Curious Girl," based on the Grimms' "Frau Trude," was revelatory for this Kay. She saw the possibility for queerly reading that tale of a girl's willfulness, as will be evident later in this book. Since those days in Canada, Kay has continued to dedicate time in her Performed Story in Culture classes at New York University to feminist and queer readings of the Grimms, and Kay and Pauline have both worked, sometimes alone and sometimes in tandem, to keep the *Transgressive Tales* project moving forward.

Kay and Pauline acknowledge and express their gratitude for three grants that have served as magical fiduciary objects aiding us in our quest: two from the University of Winnipeg and one from the Research Development Initiatives of the Social Sciences and Humanities Research Council of Canada (SSHRC). They invaluably funded meetings, research assistance, administrative expenses, the index, and getting the word out about the project early on. In particular, we thank all our friends at the University of Winnipeg Research Office, especially research goddess Jennifer Cleary, and Garry Pinard of SSHRC. Appreciation is also extended to the Performance Studies Department at New York University, especially department chair José Muñoz, for allowing a maverick folklorist to teach and learn from marvelous students over the past ten years. The fruits of that labor are evident in the work of four students—Andrew Friedenthal, Elliot Mercer, Joy Brooke Fairfield, and Kevin Goldstein—presented herein. We were fortunate to count on the able and enthusiastic research and editorial assistance of Emilie Anderson-Grégoire, Joy Brooke Fairfield, Bettina Hutschek, Jeana Jorgensen, Morgan Levy, Kendra Magnusson, Krista Miranda, and Vanessa Roberts. We thank Bettina Hutschek for her compelling, entertaining, and queerly quirky line drawing illustrations.

We also thank many fellow travelers, whose work inspired us but did not make it into the final text. From a *Transgressive Tales* forum at the American Folklore Society meetings in Atlanta, Georgia, in 2005, we would like to acknowledge the following: Regine Joseph's rethinking of illicit intergenerational desire in "The Old Beggar Woman"; Joe Goodwin's riff on the stereotypically feminine characteristics of male heroes in tales such as "The Golden Goose" (ATU 571/513B); Kathleen Manley's reading of A. S. Byatt's short story "The Thing in the Forest" as a "re-situation" (de Caro and Jordan 2004) of the Grimms' "Snow White and Rose Red" (ATU 426); and Camilla Mortensen's examination of counternarratives of female agency embedded in tales of banished girls such as "The Handless Maiden" (ATU 706) and "Love Like Salt" (ATU 923). At the Folklore Studies Association of Canada meetings in Sherbrooke, Quebec, in 1999, some of Kay's University of Winnipeg seminar students presented their term papers to a wider audience. Nathalie Cohen reinterpreted "Mistress [Frau] Trudy [Trude]" as part of a canon of queer-positive and celebratory literature for a desirably queer world; Maria Fowler revisited "Mother Holle" in terms of a conflict between society's laws and the body's desires; and Kathleen Shellrude looked at "The Girl Without Hands [The Handless Maiden]" as a journey to queer desires satiated by an/other woman.

On the difficult and sometimes treacherous road to publication, our magical helpers were Annie Martin, Donald Haase, Kristin Harpster, and Maya Rhodes of Wayne State University Press, who cleared seemingly immovable objects from our path and lighted the way when no others could see it. Other helpers included the two anonymous reviewers for WSU Press, who matched warm appreciation with careful attention and intellectual rigor; fabulous copy editor Carissa Vardanian, who answered all queries with preternatural speed and efficiency; and John Dobson, who constructed the index in a trice! Pauline adds a note of thanks to Kel Morin-Parsons, whose LOL e-mails helped get her through the last day of editing before sending the first draft manuscript to the press. Kay thanks her own "happily ever after" princess, Mary Sanger. And, finally, we hope this work finds favor with the spirit of the late, great Eve Kosofsky Sedgwick, a transgressive gal extraordinaire!

Transgressive Tales flavors the cauldron of fairy-tale interpretation with queer, gay, trans, and feminist spice, showing that old stories forever contain new meanings. We lift the lid off specific tales that forefront unconventional relational and sexual possibilities and problems that remain undertheorized in the scholarly literature on the *Household Tales*. We preheat the oven with a few theoretical concepts, then our transgressive colleagues toss fresh ingredients into the pot in their interpretive papers. We close with some new recipes in the form of transgressive versions of already transgressive tales. Delicious! And nutritious!

INTRODUCTION

Once Upon a Queer Time

KAY TURNER AND
PAULINE GREENHILL

> Transgression carries the limit right to the limit of its being.
> —Michel Foucault, "A Preface to Transgression"

OPENING FORMULA

In the two hundred years or so that the Grimm brothers' *Kinder- und Haus-märchen* (*KHM, Children's and Household Tales*) has circulated in publication, its stories have been reproduced in countless editions; translated many times; interpreted by scholars, writers, and artists; and rewritten from a number of theoretical and political perspectives. The *KHM* has inspired compelling interpretations representing a wide variety of cultures, historical periods, and disciplinary directions. Indeed, the Grimms' versions, arguably more than those of other compilers and scholars, have shaped and defined academic and popular understandings of the fairy-tale genre. Thus, this work focuses primarily, though not exclusively, on the Grimm oeuvre.

In the history of narrative and folklore scholarship, the Grimms' *KHM* became canonical despite scholarly skepticism about the collection's authenticity in representing oral tradition or the stories as originally told. The first edition of the *KHM* was published in 1812 and 1815, and over a period of forty years, the brothers, especially Wilhelm, revised, edited, sanitized, and bowdlerized the tales, publishing the seventh and final edition in 1857.

Indeed, a source of continuing intrigue in analyzing the Grimms' redactions stems from their assiduous and continuous expurgation and removal of sexual—read heterosexual—details.[1] Maria Tatar (e.g., 1987, 1992) and Jack Zipes (e.g., 1983a, 1988a, 1988b), among others, have followed this story within the story of the fairy tales' emergence. For example, by the time "Little Red Cap" (ATU 333) had been worked over, by Charles Perrault at the end of the seventeenth century, then by the Grimms at the beginning of the nineteenth century, Red's bawdy striptease for the wolf masquerading as grandmother had disappeared along with references to peeing in the bed and the scatological "making cables."[2]

But if the Grimms and other earlier and later collectors attended vigilantly to the task of excising heterosex, they likely never even thought about ridding the tales of homosexual implications or other counternormative, counterhegemonic queer alliances. We nevertheless note a lack of transgender—cross-dressing or sex change—in their collection (see, for example, chapter 8 in this volume) but frequent expression of transbiology—man to frog or woman to swan, for example. Yet despite the Grimms' repeated moves to expurgate sexual, nonretributively violent, and class-inappropriate references and interactions within the tales, these stories don't just provide instruction in compliant behavior for children but offer considerable significance for adults. Awash in perverse possibilities, they beg for a queer(y)ing. Hence, the fertile ground we plow in this book.

The long-lived history of oral and literary fairy tales offers remarkable testimony to their enduring popularity. Certainly no other folk narrative genre has been as widely told and retold, interpreted and reinterpreted, or translated into other art and performance forms: ballet, folk dance, films, novels, short stories, games, cartoons, and graphic and other visual arts.[3] Writers from A to Z have reworked the genre—from Margaret Atwood (1993), A. S. Byatt (1998), and Angela Carter (1979a) to Eudora Welty (1942) and Fay Weldon (1977) (see, e.g., Preston 1995; Bacchilega 1997; de Caro and Jordan 2004; Roemer and Bacchilega 2001). *Transgressive Tales* is in league with those who have found much to say about the profound meanings of fairy tales: the psychological reflections of Marie-Louise von Franz (1996), Alan Dundes (1993), and Bruno Bettelheim (1976); the culturally and socially attentive scholarship of Ruth Bottigheimer (e.g., 1987); the wide-ranging historical scholarship of Jack Zipes (e.g., 1979); the lesbian reworkings of Emma Donoghue (1997; see Orme 2010) and Jeanette Winterson (1989; see chapter 6 of this volume); the fierce reimaginings of Angela Carter (1979a; see chapter 5 of this volume); the art of Cindy Sherman and Meret Oppenheim (discussed in Marina Warner 1994) as well as of Kiki Smith (see Bernheimer 2006) and Carrie May Weems (see Watts 1993); the postmodern interpretations of Cristina Bacchilega (1997 and chapter 1 of this volume) and Jessica Tiffin (2009); the essays collected by Christine A. Jones and Jennifer Schacker (2012); and the feminist revisions of Kay Stone (e.g., 2008), Cathy Lynn Preston (2004), Maria Tatar (e.g., 2004b), Marina Warner (e.g., 1994), and those compiled and discussed by Donald Haase (2004a, 2004b). Yet, as Vanessa Joosen (2011) points out, queer readings seem absent from feminist fairy-tale criticism, and even in Haase's collection, only one article, by Patricia Anne Odber de Baubeta (2004), mentions such interpretation, dealing with late twentieth-century examples.

QUEER(Y)ING TALES

Transgressive Tales opens exploration of some specifics of the imaginative worlds of fairy tales—queer, lesbian, homosexual, transgender, and transbiological—for their function not only as fantastical creations but also as incarnations calling for sustained and informed inquiry. Surely the genre is not only the fair(y)est of them all but also the queerest of them all. Applying contemporary queer eyes to the Grimm guys, the lens shifts focus from normative sexual dynamics—like the happy ending of wedded heterosexual bliss—or patriarchal moral lessons—like the punishment of curious girls—to the tales' internal struggles, suggestive of multiple and more complex desires and their perversely performative nature.[4] Fairy tales, oral or literary in derivation, feature human and non-human principal characters in developed fictional narratives, along with elements of wonder and the supernatural. In the realm of the simultaneously weird and wonderful, traditional fairy tales may be peerless. The worlds they imagine, and the characters who inhabit them, have always been drawn far beyond the limits of the actual world and its characters. Imaginative worlds can, arguably, open conceptualization. As Jack Zipes put it,

Folk and fairy tales remain an essential force in our cultural heritage, but they are not static literary models to be internalized for therapeutic consumption. Their value depends on how we actively produce and receive them in forms of social interaction which leads toward the creation of greater individual autonomy. Only by grasping and changing the forms of social interaction and work shall we be able to make full use of the utopian and fantastic projections of folk and fairy tales. (1979, 177)

Transgressive Tales thus willfully crosses boundaries of scholarship, and we read the Grimms anew—and askew.

Fairy tales are queer, at the very least, in the nineteenth-century usage of the term, to mean odd, strange making, eccentric, different, and yet attractive. Roderick McGillis, addressing "the queering of fairy" in George MacDonald's literary fairy tales, comments, "By queer, I mean what MacDonald and his contemporaries meant by the word: that which is puzzling or confusing" (2003, 88). But the genre and its tales also explore queerness in the sense given by twentieth- and twenty-first-century understandings (see Pugh 2008); they implicate lives and theories relating to sexes and sexualities beyond the mainstream and deviating from the norm (see Seifert 2008). Annamarie Jagose helpfully deconstructs the term, noting that "some claim that it radically erodes the last traces of an oppressive gender coherence, whereas others criticise its pan-sexuality as reactionary, even unfeminist" (1996, 2–3). Queer, she argues, can be understood in terms of "those gestures or analytical models which dramatise incoherencies in the allegedly stable relations between chromosomal sex, gender and sexual desire. Resisting that model of stability—which claims heterosexuality as its origin when it is more properly its effect—queer focuses on mismatches between sex, gender, and desire" (3).

Yet defining principles of queer also include an emergent body of literature that addresses issues specifically dealt with in fairy tales: concerns about marginalization, oddity, and not fitting into society generally. Queerness, then, embraces more than sex/gender/sexuality to deal with the problematics of those who for various reasons find themselves outside conventional practices. As Lee Edelman defines the term, *queerness* "marks the excess of something always unassimilable that troubles the relentlessly totalizing impulse informing normativity" (Dinshaw et al. 2007, 189). Such excess is discoverable in the traditional fairy tale. Nevertheless, with only a few exceptions (e.g., Solis 2007; Greenhill 2008),[5] queer fairy-tale readings have looked at revisions and rewritings, not at traditional texts (see Joosen 2011, 111–17).

Trans theorist Susan Stryker distinguishes queer from transgender theory: "If queer theory was born of the union of sexuality studies and feminism, transgender studies can be considered queer theory's evil twin: it has the same parentage but willfully disrupts the privileged family narratives that favor sexual identity labels (like *gay*, *lesbian*, *bisexual*, and *heterosexual*) over the gender categories (like man and woman) that enable desire to take shape and find its aim" (2004, 212). Under trans, we include both transgender and transbiology. Here, *transgender* signals a disconnection between conventional gender identity (social, cultural, psychological) and canonical sex identity (biological, physiological). As an encompassing term, it includes transsexuals, who identify as another sex than that of their birth, who may or may not want or enact hormonal or surgical interventions to match their sex identity to their gender identity; intersexuals, whose biological identity includes markers of both male and female; cross-dressers or transvestites, who clothe themselves as another sex; and genderfuckers, who feel their sex/gender identity to be between, beyond, or in addition to the binaries of male and female.[6] We recognize that these are not the only or even the least contested uses of the term (see, e.g., Heyes 2000; Hird 2002a; Namaste 2005; Noble 2006; Stryker and Whittle 2006).

Transbiology is a more recently developed and broadly interpretable concept. Scholars such as Sarah Franklin (2006), Judith Halberstam (2008), Myra Hird (2004, 2006), and Noreen Giffney (Hird and Giffney 2008) have begun to map the territory, but we retroactively include much anticipatory scholarship (Berger and Walker 1989; Haraway 1991, 1997). Franklin calls transbiology "a biology that is not only born and bred, or born and made, but *made and born*" (2006, 171). When manufacture precedes parturition, she includes cloning, stem cell research, and embryology. She notes, "It is a world of cyborgs, but also of mixtures in which it is the symmetry of parts that allows translation, so that the mouse, the sheep, the cow, the pig and the dog move together as animal models susceptible to re-engineering and improvement" (176). The fairy tale, like myth, imaginatively anticipates the transbiological wonders and worries of today. Transbiology here includes animals or humans who masquerade as or transform into another species (in whole or in part) and/or who otherwise mess with hard-and-fast distinctions between species, including between human and non-human.

Perhaps more than any other kind of folk narrative, the fairy tale's generic conventions define a kind of queerness in the story's own form. This quality, first and foremost due to the interpenetration of fantasy and reality and the acceptance of a magical world within the tales, allows for eccentricity and strange making. It also invites ambiguity and ambivalence, which often spill into the arena of sex and gender. Queerness and temporality uniquely meet in the fairy tale. Elizabeth Freeman calls normative temporality "a mode of implantation through which institutional forces come to seem like somatic facts" (2007, 160). If straight time acts more like a straitjacket, the queer time of fairy tales invites participation in the realm of enchantment. The experience of enchantment knocks out previously binding temporalities and dominances; it refreshes potentiality. The fairy-tale surface story may be moralistic, socially restrictive, and gender/sexuality normative, but the fairy tale's deep structure, represented by the realm of enchantment, is antimoralistic, agency oriented, and gender/sexuality expressive in terms that challenge normativity. As Tiffin puts it, while the fairy tale's "basic principles—life, death, love, hate, quest, challenge, reward, punishment—are those of human existence, the world in which such principles are enacted is significantly different from the real, so that normal expectations are completely transcended" (2009, 13). Transcending the normal, we argue, opens possibilities for rising above sociocultural expectations.

A second feature, the fairy tale's use of ordinary people as primary protagonists often faced with the psychosexual challenges all humans face (love, marriage, desire, jealousy), centers a number of narratives on the quest for identity and thus makes them sources for expressing unconscious fears and desires. Steven Swann Jones summarizes this feature, following the extensive work of Max Lüthi, saying, "Fairy tales are dominated by the fantastic perspective, which is a product of the unconscious, intuitive and imaginative aspects of the mind" ([1995] 2002, 12). Or, as Tiffin argues, "Fairy tale symbols function resonantly rather than illustratively to suggest multiple meanings rather than to illustrate one aspect of reality" (2009, 15).

If queer and trans interpretations have hitherto been lacking in that mix of multiple meanings, we now liquidate that lack, remembering the wise words of one famous old story maker, Gertrude Stein: "It takes time to make queer people" ([1925] 1968, 21). Our time has come. And at the heart of our project are queer fairy tale listeners or readers. They may be straight, gay, bi, trans; young, old, middle-aged; come from Boston or Beijing. But what distinguishes them most of all is a propensity for what Bonnie Zimmerman (1993) calls "perverse reading." Our perversity willfully turns away from the conventionally correct or responsible. That's just the kind of riot grrrl scholars we are. But we have, nevertheless, some eminently respectable forebears. We follow on feminist reader-response and German reception theory, which clear the way for a direct acknowledgment of the potential for queerly reading the Grimms. For example, in a critique of Heinz Rölleke's implicit campaign for "responsibility" in tale scholarship—his insistence on an objective evidentiary history of each narrative—Haase comes to the aid of the irresponsible and, we would add, the perverse. Defending the fairy tale's tendency to invite multiple levels of interpretation, he maintains that "1) fairy tales consist of chaotic symbolic codes that have become highly ambiguous and invite quite diverse responses; and 2) these responses will reflect a recipient's experience, perspective, or predisposition" (1993, 235). Ultimately, he maintains, the significance of the fairy tale lies in its reception (234). Haase is in synch with queer scholar Freeman who, writing on the dialectic between sex and temporality, suggests that "as new readerly responses become possible, new modes of writing emerge and older modes become suddenly, dazzlingly accessible to us. Readerly responses, erotic in the broadest sense of the term, depend on the sensations possible, thinkable, and tangible in a particular historical period" (2007, 168).

And so the queer eye lands on a fairy tale and begins to read, to work. For according to Roland Barthes, reading *is* a kind of work: "To read, in fact, is a labor of language" (1974, 11). The written fairy tale offers an ideal working text in Barthes's sense; it impels the labor of dialogic interaction. Reader and text participate in a making of meanings similar to those associated with the oral precedents of teller and story. A fairy tale cannot finally or necessarily mean anything; it can only reveal particular meanings through the performance of the reading act. Theorizing is but one part of that revelation, which is why this book offers in closing two complete tales as well as analyses/interpretations.

But fairy tales—and theory—also offer pleasure. "The pleasure of accepting wonder in experiencing the fairy tale is . . . complex, based both in the enjoyment of the marvelous and in the geometric pleasures of pattern" (Tiffin 2009, 19). For us, part of the enjoyment relates to four recurring qualities—the eroticized, tabooed, perverse, and women focused. All provide alternatives and sometimes even active resistance to mainstream cultural constructions. These four are sometimes quite overt, and sometimes "secret messages . . . inscribed in plain sight" (Tatar 1987, 177). By no means discrete, they interweave in complex fashion in the tales, as they do in other symbolic manifestations of discourse. We use the familiar tale of "Little Red Riding Hood" as a demonstration (see, e.g., Dundes 1989; Zipes 1983b). As with every orally based fairy tale, multiple versions exist, and like most that have become popular and literary over the past three hundred years, significant aspects have been expurgated as they increasingly have been directed toward children.

In terms of eroticism, many fairy tales express, explore, and celebrate sexual content. Some folklore scholars (e.g., S. S. Jones [1995] 2002) argue that traditional stories must be subdivided (implicitly on the basis of their sexual and violent content) into those intended for small children, those for developing adolescents, and those for mature adults. Yet we need not simply accept this distinction as inevitable, especially given that audience members will understand texts differently (see, e.g., Radner 1993; Falassi 1980). Our project is more interested in how the erotic—ever fluid and subjective—can be said to radiate across time. In "Little Red Riding Hood," the wolf's intentions toward Red may be understood as fulfilling desires for food, for sex, or both. As eloquently argued by Rosalind Coward, food and sex inter-refer in many aspects of Euro–North American discourse,[7] from the terms of endearment that are also food terms—honey, sweetheart, peach, sugarplum (1985, 87)—to the ways in which appetites for food and sex are equally deemed illicit and pornographic, especially for women (102; see also Greenhill 1998 and chapters I and II of this volume).

A second aspect of the tales involves their citation, indeed glorification, of a series of cultural taboos; as Maria Tatar succinctly puts it, the Grimm tales deal with "murder, mutilation, cannibalism, infanticide, and incest" (1987, 3). For example, references to the wolf eating Red and her grandmother implicate a kind of cannibalism (see also Tatar 1992, 2004a). Marianna

Torgovnick (1990, 179) articulates how cannibalism becomes so much a quintessential "unthinkable" as to stand metonymically for the primitive and savage itself. Although cannibalism signifies eating one's own species, its primary meaning involves humans eating humans, an activity so proscripted that the tale mitigates it. While the wolf (the eater) is arguably not perfectly human (and thus unlike his food), his ability to speak and disguise himself marks him as not perfectly wolf, either. Note that other Grimm tales are not so sensitive on this practice; "The Juniper Tree" (ATU 720) involves a kind of incestuous cannibalism, where a father eats his own son, murdered by the mother, as a black pudding or stew (see Greenhill and Brydon 2010). Yet, in this volume, Turner discusses the evolution of the witch Frau Trude's (in ATU 334) desires from cannibal to connubial, thus further complicating the relationship between the sensual and the criminal in Grimms' tales.

Perversity in the fairy tales arises because when sex and sexuality are involved or implicated, they do not necessarily take the form of mainstream heterosexual practices. Certain tales present a choice to turn away from heteronormativity. Fairy tales reference same-sex erotic attraction, symbolically yet multivocally. One could argue that the Grimm tales, for example, largely reference a female-centered world, where relationships between women—whether or not they are sexualized and/or eroticized—become the primary areas of concern (see, e.g., chapters 7 and 11 of this volume). They also open possibilities for understanding female desires and women's *jouissance* outside heterosexual relationships (see chapter 1 of this volume).

Finally, some feminist readings of the Grimm tales and their analogues (e.g., Gilbert and Gubar 1984; de Lauretis 1984) would see Little Red as the victim, both sexually innocent and passive in the face of the wolf's phallic male persona and requiring rescue by the equally phallic male huntsman (also discussed by Stone 1986). Yet female figures—Red, her mother, and her grandmother—are pivotal. Further, versions of some Grimm stories are virtually patriarch(y) free. Collected almost entirely from women, to a large extent their women-centeredness survived the Grimms' various redactions and expurgations. Woman centering and lesbian orientations signify in the doubling of the female image—reflections in mirrors, for example—or in the reproduction of female counterparts—sisters with parallel but different qualities, mothers and stepmothers, and so on (see Greenhill 2008). For example, as Kay Turner discusses in this volume, a tale like "Frau Trude" could be read as a warning to girls against disobeying their parents, with the horrible outcome of being turned into a burning log by an evil female figure. Or alternatively, it celebrates the transformative potential of the transgressive same-sex relationship between an old witch and a young acolyte.

Feminist scholarship has added much to our understanding of these tales. But in contrast to the wealth of feminist material, queer and trans fairy tale interpretations, beyond reinventions and new tellings (see, e.g., Donoghue 1997), are rare. Many scholars, including those represented in this volume, have found such rewritings compelling (see, e.g., Bacchilega 1997). That critical literature can nevertheless potentially be extended by the work here, using queer and trans perspectives on the Grimms to unlock new appreciation for the lasting power of the fairy-tale genre. A queer interpretation of "Little Red" awaits the duly-inspired scholar.

Queer Theory and Fairy Tales

Annamarie Jagose lauds queerness for "its definitional indeterminacy, its elasticity. . . . Part of queer's semantic clout, part of its political efficacy, depends on its resistance to definition" (1996, 1). Certainly, the extensive discourse in GLBTQ scholarship on the diverse meanings of queerness is daunting. But for our introductory purposes, Alexander Doty, in his work on film, helpfully outlines how the concept of queer is theoretically employed. His catalog suggests the various and sometimes contradictory uses of the term:

1. As a synonym for either gay, or lesbian, or bisexual.
2. In various ways as an umbrella term
    (a) to pull together lesbian, and/or gay, and/or bisexual with little or no attention to differences. . . .
    (b) to describe a range of distinct non-straight positions being juxtaposed with each other.
    (c) to suggest those overlapping areas between and among lesbian, and/or gay, and/or bisexual, and/or other non-straight positions.
3. To describe the non-straight work, positions, pleasures, and readings of people who don't share the same "sexual orientation" as the text they are producing or responding to. . . .

4. To describe any non-normative expression of gender, including those connected with straightness.
5. To describe non-straight things that are not clearly marked as gay, lesbian, bisexual, transsexual, or transgendered, but that seem to suggest or allude to one or more of these categories, often in a vague, confusing, or incoherent manner. . . .
6. To describe those aspects of spectatorship, cultural readership, production, and textual coding that seem to establish spaces not described by, or contained within, straight, gay, lesbian, bisexual, transsexual, or transgendered understandings and categorizations of gender and sexuality—this is a more radical understanding of queer, as queerness here is something apart from established gender and sexuality categories, not the result of vague or confused coding or positioning. (2000, 6–7)

Thus, queer theory's defining principles problematize sex, gender, and sexuality. They refigure the possibilities of relationality along lines that challenge fixed or normative categories but also address concerns about marginalization, oddity, and not fitting into society generally. Our queering of the fairy tale is, as much of queer theory proposes, a taking stock of various unspeakable and unspoken desires. But as Jonathan Goldberg and Madhavi Menon insist, it is also about "reckon[ing] with desire itself, not as an essence to be explained but as a formation that rarely has a single objective correlative by which to be measured" (2005, 1611). In a sense, the entire *Transgressive Tales* project hinges on agreeing with the critical importance of understanding desire(s) *as*, and *in*, formation.

Trans theory explores the potential for expressing individual and collective identities that reverse, transcend, complicate, or deny sex/gender binaries of male or female or species binaries of human or animal. Transgender theory addresses in particular how a lack of correspondence between gender identity (social, cultural, psychological) and sex identity (biological, physiological) could illuminate understandings not only of sex and gender but of the sociopolitical (in)formation around character and humanness. Transbiology theory concerns scientific and popular representations of animals (including humans who masquerade as or transform into another species or vice versa and/or who mess with hard-and-fast distinctions between species). It demonstrates the awkward knottiness/naughtiness of the boundary between human and non-human.

It's sometimes hard to fathom how extensive has been the absenting and denial of queer and trans culture readings in folklore studies. Much of that process has taken the form of a dogged heterocentric norming of manifest queer content.[8] For example, A. L. Lloyd explains away the many British traditional and broadside ballads that feature women dressing as men and going to sea or to war—and being the object of sexual attraction by women as well as men—as a heterosexual fantasy in the homosocial male context of barracks or ship's cabin (discussed in Greenhill 1995). And Barre Toelken explains the floating verse "Sister's gonna kiss my ruby red lips / And I don't need no man" as anything but the obvious lesbian relationship it indicates (discussed in Greenhill 1997). Presumptions absenting queer culture from discussions of literary texts were sardonically enumerated by the late great Eve Kosofsky Sedgwick:

1. Passionate language of same-sex attraction was extremely common during whatever period is under discussion—and therefore must have been completely meaningless. Or
2. Same-sex genital relations may have been perfectly common during the period under discussion—but since there was no language about them, they must have been completely meaningless. Or
3. Attitudes about homosexuality were intolerant back then, unlike now—so people probably didn't do anything. Or
4. Prohibitions against homosexuality didn't exist back then, unlike now—so if people did anything, it was completely meaningless. Or
5. The word "homosexuality" wasn't coined until 1869—so everyone before then was heterosexual. (Of course, heterosexuality has always existed.) Or
6. The author under discussion is certified or rumored to have had an attachment to someone of the other sex—so their feelings about people of their own sex must have been completely meaningless. Or (under a perhaps somewhat different rule of admissible evidence)
7. There is no actual proof of homosexuality, such as sperm taken from the body of another man or a nude photograph with another woman—so the author may be assumed to have been ardently and

exclusively heterosexual. Or (as a last resort)

8. The author or the author's important attachments may very well have been homosexual but it would be provincial to let so insignificant a fact make any difference at all to our understanding of any serious project of life, writing, or thought. (1990, 52–53)

Despite folklore and fairy-tale studies' lack of engagement with it, queer theory has gained in both academic sophistication and scholarly reputation over the last twenty-five years.[9] Queer theory quite fittingly emerges in our focus on the fairy-tale genre's frequent refusal to confine sexuality to strictly heterosexual norms. As we have continued to think about queering the Grimms over the years, we have come to feel that the tales scream out for queer and trans theory. We counter Rölleke's admonition/dictation with our own call for responsibly *irresponsible* analysis. Admitting the impossibility of exhaustively outlining what queer theory can offer readings of the fairy tale, we instead demonstrate some of its multiple pathways, strewn with delicious bread crumbs of discovery and provocation. Here we name in programmatic fashion certain arenas of queer theory and its discourse that seem most applicable to fairy-tale analysis. Dependent on the feminist and gay and lesbian theories that precede it, and inspiring the trans theory that comes after it, queer theory nonetheless critiques the subject beyond identity in trenchant ways, including the following:

1. Queer theory problematizes all forms of gender, sex, and sexuality, addressing "the political ramifications, the advantages and dangers, of culturally 'fixed' categories of sexual identities and the ways in which they may . . . be performed, transgressed and queered" (Goldman 1999, 525).

2. These moves consequently query what is conventionally seen as "the family," its historical and social construction and its possibility for transformation into new forms.

3. Queer theory neither privileges nor denies the power of evidence or proof but also, following Raymond Williams (1977) on "structures of feeling," relies on categories of knowledge and experience that are felt and intuited, and often expressed in art.[10]

4. Queer theory questions all forms of dominant social and political

relationships in the interest of transforming the world, effecting what José Esteban Muñoz calls "queer worldmaking," the disidentificatory performance through art and other means of alternative views that "disavow that which majoritarian culture has decreed as the 'real'" (1999, 196).

5. Queer theory accepts what Sedgwick calls the "performative aspects of texts, and . . . what are often blandly called their 'reader relations,' as sites of definitional creation, violence, and rupture in relation to particular readers, particular institutional circumstances" (1990, 3).

6. Queer theory claims, again quoting Sedgwick, "that something about *queer* is inextinguishable. Queer is a continuing moment, movement, motive—recurrent, eddying, *troublant*. The word 'queer' itself means *across*—it comes from the Indo-European root—*twerkw*, which also yields the German *quer* (transverse), Latin *torquere* (to twist), English *athwart*. . . . The queer . . . is transitive—multiply transitive. The immemorial current that queer represents is antiseparatist as it is antiassimilationist. Keenly, it is relational, and strange" (1993, xii).

Though the foregoing is no exhaustive list to be sure, it lays the ground for many of the essays in this book and allows us to give further consideration to our perverse readings of the tales. We want to say a bit more about ephemerality, queerness, and fairy tales. Queer theory privileges the ephemeral, momentary sites and phenomena that appear and quickly disappear (see, e.g., Muñoz 1996). Deciphering these sites can be accomplished through an understanding of coding, and Joan N. Radner's *Feminist Messages* (1993) is as useful for queer readings as it is for feminist ones. Queer people survive by learning to read implicitly coded messages—where even the presence of coding can be disputed, so that both senders and receivers can be protected from the consequences of their decodings. Queer readers learn to read signals that others cannot read. Codes simultaneously conceal and reveal hidden messages. Queerness is also a site of ephemeral sexualities. Muñoz remarks that "queerness has existed as innuendo, gossip, fleeting moments, and performances." Ephemeral acts of queerdom "stand as evidence of queer lives, powers, possibilities" (1996, 6). The queer reader of fairy tales is attuned to such innuendo, to fleeting moments of unconventional engagement in the stories, especially sexual engagement.

We also invite a reinvestment in analytical modes that may gain new life by being theoretically queered. For us, structural analysis—the good old-fashioned kind Claude Lévi-Strauss, Dundes, Elli Köngäs Maranda, and others performed on traditional narratives decades ago—still stands up as a way to unloose tales from their superficial, syntagmatic drive. Dundes said it best years ago when he claimed that "structural analysis is not an end in itself, but is rather a means to other ends, ends such as gaining an understanding of concrete human behavior and thought" (1971, 173). For queer readers, structural analysis gives what Lévi-Strauss, in analyzing myth, called a certain potential to undo the perversion of unilinearity. His famous instruction reads thus: "The myth will be treated as would be an orchestra score perversely presented as a unilinear series and where our task is to re-establish the correct disposition" (1955, 432). Here those terms *perverse* and *correct* return, in direct opposition to our previous sense. Where the willful is the unilinear, our task is to correct this perversity with "the correct disposition"; that is, to assert the paradigmatic—the music—over the syntagmatic. This move amounts to a reordering or restructuring in an attempt to reveal the narrative's latent content. It also allows for a deeper look at its transformations and projections along social and sexual lines and especially makes analysis of minor characters and symbols more central (see K. Turner 2009).

As Dundes suggests, "The manifest/latent dichotomy gives the structural analyst a role comparable to the psychoanalyst who must see through or past the manifest content in order to reveal the 'true' secret organization and meaning of a folk narrative" (1971, 172). This search for the subject and for what Mieke Bal calls "narrative subjectivity" reveals it as a network, not an unquestionable identity (see Bacchilega 1997, 13). A queer reader intuitively seeks a tale's structural distinctions—polarities, binaries, or relational chains—that fail to conform to heteronormative claims. The "correct" binary for the queer reader may not be father/prince or mother/princess. In a number of the tales, including "Frau Trude" (ATU 334), "Mother Holle" (ATU 480), "Rapunzel" (ATU 310), "The Robber Bridegroom" (ATU 955), and "The Three Spinners/Spinsters" (ATU 501), the polarity girl/witch or girl/old woman serves as the source of dramatic tension for the queer reader. This tension can be a latent—or sometimes very manifest—sexual one, as Frau Trude and Rapunzel exemplify. Other problems of relationship, including the denaturalization of the normative family, can also be worked out in the orchestra of queer structural analysis.

Transgender theory (Greaney 1999; Stryker 2004; Stryker and Whittle 2006) "invites an interpretation of gender as precarious outcome, achieved at significant cost" (Hird 2002b, 51). Transgender moves may be obvious in tales like "The Shift of Sex" (ATU 514) where a girl literally transsexes into a boy in most versions (see Greenhill and Anderson-Grégoire, forthcoming). But arguably, gender fucking manifests whenever girls and women do work more associated with boys and men, as in "Mutsmag" (ATU 327B/328), or boys or men demonstrate "femmey" characteristics of sensitivity and physical weakness, like Mutsmag's counterparts the boy Thirteen and quite a few Jacks (ATU 328). Indeed, for all the genre's passive ingenue princesses who wait for brave handsome princes to rescue them, there remain characters who hardly instantiate mainstream notions of hegemonic masculinity or femininity. Transgender in folklore genres has also been underresearched (exceptions include Greenhill, forthcoming; Mills 1985), but the extensive use of the element of disguise (including cross-dressing) in folktales has received some consideration (e.g., Muhawi 2001).

In transbiology, we would argue, the concepts of biology and humanity both transform, and the allegedly rigid boundaries between species become permeable.[11] Literary scholar Howard Bloch points out how "the fable is a repository of anxiety about changing social status, capturing in terms of animal species the relation between nature and culture in the determination of social worth. . . . The motif of changing habitat, body type, or species is a thinly veiled metaphor for the principle of social mobility" (2004, 71–73). Social anthropology has explored in depth how animal metaphors and taboos actually express notions about human culture (e.g., R. Willis 1974; Douglas 1966; Lawrence 1990; Leach 2000; Waddell 2003). Historian Harriet Ritvo (1997, 2004) points out the complexities of animal taxonomy and the use of the term *monster* to describe animals that do not fit what are considered normal (human) heterosexual patterns, such as creatures which are intersexed or "hermaphrodite." In classical Greece and Rome, as well as in medieval and Renaissance Europe, human-faced animals were frequently depicted (Rowland 1973). Making animals stand for humans takes place in fairy tales, too, but human-animal (and vice versa) transformations also offer possibilities that implicate not only those relationships but also sex/

gender dichotomies and misplaced, inexpressible, or otherwise wanton desires.

Disguise as an animal in fairy tales (e.g., "Allerleirauh" [ATU 510B], see chapters 4 and 10 of this volume) is not uncommon, but the transbiological implications have been underexplored (e.g., Greenhill 2008). If linked with current concerns in transbiology and ethics (e.g., Haraway 2003; Braidotti 2009), interpretation of the fairy tale may find a new frontier in its consideration of otherness. Rosi Braidotti calls for an end to animals as metaphor for human qualities. Rather, she encourages thinking "in terms not of established categories but rather of encounters with anomalous and unfamiliar forces, drives, yearnings, and sensations, spiritual and sensorial stretching of the body's capabilities." She says this requires a "qualitative leap" (2009, 531)—and perhaps the fairy tale will provide one means of jumping to a new understanding of transbiological relations.

Fairy tales are emancipatory not in their content but in their reception (Haase 1993, 244); they are good to think and good to feel. We draw on queer theory to better understand the chaotic, fantastic, manipulated, and highly compressed fairy tale. We draw on queer theory not to free the fairy tale from its history but to understand further the complexities of that history—its multiple tellings and readings over time—as a source for solving problems pertaining to the individual, the social being in his or her own history.

TRANSGRESSIVE CONTENTS

But what, specifically, can you as our gentle reader look forward to in *Transgressive Tales*? By dividing the book into parts, we encourage your attention to certain themes. In "Faux Femininities," Cristina Bacchilega, Kevin Goldstein, Jeana Jorgensen, and Margaret R. Yocom address less familiar Grimm tales, arguing that a process of destabilizing mainstream notions of heterofemininity works within these stories. Bacchilega asks what makes a female character "clever" in the Grimms and discovers that women tricksters actively enjoy exceeding the social, narrative, and rhetorical limitations of their gendered locations. Not surprisingly, given the already noted confluence of food and sex in fairy tales—as in contemporary Euro–North American cultures—their pleasures are simultaneously gustatory and erotic. And eating and sexual pleasure are also surprisingly similar for Clever Gretel, who is very manifestly the author of her own fate, and Clever Else, who at least initially appears to be the victim of others' misunderstandings. Both tales employ their protagonists' artistry and humor—though Gretel's is arguably more deliberate than Else's—in response to patriarchal attempts to thwart their needs and wishes.

Bacchilega says that both characters have "an appetite for an alternative"—and the same could be said for characters in "The Goose Girl at the Spring," as described by Goldstein. Like Gretel and Else, the old woman/wise woman/witch goes against narrative and social expectations for one of her age and gender. Her bond with the young princess is mutual and significantly strong. Goldstein broadens our understanding of this benevolent female aide, thoughtfully analyzing her complex status as old woman, wise woman, and midwife, and as a marginal figure demanding recognition. Spinning the tale and the act of spinning within the tale offer a silent testimony to possibilities and limitations for female characters who venture outside the norm.

All these tales avoid heteronormative expectations for their female characters—but in "The Maiden Who Seeks Her Brothers," as discussed by Jorgensen, it's difficult to fit any of the main protagonists into conventions. And again food (or alleged food, inappropriate food, cannibalized food) enters into an equation with sexuality. But this is not the joyous food that Gretel eats, or even the beer that Else spills; instead it's the blood of procreation, of menstruation, of women's fearful sexuality—feared by other women, not by men, who are instead (perhaps equally inappropriately) interested in tasting it themselves (see Kane 1988). Of course in this case the feeling is mutual; the heroine loves her brothers and father as much (and apparently as indecently) as they love her. This familial queering leads beyond an exploration of femininities and directly into the exploration of sexualities.

Margaret Yocom's work on "Allerleirauh"/"All Kinds of Fur" shows the difficulty of assigning pronouns to a figure who is both but also neither male and/or female and who messes with the transbiological boundary between humans and other animals. A tale constituted in what Yocom calls "ambiguous pronouns and ambiguous bodies," it is ripe for queer decoding. Though Allerleirauh finally resolves into a female figure, she travels through a variety of positions to get there. Yocom knowingly places her analytical emphasis on the long middle section of the tale, where the heroine's journey is expressive of the kind of multiple ambiguities that can make diverse meanings for readers.

In the second section, "Revising Rewritings," Kimberly J. Lau and Jennifer Orme address the intertexts between traditional, oral versions of two tales—"Sleeping Beauty" and "The Twelve Dancing Princesses"—and rewritings by Angela Carter and Jeanette Winterson that foreground queer possibilities in these texts. Lau addresses how Carter's "The Lady of the House of Love" combines vampire and fairy tale to make explicit not only the necrophilia inherent in the collected version (for the Grimms, "Little Brier Rose") but also the anything-but-passive possibilities of a somnambulist title character who is no innocent persecuted heroine (see Bacchilega 1993).

Orme's chapter considers how even a rewriting of a story of overtly transgressive women (the twelve princesses disobey express directions from their father the king and do so covertly and, at least at first, quite success-fully) by a lesbian writer resists designation as inherently queer. Though it is one of the few Grimm tales in which wayward women escape the severe punishment of a gruesome death, and one in which women work together for their own common interests, in Winterson's version they do not all have the same desires and interests. Some are arguably heterosexual, others more obviously far from that position. Both chapters show how, once having ap-proached these familiar stories with a queer eye, they can be shown to hold complex meanings derived from aspects of the characters not conventionally explored.

Andrew J. Friedenthal's chapter begins at a different point—not with queer rewritings, but instead with the straight Disney version of "Snow White." Arguing that the queer possibilities of the title character manifest in the tale that pairs her with her sister, Rose Red, Friedenthal finds the latter's relative muting in Euro–North American culture a suppression of lesbian implications. Happily, he notes that Rose Red finds a simpatico and potentially—if not overtly—queer milieu in graphic novels and comics. Here, sexy Rose Red plays freely with her possible transgressive significations. But Friedenthal also finds the intimate friendships in these later readings clearly marked in the Grimms' version—prefiguring our third section.

In "Queering the Tales," Pauline Greenhill, Anita Best, and Emilie Anderson-Grégoire; Catherine Tosenberger; Joy Brooke Fairfield; and Kay

Turner turn more directly to the ways that Grimm and other tales can redirect presumptions of sexuality and marriage away from the hetero norm. Greenhill, Best, and Anderson-Grégoire look at Canadian versions—one English and one French—of a composite tale about the adventures of a masculine girl, Peg Bearskin or La Poiluse, whose final sought-for reward is femininity and marriage to the best-looking, most prized prince. By being equally good at conventionally masculine tasks like war making and troll conquering and feminine tasks like cooking, s/he finally transsexes into the woman she clearly wants to be. Peg and La Poiluse underline the absence of these kinds of characters in the Grimms.

Tosenberger, beginning with her own reaction to "Fitcher's Bird" ("Rescue by the Sister"), shows how this tale simultaneously invokes and undermines the male gaze and performative femininity. True and false brides abound, yet no marriage results. But rather than establishing gender expectations and then undermining them, Tosenberger suggests, this tale exposes a heroine who acts well beyond narrative conventions (including those in similar Grimm and international tales).

Fairfield addresses a different queer character, Princess Mouseskin, who, like Fitcher's Bird, takes on an animal disguise but whose actions seem unplanned and unconscious in comparison to the latter. Initially, the princess is as uninterested in marriage and heterosexual relations as the protagonist of "Fitcher's Bird." And though in the end she pairs with a prince, her journey to "maturity," Fairfield argues, entails not growing *up*, but queerly growing *sideways* (see Stockton 2009). This heroine enacts what Fairfield calls "repeated performances of incomplete becoming" or partial transformations, yet such "sideways growth" puts her very much in charge. Her sensual focus on food (again) and interest in roles not usually considered princessly—mousehood, manhood, servanthood, and princehood—mark her as a queer figure who benefits from her exploration of difference.

Turner investigates compelling attractions between an older woman and a girl in "Frau Trude." The story tells of a girl who, against the interdiction of her parents, goes out of curiosity (equaling desire) to a witch—also characterized as a flame-headed devil—who has been waiting for her for a long time. No typically gruesome devouring of flesh ends this version of ATU 334, but rather a quite marvelous union occurs between the fiery hag and the girl transformed by her into a burning log. Fire meets fire in elemental passion. Turner reads "Frau Trude" as a paradigmatic tale of cross generational, same-sex desire—the "lost motif" of attractions, seductions, and affections between older and younger women that motivates action in other tales, such as "Rapunzel." Using her analysis to introduce the work of numerous queer scholars into fairy-tale interpretation, she invites an encounter with normative taboo reconsidered as transformation.

In "Beyond the Grimms" we present versions of already queer stories. Margaret A. Mills leads us away from Eurocentric narratives and perhaps wins the prize for most outrageous transgressive tale in her recounting of an Afghan boxwoman type, featuring the kind of women tricksters found pervasively in Islamic popular literature and tradition. This particular story, performed by Safdár Tawakkolí and collected by Ravshan Rahmoní, features a powerful woman who exerts extraordinary control over men. Again, this work underlines the absences in the Grimms—not only of riot grrrl characters, but also of the language and interactions of actual tellings of folktales and fairy tales. Elliot Mercer's hilarious "queer adaptation" of "The Grave Mound" (similar to ATU 815, containing an episode of ATU 1130) shows how the moral lessons of the Grimms' time can sometimes apply in surprising contexts. Of these, we will say no more.

Closing Formula—We Went Upstairs, Our Tale Was True

Almost exclusively, *Transgressive Tales* queers female protagonists. A different project might center on masculine subversions, including homosexuality, but our project makes a meeting between feminist and queer scholarly positions that leads us vitally to fraus and fur girls. By their adventuresome nature, their insistent self-possession, their refusal to succumb passively to authoritarian dictates, and their disinterest in necessarily choosing to partner appropriately (i.e., normatively and singularly), these characters open doors to new possibilities for understanding the diversity of women's desires and affective attachments, their ways of feeling and knowing.

A wholly new approach to the fairy tale, such as we offer here, views the genre not so much as morally transparent—aimed at teaching lessons—but rather as transgressively emergent and part of what Carolyn Dinshaw calls "contingent history in the postmodern sense—its forms are intelligible but do not emerge out of teleological necessity" (1999, 2–3). Our mode of inquiry moves in the direction of the ambiguous, ambivalent, and indeterminate, even the contradictory. A queer sense of contingency helps us freshen our understanding of the highly ambivalent world of the fairy tale, imbued as it is with fantasy, magic, temporal instability, and transformations, all bound up around wish fulfillment, dreams, family troubles, relational anxieties, status, love, and sex. Freud worked on dreams, but he might have just as well interpreted the fairy tale to exemplify his sense of the human psyche as that realm where the law of noncontradiction does *not* apply. Instead ambivalence reigns, giving license to the coexistence of opposites, and not always for the sake of their ultimate resolution, but sometimes for the perverse differences they inspire.

The fairy tale owes much of its longevity to contingencies and contradictions associated with desire and pleasure. We might even say that the fairy-tale genre conjured the postmodern in its early signaling of the contingent nature of signs and systems of representation, especially in the realm of sex and social relations. This genre, which poses so pointedly and yet so strangely—so queerly—the big questions of life, still offers plenty of room for interpretive shifts and shake-ups as its stories are encountered anew, from generation to generation.

Notes

1. Though Vanessa Joosen notes that "in a few rare instances, critics have attributed Jacob Grimm's lifelong bachelor status to suppressed homosexuality" (2011, 11).

2. Perrault also added a moral, warning women and girls, "Children, especially attractive, well bred young ladies, should never talk to strangers, for if they should do so, they may well provide dinner for a wolf. . . . There are various kinds of wolves. There are also those who are charming, quiet, polite, unassuming, complacent, and sweet, who pursue young women at home and in the streets. And unfortunately, it is these gentle wolves who are the most dangerous ones of all" (Ashliman 1996–2011).

The Grimms introduced a patriarchal male rescuer in the form of the woodsman (see, e.g., Greenhill and Kohm 2009 on live-action film versions exploring pedophilia). David Kaplan's short film, *Little Red Riding Hood* (1997), starring the then teenaged Christina Ricci as Red and Timour Bourtasenkov as the beautiful, dancing wolf, more closely resembles the oral French tales (see Verdier 1980; Velay-Vallantin 1998).

3. See, e.g., Greenhill and Matrix (2010) for discussions of film versions.

4. Similarly, Michelle Ann Abate's (2008a, 2008b) work on tomboys in literature suggests the need to focus not on the compliant ends in stories like *Little Women*, where the erstwhile gender bender grows up to instantiate a more normative sex and sexuality, but instead the resistant middles of those tales, where the tomboy revels in her transgressive social desires.

5. And note that Greenhill's 2008 article was originally intended for this collection.

6. Jacquelyn N. Zita calls "genderfuck" "tampering with the codes of sex identity by mixing male and female, masculine and feminine, man and woman signifiers on one body" (1992, 125).

7. Here and elsewhere, we use "Euro–North American" quite deliberately, because the discourses of African American, Arab American, and other settler cultures, as well as those of First Nations and aboriginal folks, often differ sharply from the hegemonic, dominant cultures of white people of European origin.

8. A few exceptions include Marjorie Garber's (1992) reflection on Red Riding Hood and the wolf, Greenhill's (1995, 1997) consideration of same sex attraction in ballads, and Ruth Vanita's (2005) treatment of same-sex reproduction in an Indian tale.

9. See, e.g., Bersani (1996, 2009); Butler ([1990] 1999, 1993, 2004); Cvetkovich (1998, 2003); de Lauretis (1994); Dinshaw (1999); Doty (1993, 2000); Freccero (2006); Freeman (2007, 2010); Halberstam (1998, 2005); Jagose (1996, 2002); Kirsch (2000); Muñoz (1996, 1999, 2009); Sedgwick (1985, 1990, 1993); Stockton (2009); Sullivan (2003); Michael Warner (1993); Weed and Schor (1997); Wilchins (2004).

10. Raymond Williams refers his meaning of "structures of feeling," specifically to art and literature, "where the true social content is in a significant number of cases of this present and affective kind, which cannot be reduced to belief-systems, institutions, or explicit general relationships" (1977, 133). Phillip Brian Harper's work uses the evidence of felt intuition in relation to racial prejudice and homophobia. He argues for the necessity of taking recourse to the evidence of things not seen, not provable: "Minority existence itself induces speculative rumination—felt intuition—because it continually renders even the simplest and most ephemeral social encounters as possible cases of discrimination" (2000, 643). On the positive

side, ephemeral social encounters in fairy tales—the kind that often occur between protagonists and anomalous beings—are just the kind that illuminate queer possibilities and alliances.

11. Further, Hird argues against "the idea that biology itself consistently distinguishes between females and males. Nature . . . offers shades of difference and similarity much more than clear opposites" (2000, 348).

FAUX FEMININITIES

1

Whetting Her Appetite

What's a "Clever" Woman To Do
in the Grimms' Collection?

CRISTINA BACCHILEGA

> She showed me the sparkle in my eyes, how wide
> my skirt could spread, how to waltz without getting dizzy.
> —Emma Donoghue, *Kissing the Witch*

Only two tales in the Grimms' *Kinder- und Hausmärchen* are titled after a named "clever" heroine, and both of them are jocular or comic tales: the protagonist of "Clever Gretel" is the one playing word and mind games, while the title character in "Clever Else" is the one played. "Clever" (the English-language standard translation of the Grimms' *klug*) does not have positive connotations in either case, as "Clever Gretel" exemplifies unsuitable and punishable behavior in a lower-class woman, and the qualifier in "Clever Else" and other Grimm titles ("Clever Hans," for instance) ironically points to its opposite meaning (Uther 2008, 72). The joke, then, seems to be on the two women characters, but does it have to be? Perhaps not, when we read the two tales and characters together, as related to each other in their "cleverness" and transgressive potential. If "clever" in these two tales is a gendered and subordinate construct, I am going to focus on Gretel's and Else's queer exuberance and rule-breaking actions—however different their form and outcome are—to see how (Gretel) and if (Else) they, as trickster figures, exceed the limits that are socially, narratively, and rhetorically set for them.[1]

In "Clever Gretel" ("Das kluge Gretel," KHM 77 in the Grimms' German collection and in Jack Zipes's translation, *Complete Fairy Tales of the Brothers Grimm*), the protagonist is a cook tasked with preparing two chickens for her master and his guest. Inspired by the roast's aroma and the wine she's been drinking, Gretel starts by nibbling away at a chicken wing and, since the guest is late and the food is ready, she joyously ends up eating both chickens herself. When the guest finally arrives, she warns him that her master is sharpening his knife to cut off the man's ears; and when the caller runs away, she tells her master that his guest has stolen the chickens. The tale ends with Gretel's master running after his guest: "With the knife still in his hand, he screamed, 'Just one, just one!' merely meaning that the guest should at least leave him one of the chickens and not take both. But the guest thinks that his host is after just one of his ears," so he runs off even faster (Zipes 1987, 312–13).

The *Types of International Folktales* classifies "Clever Gretel" as ATU 1741, "The Priest's Guest and the Eaten Chickens" (Uther 2004, 2:409), to be found among "Anecdotes and Jokes," and more specifically among jokes where a "clergyman is tricked" (ATU 1725–1774). Over the years I've told "Clever Gretel" in the classroom several times partly because it is an entertaining story that brings home the point that the brothers Grimm did not collect and publish tales of magic alone. We know that the brothers adapted it from Andreas Strobl's *Ovum paschale* (1700), a collection of stories deemed appropriate for Easter sermons, where it exemplified unsuitable behavior in a lower-class woman. In Strobl's version, the tale ends poorly for Gretel, who is left living in misery without the support of her master, but the Grimms did away with the moralizing coda that punishes the cook's one-upping him.[2] Sensitive to the social appeal of Gretel's "turning the table on her master," Jack Zipes has read the Grimms' version as a "tall tale"; he explains, "What begins as a common, seemingly realistic event with a common character is gradually exaggerated and turned into a fantastic event" where "the cook emancipates herself" (Zipes 1995a, 157). Angela Carter, who included the story in her anthology, *The Virago Book of Fairy Tales*, also emphasized, but from a different angle, the fantastic aspect of "sassy Gretel" as "a direct reflection of middle-class fears of what the servants get up to down there in the kitchen" (1990, 236).

Joke, moralizing parable, tall tale, fantasy: the genre codification of "Clever Gretel" is, in spite of the authoritative Aarne-Thompson-Uther label, not all that stable. I used to read this tale to my daughter when she was little, and it was one of our favorites from Angela Carter's (1990) collection, where it is grouped with others featuring "Clever Women, Resourceful Girls and Desperate Stratagems."[3] Bruna would smile knowingly as we neared the end of the tale, which, in some way, brought home to me why Angela Carter called it a "genial" tale (236); I have interpreted this categorization to mean that there is something cheerful, but also creative and inspiring, even tutelary, about it.

The play of double entendres certainly marks "Clever Gretel" as a joke, but reading it *only* as a joke seems to be dismissive of Gretel's own cheer and wordplay throughout the story. It is on her, on Gretel, that I intend to dwell in order to limn what is genial about the tale. While I appreciate the points that "Clever Gretel" employs "tall tale" strategies, and that Gretel's "emancipation" is "fantastic," I propose to focus on this "clever" character's appetite, rule-breaking behavior, and playful verbal deception as connecting her with another larger-than-life or unrealistic narrative mode, that of the trickster.[4]

The Grimms' tale begins not with a "common" event (the master telling the cook to prepare a meal for him and his guest) but by introducing us to Gretel. And she is represented from the very beginning of the story as quite uncommon:

There was once a cook named Gretel, who wore shoes with red heels, and when she went out in them, she whirled this way and that way and was as happy as a lark. "You really are quite pretty!" she would say to herself. And when she returned home, she would drink some wine out of sheer delight. Since the wine would whet her appetite, she would take the best things she was cooking and tasted them until she was content. Then she would say, "The cook must know what the food tastes like!" (Zipes 1987, 312)

Gretel wears red and transgressively stands out, inside the kitchen, where she works as a cook, as well as when she steps out of the kitchen. She wears red, not a red cap, the sign that shows off in Charles Perrault's "Little Red Riding Hood" the onset of puberty, but shoes with red heels. These are not the "red-hot iron shoes" in which the queen in the Grimms' "Snow White" is forced to dance herself to death, or the unstoppable red dancing shoes that take over Karen's life in Hans Christian Andersen's pious story. Gretel's sexuality is not so much a display for others or a tell-tale sign of how she deserves punishment; rather these red heels peep out to tell us "there is always more going on than meets the eye," that this cook is "dedicated to the pleasure principle" (A. Carter 1990, xii), a characteristic that Carter associated—in a provocative more than a romanticizing way—with the genre of the folk and fairy tale.

When Gretel goes out in her red-heeled shoes she finds such pleasure in her whirling dance that she is delighted with herself. Having returned to the home where she works as a cook, she persists in nurturing that "sheer delight" by imbibing some of her master's wine. This only "whets her appetite," and she partakes of the best morsels of what she has prepared. Gretel's sexually playful body finds its pleasures outside and inside her master's house, but differently: when she is "out" she is free to exhibit her desire and to recognize its beauty; when she is inside the master's house, if she is to retain her "delight," she must transgress, steal, and deceive. So she does just that, and with much self-awareness: her words—"The cook must know what the food tastes like"—are both a rationalization that protects her as a subaltern in the master's house (after all, eating the forbidden food is a "service" to him) and also an active, if circumscribed, questioning of the social relations that alienate her from the fruit of her own labor. Delight in her body and playful deception both feed her autoerotic pleasure or *jouissance.*

That in other versions of this tale the heroine tricks not her "master" but her husband confirms that Gretel's transgressive desires are sexual—"The wife and her lover secretly eat (nibble at) the fowl" (Uther 2004, 2:409)— but not *just* sexual. Food is a matter of survival, and the cook/wife protests against wasting food.[5] The laws she disobeys and the authorities she tricks have to do with the hegemony of alienating class and labor relations (cook feeding and serving the master), heterosexual patriarchy (wife favoring the husband's well-being and ensuring his reproduction), and even religion: the "clever" woman's master is in many versions a priest, and his guest is a clergyman. When Gretel consumes, to her full enjoyment, a lot of wine and the two chickens she has roasted, she is also showing she has no taste for the wine and bread symbolic of (self-)sacrifice in the Christian tradition.[6] She is not content to represent lack when producing nourishment is her daily pleasure.

A Sicilian version, "Lu burgisi e lu pridicaturi" ("The Bourgeois Man and the Preacher") collected by Giuseppe Pitrè, is evidence of the three-pronged protest of the woman protagonist. "There is a custom here that, when a visiting preacher makes the rounds during Lent, the bourgeois population is supposed to invite him to their homes, and they spend a small fortune on this entertainment as they compete over who can do it best" (Zipes and Russo 2009, 1:633). The wife of one of these bourgeois men "was not at all pleased by this behavior because her husband was the stingiest miser imaginable regarding her own needs, but when it came to the clergy he spent money like water." The husband denies her not only pleasure but satisfaction (having enough) in the everyday and then demands that she cook delicacies—three pigeons in this case—for those she must serve. Having eaten the tasty birds herself, she flatters the preacher who's just arrived: "You honor us with your presence today. . . . And what a beautiful pair of eyes. . . . I will certainly shed tears when they are gone." When she explains that her husband is "crazy about eyes," gouging them out and eating them, and that "when a new preacher arrives, [the husband] uses the pretext of inviting him to dinner and then gouges his eyes out," the preacher is quick to run off. We know the rest of the story, with the bourgeois man running after the preacher to get his dinner back and the preacher running away for fear of having his eyes poked out. Rosa Brusca, the woman who told Pitrè the story he published in 1875, concludes, "From that day on [the man] abandoned his habit of inviting the visiting preacher to dinner, and that's how his wife freed herself of this dreadful annoyance" (Zipes and Russo 2009, 1:633–34). The Sicilian tale and storyteller place this "clever" woman's success within larger and oppressive dynamics of power that include class and the institution of the church as well as that of the patriarchal family.

The woman protagonist of "Lu burgisi e lu pridicaturi" is successful in bringing to an end a particularly annoying and expensive display of the husband's disregard for her needs, but she was and remains dissatisfied with her daily life. We do not know much about her beyond this displeasure, her being "sulky" and "a bit of a glutton." In my view, she takes apparently extreme measures—lying to a religious authority—to address her husband's excess, what outrages her once a year, not his habitual stinginess. This Sicilian version features a "clever" and resourceful woman, but she is not—like the Grimms' Gretel—larger-than-life in the everyday, whirling about in her red shoes and delighting in herself. Gretel is a philosopher of pleasure—articulating heteroglossia and embodied knowledge at the same time that she asserts her right to nurturing, not just feeding, herself. More than a survivor, Gretel is an artist of enjoyment.

Gretel's appetite itself in the tale is extraordinary because she is neither wanting (it is implied that she does have "enough" since she treats herself regularly to tasting what she cooks) nor apologetic.[7] Once we realize she's eaten two full chickens, her initial action of daintily cutting off a wing that is burning on the spit is clearly a joke itself. Her master had asked her to roast *two* chickens—not three pigeons as in the other tale—possibly one for each of the men. I surmise that perhaps a not-so-plump wing was meant for Gretel, the cook, but no more than that. Gretel's labor and domestic art were going to be minimally if at all compensated. Though *she* has produced the roasted birds as edible food, she knows, and we as readers know, that once she starts eating more than a taste, she is partaking of what—in the social world of the tale—is definitely not hers. In a perversion of the Christian ritual, the wine inebriates her but also purifies her from guilt, as she says to herself, "Have another drink and eat it all up! When it's gone, there'll be no reason for you to feel guilty. Why should God's good gifts go to waste?" (Zipes 1987, 313). She does not hesitate, in the absence of her master and his guest, to feast on the juicy birds, to feast herself as worthy of the "good gifts." Alone in her pleasures, she (re)incorporates, in a sensual response to the physical properties of the food ("The chickens are really good! It's a crying shame not to eat them all at once!" [313]), what she knows to be "good" and tasty. Counter to the imagery of the angel of the house and the self-sacrificing motherly figure, Gretel fulfills her desire by feeding herself exclusively. Defying fairy-tale/folktale coding in particular, she is a far cry from the all-giving (dead) mother of the Grimms' "Cinderella." Gretel in her feasting departs, fully if momentarily, from participation in an economy where the fruit of her labor ("she killed two chickens, scalded them, plucked them, stuck them on the spit, . . . placed them over the fire to roast . . . basted them with butter" [312]) is exchanged between men.[8]

I've been pointing out that Gretel's autoerotic behavior and orality position her oddly in at least two ways: as a social subaltern whose appetites are in excess of her dependent standing and as a gendered subaltern who does not aspire to heterosexual domesticity. Rather than representing temporary phases in a normative script of sexual and social development, her autoeroticism and orality mark her as "growing sideways," a queer character who increases "in quantity, size, and degree" but "oddly beside" herself (Stockton 2004, 279). As an artist of enjoyment, she is neither an innocent child nor a quiescent woman, the Grimms' most popular fairy-tale heroine types.

Gretel's speech to herself and to the two men further amplifies and puts into discursive action her oral gratification, exemplifying how the "trickster's intelligence springs from appetite in two ways" (Hyde 1998, 22): she satiates herself and then, refusing to participate in the two men's game, she plays *with*, rather than to or against, their rules. "In the invention of traps, [the] trickster is a technician of appetite and a technician of instinct" (19). First, let's consider how much Gretel talks in the story and how much she talks to herself. As Kay Turner observes, Gretel's "self-reflexive and self-referential speech queers her to all those silent, long suffering" heroines in the Grimms' collection. "Talking to oneself is usually equated with craziness, but here we see that talking to oneself is a kind of queer magical act" (Kay Turner, personal communication), a strategy of antinormative self-articulation. Second, even when taken at face value, Gretel's words to the two men produce a tricky message. Gretel upholds the norms of hospitality and good manners, but this code is inappropriately performed given her socially subaltern status: she whispers advice to the guest ("Get out of here as quick as you can! If my master catches you, you'll be done for"

[Zipes 1987, 313]), and she screams at her master about his poor judgment ("What kind of guest did you invite!" [Zipes 1987, 313]). Furthermore, as she whispers and shouts, her words expose the violence of the norm: the two men were to share a meal, and in the exchange of hospitality rituals, over the chickens she cooked, test the terms of their interaction, the place of hostility or competition in it. Even as one goes to the other's house, the two men do not seem to trust each other, and each one fears losing to the other. Each man's reaction to her "clever" words confirms Gretel's intuition of the threat that the men fear they may pose to each other: they are strangers, and they could easily become enemies.[9] Their sharing a meal was to be the stage for a symbolic negotiation that Gretel knowingly and successfully preempts.

In some versions the Gretel figure calls a spade a spade more explicitly than in others.[10] The Grimms have the guest running as fast as he can to protect his ears from the other man's alleged violent desire. But the tale's earliest versions, such as the twelfth-century French fabliau "Les perdris" and the thirteenth-century anecdote "Der Hasenbraten" (The rabbit stew), have the guest fleeing because he thinks the host wants to cut off his testicles (Van der Kooi 2002, 1309).[11] And in some modern variants, "the wife tells the guest that her husband intends to put the pestle up his backside (oven-fork in his mouth)" (quoted in the entry for ATU 1741, Uther 2004, 2:409). In the desexualized Sicilian version I discussed earlier, cannibalism (the master, she claims, will gouge out the guest's eyes to eat them) can perhaps be read as displacing and also intensifying the sexual threat of castration. Whether it is the guest's masculinity or the host's property (the chickens) that is at stake, the Gretel figure articulates—verbally performs—their hostility by invoking, and at the same time making a sham of, the rules of propriety. Gretel's "clever" words and actions do not simply free her from facing the consequences of her transgression; they disturb the homosocial exchange between the master and his guest, unmasking the violence on which it rests.[12]

In "Commodities among Themselves," feminist philosopher Luce Irigaray wrote that heterosexuality "is nothing but the assignment of economic roles: there are the producer subjects and agents of exchange (male) on the one hand, productive earth and commodities (female) on the other" (1985, 192). This economy is sustained by a homosocial heteronormative order that forbids same-sex pleasures. I see Gretel speaking not so much as a woman but as a trickster, who, Victor Turner observed, often holds an "uncertain sexual status,"[13] and from a position that "cleverly" queries this heteronormative symbolic order (quoted in Hyde 1998, 580).

Notably, the conclusion of the Grimms' tale, which I quoted at the start of this chapter, zooms in on the two men—one running after the other, a domestic tool (the carving knife) turned weapon between them, each convinced of having been betrayed by the other. Gretel is not in focus. But whenever I've told "Clever Gretel," at school or at home, I've brought the tale to closure by refocusing on Gretel. Do you see Gretel, as I do, wearing red-heeled shoes? And what is Gretel doing in the house, her belly full and her words powerful? As I've told it, "Gretel laughs and laughs and laughs."[14] And with every telling, my daughter would be smiling with her. I can't say what Bruna's smiling was about, but she tells me—now that she is a young woman—she remembers wanting Gretel's red shoes. An inspiring effect? For myself as a teller I have been aware that Gretel's tricky orality offers a fun recipe not only for "getting away with it" but for knowing oneself and the world. I am not advocating stealing and deceiving as a way of life, of course, but affirming that Gretel's sideways, trickster-like, risk-taking actions and words unhinge the world as we are socialized to accept it. Gretel is indeed "clever," as the Grimms' translated title characterizes her, meaning she displays mental alertness and is quick with her words. But in excess of "clever," her story is "genial" because, as a transgressive decoder of the heteronormative patriarchal symbolic order (and one who does not have to use such words to do so), Gretel is oddly and joyously wise in her queerdom.

It is the title of the Grimms' tale that anchors our interpretation of Gretel's actions and words as "clever," the standard English-language translation of *klug*. Since the German adjective carries the meaning of "prudent," the title can be read ironically, and indeed in the text by Andreas Strobl on which the Grimms drew for their tale (Van der Kooi 2002), the dissolute cook is punished for her dissolute behavior.[15] On the one hand, the English-language "clever" moves us away from such a moralistic interpretation, and it also maintains some distance from "cunning," which would vilify Gretel's quick mindedness. On the other hand, as I have just suggested, if the attribute "clever" fits, it may be too snug a fit, setting limits to the recognition of Gretel's knowledge and good judgment. No one in the story world calls Gretel "Clever Gretel," and I wonder if, as per Louis Althusser's (1971, 174–83) famous scene of the ideological interpellation of the subject, she would turn around to answer that call, or demand to be recognized as "world wise."[16]

Such self-confidence is quite unlikely in the protagonist of "Clever Else," at whom the epithet "clever" is hurled with such irony that it is almost an insult. Unlike "Clever Gretel," "Clever Else" ("Die kluge Else," KHM 34) has not been part of my storytelling or teaching repertoire, so my relationship to the tale is different. I'm fond of Gretel, while, as a character, Else upsets and intrigues me. My reading emerges not from delight and familiarity, as it did with "Clever Gretel," but from dissatisfaction with how plainly in sight Clever Else's foolishness is taken to be. Does she have no tricks up her sleeve?

The protagonist of "Clever Else" is a young woman whose family is hoping for her to marry. When Hans finally comes along, he insists that his future wife must be really "smart," and Else's parents assure him that she is, as they entertain the suitor with food and beer. Sent to the cellar to fetch beer, Else notices a pickax hanging right above her and begins to weep as she imagines the child she might have with Hans going to fetch beer in the cellar himself and being killed by the ax. When family members come to the cellar, one by one, to enquire about what's taking so long with the beer, Else brings them to tears as well with this sad story. (The illustration that often accompanies the tale shows what the narrator leaves to the reader's imagination—the beer is spilling out of the cask as everyone in the household, following Else's lead, sobs over a "possible" future [e.g., Zipes 1987, 141].) Hans apparently takes all this as evidence of Else's cleverness and marries her.

The tale is not over, focusing next on a single day of the couple's married life. When Hans finds Else fast asleep in the field instead of cutting wheat, he drapes a "net with bells used for catching birds" over his sleeping wife, returns home, and locks the door. Hans's practical joke—which enacts the verbal "I caught you!"—is not understood as such by Else when she wakes up; instead, moving in the dark with all the bells jingling about her (another popular illustration accompanying the tale), she is unable to recognize herself. "Is it me, or isn't it me?" asks Else. After a brief exchange with Hans that is a classic comedy of errors, Else becomes further confused,

"Oh, God, then I'm not me." Hans seems unaware that he's locked Else out of the house, and nobody else wants to open the door at night to a strange being with bells ringing at every step: "Since there was no place for her to go, Clever Else ran out of the village, and nobody has ever seen her" (Zipes 1987, 140–43).

Like "Clever Gretel," "Clever Else" has been mostly received as a joke, which it is.[17] But again I am going to suggest that—in thinking about the representation of gender and sexual relations of power—something can be gained by transgressing that generic threshold of interpretation. So in the next section of this chapter—the other side of my argument—I focus on how the act, circulation, and double meaning of Else's interpellation as "clever" function quite differently than in the case of Gretel. In the process, I will speculate on Else's (admittedly unpromising) trickster potential for counterappropriating her name, "Clever Else."

Unpacking a joke is a thankless task, but here I go. The irony of the girl's (nick)name will be apparent to readers; however, it seems not to be to her family. The tale's first line—"There once was a man who had a daughter called Clever Else" (Zipes 1987, 140)—introduces us to the protagonist via her father, and "clever" is not just the Grimms' but her family's interpellation of Else. "Clever Else" is a proper name—the girl is known within the social world of the story as such—in addition to being an attributive phrase ("clever Else"); and this interpellation and assertion both are repeated face value throughout the story by the girl's family and Hans. This is a noodle story with more than one noodlehead. When Else's parents weep with her at the fate of an imaginary grandson, while the beer goes to waste in front of them, are they unwittingly showing that the apple does not fall far from the tree? It seems so, given that other versions of ATU 1450 end with the suitor leaving the heroine with her family after the ridiculous beer-spill scene proves the girl's (and her family's) foolishness.[18] In contrast, in the Grimms' tale, Hans's statement when he witnesses the same scene is proof of how his foolishness matches hers: "Since you are such a clever Else, I'll have you for my wife" (142). Married to her "for some time," he can still exclaim to himself, "What a clever Else I've got" (143). The ridiculous reiteration of "Clever Else" and "clever Else" in the characters' dialogue, then, builds up to the literal disappearance of "Clever Else," this time in the narrator's words, as she becomes a joke.[19] Clever Else, the narrator asserts, will not be seen again as she cannot possibly be "clever Else." And eventually the irony exchanged between narrator and reader retroactively permeates the tale's title as well, turning "Clever Else" into a disparaging title, a put down.

The act of naming "Clever Else" inaugurates a process by which this man's daughter is tasked with living up to a project that the repeated performance of her name will reinforce; but the reiteration within the story world of "Clever Else," as a performative utterance of illocutionary force, does *not* work.[20] Similarly, the characters' verbal recognition of Else as "clever" is repeatedly shown to be a misrecognition. It is via the repeated failure of these speech acts in the story world that rhetorically—with the authorization of the narrator and reader—"Clever Else" becomes a name for the stereotype of "fool" and more precisely "foolish woman."[21]

Having unpacked how this gendered type is constructed rhetorically— through acts of language—moves me to counter it by refocusing on Else's actions and words in response to her interpellation as "Clever Else." Judith Butler, whose analysis of gender as performative I have been drawing on, revises Althusser by noting that "interpellation can function . . . without anyone ever saying 'Here I am!'" and in fact with one asserting, "'That is not me, you must be mistaken!'" Despite one's protest, "the name continues to force itself upon you, to delineate the space you occupy, to construct a social positionality" (Butler 1997, 33).[22] We are not told how the tale's protagonist responds to being hailed over and over again as "Clever Else." Does she protest or does she inhabit her name? I see her as doing both, and I will qualify my reading by stating that I do not thereby imagine the character as fully conscious of or accountable for either position: her actions and words speak for her.

The social norm that the naming of "Clever Else" signifies is, from the start and throughout the tale, that of the marriageable woman. Her father markets her as "Clever Else" and Hans recognizes her as "clever" when he agrees to marry her. While Hans's action is, as already discussed, the outcome of misrecognition, his statement can also be read as the assertion of her value as a wife. What Else is worrying about in the cellar is, after all, *Hans's* future, personified in the imagined *son* she will give him; and in doing so, whatever the reason, she is displaying no worries about her own immediate safety. Witness to her selflessness and overwhelming concern for him, Hans states, "I certainly don't need any more brains than that for my household" (Zipes 1987, 142). He may very well be aware that she is not *kluge*, but she may be *gescheit* enough to be his wife, which is what Hans asked for in the German text: a sensible wife, sensible according to him.[23] And as a matter of fact, he continues to think of her as "Clever Else" until she puts herself first—eating "some good porridge" and choosing to rest before working as Hans has tasked her to do: "What should I do first, cut the wheat or sleep? I think I'll sleep first" (Zipes 1987, 143). What's transgressive about her appetite is not its abundance—as in Gretel's case—but that it comes first, before her duty. Once he sees this "other" Else, Hans—unconsciously perhaps in this version, but not others—locks his wife out of the home: he makes her into a social pariah, while at the same time holding on to his image of her ("'Hans, is Else inside?' 'Yes,' answered Hans. 'She's here.'" [143]). Regardless of his awareness, it is no stretch of the imagination to read Hans's actions as punishment of an unruly wife. "Hansens Trine," the precursor of "Die kluge Else" in the Grimms' 1812 first edition, ends with the statement that this is how Hans got rid of his lazy wife (Bolte and Polívka 1913, 335).[24]

This reading of how cleverness and foolishness are related to the exchange and use value of the woman as "marriage material" in the tale finds some support outside of the text. ATU 1450, the "Clever Else" tale type, is placed not only within the larger category of "Anecdotes and Jokes" in the *Types of International Folktales*; it is the first tale in the smaller grouping, "Looking for a Wife" (types 1450–74) (Uther 2004, 2:225). Furthermore, when, in an Italian version of "Clever Else" (as discussed in the 1888 *Book of Noodles*) the groom becomes aware of the farce going on in the cellar, he comments, "You stupid fools! Are you weeping at this and letting the wine run into the cellar? . . . It shall never be said that I remained with you. I will roam the world, and until I find three fools greater than you, I will not return home" (Clouston 1888, 199). Confronted with the foolishness of his wife and in-laws, this groom finds it necessary to go on a quest. However, this is not a quest for another wife; rather, it is for him to save face and continue to assert his superior judgment. Some foolishness on the part of a wife is more than acceptable as long as it is clear that the husband has not bought into it and that the fool is doing his bidding.

But as Butler emphasizes in *Excitable Speech*, even the hailing of a subordinate subject is enabling, "producing a scene of agency from ambivalence, a set of effects that exceed the animating intentions of the call" (1997, 163). If proving herself as "marriage goods" is the project that Clever Else has been set up to accomplish ("Clever Else had to prove she was really smart" [Zipes 1987, 140]), her actions and words do *not* overall—whether via incompetence, resistance, or both—represent her as being on task.[25] The first direct encounter readers have with her as an actor or agent—rather than as a construct of her parents' and suitor's discourse—occurs when she is asked to perform a domestic duty, going to fetch beer in the cellar: "Clever Else took the pitcher from the wall, went down to the cellar, and along the way played with the lid by flapping it to pass the time" (140). I cannot help but think of this dillydallying in comparison with the behavior of Charles Perrault's female protagonist in "Bluebeard" who "raced down a little staircase so fast that more than once she thought she was going to break her neck" (Tatar 1999, 145). We cannot be sure of what motivates Perrault's heroine, who has just wedded Bluebeard, to race down the stairs, but her behavior has often been attributed to curiosity about him and the hope that perhaps by gaining forbidden knowledge she will consolidate her position in the marriage. In contrast, Clever Else amuses herself flapping the lid of the pitcher, playing on her own—I am tempted to say with herself—"to pass the time" as she embarks on the task that, it is implied, will ingratiate her to Hans. She takes *her* own time. Clever Else's actions can be read as a symptom of her reluctance to follow the script, a holding back, a sign of caution—if not of protest, of disinterest.

The narrator then shows Clever Else being careful—prudent or cautious as *klug* also implies—not to hurt herself in the cellar, sitting on a stool so as not to injure her back by stooping to get the beer from the keg, a detail that is supposed to accentuate the ridiculousness of her reaction to seeing the pickax "hanging directly above her" (Zipes 1987, 140). How foolish of her to build "air castles" and weep over them when she is in actual danger![26] But what if she is very much aware of that pickax hanging over her, an externalization of the marriage script, and the scenario she cries over is the hyperbolic futility of her self-sacrifice in a prescribed role of wife and mother? Her actions—her weeping and her repeated telling of the story—I want to suggest, may well be an embodied request for help in the face, not so much of the doom she envisions in this future, but of the impending marriage we are not told she wants for herself.

If it is a coded message, Else's plea for help goes unheard, as the various members of the household continue in their misapprehension of her "cleverness." Her repeated performance "tricks" them but fails her because, rather than playing with the rules—as Gretel does—she is in her tale repeating the story of how she is played by the rules. The other characters (Hans explicitly) assume she is simply reenacting a normative script, that of the selfless mother and wife. They recognize her forecasting prudence, but not the immediacy of her predicament; nor do they recognize the role they could play in helping her free herself from it.[27]

The two are married as the script has it, but we know this is not the end of Clever Else's story. After Hans unwittingly recognizes Else's erratic subjectivity—her acting outside of her subordinate role as wife—Clever Else wakes up to the project of recognizing herself outside of her father's or husband's home, besides herself as she has been scripted. The "jingling all around her" surprises Else as she wanders in the dark of night; it frightens her when she is no longer recognized as belonging in the home or in the village; but by the end of the tale, she is taking action based on her own answer to the question of who she is. The textual narrator concludes: "Since there was no place for her to go, Clever Else ran out of the village, and nobody has ever seen her again" (Zipes 1987, 143). Within the normative discourse that interpellated her as "Clever Else," this is a dead end, at which point her name becomes a joke, a tale type, a stereotype, and a warning. But if we refocus our attention on Else's words and actions, once she acknowledges that her place is not in Hans's home or social order—"then I'm not me"—that frees her to run out of the village. For the first time, Else's place is not preallocated for her. When she acknowledges verbally that she is not the "clever" (*gescheit*) woman Hans expects her to be, she is no longer on his mind, but she is hardly out of *her* mind. In fact, by no longer trying to fulfill the expectations of others, her father and husband especially, she may have found her own way. She is on the road—"still always on the road, future still uncertain," as Pauline Greenhill (2008, 164) writes of the heroine of another Grimms' tale—and quite possibly, as I see her, on the road to make a future for a Clever Else that is not limited to a heteropatriarchal definition of "clever." In this view, the bells announce her taking the chance to "grow sideways" (Stockton 2004), her reappropriation of herself as a trickster of a kind.

If "tricksters seem by turn wise and witless" (Hyde 1998, 77), I am suggesting that those of us who are interested in the politics of gender and sexuality of the brothers Grimm tales can gain from reading *both* "clever" Gretel and "Clever Else" as trickster figures. The interpellation of Gretel and Else as "clever" in the two stories' titles is generally understood to have opposite meanings; and the outcomes of their language and mind games also seem quite divergent: Gretel the cook takes over the master's household (if only temporarily), while Else is no longer allowed into her husband's home. Gretel's trick works, and Else's does not, but that opposition need not be the point or the end of their stories. *Together*, in different ways but beside each other, Gretel and Else trump the norms of gendered domesticity.

Whether they are recognized as "clever" or "foolish," Gretel and Else embody a knowledge that exposes the social and symbolic order of heteronormative patriarchy, and they embody an appetite for an alternative. As Butler writes, "The terms by which we are hailed are rarely the ones we choose . . . but these terms we never really choose are the occasion for something we might still call agency, the repetition of an originary subordination for another purpose, one whose future is partially open" (1997, 38). I have proposed refocusing on the act, circulation, and double meaning (clever/not wise and clever/marriageable) of each heroine's interpellation as "clever" to remark on that agency and to make at least three points. In each story the heroine's speech acts and actions, respectively playful and erratic, transgress the bounds of propriety and property from the start, running counter to normative domesticity, in respectively open and coded ways. If we agree that these tales are jokes, in Gretel's case I suggest that we laugh with her, and in Else's that we consider how laughing at her performs a certain violence. And, whether sage or fool, Gretel and Else are each represented as "clever" but dispensable figures who end up falling outside of the frame—visual and narrative—of the Grimms' tales. To redeploy these narratives, I therefore have suggested taking these steps: relating Gretel and Else one to the other as queerly "world wise" tricksters and relating to each of them as agents who need not be defined by the Grimms' frame.

Notes

I dedicate this chapter to Donatella Izzo. My thanks to Jeana Jorgensen for providing me with invaluable research assistance in this project and to Ulrich Marzolph for sharing his extensive knowledge of the two tale types (especially in their Muslim versions) I discuss in this chapter. Esther Figueroa, Pauline Greenhill, Donald Haase, Uli Marzolph, Carmen Nolte, Jennifer Orme, Bruna L. B. Rieder, John Rieder, Cornelius Rubsamen, and John Zuern responded either to drafts or to specific queries concerning German-language meanings, helping me clarify my points. For this chapter specifically, and over many years, Kay Turner provided inspiration; her witty and sideways comments have enriched my thinking. Inaccuracies and limitations are entirely my own.

1. Here and throughout the chapter, "queer" refers to antiheteronormative behaviors that are at odds within dominant social and sexual practices.

2. The Grimms refer to possibly having heard "Clever Gretel" in the oral tradition, but they quote and make use of Andreas Strobl's *Ovum paschale* (1700) and of Hans Sachs's "Die vernascht maid" (1536). The latter was found by Sachs in Johannes Pauli's manuscript collection of jokes and anecdotes "Schimpf und Ernst" (1522, no. 364) and was read by the Grimms in a collection by Achim von Arnim (see "Das kluge Gretel" in Bolte and Polívka 1915, 129–31).

3. Note how Carter's heading for this group of tales contrasts with the ATU title, "The Priest's Guest and the Eaten Chicken," which does not even mention the tale's protagonist or her gender. For a significant critique of gender-related biases in the type and motif indexes of Aarne and Thompson, see Torborg Lundell (1989).

4. As Susan Wyatt (2005, 5–6) notes, "Most of the time, the trickster is represented as a male figure such as Hermes or as an animal such as Coyote or Raven. However, a woman can also play the part of the trickster as Penelope does with her unweaving. In stories of women tricksters, the archetype is usually a role that is taken on to evade the control, threats, or ineptness of their men or their culture rather than intrinsic to their nature, as in Grimm's tale of 'Clever Gretel' (1987) or the tale of the cunning wife in 'The Butcher's Tale' (Burton 1997) or the story of the teller of this tale, 'Scheherazade.'" See also Lundell's (1989) and Marilyn Jurich's (1998) explanations of how female tricksters have been ignored in tale type and motif classification as well as in general discussions of the trickster figure.

5. Ruth B. Bottigheimer (1996) notes that "Clever Else" conveys a critique of people who waste food.

6. In her refusal of self-sacrifice, Gretel's behavior departs significantly from what Lewis Hyde identifies as the trickster's "slipping the trap of appetite" by turn-

ing intentionally to "the invention of self-sacrifice"—the giving up of "the organ of that appetite, his odious belly" (1998, 38).

7. The importance of food cannot be overestimated in folk and fairy tales. My reading accentuates the association of food and meals with sexuality, ritual, and violence (see Marina Warner 1994; Nikolajeva 2008; Everett 2009). What is striking about Gretel's behavior is her *not* sharing the meal. In addition to refusing self-sacrifice, her keeping the food to herself could be seen as a regenerative incorporation of the men's power, as I later suggest. In fairy-tale/folktale coding, the all-giving mother is contrasted with the vengeful stepmother in "The Juniper Tree" who cooks up her stepchild as stew for her husband. When mother figures do not share food, it is usually because there is none (the stepmother in "Hansel and Gretel") or because she is a cannibalizing ogress/witch (the witch in "Hansel and Gretel" or the mother-in-law in some versions of "Sleeping Beauty").

8. In "Cinderella," the fruit of the mother's labor is her child, the protagonist who is then exchanged between her (absentee) father and the prince (see Rubin 1975).

9. In the case of the master and guest in "Clever Gretel," the possibility of negotiations between them is made impossible by Gretel's articulation of the hostility they both fear. The Latin *hostis*, as per Jacques Derrida's investigation of the relationship between host and guest, houses both hospitality and hostility, opening up the dangers of "hosting" to being held "hostage"—either to the host's or to the guest's rules. Derrida's analysis in *On Hospitality* is further politicized and emplaced by Paul Lyons (2006). In a brilliant "deconstructive-restorative" reading (Obeyesekere qtd. in Lyons 2006, 3) of textual encounters (scholarly, fictional, and touristic) between American and Pacific people, Lyons focuses on friendship "as a complex counterpoint to that of fear semiotics (based on the putative endemic violence of the 'cannibal')" (19).

10. That ears and testicles are allomotifs is not uncommon. In his analysis of different versions of the folksong "Do Your Ears Hang Low?" Alan Dundes (1997, ix–xii, 34) showed how ears can symbolize both female and male sexual organs. His comment about the origin of the word "contest" in English (*con testis*, with testicles) furthers my reading of the two men's behavior as a homosocial competition that Gretel disables.

11. "The Woman Who Humored Her Lover at Her Husband's Expense," which is included in Richard Burton's *1001 Nights* from the eighteenth-century Wortley-Montague manuscript, is explicit about the sexual nature of the woman's transgression (she has a lover and wants to feed him baked goose) *and* the threat to the guest (his testicles will be cut off). There is no threat of cannibalism though (Marzolph and Van Leeuwen 2004, 452).

12. In this homosocial economy of desire, possessing the phallus—"the phallic

mirage" as Luce Irigaray sees it—is what allows one to be a subject—rather than an object—of exchange (see 1985, 170–91).

13. Hyde quotes Victor Turner's observation that "most tricksters have an uncertain sexual status" (1998, 580), and perhaps the use of the "neutral" article *das* rather than *die* in the tale's title, "Das kluge Gretel" linguistically marks Gretel's queering status in the tale.

Given that I do not speak German, on the one hand, I hesitate to make any points that are purely based on language usage in the Grimms' texts. On the other, I am also reluctant not to treat translations as such and want to address—within limits and with the acknowledged help of the dictionary and native speakers—problems of meaning that a translation may either gloss over (in this case) or limn (see note 21).

14. Hélène Cixous's (1981) "The Laugh of the Medusa" is relevant here.

15. As mentioned earlier, the Bavarian priest Strobl (1641–1706) scolds the maid for her rule-breaking behavior. The Grimms edited Strobl as detailed in "Das kluge Gretel" (Uther 2008).

16. The meaning of the word *klug* extends to "world wise." See the Grimms' (1854–1960) German dictionary, *Deutsches Wörterbuch*.

17. In *The Types of International Folktales*, the tale type "Clever Elsie" (ATU 1450) appears to be named after the Grimms' text (Uther 2004, 2:225), which, however, is accounted for in its entirety only once we combine ATU 1450 with another tale type, "The Woman Does Not Know Herself" (ATU 1383). ATU 1450 is also related to "The Woman Goes to Get Beer" (ATU 1387) and often combined with "The Husband Hunts Three Persons as Stupid as His Wife" (ATU 1384). Regardless of how many tale types it is associated with, "Clever Else" is classified among "Anecdotes and Jokes." For further information see Johannes Bolte and Georg Polívka (1913), Bottigheimer (1996), and Uther (2008).

18. See ATU 1450 plot and variants in Uther (2004, 2:225–26).

19. In this chapter, I refer to the "narrator" as the textual or narrative voice, rather than the oral storyteller. Dorothea Viehmann, one of the standard contributors to the Grimms' tales, is identified as the teller of "Clever Else" (Bolte and Polívka 1913, 335–42).

20. In *Bodies That Matter: On the Discursive Limits of "Sex,"* Butler (1993, 232) elaborates on the understanding that gender is performative by explaining how, masking itself as recognition, the repeated interpellation of a subject (in her example "It's a girl!") sets up the process of fulfilling an assignment or living up to a norm. The success of the performative depends on the repeated citation of the norm, and yet within certain performances the weakness of that norm may also be exposed. In

the book's section "Performative Power," Butler specifically states that Eve Sedgwick's "reflections on queer performativity ask us not only to consider how a certain theory of speech acts applies to queer practices, but how it is that 'queering' persists as a defining moment of performativity" (224).

21. It should be noted that this gendering of the fool par excellence is not typical of all versions. In *Arabia Ridens*, Ulrich Marzolph (1992, 264, no. 1229) translates and comments on the following Arabic variant:

> Abu al-'Anbas said: I once walked through the streets because of some mat-
> ter when suddenly a woman addressed me asking me: "Do you want me to
> marry you to a young woman [or: a slave-girl] that will bear you a son?" I
> said: "Yes!" She continued [lit.: said]: "You will send him to school, he will go
> there, play [with the other children], climb on the roof, fall down and break
> his neck!" [After this sentence] she cried and lamented [as if her words had
> already become true]. I got frightened and said [to myself]: "She is [certainly]
> mad!" And I walked away.
>
> [Soon after] I saw an old man [sitting] at the door [of his house]. He asked
> me: "What's up, my friend?" And I told him what had happened [lit.: told him
> the story]. When I reached the point of her wailing, he said in an important
> mood: "Certainly women have to wail when a relative of theirs [lit.: a dead one]
> dies." Now this man is more stupid and more ignorant than her!
>
> The misogyny of ATU 1450 and other European jocular tales—as well as the
> gender bias of their classification—is not traceable to Muslim antecedents. A
> prominent example is ATU 1353, "The Old Woman as Trouble Maker," where
> the male slave in the old Arabic versions (dating from the ninth century) is
> replaced in European versions by a woman who is "worse than the devil."
> (Marzolph 2006, personal communication)

22. The passages I am quoting are part of the introduction, "On Linguistic Vul-nerability," of Butler's (1997) *Excitable Speech: A Politics of the Performative*, which develops into a powerful critique of the confusion between speech act and action, on which advocating censorship (of hate speech and pornography as well as of ho-mosexuality in the current US military policy) rests. While I hope not to be empty-ing out the "politics" of the performative in my reading, I want to acknowledge the incommensurability of the point and text I am working with and Butler's real-life politics and examples.

23. Hans, in the Grimms' German version, has required that Else be *gescheit*, which Zipes translates as "smart," in order to become his wife. The two terms, *klug* and *gescheit*, are, according to dictionaries and experts, almost synonymous, and

Hans does refer to Else as *kluge* when he decides to marry her: "Weil du so eine kluge Else bist, so will ich dich haben" (Rölleke 1980, 1:191). However, the opposite of *gescheit* has more to do with "being out of one's mind" than with "being dumb" (Carmen Nolte, personal communication).

24. In their entry on "Die kluge Else," Bolte and Polívka (1913, 335–42) summarize this 1812 version, which has Hans cutting his wife's long skirt short while she is asleep; when she wakes up in the dark and in this unusual state, she becomes confused about who she is. A note by the Grimms apparently states that the cutting of the skirt references an ancient legal custom; I take this to mean that the husband has withdrawn his legal support from the woman, that her status as wife is being taken away. Bolte and Polívka also refer to a sixteenth-century poem by Heinrich Götting in which it is said that the suitor does not want his future wife anymore after he witnesses her foolishness, because he is quite displeased with her.

25. "Incompetence" is one of the strategies discussed in Joan N. Radner's (1993) collection *Feminist Messages: Coding in Women's Folk Culture*.

26. I refer here to the title for another tale type, "The Man and His Wife Build Air Castles" (ATU 1430), grouped under "The Foolish Couple, 1430–1439" classificatory umbrella (Uther 2004, vol. 2).

27. In a recent online article, "A Fairy Tale for Our Time," Alberto Manguel (2009) revisits "Clever Else" in order to comment on the importance of agency as we confront the "world economic crisis." Drawing on the understanding that "fairy tales have a way of surreptitiously explaining much of what is dark and frightening in our world," Manguel goes on to compare the meaning and irresponsible reception of Else's story in the cellar to hegemonic representations of and responses to the current economic crisis in the media: "We too have been called into the cellar to bear witness to something imminent and to bemoan a tragedy that has not yet taken place—instead of, for instance, removing the pickaxe that seems to threaten the life of a nonexistent child. There is a difference between grave concern about the state of things caused by a corrupt and greedy economic system, and the imposed sense of impending doom for which no one is held criminally responsible."

2

Nurtured in a Lonely Place

The Wise Woman as Type
in "The Goose Girl at the Spring"

KEVIN GOLDSTEIN

In her eloquent analysis of the Grimms' fairy tales, Maria Tatar notes that, owing to Wilhelm Grimm's inclination to censor, "stepmothers and cooks are almost always thinly disguised substitutes for [depraved] biological mothers" (2003, 144). Indeed, from witches to mothers-in-law, any number of types may be enlisted to perform the role of female villain. In contrast, biological mothers are typically either passive or long deceased. Ruth Bottigheimer argues that, in the centuries preceding the Grimms' work, a radical shift occurred in literary depictions of women: "Girls had become frightened damsels, their mothers had retreated into the shadows, and maids and sisters who had formerly lent their mistresses a helping hand had disappeared" (2004, 37). In short, the heroine of the Grimms' tales, bereft of many female aides, denied even her wits, is left routinely helpless, dependent on men.

Nonetheless, these trends cannot account for the fairy tale tradition in toto. Having noted this apparent vacuum of female aids, we can begin to people that void, for female donors and helpers linger yet in the *Kinder- und Hausmärchen*.[1] Tatar catalogs the evil mother's literary surrogates, but allomothers too dwell within the tales.[2] One such allomother is the old woman found in "The Goose Girl at the Spring" ("Die Gänsehirtin am Brunnen"). Neither passive mother nor villain, her identity becomes the central concern of the tale's coda: "One thing is sure: The old woman [*Alte*] was not a witch [*Hexe*], as people believed, but a wise woman [*weise Frau*] who meant well" (Zipes 1987, 570). The aim of this investigation is to untangle the sociolinguistic forces animating this speech act. What does the phrase "wise woman" do, both within the tale and the tale's cultural matrix? Because this cultural matrix is profoundly layered, what is warranted is a diachronic analysis of "wise woman" as a sign. To borrow John Miles Foley's term, one must discern the "traditional referentiality," the implicit cultural content, embedded within this speech act (1999, xiv).

To achieve this end I will undertake a two-tiered analysis. First, I will contextualize the story within the fairy-tale tradition and within broader sociohistorical trends in early modern Europe: the Grimms' cultural inheritance. Second, I will apply these findings to the story itself, reflecting on what precisely the story performs within its traditional and sociohistorical milieu. Thus a concern with traditional referentiality necessarily extends to the implications of "wise woman" as a speech act in early modern Europe: How does the term interpellate its subject? Ultimately, why is it significant that the old woman is not a witch but a wise woman and, furthermore, one who attended the birth of the princess? To engage these questions, I will traffic not merely in deductive reasoning but, like fairy tales themselves, in magical thought. In lieu of hard evidence, I shall hope that metonymic and metaphorical association, the twin currencies of oral tradition's semiosis, will bear quiet witness to the historical interrelation of "old woman" (*Mütterchen, Alte*), "wise woman" (*weise Frau*), and "midwife" (*Geburtshelferin*) in the European imagination.

"The Goose Girl at the Spring" begins by introducing the old woman (*Mütterchen*), who lives in a lonely place (*einer Einöde*) and gathers grass each day to feed her geese (Zipes 1987, 518; Uther 1996, 3:93). She is amiable, but ostracized, suspected of being a witch. One day a handsome count's son comes upon her and is soon engaged to carry her load. He struggles uphill with the unbearable weight and after much effort arrives with the old woman at her home, greeted by her many geese as well as her robust and ugly daughter. The old woman rewards the count with a box carved from a single emerald. After wandering three days, he arrives at a castle where, upon presenting the emerald box to the royal couple, the queen recounts how her daughter had the ability to weep pearls and jewels but was banished by the king for comparing her love for him to her love for salt. Despite the king's subsequent contrition, they were never able to find their daughter again. But the emerald box contains a pearl just like those her daughter wept, which encourages the queen that her daughter yet lives.

One night, after spinning, the old woman sends her daughter out to "do [her] work." She goes to a spring, removes a false layer of skin, revealing her beauty, bathes herself, and weeps. Hearing a sudden sound—as we later discover, the sound of the count falling from a nearby tree at this marvelous sight—she slips back into her false skin and flees. Returning to the house, the old woman tells her that she will soon be leaving. The count, together with the king and queen, arrive at the old woman's door, where she welcomes them, well aware of their identity. After admonishing the king for banishing his daughter, she calls for the princess. The royal family reunites happily; the old woman rewards the princess for her work by giving her the pearls she has wept as well as the house. At once the old woman disappears and the house transforms into a palace. The storyteller then intervenes, continuing the story that her grandmother had ended prematurely in a lapse of memory: she declares that the princess marries the count and that certainly the old woman was no witch but a wise woman, who was present at the princess's birth and gave her the gift of weeping pearls instead of tears.

This intervention marks a rare exegetical performance in the Grimms' collection, one which aims to resolve the ambiguity enveloping the old woman. Because she inhabits a liminal space, she troubles the binary between the good—if passive or absent—mother and the antimother—the malevolent witch or stepmother. Neither the passive mother nor the female villain, she is the donor-helper. Yet her relationship to the princess remains essentially mysterious, her motives for aiding the heroine left unexplained.

The princess's tears manifest her affective relationship to the social world. Her character is marked by continual emotional disclosure; her seemingly opaque affirmation of love only reveals her sincerity, her lack of artifice. In contrast, the old woman must be sought in her silence, in her equally benevolent and self-annihilating behavior. This silence provides the opening for a queer reading of the tale, wherein we find the queerness of the wise woman, of the midwife, of the allomother, whose bond to the princess circumvents both marriage contract and kinship network.

"The Goose Girl at the Spring" recounts a world of profound reversals, inversions where merit is found precisely where demerit was declared. The story vindicates both outcast women. Poverty becomes wealth. The marginal becomes central. What is more, the strength of man proves slight compared to the strength of an old woman. First, the rich count struggles to carry the old woman's load,[3] and, second, the very figure of the active male becomes subverted: the actions of the count merely follow from the designs of the old woman's magic. The old woman, in turn, represents the unspoken center of the tale. She orchestrates the action of the story, literally spinning the plot. She has at her side the magic of nature, messages are conveyed to her by the night owl's call, and she has the power to transform tears into pearls, young maidens into geese, poverty into wealth, beauty into ugliness, and vice versa.

As the story begins, we approach the old woman with trepidation; at first glance, she represents a thoroughly ambiguous character. Given the malevolence of so many other marginal, elderly females in the Grimms' tales, the suspicion on the part of her neighbors is mirrored in the reading or listening audience. Our expectation is that she will do harm, but the narrative subverts our expectations. Intriguingly, only male characters assume she is a witch: a father warns his son of the claws hidden beneath her gloves, and the prince is only relieved of this prejudice when the princess disrobes at the spring. In contrast, in the context of the transmission of the tale itself, from grandmother to granddaughter, the latter makes another claim: the old woman was a wise woman. One might argue that this literary reparation, carried out for the libel committed against the old woman, is prompted by the grandmother's abrupt ending, ostensibly due to a lapse of memory. Her silence is an incitement to her granddaughter to collaborate, to affirm for herself the injustice of the libel.

These competing truth claims, one passed patrilineally, the other matrilineally, mirror the ambiguity inherent in the figure of the wise woman. The old woman is both the subject of accusation and a benevolent practitioner of magic. What is more, present at the birth of the princess, she gives the princess a loving home during her exile. Stylistically, the tale could end with a simple assertion that the new couple lived happily ever after, but the narrator lingers over the old woman. Why does this figure invite such a response?

As listeners, we are left with an apparently constative utterance[4]—namely, that the old woman was not a witch but a wise woman,[5] and, further, that she was probably present at the birth of the child. Yet this apparent resolution only draws further attention to the mysterious old woman. We are left first with her sudden, shocking physical absence. All that remains is a vague melancholy, the melancholy that comes in the wake of an unjust ostracism, an unreciprocated kindness. It is rare that the donor enjoys the last lines of a Grimm fairy tale, yet the old woman haunts this tale, haunts its listener-narrator, and finally haunts us. It is as if the narrator, possessed, speaks with the authority of the old woman, who demands that we recognize her. Whence comes this voice?

PROVENANCE

The story is based on Andreas Schumacher's Austrian dialect story "D' Ganshiadarin" (Vienna 1833), translated into High German by Hermann Kletke as "Die Gänsehüterin" and published in Berlin in 1840 (Zipes 1987, 723). Aside from this literary source, we have recourse to comparative scholarship locating the tale in broader fairy-tale—both oral and literary—traditions. In terms of tale type, "Die Gänsehirtin am Brunnen" partially conforms to ATU 923, or "Love like Salt." It is thus a variant of tales such as "Cap O' Rushes" from England, "The Necessity of Salt" from Austria, and "Water and Salt" from Sicily (Uther 2004, 1:555–56). Due to its innocent persecuted heroine, ATU 923 bears a relationship to ATU 510A, or the "Cinderella" cycle, and, in turn, to 510B, "Peau d'Asne," with motifs such as the king who tries to marry his daughter and the heroine who takes on a disguise.[6] In addition, ATU 533 involves the motifs of the innocent persecuted heroine who tends geese and the transformation of tears into pearls (Goldberg 1996, 189–90).

Two motifs shared among these tale types require specific mention, namely, disguise and the benevolent female aid. First, the motif of disguise by an animal skin is particularly pervasive. The so-called goose girl is not clothed in the skin of an animal but apparently that of an old woman's corpse; nonetheless, as her name implies, she is deeply associated with transformation into bestial form. The innocent persecuted heroine in 510B often disguises herself—by making herself ugly—to guard against unwanted male advances, often those of a lecherous father. There is thus a link between the father who banishes his daughter for a perceived want of affection ("love like salt," *King Lear*) and the father who drives his daughter away by his incestuous designs.

The motif of the benevolent woman coming to the innocent persecuted heroine's aid deserves special attention. Here we have an old woman, but one who the storyteller explicitly argues is a wise woman. In the Cinderella stories (tale type 510A), owing to the French literary fairy tales of Charles Perrault, she is familiarly known as the fairy godmother, but such a title is in fact rarely found in the broader fairy-tale tradition. In one Swedish variant, for instance, the figure is explicitly called a midwife (Cox 1893). In the Grimms' "Cinderella," the spirit of the heroine's mother comes to her aid. In another Grimms' tale, "Spindle, Shuttle, and Needle," it is her actual godmother who in death aids the heroine. Alternatively, in the Italian tale "Water and Salt" an old woman comes to the aid of the banished princess. In the Austrian variant, "The Necessity of Salt," a female innkeeper-cook occupies the role. In the Grimms' "The Maiden without Hands" (ATU 706), which parallels our story through motifs such as the father's betrayal (he is coerced by the devil to cut off his daughter's hands) and the mutilation of beauty, a kind of angel–wet nurse helps the innocent persecuted heroine (Zipes 2001). Furthermore, the old woman's gift of weeping pearls instead of tears points to a convergent or parallel development with the Sicilian popular tradition, where angels were thought to be capable of transforming the tears of unbaptized children into pearls (Cox 1893).

Thus, the figure of the female aide, often capable of employing magic, pervades these tale types. Yet what account can be made of this figure in the popular imagination of early modern Europe? Etymologies provide a glimpse into this network of beliefs. Consequently, let us consider some etymologies that trace this intriguing link between *old woman, wise woman, godmother*, and *midwife*, beginning with the word for midwife in various Indo-European and Semitic languages. The term *wise woman*, to denote midwife, has been in existence since antiquity. In Talmudic literature, one finds the Mishnaic Hebrew word *hachama*, meaning wise woman, in reference to midwives (Ben-Moshe and Klein 2008). French (*sage-femme*) and Dutch (*vroedvrouw*) speakers also use the term *wise woman* to refer to midwives. In German, wise woman (*weise Frau*) may mean midwife, although the more common word, in modern usage at least, has been *Geburtshelferin* (birth-helper) or *Hebamme* (lift-nurse).

The word *Amme* itself, aside from its more general meaning of nurse or wet nurse, has a very exciting archaic signification: foster mother. In Spanish, the word for midwife is *comadrona*, which has an historical relationship to *comadre*, or godmother. Similarly, the Italian word *comare/commare* underwent a shift over time from denoting comother, or perhaps godmother, to midwife, at least until the seventeenth century. Today *comare* simply means a gossip or crony.[7] In English, the now obsolete word *cummer* bears a similar trajectory, having been used to refer to a godmother, intimate friend, midwife, or wise woman before the nineteenth century (Marina Warner 1994, 33). The English word *midwife* has its root in the Old English, meaning "with woman." Another intriguing case is the Romanian word for midwife, *moaşă*, which is a feminized form of *moş*, or old man. We thus see a pattern across languages linking wise woman and midwife, and in turn midwife and comother or godmother and even aged woman, the last of which could itself refer back to wisdom.

These philological relationships necessitate a reevaluation of the term *wise woman* as employed in "The Goose Girl at the Spring." Is it possible that *weise Frau* would have enjoyed an unproblematic denotation in the medieval and early modern periods, a semantic self-evidence that required no further clarification through centuries of oral and finally literate transmission? What is the "storyteller" telling us when she declares that the old woman was not a witch but a wise woman? At the same time, in pondering these questions we must recognize the diachronic depth of the phrase, a depth borne out by the etymologies. The textual phrase *wise woman* contains within it multitudinous speech acts enacted over centuries by thousands of men and, more substantially, women. It is a signifier grown heavy with meaning, which carries a vestige of those mothers, spinners, wet nurses, godmothers, and midwives who told tales and died without celebrity. This composite, embodied in the fairy-tale character, reflects the history of its transmission-genesis. Each telling grafts onto the tradition as a whole. We might imagine a midwife or an old spinner mapping her own experience onto that of the old woman. As in Walter Benjamin's (1968, 92) image of the vessel in which the handprints of the potter cling to the hardened clay, the old woman bears the handprints of the countless women who bore her along.

With this in mind it behooves us to further contextualize the character of the old, wise woman within the popular imagination of early modern Europe. Who is the wise woman, this other mother, who takes responsibility for outcast girls without the slightest hesitation, as if it were the most natural thing to do? This woman who was present at the birth of the princess? It would be a crude thesis that argues that she is in fact a midwife, or a godmother, or a wise woman. Such an argument demands a finality that the oral tradition as such renders untenable. If the tradition is fluid, then the character of the old woman reflects that fluidity. Hence we must understand her character as the focal point of a network of associations, of referentiality, which links "wise woman" and "midwife" with the practice of magic. Evidence of this historical relationship is not found solely in an archive but in magical—that is to say poetic—thinking itself.

EARLY MODERN TYPES

One prominent misconception in desperate want of nuance concerns the conflation of wise woman—or midwife—with the exclusively malevolent use of magic, namely witchcraft. It is difficult to ascertain at what point (or points) the figure of the marginal, elderly female became subject to the suspicion of being a witch, *Hexe, bruja, sorcière, strega,* or *vrajitoare.* Nonetheless, in order for the suspicion of the townspeople in "The Goose Girl at the Spring" to be intelligible, such an association must at least be plausible. On the one hand, this suspicion could be seen as the invention of literate, bourgeois men and women of the mid-nineteenth century projecting onto the contemporary peasant class or the peasants of remote history. On the other hand, it could be seen as the common folk knowledge of peasants throughout late medieval and early modern Europe. Unfortunately, both of these possibilities risk becoming caricatures.[8]

Nevertheless, a link between "wise woman" and "midwife" does not necessarily entail a strong historical link to witchcraft or, better, accusations of witchcraft. As concerns midwives, recent scholarship has done much to dispel the widely held belief that they were the frequent subjects of clerical prosecution in the early modern period. Examining accusations of necromancy in Europe and particularly Finland, Raisa Toivo (2008, 177) concludes that court depositions contradict the midwife-witch theory. In her view, most scholars give too much credence to a few works by demonologists (above all the *Malleus Maleficarum*) without considering whether such polemics had a significant cultural impact. In reality, midwives were far more likely to arrive in court as witnesses or to inspect an accused witch for the devil's mark. For example, in sixteenth- and seventeenth-century Scotland, only one in five hundred accused witches were midwives (Harley 1990, 14). David Harley, in the same vein as Toivo, argues that midwives were rarely accused of witchery because they garnered respect as influential members of their communities, not marginal women. Jonathan Durrant (2007, 193), in his analysis of early modern Germany, characterizes midwives as one of several nexus points for female networks within the community.

This does not mean that midwives were not associated with the use of magic but simply that, in some locations, they were rarely persecuted as witches. In early modern France, for example, popular belief held that midwives could predict, facilitate, or block conception, render women infertile and men impotent, or, alternatively, ensure fertility. Midwives were thought to have the power to divine future fertility through an interpretation of the umbilical cord, as well as to transform nature, making beautiful children ugly and ugly children beautiful (H. Tucker 2003, 61–65). Cataloging these magical powers, one notes an evident dichotomy between the benevolent and malevolent midwife. Louise Bourgeois, midwife to Marie de' Medici, writes in "Instruction à ma fille" that the midwife is privy to secrets, and that "there are two paths that are easy to take: one is the path of salvation and the other, damnation" (57).

Indeed, it is precisely this question of damnation that concerned the inquisitors of the Catholic Church. At least as early as the *Malleus Maleficarum*, demonologists obsessed over the potential evils the midwife was liable to commit, unobserved in that exclusively female arena, the birth chamber. Fears swelled around satanic baptism and the slaughter of infants for use in ointments or malicious potions (Forbes 1966, 119). Although emergency baptisms by the midwife had the sanction of the church as early as the seventh century,[9] the matter gained special priority during the Reformation (Wiesner 1993, 85–86). The 1491 Wurzburg Synodal Statutes meticulously regulated the performance of baptism, particularly how biological by-products were to be disposed of after deliveries. In addition, they demanded that midwives employ no superstitious practices during the delivery.

However, once again, there is a distinction to be made between the witch crazes as a clerical versus a popular phenomenon. Harley (1990, 8) argues that the so-called midwife-witch was largely a literary convention that failed to substantially influence popular perceptions. Richard Horsley (1979, 693–94) claims that, although the victims of the inquisition's prosecutions (the majority of them poor, elderly women) could be accused by magistrates of either white or black magic equally, peasant depositions in Britain and the continent reveal a distinction between the wise woman who heals and the sorcerer who bewitches. Hence there exists a broad division between the prosecutions carried out by trained demonologists and the opinions at the village level. Nevertheless, Horsley further maintains that, in Austria, a particularly large percentage of accused persons appear to have been primarily wise women. These would include women who practiced herbal and magical healing and offered love charms, protective and fertility magic, and sometimes midwifery. Thus an observable incongruity emerges between, on the one hand, accusations made by magistrates, clerics, and individuals under torture and, on the other hand, the testimony of uncoerced individuals.

In short, the figures of the wise woman and the midwife overlap in social function in the cognitive scripts of early modern Europeans, developing over time into a kind of composite character that embodies certain cultural binaries between magical healing and medical practice or the place of women in the public versus private realms. Clearly these types do not always and everywhere represent the same person, yet their many points of correspondence create the conditions for metonymic association through the continual process of reassembly and renewal that characterizes the oral tradition. This composite figure functions in a dual role as both the wise woman who can treat disease through thaumaturgy, versed in verbal charms as well as herbal remedies, and also increasingly as a civil servant, regulated by municipal statutes and regulations. In Germany, for example, midwives became sworn city officials as early as the fifteenth century—1417 in

Nuremberg, 1456 in Frankfurt, 1480 in Munich, and 1489 in Stuttgart—and continued to serve in this capacity until at least the end of the eighteenth century. And even at the height of the witch craze in Germany, city records show a continued concern on the part of municipal authorities with the honesty and competence of midwives rather than any potentially diabolical affiliations (Wiesner 1993, 88).

The reputation of the midwife was essential in her trade as "it was her chief credential and only advertisement" (Harley 1990, 6). The very success of the midwife required that she be respectable and trustworthy, two characteristics that for much of the early modern period necessarily involved the proper, beneficent use of magic. Rolande Graves, discussing women and childbirth in France from the Middle Ages to the Enlightenment, claims that precisely because of the inherent risks of childbirth, a risk only exacerbated by the services of an untrained midwife, "a knowledgeable and caring midwife was not only called on to do her duty, but was often 'adopted' by the family who came to look upon her as a friend—someone to rely on at desperate times" (2001, 67). Thus the image of the persecuted wise woman–midwife is not entirely accurate or at least not applicable across Europe. What must remain clear is that there has always been a space in the European imagination for benevolent thaumaturgy, namely as it concerns the wise woman and/or midwife. This was the case even or perhaps especially at moments when clerical persecution predominated.

Having created this necessarily partial portrait of the potent, if ambiguous, significations of "wise woman" across early modern Europe, we discover the broad semantic network of traditional referentiality the phrase engages. "Wise woman" is meant to reorient our understanding of the old woman. Nonetheless, any analysis of the old woman must run parallel to an analysis of the princess. We arrive at the old woman via the princess.

The Princess at the Spring

For much of the tale, the princess's behavior is characterized by a deep disquiet. When we first encounter the heroine, she nervously inquires about her long absent "mother." Later, when the old woman says that they can no longer stay together, she responds with anguish, pleading not to be cast out. The trauma of her kin-inflicted exile is palpable in these moments. Perhaps even more than in these exchanges, the princess appears deeply pathetic in the titular scene at the spring. This pathos requires further examination. At the start of the scene, the princess and the old woman sit spinning. For the first time, we witness the princess in complete tranquility. Her silence literally reveals her quietude, the intimacy she shares with the old woman—her home, her mother. The night owl disturbs this silence, and the old woman speaks: "Now, my little daughter, it's time for you to go outside and do your work" (Zipes 1987, 567).

A great deal pivots on this statement. If the old woman has indeed engineered the plot,[10] selecting the suitor who will in turn reunite the royal family and marry the princess, then the phrase "do your work" serves a teleological function. At the spring, the princess bathes herself, unknowingly preparing for her betrothal. Equally unknown to her, she is carrying out a courtship ritual, for her suitor watches from a distant tree. If we are to take the old woman at her word when she says "I know everything already," then she is aware that the count awaits. Perhaps the night owl carried this very message. In this peculiarly intricate scene, a performance takes place under the old woman's direction, though both performer and spectator are ignorant of their roles. We alone are privy to the script. We watch from a distant perch.

Bottigheimer (1986, 115; 1987, 51–80) argues that mid-nineteenth-century Germany idealized the silent, weak woman. The modern fairy-tale heroine, characterized above all by a long-suffering victimhood, can be traced to the nineteenth-century German and German-influenced tale collections (Bottigheimer 2004, 49). In this context, the goose girl at the spring performs this ideal. She transforms herself before the count's eyes—but not before transforming before our eyes—from a strong, old, ugly woman to a weak, young, beautiful one. Her weeping only serves to reinforce her vulnerability, her abasement, her "femininity." She is the very image of the fairy-tale heroine: close to nature, passive, isolated, degraded.

Furthermore, notions of female virtue were intimately related to the practice of spinning. Bottigheimer argues that notions of selflessness, generosity, poverty, spinning, and femininity were joined together in nineteenth-century German culture. For Bottigheimer, "The Goose Girl at the Spring" exemplifies this connection: "Spinning is the symbol for and the visible attribute of the penury and personal degradation into which a princess is plunged when she is deprived of male protection" (1987, 119). For no cause save her own sincerity, the princess suffers the loss of her father's protection, enduring three years of degradation. She weeps at the spring, watching the reflection of a princess who has been lowered to such an extent that she must spin for hours on end. In this reading—by no means the only possible one—the spinning scene symbolizes the nadir of her trial, just before her climactic restoration.

Unfortunately, such an interpretation is not substantiated by the text. The princess never voices disdain for her lowly position but instead displays a powerful bond with the old woman. Unlike Rapunzel, who is all too happy to part with Mother Gothel,[11] the princess is distraught at the notion of leaving the old woman. To understand the princess's feelings toward her guardian one must first understand her motives for weeping at the spring. Yet her tears are enigmatic. Indeed, the princess herself is enigmatic. Evidence of her emotional life rests almost entirely on a handful of events: distress when the old woman is gone; distress when she discovers she may be cast out yet again; tears (reported) when she is initially exiled; tears at the spring; tears at her reunion with her family; and a childish blush when she sees the count. The princess emotes continually, but the referents of her feelings are not always clear.

With this in mind, let us consider two scenes in opposition to each other: the aforementioned spinning scene, and what we might call the Lear scene in which the king seeks verbal affirmations of his daughter's love. In the latter scene, the princess keeps quiet, not knowing what to say. When her father entreats her, she at first says she cannot compare her love with anything, and, finally, she compares her love for her father to her love of salt. As we well know, this invokes her father's rage and invites the princess's exile. In contrast, the spinning scene with the old woman is characterized above all by its silence. This love requires no verbal affirmation. Silence may have typified feminine virtue in the Grimms' cultural matrix, indeed this is part of what the tale performs, but nevertheless we should not underestimate its versatility as a narrative device. No scholar would claim that silence has a single signification in the Grimms' tales. In fact, many kinds of silence inhabit the collection, with many significations. Perhaps the silence of the spinning scene alludes both to an ideal of female virtue and, somewhere within the tale's dim history, to a bond that elides that ideal.

What form might this bond have taken, hidden within silence, nurtured in a lonely place? As our etymologies tell us, "midwife," "wise woman," "godmother," and "old woman" have intermingled as signs throughout the last millennium. The line is not always clear between the mother and the other mother. The intimacy of the birth chamber—an exclusively female arena until the last half of the seventeenth century and the gradual encroachment of the male surgeon-obstetrician (Wilson 1995, 25–41)—has the potential to generate metonymic associations between the midwife, who, in her magical power to influence the delivery, seems to comother the child and the godmother, who is present at the baptism. Just as the baptism and the birth scene could at times conflate, so too perhaps could the roles of mother, midwife, and godmother have the tendency to overlap in the cultural imaginary.

Two mothers inhabit our story, one passive, or at least incapable of defending her daughter, and the other active, carefully devising a plan to reinstate her daughter. It is worth noting that the princess calls only one person "Mother," namely the old woman. Nonetheless, this comother, or allomother, is ultimately excluded from the life she helps engender and protect. The story subtly explores the tension inherent to the presence of the other mother, a female present at the birth who is, in a sense, cogenerative with the mother and instrumental in the child's survival, and ultimately concludes that the two cannot coexist. The mother returns and the other mother disappears.

Somehow, the old woman and the princess cannot coexist. As the former says, "Don't you remember . . . that you came to me three years ago on this day? Your time is up. We can no longer stay together" (Zipes 1987, 569). As it turns out, it is the old woman whose time is up. She sets about cleaning the house, preparing for the arrival of the royal couple, the count, and her own demise. In so doing, she initiates a ritual of transformation, scrubbing and sweeping away her own life. Slowly, but diligently, she scrubs away the days, the months, the years she shared with the princess—and those they might yet have shared. She tears into her past to satisfy a vague imperative. She spins the plot, yet some still greater force has fixed the duration of the union.[12] What seems to drive the narrative is an unquestioned belief that a life shared by two women is not enough. Indeed, the final unveiling of the princess constitutes a fundamental rupture.[13] The old woman offers her, like a bride, to the count. In the peculiar arrangement of the scene, the royal couple seems more like the groom's parents than the princess's. The plot culminates in the dissolution of one relationship and the beginning of another. This final scene dramatizes the inevitable separation that patrilocality entails.[14]

Yet something resists and arrests the plot. This final parting provides a new way to read the spinning scene, for suddenly that long silence at the loom carries the melancholy of imminent loss, a kind of mourning. Herein the tale's competing narrative voices become manifest. For the Grimms— as well as many others—the helper or donor is meant to aid the heroine, and, almost invariably, success is equated with marriage. Yet what makes "The Goose Girl at the Spring" unique in the Grimms' collection is the very hesitation that precedes the betrothal: the lingering silence the two women share as they sit spinning. The narrator tells us that they spin for two full hours, yet this part of the tale is literally unobservable—it is a span of time that does not belong to us. Given that it contributes nothing to the union of the count and the princess, this scene serves no function within the plot. In fact, it arrests the plot, arrests the very web the old woman is spinning for herself.

When is protection excessive? Bottigheimer (1987, 119) argues that "self-lessness," "generosity," "poverty," "spinning," and "women" all formed a complex in nineteenth-century Germany. The old woman's virtue is linked with the sacrifice she offers, yet what virtue lies in self-destruction? The strange silence that pervades the tale—the loving silence and the melancholy silence of the spinners, the purposeful silence of the grandmother—finally refers back to the motif of the protective disguise. Hidden within the tale is a woeful quiet.

In turn, the motif of disguise demands a reconsideration of the false skin that conceals the beauty of the princess. Just before the old woman sends her out to the spring, the princess speaks at relative length, begging not to be put out by her adopted mother. It is after this moment of complete vulnerability—laying herself figuratively bare—that she must take off her "false" skin and put on a silk dress. Given her patent attachment to the old woman, given the performance she must now enact, the careful reader must ask, Which is the true skin, which the disguise? The beauty of the princess immediately constitutes her as an object of male lust. In conforming to a heteronormative standard of beauty, she becomes visible to the hitherto uninterested count.

This false skin, which has ensured the invisibility of the princess, should also be read in light of the spinning scene. Just as that scene arrests the plot, deferring for a moment its heteronormative resolution, the disguise offers the princess three years of respite from male advances. The disguise thus complements the isolation of the *Einöde*, the lonely place. Nonetheless, the disguise also represents a way for the old woman to keep the princess for herself, to zealously guard the young woman's beauty.

The isolation of their abode assured these women a delimited and safe space, a place of their own. It is a place of refuge and solace, where they had the freedom to reconstitute family and, further, the dynamics of a female relationship. If we consider the ending of the story as the end of one relationship and the beginning of another, then it behooves us to consider how they mirror each other, and how the erotic content of the former—latent in this telling—is transferred to the latter. In this queer reading, the sensuality, the erotic charge of the women's relationship, emerges in the crimson blush of the silent princess.

Describing their three years together as borrowed time, as a terminal union, the two resemble doomed lovers. The sense of finitude that increasingly marks the tale with each reading only serves to heighten the intensity of the spinning scene, which becomes a funeral in life, a memorial for something slipping away. Characteristic of the literary fairy tale, we find a splicing technique that joins the scene at the royal court with the spinning scene.[15] In this incongruous shift, we note the tension between these narratives, as if the *Einöde* wishes to persist in its solitude, as if the women therein would rather spin on without interruption, silent, together.[16]

A Voice That Was Silenced

What can it mean to say the old woman was a wise woman? We circle around the question continuously and still she eludes us. Whether the phrase is an embedded allusion to the midwife and/or the godmother is unclear; the plausibility of that connection is precisely what makes it intriguing and, simultaneously, a baffling piece of evidence. The very proximity of the words *weise Frau* and *Geburt* (birth), which forms half of the compound *Geburtshelferin* (birth-helper) or midwife, seems to invite such an association. Nevertheless, to claim that one meaning may be wrought from the tale is to deny the vitality of the tradition.

These etymological and textual points of contact prove little conclusively. That being said, I believe that all the evidence taken together constitutes a sound basis to argue for not only a contemporary queer reading of the tale but a queer telling embedded historically within the tradition. The tale subtly explores the queerness of the relationship between the child and the other mother, the midwife or godmother figure who plays a crucial role in her birth and development. Their bond bespeaks a broader conception of love and family. What is more, the tale subverts our expectations of the witch type. The speech act found at the tale's conclusion engenders a feat of magic no less remarkable than those of the old woman herself: the witch (*Hexe*) becomes the wise woman (*weise Frau*). Her magic proves white, her designs benevolent. If the tale represents an amalgamation of multitudinous voices emergent in each performance, then it contains within it the memory of those wise women who populate its ineffable provenance. This is the unspoken cultural content that animates the speech act "weise Frau." To say the old woman was not a witch but a wise woman forces the phrase to transcend the level of the constative; "weise Frau" is an act of defiance that demands and engenders a radical shift in perception.

Nevertheless, this is not a utopian fantasy, and, like all fairy tales, it acts more or less within certain generic—as well as heteronormative—constraints. The princess suffers banishment, but ultimately it is the old woman whose suffering is interminable. Her work, whether gathering grass, spinning, or arranging for the happy ending of her ward, leads ultimately to nothing save her own quiet eradication. This is her telos. She offers a happiness safeguarded by her convenient absence. Having given everything to the princess, she renders herself a mere dependent, and this dependency jeopardizes the new couple's life lived happily ever after. Hence she disappears.

Whether this fairy tale, through its innumerable iterations, represented a way for women and men to work through the tensions between "parent" and "alloparent"—tensions made all the more acute as the nuclear family gained ascendancy in Western Europe—frustrates any definitive resolution.

It is an unfalsifiable claim. Thus we return to the problem of evidence. Etymologies and historical documents rarely provide the kind of answer that conclusively seals a debate. The truth is everywhere, but this very omnipresence confounds delimitation. How do we do this old woman—a fictional character, but one who bears the trace of those women who suffused her with embodied experience—justice? How does one give an account of a voice that was silenced? In lieu of evidence, we remain immersed in this silence, save the sound of her wordless spinning, her testimony.

Notes

1. Propp (1968, 39–43) distinguishes between the pure donor, who aids the hero but does not directly intervene on his behalf, and the pure helper, who does intervene. Many figures may fall under both categories.

2. The term "allomother" refers to caretakers—mostly but not exclusively female—other than the biological parents. In *Mothers and Others: The Evolutionary Origins of Mutual Understanding*, Sarah Blaffer Hrdy (2009) argues that selection for cooperative breeding was a driving force in human hypersociality and cooperative behavior in general.

3. This act mirrors that of the princess, who is led into exile with a bag of salt on her back—punishment for her poorly interpreted affirmation of love. The count's ascent may also be read as a symbolic test of his merit as a suitor.

4. In J. L. Austin's words, "To issue a constative utterance (i.e., to utter it with historical reference) is to make a statement" (1962, 6).

5. Positing that the couple lived happily ever after implies an assertion of personal belief on the part of the narrator, claiming "I believe" (Ich glaube); but in the case of the old woman's identity, there is no doubt: "One thing is sure" (Soviel ist gewiß). Indeed, this assertion runs counter to the community's belief, for the full sentence reads: "One thing is sure: The old woman was not a witch, as people believed, but a wise woman who meant well" (Zipes 1987, 570; Soviel ist gewiß, daß die Alte keine Hexe war, wie die Leute glaubten, sondern eine weise Frau, die es gut meinte [Uther 1996, 3:104]).

6. Examples of ATU 510B are Charles Perrault's "Donkeyskin" and the Grimms' "All Kinds of Fur," discussed in chapter 4 of this volume.

7. Warner emphasizes the historical relationship between the English word "gossip" and the roles of godmother and intimate friend.

8. Two works often cited by scholars are Reginald Scot's *The Discoverie of Witch-*

craft, written in 1584, and the highly problematic *Malleus Maleficarum*, written by Heinrich Kramer and Jacob Sprenger in 1486. Both works argue from opposite sides for a relationship between midwives, wise women, and magic. Kramer and Sprenger, demonologists of the Catholic Church, argue not merely that witchcraft exists but that wise women and midwives are its chief practitioners. Scot, nearly a century later, argues that witchcraft does not exist, that the person one calls a witch is nothing but a wise woman (i.e., a village healer/diviner and/or possibly a midwife). The relationship between wise woman and midwife is not always clear. It would be wholly inaccurate to argue that, in Britain or the continent, all wise women were midwives or vice versa; however, there does seem to be some overlap in social roles, coupled with a popular conception of a link between them (Horsley 1979, 697).

9. So-called emergency baptisms refer to those performed by a layperson when the newborn's life was thought to be at risk and no clergyman was present.

10. As the old woman declares, "I know everything already"; "Come in, I already know who you are" (Zipes 1987, 565, 569).

11. *Gothel* means godmother in German (Tatar 2002, 149).

12. One possibility is that their relationship is framed as one of reciprocal exchange, as in "Frau Holle" (ATU 480). One is also reminded of Perrault's "Donkeyskin" and the Grimms' own "All Kinds of Fur" and "Princess Mouseskin"—all ATU 510B variants—where the fleeing heroine is enlisted to work in a kitchen.

13. Much of the tale centers on notions of privacy and protection. In several instances, the seclusion of the old woman's home is disrupted. The night owl messenger first interrupts the women's spinning by glaring through the window with "two fiery eyes" (*zwei feurige Augen*). Likewise, the count and the royal couple look through the window at the old woman spinning, while the princess prepares herself in another room, an additional wall shielding her from prying eyes. The dual scenes at the spring play out a dialectic between privacy and voyeurism. In other words, each of these scenes extends the motif of disguise.

14. *Patrilocality* refers to social situations in which a wife resides with her husband's kin group.

15. *Splicing* refers to the union of two or more distinct narratives in order to create a single narrative.

16. I would like to take this opportunity to thank Kay Turner for her invaluable assistance in the development of this queer analysis, specifically in queering the relationship between the old woman and the princess.

3

Queering Kinship in "The Maiden Who Seeks Her Brothers"

JEANA JORGENSEN

Fantasy is not the opposite of reality; it is what reality forecloses, and, as a result, it defines the limits of reality, constituting it as its constitutive outside. The critical promise of fantasy, when and where it exists, is to challenge the contingent limits of what will and will not be called reality. Fantasy is what allows us to imagine ourselves and others otherwise; it establishes the possible in excess of the real; it points elsewhere, and when it is embodied, it brings the elsewhere home.
—Judith Butler, *Undoing Gender*

The fairy tales in the *Kinder- und Hausmärchen,* or *Children's and Household Tales,* compiled by Jacob and Wilhelm Grimm are among the world's most popular, yet they have also provoked discussion and debate regarding their authenticity, violent imagery, and restrictive gender roles. In this chapter I interpret the three versions published by the Grimm brothers of ATU 451, "The Maiden Who Seeks Her Brothers," focusing on constructions of family, femininity, and identity. I utilize the folkloristic methodology of allomotific analysis, integrating feminist and queer theories of kinship and gender roles. I follow Pauline Greenhill by taking a queer view of fairy tale texts from the Grimms' collection, for her use of queer implies both "its older meaning as a type of destabilizing redirection, and its more recent sense as a reference to sexualities beyond the heterosexual." This is appropriate for her reading of "Fitcher's Bird" (ATU 311, "Rescue by the Sister") as a story that "subverts patriarchy, heterosexuality, femininity, and masculinity alike" (2008, 147). I will similarly demonstrate that "The Maiden Who Seeks Her Brothers" only superficially conforms to the Grimms' patriarchal, nationalizing agenda, for the tale rather subversively critiques the nuclear family and heterosexual marriage by revealing ambiguity and ambivalence. The tale also queers biology, illuminating transbiological connections between species and a critique of reproductive futurism. Thus, through the use of fantasy, this tale and fairy tales in general can question the status quo, addressing concepts such as self, other, and home.

The first volume of the first edition of the Grimm brothers' collection appeared in 1812, to be followed by six revisions during the brothers' lifetimes (leading to a total of seven editions of the so-called large edition of their collection, while the so-called small edition was published in ten editions). The Grimm brothers published three versions of "The Maiden Who Seeks Her Brothers" in the 1812 edition of their collection, but the tales in that volume underwent some changes over time, as did most of the tales. This was partially in an effort to increase sales, and Wilhelm's editorial changes in particular "tended to make the tales more proper and prudent for bourgeois audiences" (Zipes 2002b, xxxi). "The Maiden Who Seeks Her Brothers" is one of the few tale types that the Grimms published multiply, each time giving titular focus to the brothers, as the versions are titled "The Twelve Brothers" (KHM 9), "The Seven Ravens" (KHM 25), and "The Six Swans" (KHM 49). However, both Stith Thompson and Hans-Jörg Uther, in their respective 1961 and 2004 revisions of the international tale type index, call the tale type "The Maiden Who Seeks Her Brothers." Indeed, Thompson discusses this tale in *The Folktale* under the category of faithfulness, particularly faithful sisters, noting, "In spite of the minor variations . . . the tale-type is well-defined in all its major incidents" (1946, 110). Thompson also describes how the tale is found "in folktale collections from all parts of Europe" and forms the basis of three of the tales in the Grimm brothers' collection (111).

In his *Interpretation of Fairy Tales*, Bengt Holbek classifies ATU 451 as a "feminine" tale, since its two main characters who wed at the end of the tale are a low-born young female and a high-born young male (the sister, though originally of noble birth in many versions, is cast out and essentially impoverished by the tale's circumstances). Holbek notes that the role of a low-born young male in feminine tales is often filled by brothers: "The relationship between sister and brothers is characterized by love and help-fulness, even if fear and rivalry may also be an aspect in some tales (in AT 451, the girl is afraid of the twelve ravens; she sews shirts to disenchant them, however, and they save her from being burnt at the stake at the last moment)" (1987, 417). While Holbek conflates tale versions in this description, he is essentially correct about ATU 451; the siblings are devoted to one another, despite fearsome consequences.

The discrepancy between those titles that focus on the brothers and those that focus on the sister deserves further attention. Perhaps the Grimm brothers (and their informants?) were drawn to the more spectacular imagery of enchanted brothers. In Hans Christian Andersen's well-known version of ATU 451, "The Wild Swans," he too focuses on the brothers in the title. However, some scholars, including Thompson and myself, are more intrigued by the sister's actions in the tale. Bethany Joy Bear, for instance, in her analysis of traditional and modern versions of ATU 451, concentrates on the agency of the silent sister-saviors, noting that the three versions in the Grimms' collection "illustrate various ways of empowering the hero-ine. In 'The Seven Ravens' she saves her brothers through an active and courageous quest, while in 'The Twelve Brothers' and 'The Six Swans' her success requires redemptive silence" (2009, 45).

The three tales differ by more than just how the sister saves her brothers, though. In "The Twelve Brothers," a king and queen with twelve boys are about to have another child; the king swears to kill the boys if the newborn is a girl so that she can inherit the kingdom. The queen warns the boys and they run away, and the girl later seeks them. She inadvertently picks flow-ers that turn her brothers into ravens, and in order to disenchant them she must remain silent; she may not speak or laugh for seven years. During this time, she marries a king, but his mother slanders her, and when the seven years have elapsed, she is about to be burned at the stake. At that moment, her brothers are disenchanted and returned to human form. They redeem their sister, who lives happily with her husband and her brothers.

In "The Seven Ravens," a father exclaims that his seven negligent sons should turn into ravens for failing to bring water to baptize their newborn sister. It is unclear whether the sister remains unbaptized, thus contributing to her more liminal status. When the sister grows up, she seeks her brothers, shunning the sun and moon but gaining help from the stars, who give her a bone to unlock the glass mountain where her brothers reside. Because she loses the bone, the girl cuts off her small finger, using it to gain access to the mountain. She disenchants her brothers by simply appearing, and they all return home to live together.

In "The Six Swans," a king is coerced into marrying a witch's daughter, who finds where the king has stashed his children to keep them safe. The sorceress enchants the boys, turning them into swans, and the girl seeks them. She must not speak or laugh for six years and she must sew shirts from asters for them. She marries a king, but the king's mother steals each of the three children born to the couple, smearing the wife's mouth with blood to implicate her as a cannibal. She finishes sewing the shirts just as she's about to be burned at the stake; then her brothers are disenchanted and come to live with the royal couple and their returned children. However, the sleeve of one shirt remained unfinished, so the littlest brother is stuck with a wing instead of an arm.

The main episodes of the tale type follow Russian folklorist Vladimir Propp's structural sequence for fairy-tale plots: the tale begins with a villainy, the banishing and enchantment of the brothers, sometimes resulting from an interdiction that has been violated. The sister must perform a task in addition to going on a quest, and the tale ends with the formation of a new family through marriage. As Alan Dundes observes, "If Propp's formula is valid, then the major task in fairy tales is to replace one's original family through marriage" (1993, 124; see also Lüthi 1982). This observation holds true for heteronormative structures (such as the nuclear family), which exist in order to replicate themselves. In many fairy tales, the original nuclear family is discarded due to circumstance or choice. However, the sister in "The Maiden Who Seeks Her Brothers" has not abandoned or been removed from her old family, unlike Cinderella, who ditches her nasty stepmother and stepsisters, or Rapunzel, who is taken from her birth parents, and so on. Although, admittedly, "The Seven Ravens" does not end in marriage, I do not plan to disqualify it from analysis simply because it doesn't fit the dominant model, as Bengt Holbek does when comparing Danish versions of "King Wivern" (ATU 433B, "King Lindorm").[1] The fact that one of the tales does not end in marriage actually supports my interpretation of the tales as transgressive, a point to which I will return later.

Dundes's (2007) notion of allomotif helps make sense of the kinship dynamics in "The Maiden Who Seeks Her Brothers." In order to decipher the symbolic code of folktales, Dundes proposes that any motif that could fill the same slot in a particular tale's plot should be designated an allomotif. Further, if motif A and motif B fulfill the same purpose in moving along the tale's plot, then they are considered mutually substitutable, thus equivalent symbolically. What this assertion means for my analysis is that all the methods by which the brothers are enchanted and subsequently disenchanted can be treated as meaningful in relation to one another. One of the advantages of comparing allomotifs rather than motifs is that we can be assured that we are analyzing not random details but significant plot components. So in "The Six Swans" and "The Seven Ravens," we see the parental curse causing both the banishment and the enchantment of the brothers, whereas in "The Twelve Brothers," the brothers are banished and enchanted in separate moves. Even though the brothers' exile and enchantment happen in a different sequence in the different texts, we must view their causes as functionally parallel. Thus the ire of a father concerned for his newborn daughter, the jealous rage of a stepmother, the homicidal desire of a father to give his daughter everything, and the innocent flower gathering of a sister can all be seen as threatening to the brothers. All of these actions lead to the dispersal and enchantment of the brothers, though not all are malicious, for the sister in "The Twelve Brothers" accidentally turns her brothers into ravens by picking flowers that consequently enchant them.

I interpret this equivalence as a metaphorical statement—threats to a family's cohesion come in all forms, from well-intentioned actions to openly malevolent curses. The father's misdirected love for his sole daughter in two versions ("The Twelve Brothers" and "The Seven Ravens") translates to danger to his sons. This danger is allomotifically paralleled by how the sister, without even knowing it, causes her brothers to become enchanted, either by picking flowers in "The Twelve Brothers" or through the mere incident of her birth in "The Twelve Brothers" and "The Seven Ravens." The fact that a father would prioritize his sole daughter over numerous sons is strange and reminiscent of tales in which a father explicitly expresses romantic desire for his daughter, as in "Allerleirauh" (ATU 510B), discussed in chapter 4 by Margaret Yocom. Even in "The Six Swans," where a stepmother with magical powers enchants the sons, the father is implicated; he did not love his children well enough to protect them from his new spouse, and once the boys had been changed into swans and fled, the father tries to take his daughter with him back to his castle (where the stepmother would likely be waiting to dispose of the daughter as well), not knowing that by asserting control over her, he would be endangering her. The father's implied ownership of the daughter in "The Maiden Who Seeks Her Brothers" and the linking of inheritance with danger emphasize the conflicts that threaten the nuclear family. Both material and emotional resources are in limited supply in these tales, with disastrous consequences for the nuclear family, which fragments, as it does in all fairy tales (see Propp 1968).

Holbek reaches a similar conclusion in his allomotific analysis of ATU 451, though he focuses on Danish versions collected by Evald Tang Kristensen in the late nineteenth century. Holbek notes that the heroine is the actual "cause of her brothers' expulsion in all cases, either—innocently—through being born or—inadvertently—through some act of hers" (1987, 550). The true indication of the heroine's role in condemning her brothers is her role in saving them, despite the fact that other characters may superficially be blamed: "The heroine's guilt is nevertheless to be deduced from the fact that only an act of hers can save her brothers." However, Holbek reads the tale as revolving around the theme of sibling rivalry, which is more relevant to the cultural context in which Danish versions of ATU 451 were set, since the initial family situation in the tale was not always said to be royal or noble, and Holbek views the tales as reflecting the actual concerns and conditions of their peasant tellers (550; see also 406–9).[2] Holbek also discusses the lack of resources that might lead to sibling rivalry, identifying physical scarcity and emotional love as two factors that could inspire tension between siblings.

The initial situation in the Grimms' versions of "The Maiden Who Seeks Her Brothers" is also a comment on the arbitrary power that parents have over their children, the ability to withhold love or resources or both. The helplessness of children before the strong feelings of their parents is corroborated in another Grimms' tale, "The Lazy One and the Industrious One" (Zipes 2002b, 638).[3] In this tale, which Jack Zipes translated among the "omitted tales" that did not make it into any of the published editions of the *KHM*, a father curses his sons for insulting him, causing them to turn into ravens until a beautiful maiden kisses them. Essentially, the family is a site of danger, yet it is a structure that will be replicated in the tale's conclusion . . . almost.

But first, the sister seeks her brothers and disenchants them. The symbolic equation links, in each of the three tales, the sister's silence (neither speaking nor laughing) for six years while sewing six shirts from asters, her seven years of silence (neither speaking nor laughing), and her cutting off her finger and using it to gain entry to the glass palace where she disenchants her brothers merely by being present. The theme unifying these allomotifs is sacrifice. The sister's loss of her finger, equivalent to the loss of her voice, is a symbolic disempowerment. One loss is a physical mutilation, which might not impair the heroine terribly much; the choice not to use her voice is arguably more drastic, since her inability to speak for herself nearly causes her death in the tales.[4] Both losses could be seen as equivalent to castration.[5] However, losing her ability to speak and her ability to manipulate the world around her while at the same time displaying domestic competence in sewing equates powerlessness with feminine pursuits. Bear notes that versions by both the Grimms and Hans Christian Andersen envision "a distinctly feminine savior whose work is symbolized by her spindle, an ancient emblem of women's work" (2009, 46). Ruth Bottigheimer (1986) points out in her essay "Silenced Women in Grimms' Tales" that the heroines in "The Twelve Brothers" and "The Six Swans" are forced to accept conditions of muteness that disempower them, which is part of a larger silencing that occurs in the tales; women both are explicitly forbidden to speak, and they have fewer declarative and interrogative speech acts attributed to them within the whole body of the Grimms' texts.

Ironically, in performing subservient femininity, the sister fails to perform adequately as wife or mother, since the children she bears in one version ("The Six Swans") are stolen from her. When the sister is married to the king, she gives birth to three children in succession, but each time, the king's mother takes away the infant and smears the queen's mouth with blood while she sleeps (Zipes 2002b, 170). Finally, the heroine is sentenced to death by a court but is unable to protest her innocence since she must not speak in order to disenchant her brothers. In being a faithful sister, the heroine cannot be a good mother and is condemned to die for it. This aspect of the tale could represent a deeply coded feminist voice.[6] A tale collected and published by men might contain an implicitly coded feminist message, since the critique of patriarchal institutions such as the family would have to be buried so deeply as to not even be recognizable as a message in order to avoid detection and censorship (Radner and Lanser 1993, 6–9). The sister in "The Six Swans" cannot perform all of the feminine duties required of her, and because she ostensibly allows her children to die, she could be accused of infanticide. Similarly, in the contemporary legend "The Inept Mother," collected and analyzed by Janet Langlois, an overwhelmed mother's incompetence indirectly kills one or all of her children.[7] Langlois reads this legend as a coded expression of women's frustrations at being isolated at home with too many responsibilities, a coded demand for more support than is usually given to mothers in patriarchal institutions. Essentially, the story is "complex thinking about the thinkable—protecting the child who must leave you—and about the unthinkable—being a woman not defined in relation to motherhood" (Langlois 1993, 93). The heroine in "The Six Swans" also occupies an ambiguous position, navigating different expectations of femininity, forced to choose between giving care and nurturance to some and withholding it from others.

Here, I find it productive to draw a parallel to Antigone, the daughter of Oedipus. Antigone defies the orders of her uncle Creon in order to bury her brother Polyneices and faces a death sentence as a result. Antigone's fidelity to her blood family costs her not only her life but also her future as a productive and reproductive member of society. As Judith Butler (2000) clarifies in *Antigone's Claim: Kinship between Life and Death*, Antigone transgresses both gender and kinship norms in her actions and her speech acts.

Her love for her brother borders on the incestuous and exposes the incest taboo at the heart of kinship structure. Antigone's perverse death drive for the sake of her brother, Butler asserts, is all the more monstrous because it establishes aberration at the heart of the norm (in this case the incest taboo). I see a similar logic operating in "The Maiden Who Seeks Her Brothers," because according to allomotific equivalences, the heroine is condemned to die only in one version ("The Six Swans") because she allegedly ate her children. In the other version that contains the marriage episode ("The Twelve Brothers"), the king's mother slanders her, calling the maiden "godless," and accuses her of wicked things until the king agrees to sentence her to death (Zipes 2002b, 35). As allomotific analysis reveals, in the three versions, the heroine is punished for being excessively devoted to her brothers, which is functionally the same as cannibalism and as being generally wicked (the accusation of the king's mother in two of the versions).

In a sense, the heroine's disproportionate devotion to her brothers kills her chance at marriage and kills her children, which from a queer stance is a comment on the performativity of sexuality and gender. According to Butler, gender performativity demonstrates "that what we take to be an internal essence of gender is manufactured through a sustained set of acts, posited through the gendered stylization of the body" ([1990] 1999, xv). This illusion, that gender and sexuality are a "being" rather than a "doing," is constantly at risk of exposure. When sexuality is exposed as constructed rather than natural, thus threatening the whole social-sexual system of identity formation, the threat must be eliminated.

One aspect of this system particularly threatened in "The Maiden Who Seeks Her Brothers" is reproductive futurism, one form of compulsory teleological heterosexuality, "the epitome of heteronormativity's desire to reach self-fulfillment by endlessly recycling itself through the figure of the Child" (Giffney 2008, 56; see also Edelman 2004). Reproductive futurism mandates that politics and identities be placed in service of the future and future children, utilizing the rhetoric of an idealized childhood. In his book on reproductive futurism, Lee Edelman links queerness and the death drive, stating, "The death drive names what the queer, in the order of the social, is called forth to figure: the negativity opposed to every form of social viability" (2004, 9). According to this logic, to prioritize anything other than one's reproductive future is to refuse social viability and heteronormativity—this is what the heroine in "The Maiden Who Seeks Her Brothers" does. Her excessive emotional ties to her brothers disfigure her future, aligning her with the queer, the unlivable, and hence the ungrievable. Refusing the linear narrative of reproductive futurism registers as "unthinkable, irresponsible, inhumane" (4), words that could very well be used to describe a mother who is thought to be eating her babies and who cannot or will not speak to defend herself.

The heroine's marriage to the king in two versions of the tale can also be examined from a queer perspective. Like the tale "Fitcher's Bird," which queers marriage by "showing male-female [marital] relationships as clearly fraught with danger and evil *from their onset*," the Grimms' two versions of ATU 451 that feature marriage call into question its sanctity and safety (Greenhill 2008, 150, emphasis in original). Marriage, though the ultimate goal of many fairy tales, does not provide the heroine with a supportive or nurturing environment. Bear comments that in versions of "The Maiden Who Seeks Her Brothers" wherein a king discovers and marries the heroine, "the king's discovery brings the sister into a community that both facilitates and threatens her work. The sister's discovery brings her into a home, foreshadowing the hoped-for happy ending, but it is a false home, determined by the king's desire rather than by the sister's creation of a stable and complete community" (2009, 50).

The manner in which the king discovers the heroine is also questionable in ATU 451. In "The Twelve Brothers," a king comes upon the heroine while out hunting and fetches her down from the tree in which she sits; in "The Six Swans," the king's huntsmen carry her down from a tree after she throws down all of her clothing except for a shift, after which she is taken to the king. The implication that the heroine is actually the king's quarry subtly exposes the workings of courtship as a hunt or chase with clearly prescribed gender roles. In both cases, the king weds her for her beauty, and the heroine silently acquiesces. The heroine is slandered in her own home, and, tellingly, her marriage is not stable until her brothers are returned to human form. As Holbek notes, "There is an intriguing connection between the brothers and the king: the heroine only wins him for good when she has disenchanted her brothers" (1987, 551). This suggests that issues with the natal family must be worked out before a new family can be successfully formed.

Anthropological methods also help to illuminate the kinship dynamics of this tale. In particular, the culture reflector theory is useful, but only to a degree, as ethnographic information about nineteenth-century German family structure is limited. More generally, European families in the nineteenth century were undergoing changes reflecting larger societal changes, which in turn influenced narrative themes at the time. Marilyn Pemberton writes, "Family structure and its internal functioning were the keys to encouraging the values and behavior needed to support a modern world which was emerging at this time" (2010, 10). The family in nineteenth-century Germany faced upheavals due to industrialization, wars, and politics, as the German states were not yet unified. Jack Zipes situates the Grimms in this historical context: "The Napoleonic Wars and French rule had been upsetting to both Jacob and Wilhelm, who were dedicated to the notion of German unification" (2002b, xxvi). And yet the contributors to a book titled *The German Family* suggest that the socialization of children remained a central function of the family structure (Evans and Lee 1981). The German family was the main site of the education of children, with the exception of noble or bourgeois males who could be sent to school, until the late nineteenth century (Hausen 1981, 66–72). Thus we may expect to see in the tales some reflection of the family as an educational institution, even if the particular kinship dynamics of the Grimms' historical era are still being illuminated.

Two Grimm-specific studies support this. August Nitschke (1988) uses historical documents such as autobiographies and novels to demonstrate that nineteenth-century German mothers utilized folk narratives from oral tradition to interact with their children, both as play and instruction. Ruth Bottigheimer's (1986) historical research on the social contexts of the Grimms' tales shows how by the nineteenth century, women's silence had come to be a prized trait, praised in various media from children's manuals to marriage advice. This message was in turn echoed in the Grimms' tales, with their predominantly speechless heroines, a stark example of a social value reflected in the tales. Additionally, Bottigheimer notes that it "was generally held in Wilhelm's time that social stability rested on a stable family structure, which the various censorship offices of the German states wished to be presented respectfully, as examples put before impressionable minds might be perceived as exerting a formative influence" (1987, 20). Thus, rigid gender roles and stable families came to be foregrounded in the Grimms' tales.

Moving from the general reflection of social values to kinship structures in folktales, I would like to draw a parallel between German culture and Arab cultures based on how many of the tales in the Grimms' collection feature a close brother-sister bond. The folktales Ibrahim Muhawi and Sharif Kanaana collected from Palestinian Arab women almost all feature close and loving brother-sister relationships. Muhawi and Kanaana read these relationships in light of their hypothesis that the tales present a portrait of the Arab culture, sometimes artistically distorted, but still related. Based on anthropological research, they note that the relationship between the brother and the sister is warm and harmonious in life, and it is one of the most idealized relationships in the folktale. Clearly I am not trying to imply in a reductionist fashion that German and Palestinian Arab cultures are the same, though a number of their folktale plots overlap; rather, I am stating that if we have evidence that the tales reflect kinship arrangements in one culture, then perhaps something similar is true in a culture with similar tales. Perhaps the Grimms' tales, collected and revised in a society where families still provided an educational and nurturing setting permeated by storytelling traditions and values, contain information about how families can and should work. Sisters and brothers may have needed to cooperate to survive childhood and the natal home, and behavior that the narrative initially constructs as self-destructive might guarantee survival later on.

Hasan El-Shamy's work on the brother-sister syndrome in Arab culture provides a second perspective on siblings in Arab folktales. In his monograph on a related tale type, ATU 872* ("Brother and Sister"), El-Shamy summarizes a number of texts and analyzes them in the context of an Arab worldview.[8] What these texts have in common with "The Maiden Who Seeks Her Brothers" is that the sister-brother dyadic relationship is idealized and provides the motivation for the plot.[9] However, since the brother-sister relationship is so strong emotionally as to border on the potentially incestuous, the desire of the brother and sister to be together must be worked out narratively through a plot that makes sense to its tellers and the audience so that "the tale reaches a conclusion which is emotionally comfortable for both the narrator and the listener" (1979, 76). Thus in Arab cultures, this tale type makes meaningful statements about the proper relationships between brothers and sisters, both reflecting and enforcing the cultural mandate that brothers and sisters care for one another.

The brother-sister relationship in the same tale or related tales in different cultures can take on various meanings according to context; as discussed previously, Holbek interprets ATU 451 as a tale motivated by sibling rivalry, while El-Shamy interprets related tales as expressing a deep sibling love. Both scholars interpret the tales drawing on information from their respective cultures and yet reach different conclusions about the psychology underlying the tales. The importance of cultural context is thus paramount, and in the case of the Grimms' inclusion of three versions of "The Maiden Who Seeks Her Brothers" in their collection, the life contexts of the collectors also feature prominently.

The life histories of the Grimm brothers themselves influenced the shaping of this tale in very specific ways. Jacob and Wilhelm Grimm came from a family that was once affluent but become impoverished when their father died, and for much of their lives, Jacob and Wilhelm struggled to provide an adequate income on which to support their aging mother, their sister, and their four surviving brothers. Jacob never married but rather lived with Wilhelm and his wife and children (Zipes 2002b, xxiii–xxviii; see also Tatar 1987).[10] The correspondence between Jacob and Wilhelm "reflects their great concern for the welfare of their family," as did their choices in obtaining work that would allow them to care for family members who were unable to work (Zipes 2002b, xxv). Hence one reason "The Brothers Who Were

Turned into Birds" appears in their collection three times could be that its message, the importance of sibling fidelity, appealed to the Grimms. Zipes comments on the brothers' revisions of the text of "The Twelve Brothers" in particular, noting that they emphasize two factors: "the dedication of the sister and brothers to one another, and the establishment of a common, orderly household . . . where they lived together" (1988b, 216). Overall, the numerous sibling tales that the Grimms collected and revised stressed ideals "based on a sense of loss and what they felt should be retained if their own family and Germany were to be united" (218).

Though the love between (opposite-gendered) siblings is emphasized in the Grimms' collection as a whole, as well as in their three versions of "The Maiden Who Seeks Her Brothers," there is also ambivalence. As fundamentally human emotions, love and hate are sometimes transformations of each other, as misplaced projection or intensified identification.[11] Thus Holbek's and El-Shamy's seemingly opposing interpretations of brother-sister tales can be reconciled, since each set of tales, in their cultural context, grapples with the question of how brother-sister relations should be. The Grimms' tales veer more toward sibling fidelity, but there is a marked ambivalence in "The Twelve Brothers" in particular. When the sister sets out to find her twelve brothers, she encounters the youngest one first, who is overjoyed to see her. However, he tells her that the brothers vowed "that any maiden who came our way would have to die, for we had to leave our kingdom on account of a girl" (Zipes 2002b, 33). The youngest brother tricks the older brothers into agreeing not to kill the next girl they meet, after which the older brothers warmly welcome their sister into their midst. The initial hostility of the brothers toward their sister, though narratively constructed and transformed, could also represent the Grimms' ambivalent feelings about their family: as a family that frequently suffered hardship and poverty, there must have been some strain in supporting all of their siblings. As eldest, Jacob in particular bore many of the responsibilities. Zipes notes, "It was never easy for Jacob to be both brother and father to his siblings—especially after the death of their mother, when they barely had enough money to clothe and feed themselves" (9). Including and revising brother-sister tales may thus have been a way for the Grimms to navigate their own complicated feelings toward their many siblings by achieving a narrative resolution for an initial situation fraught with resentment.

The message of sibling fidelity also upholds social norms in a patriarchal, patrilocal society, for brothers and sisters would not be competing for the same resources. In contrast, many of the Grimms' tales (and fairy tales in general) feature competition between women for resources, a struggle that ultimately disempowers women. Maria Tatar comments on the heroines in the Grimms' collection who, lowly by day, beautify themselves at night in dresses "that arouse the admiration of a prince and that drive rival princesses into jealous rages" (1987, 118). Classical texts of ATU 510A ("Cinderella") in particular tend to present women competing for eligible men, portrayals that have drawn attention from feminist critics (Haase 2004a, 16, 20). Kay Stone's reception-based research on gender roles in fairy tales reveals that readers are aware of the competition between women featured in the tales, "a competition our society seems to accept as natural" (1986, 137).

Inasmuch as "The Maiden Who Seeks Her Brothers" depicts a woman leaving her birthplace and getting married, it upholds the patriarchal mandate that anthropologist Gayle Rubin (1975) identified as "the traffic in women." According to Rubin's theory, men cement their homosocial bonds by exchanging women as wives, essentially as commodities. Yet in each of the versions of this tale type in the Grimms, the sister continues to live with her brothers at the tale's conclusion. The brothers do not necessarily take wives of their own, which in two versions leads to an odd arrangement where the brothers live with their sister and her husband. The nuclear family is replicated, but with the addition of the bachelor brothers, thus altering the original family that was present at the opening of the tale. This familial constellation, which may have been recognizable to the extended family structures of nineteenth-century Germany, nonetheless does not conform to heteronormative ideas of the ideal nuclear family.[12] Instead, it parallels the extraordinary image of the littlest brother in the third tale left with a wing instead of an arm because his disenchantment was incomplete—a compelling icon of fantasy penetrating reality, demanding to be made livable. The brothers form a queer appendage when added to the family unit of the heterosexual couple plus their children, and the visibly liminal status of the winged littlest brother highlights the oddness of the brothers' inclusion.

This third tale, "The Six Swans," is more specifically woman centered and queer than the other two, as it begins with female desire (the witch ensnaring the father/king to be her daughter's husband) and female inventiveness (the father/king's new wife sewing and then enchanting shirts to turn the king's sons into swans).[13] The sister then defies the father/king's authority by refusing to come with him, where the new wife is ostensibly waiting to dispose of the remainder of the unwelcome offspring. The sister wanders until she finds her brothers and undertakes to free them by remaining silent for six years while sewing them six shirts from asters. Her efforts are nearly thwarted by her new husband's mother, who steals her children and attempts to frame her for murder. It is notable that the women in this tale who are the most active—the witch, the witch's daughter who becomes stepmother to the siblings, and the old woman who is mother to the sister's husband—are the most villainous. The sister, in contrast, turns her agency inward, acting on herself in order to remain silent and productive. Her agency, the most positively portrayed female agency in this tale, is thus queer in the sense that it resists and unsettles; it acts while negating action, it endures while refusing to respond to life-threatening conditions. That agency should be complex and contradictory makes sense, for, according to Butler, "If I have any agency, it is opened up by the fact that I am constituted by a social world I never chose. That my agency is riven with paradox does not mean it is impossible. It means only that paradox is the condition of its possibility" (2004, 3). The sister's agency, so quiet as to be almost unnoticeable, is nevertheless not congruent with being silenced.

The queerness of this tale also manifests in transbiology. Judith Halberstam discusses the transbiological as manifesting in "hybrid entities or in-between states of being that represent subtle or even glaring shifts in our understandings of the body and of bodily transformation" (2008, 266). More specifically, transbiological connections "question and shift the location, the terms and the meaning of the artificial boundaries between humans, animals, machines, states of life and death, animation and reanimation, living, evolving, becoming and transforming" (266). The transitions and affinities between humans and animals in "The Maiden Who Seeks Her Brothers" interrogate the very notion of humanity as a discrete state. If the heroine's brothers are birds, how can they still be her brothers? The tale seems to affirm a kinship between humans and animals, allowing for the possibility that family bonds transcend species divisions. The heroine herself is close to an animal state, especially during her silent time sewing in the forest. Viewing the heroine's state from a transbiological perspective helps illuminate Bottigheimer's statement linking muteness and sexual vulnerability, when she describes how, in "The Six Swans," "against all contemporary logic the treed girl tries to drive off the king's hunters by throwing her clothes down at them, piece by piece, until only her shift is left" (1987, 77). This scene does in fact make sense if the heroine is read to be in a semi-animalistic state, having renounced some of her humanity. Shedding human garments is akin to shedding social skins, layers of human identity, though her morphological stability betrays her when the king perceives her as a beautiful human female and decides to wed her.

However, the fact that this remains a human-centered tale renders its subversiveness incomplete. We never learn what the brothers think and feel while they are enchanted; do they keep their sister company as she silently sews shirts for them? Do they retain any fragments of their human identities or memories while in swan or raven form? The fact that the brothers fly to where their sister is bound to a pyre, about to be immolated, suggests that they acknowledge some kind of tie to her. The brothers' inability to use their bird beaks to form human speech parallels the sister's silence, rendering both brothers and sister unintelligible in human terms. For the brothers to become human again, they must be framed as legibly human. Bear notes the importance of "publicly dressing the swans as human beings" in order to disenchant them in certain versions of "The Maiden Who Seeks Her Brothers" (2009, 55). In "The Six Swans," the heroine tosses the shirts she had sewn onto the swans as they fly near the pyre to which she is bound. In "The Twelve Brothers," the brothers as ravens swoop into the yard where the sister is about to be burned at the stake, at which point the seven years of the sister's silence elapse. Exactly at that moment, "just as they touched the ground, they turned into her twelve brothers whom she had saved" (Zipes 2002b, 35–36). In "The Seven Ravens," the brothers assume human form after flying into their home as ravens, and when they go to their table to eat and drink, they notice signs of the sister's presence and exclaim, "Who's been eating from my plate? Who's been drinking from my cup? It was a human mouth" (92). The sister's presence is enough to disenchant the brothers, but it is significant that her humanness causes them to comment and initiates the transformation. Thus, in each of these three tales, the brothers must reengage with human activities—wearing clothing, acknowledging their relationship with gravity and the ground, and eating in human fashion—in order to become human once again.

To explore the issues presented by these tales further, I return to the comparative method, asking why three versions of this tale type really needed to be published in one collection, and what the differences between the versions can tell us. Queer and anthropological perspectives on the brother-sister relationship each illuminate the meanings of tales where brothers and sisters love each other excessively—both as taboo and survival strategy. Parental love is almost always destructive, whether it is excessive fatherly love or a stepmother's desire to be the sole loved object. We learn from the anomalous ending of the text "The Seven Ravens" that neither silence nor heterosexual marriage is required for this tale type to work as a story, to make sense narratively. In that tale, the sister disenchants her brothers when she arrives at their domicile and drops a ring into one of their cups as a recognition token, at which point the seventh brother says, "God grant us that our little sister may be here. Then we'd be saved!" (Zipes 2002b, 92). After the brothers are transformed back into humans, they "hugged and kissed each other and went happily home" (93). Here, enfolding back into the nuclear family is the happily ever after—the only price was the sister's little finger and her sacrifice to seek her brothers. In the texts where marriage does occur, it is queered by danger and ambivalence. According to my allomotific analysis, silence is but one method of disenchantment. A sacrifice of another sort will do: the sacrifice of a "normal" marriage, the sacrifice of a reproductive future. Yet these things seem a small price to pay for the reward of a family structure, however unconventional, bonded by love and loyalty.

As I've shown, the Grimms' versions of "The Maiden Who Seeks Her Brothers" affirm some family values on the surface, but the texts are also radical in their suggestions for alternate ways of being. The nuclear family is critiqued as dangerous, and the formation of a new marital family does not guarantee the heroine any more safety. Greenhill describes a parallel phenomenon in the tales she analyzes in her essay: "'Bluebeard' and 'The Robber Bridegroom' queer kinship by exposing the sine qua non of heterosexual relationships—between bride and groom, husband and wife—as explicitly adversarial, dangerous, even murderous" (2008, 150). The husband in "The Maiden Who Seeks Her Brothers" (when he appears) is not dangerous through action so much as inaction, by allowing his mother to slander and threaten his wife. Both men and women are alternately active and passive in this tale type, making it difficult to state to what degree this tale type exhibits female agency, a task made even more difficult when the heroine voluntarily gives up her voice. The sister's agency lies partially in negation and endurance, which is one way that the tale queers the notion of agency, despite the fact that in each of the three tales the sister takes the initiative and sets out on a quest to find her brothers. By simultaneously questioning the family and making it the sought-after object, the Grimms' three versions of "The Maiden Who Seeks Her Brothers" complicate the notion of kinship, presenting myriad possibilities for how humans and non-humans can relate to and live with one another. As a story that explores and opposes lethal and idealized families, this tale investigates themes of attachment, ambivalence, and ambiguity that were central to the Grimms' cultural context and life histories and remain relevant today.

Notes

I would like to thank Kay Turner for involving me in this wonderful project and for all of her help along the way. Thanks to Hasan El-Shamy, who went out of his way to converse with me on the interpretation of brother-sister tales. This research was supported in part by European Social Fund's Doctoral Studies and Internationalisation Programme DoRa.

1. Holbek actually dismissed the majority of the Danish versions available to him as defective or garbled versions, deteriorations from some ideal norm (Vaz da Silva 2002, 144–45).

2. Holbek's thesis specifically accounts for the marvelous elements of fairy tales by placing them in a symbolic context that is meaningful to the community of tellers: "The symbolic elements of fairy tales convey emotional impressions of beings, phenomena, and events in the real world, organized in the form of fictional narrative sequences which allow the narrators to speak of the problems, hopes, and ideals of the community" (1987, 435).

3. "The Lazy One and the Industrious One" was not published in any of the original editions of the *KHM*, hence it does not have a KHM number, though Zipes (2002b) includes it as tale 233 in his third edition of *The Complete Fairy Tales of the Brothers Grimm.*

4. Similarly, Fortuné in Madame d'Aulnoy's "Belle-Belle ou le Chevalier Fortuné" chooses not to tell those who would execute him that he is really the woman Belle-Belle and instead waits till his body reveals his sex (see Greenhill and Anderson-Grégoire, forthcoming). The protagonist who is reticent to speak and defend herself offers an interesting middle ground between fairy tales that feature a persecuted female protagonist and a protagonist who is more outgoing.

5. While Freud viewed castration as a necessary stage in the Oedipus complex, hence in gender differentiation and heterosexual desire, recent queer theorists have come to question the inevitability of these processes. Butler writes that in the process of Oedipalization, "the child presumably will become gendered on the occasion that the child takes up a position in relation to parental positions that are prohibited as overt sex objects for the child" (2004, 120). Butler then continues on to ask, "But if Oedipus is interpreted broadly, as a name for the triangularity of desire, then the salient questions become: What form does that triangularity take? Must it presume heterosexuality?" (128). Thus, in a queer reading of "The Maiden Who Seeks Her Brothers," the heroine's castration through voicelessness need not be viewed as a precursor to her passage into a static heteronormativity.

6. Joan Radner and Susan Lanser's definition of coding is useful here: it refers to "the expression or transmission of messages potentially accessible to a (bicultural)

community under the very eyes of a dominant community for whom these same messages are either inaccessible or inadmissible" (1993, 3). An element of risk is also important as it creates the conditions that make coding necessary.

7. Langlois (1993, 90–91) compares the contemporary legend to a tale published in early versions of the *KHM* and then deleted, due to its gory ending, wherein children play butcher; perhaps this is another instance of coding (and subsequent censoring) in the Grimms' fairy tales.

8. Type 872* has some motifs in common with 451, such as the slander of the sister and her expulsion, and in some cases texts of 872* open with episodes from 451 (El-Shamy 1979, 33).

9. In many of the tales of this type, the brother takes a wife (often against his sister's counsel) who falsely accuses the sister of bad behavior or magically induces pregnancy to shame her. The sister is expelled, sometimes killed and resurrected, sometimes wed; in all events, though, she is reunited with her brother and the evil wife is punished (frequently gruesomely killed).

10. The fact that the brothers continued to live together even after Wilhelm married and had children may provide another imaginative link to the denouement of the two versions of "The Maiden Who Seeks Her Brothers" wherein the disenchanted brothers live with the sister and her husband.

11. Holbek defines projection as "feelings and reactions in the protagonist's mind [that] are presented as phenomena in the surrounding world" (1987, 440). Dundes (1993) discusses projection at great length. The related concept of identification is a more general psychological process whereby people see themselves as like or want to become like others, possibly in greater amounts than is considered healthy.

12. As Butler notes about how kinship is discussed in the political sphere (e.g., in the debates surrounding gay marriage or adoption), "Variations on kinship that depart from normative, dyadic heterosexually based family forms secured through the marriage vow are figured not only as dangerous for the child but perilous to the putative natural and cultural laws said to sustain human intelligibility" (2004, 104).

13. Here I disagree with Bottigheimer's (1987, 37–39) statement that the progression of motifs and events from "The Twelve Brothers" to "The Six Swans" strips the heroine of agency and power. Assigning agency is always a tricky matter, but the heroine in "The Six Swans" does have a number of direct speech acts, and she is the only heroine in the three texts to speak after the brothers are disenchanted and thus be able to explain herself, which I view as significant evidence for her agency in "The Six Swans."

4

"But Who Are You Really?"

Ambiguous Bodies and Ambiguous Pronouns in "Allerleirauh"

MARGARET R. YOCOM

Du bist eine Hexe, Rautierchen (You are a witch, Little Hairy Animal).
—Jacob and Wilhelm Grimm, "Allerleirauh"

I just loved its "itness" for what it was.
—Claire, an intersexed person, on how he/she sees
his/her body now, quoted in Preves,
Intersex and Identity: The Contested Self

"Allerleirauh" ("All Kinds of Fur," ATU 510B) is one of the least known tales of the brothers Grimm. Few editors or publishers have been willing to include it in anything but complete editions of the tales of Wilhelm and Jacob Grimm (see Uther 2008, 160), because it opens its "Cinderella" story with a fearful taboo: a father's carnal desire for his daughter. "Allerleirauh," though, has called to me since the late 1980s when I began telling it to my graduate folklore classes and then to other audiences, including women survivors of incest.

In the tale, years after a young woman's mother dies, her father declares his intent to marry her. She demands three dresses and a mantle made of a piece of fur from each of the animals in his kingdom, thinking her father will never find such items. But he does. She puts three of her treasured possessions (a gold ring, a tiny gold spinning wheel, a tiny gold reel) and the three dresses in a nutshell. She wraps herself in the mantle of rough furs and escapes into the forest. A king's hunters find her, name her *Allerleirauh* (All Kinds of Fur), and take her to the cook in the castle where she works at lowly tasks for years. When the king holds three balls, she attends wearing the gowns. After each ball, the cook tells her to make the king's soup instead of sweeping the ashes. As she does, she puts her treasures, one at a time, into the soup bowl. The king discovers that she is the beautiful woman at the ball and marries her.

When Grimm scholars have written about "Allerleirauh," many have focused on the incest and the daughter's eventual marriage to a king. Whom she finally marries, a second king or her father, has been much debated (see Dollerup, Reventlow, and Hansen 1986, 21; Rölleke 1972, 153–59; Tatar 1992, 135). Regardless of what the Grimms intended, their 1857 text allows ambiguity to flourish: my students regularly disagree on just whom All Kinds of Fur did marry.[1] Although in this chapter I write from the two-king perspective, where incest has been averted,[2] I delight in these ambiguities for they allow readers to hear multiple possibilities and find their own stories within the text. As Maria Tatar suggests, "A fairy tale's surface events often work in tandem with latent undercurrents to generate the productive ambiguities that engage our attention as listeners and readers" (Tatar 125–26).

My focus here, though, is not on whom she marries but on the heroine herself and her journey through the gendered, sexually redolent landscape of the tale's provocative middle section. Framed by heterosexual marriage proposals, the Grimms' tale, along with the many versions of ATU 510B "Peau d'Asne" known around the world (Uther 2004, 1:295–96), spends most of its time detailing that liminal middle ground where the heroine dons gender-bending disguises and escapes her father (or brother); wanders to places of intrigue; meets creatures both familiar and strange; and, finally, reveals herself (or is revealed) as a beautiful young woman. The worldwide emphasis on this middle section of the story attests to the interest that tellers and listeners have in her long journey.

Allerleirauh travels far over land and sea, but even more compelling are her journeys back and forth among bodily locations: between human and animal, as well as among man, woman, thing, or a bodily state that combines all of the above. Over and over again, those who encounter her ask, "Who are you?" They call her "weird," "strange," and "astonishing." To them, she looks like an animal, an old man, an old woman, or all three. These corporeal ambiguities create the "undercurrents" that, as Maria Tatar (1992, 126) says, exist for readers and listeners of the fairy tale. Some see in "Allerleirauh," as I do, an undercurrent that carries the experiences of incest survivors who move back and forth among different perceptions of themselves and their bodies as they journey toward renewed life. In this chapter, I discuss another undercurrent of the tale, one that explores the experiences of queer, transgendered, transsexual, and intersexed persons. First, using multiple versions of ATU 510B, I explore the heroine's experiences in her gendered and ambiguous body; then, I focus on the ambiguous pronouns (and their corresponding possessive adjectives) of the Grimm brothers' "Allerleirauh."

ATU 510B/ATU 510B*: Gendered and Ambiguous Bodies on Display

In the compelling central section of the ATU 510 tales,[3] the heroine disguises and transforms her body over and over again, choosing coverings that both hide and heighten her gender and sex. As Ibrahim Muhawi suggests in his study of "Allerleirauh" and related Arabic tales, the beautiful gowns of the heroine are just as much a disguise as her ashy rags or her rough-fur pelt:

> There is actually a process of double masking; the beautiful dresses the heroines wear at the end are just as much of a social mask as the fur or sackcloth cloaks, the old man's skin, or the layer of ash and grime in "Cinderella" proper. In one they appear supremely feminine and desirable; in the other they are animal-like, freakish and masculine, or lowly and unworthy of attention. . . . This detail is brought out more prominently in Allerleirauh where the first disguise allying her with the animals and nature gives way to the glittering dresses that associate her with heaven and the stars, endowing her with a transcendent and irresistible beauty. The degree of desirability of the one disguise arises directly from the degree of undesirability of the other. (2001, 278)

Allerleirauh must come to understand that the gendered way she was raised cannot be her only choice if she wants to flourish on her journey; she must be willing to live in multiple ambiguous skins among people who believe that everyone lives in just one clearly discernable one. Like queer and transgendered people, the heroine must find a way to survive when others want her to behave in a way she cannot. And, like many pre-transition transsexual people, she may feel, at times, that she is living in the wrong body (Prosser 1998, 69). Claiming a skin, no matter what its makeup, is her constant focus. "To be oneself is first of all to have a skin of one's own," writes Jay Prosser, quoting Didier Anzieu (1989, 51), "'and, secondly, to use it as a space in which one can experience sensations.' Subjectivity is not just about having a physical skin; it's about feeling one owns it; it's a matter of psychic investment of self in skin" (Prosser 1998, 73). Finally, the heroine must find allies.

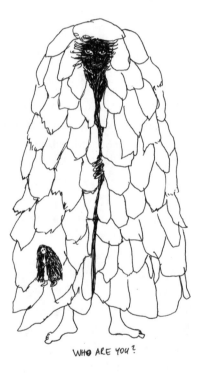

WHO ARE YOU?

In these international tales, a beautiful young woman's journey is set in motion by her father's—or her brother's—demand that she marry him.

Usually, the man falls suddenly, madly in love with her. Often her mother dies early and unexpectedly, after asking (or requiring) the king to marry no one unless she can match the dead queen's once-beautiful body in some way. The candidate should fit into the same dresses or shoes or rings, or bear the same star on her forehead, or have the same gleaming gold or gold and silver hair. No one else can be found, or the daughter tries her mother's clothing or ring on by accident. In Scotland,[4] she shows her father how well her mother's dress fits (Campbell [1862] 1969, 226–29). In North Carolina, she tries on her dead mother's wedding dress, which her father had put away; he is so angry with her that she leaves home (I. Carter 1925, 361–63). Sometimes, her unmarried brother pursues her; she is so beautiful that all men want her. Among Romanians living in the Balkans, her brother sees her combing her hair (Karlinger 1981, 181–83).[5] In Sudan, he finds a lock of her hair (Hurreiz 1977, 83–85); because he is a revered only son, her fearful parents agree to the match (Al-Shahi and Moore 1978, 110–14). In Indian versions, even though the brother is an only son, the girl's mother helps her escape (Ramanujan 1997, 74–79).

She stalls her pursuer by countering his incestuous demand with numerous requests of her own, often for objects identified with the feminine gender or the female body, made of strikingly unusual materials. In so doing, she acquires the wondrous items she will need for the challenges ahead. Sometimes she decides on the items herself, sometimes she seeks help. In Scotland, her foster mother, mother's brother, or her mother reincarnated as a little brown calf advises her to ask for gowns and shoes and chests: gowns of swan's down, moorland *canach* (bog cotton), silk standing upright with gold and silver; gowns of bird's down in the colors of sky woven with silver and stars woven with gold; a pair of glass shoes or a pair with one shoe gold and one silver; a chest that locks within and without and will travel over land or sea (see Campbell [1862] 1969, 226–29, 232–33; Bruford and MacDonald [1994] 2007, 64–69). In Denmark, the little red cow that helps the princess is, herself, an enchanted princess (Cox 1893, 231). In Italy, she turns for advice to the pope or to an enchanter (350–52). Sometimes supernatural forces intervene; although her grandmother helps her in one Slavic version, in another, the sun counsels her. Other times, the devil helps her father procure three dresses: one of the sun, moon, stars, and all the heavens; one like the sea with fishes swimming in it; and one of hollow wood (130). In Russia, she creates either three or four dolls and beseeches their aid; they split the earth open, and she escapes from her brother into an underground kingdom (Von Löwis of Menar and Olesch 1959, 47–49). In Sweden, an old man, one of the "wee folk" who live in the mountain, advises her to seek work as a scullery maid in the summer palace and gives her a magic staff that will grant her requests when she hits it against the mountain and speaks certain words (Blecher and Blecher 1993, 168–73).

One item she procures before—or sometimes during—her journey is an unattractive "skin" or covering for her body. She wears it as she journeys through forests or across seas, alone or with friends and helpful animals. In this disguise, this second skin, she appears to others as a male, female, human, spirit-world being, thing, or a living entity whose characteristics cannot be discerned. Sometimes, as in Palestine, she wraps herself in a tight-fitting sackcloth and appears to be a weird old man or a jinn (Muhawi and Kanaana 1989, 125–30). And sometimes, as in Sudan, she removes the skin from an old man and covers herself with it (Al-Shahi and Moore 1978, 110–14; Hurreiz 1977, 83–85) or has a carpenter fashion her a dress from the dawn palm (Al-Shahi and Moore 1978, 118–20). In Japan, she receives a frog's skin that enables her to become an old woman (Ikeda 1971, 75, 139). In the Basque country, the princess's donkey guardian gathers little pieces of fur from the pelts of all the palace animals. After coating her naked body with pine resin, she sticks the fur pieces all over herself and puts on a servant's dress (Karlinger and Laserer 1980, 44–54). In Slavic countries, an emperor's daughter demands a mouse-skin dress, or a princess, listening to her dead mother at the gravesite, requests a "hollow man" made of wood so that only the princess may enter (Cox 1893, 129, 130). In Norway, she asks for a wooden cloak or is advised by an old woman to demand a crow-skin cloak (327). In Russia, one princess hears the instructions of her dead mother and wraps herself in a hood made of pigskin (Afanas'ev [1861] 1985, 312–14);[6] another princess hides within a golden lantern (Haney 2001, 38–42). In Spain, the girl has a cork furniture craftsman make her a little bull gilded with gold, which she stocks with provisions, enters, and has thrown into the sea (Taggart 1990, 112–15). For Romanians living in the Balkans, she turns herself into sea foam; when she washes ashore on a far, fair island, she turns herself back into a woman (Karlinger 1981, 181–83).

Given the multiple skins of her ambiguous body, she sometimes disgusts but always intrigues those who meet her. At times, she finds them as exciting as they find her. Making use of her many layers of identity, she answers their questions with riddles about bodies. They either bring her back to their castles or open their kitchen doors to her knock. In a Basque story, a king, fishing in the mountains, invites a furry woman riding on a donkey to be his kitchen maid as soon as he hears her quick, saucy answers to his questions. "What kind of creature are you?" he asks. "Are you an animal or are you a person?" She replies,

Human am I and no animal
That, handsome youth, believe.
Under this husk lies a kernel
Many young men would crave. (Karlinger and Laserer 1980, 50)

Does he understand? Does he suspect anything? The story offers no direct pronouncement on what he thinks; but, after the young king asks two more questions and gets two more riddling answers (she tells him her name is Esaua),[7] he takes her home. In Palestinian versions, when a king's slaves see a creature completely covered in sackcloth eating the leftovers they have just thrown out, they run to their mistress. Curious, she "want[s] to have a look" at this "weird sight outside," this "strangest-looking man." They ask Sackcloth if she is "human or jinn." "I'm human," Sackcloth replies, "and the choicest of the race. But Allah has created me the way I am." Even though she says she has no "skills in particular," they invite her to work with them (Muhawi and Kanaana 1989, 127–29). In Egypt, when a slave girl sees what she thinks is a heap of skins with two bright eyes staring out, she says to her queen, "My lady, there is something monstrous crouching under our window, I have seen it, and it looks like nothing less than an *Afreet!*"[8] When the queen sees Juleidah, she comments on the "astonishing creature" and asks, "What is it?" and "Who are you?" The queen decides, "We shall keep her to amuse us" (Bushnaq 1986, 195–96). In Italy, the palace guard stutters as he debates whether or not to make her the royal goose herder: "The geese will be frightened if they see such a . . . such a . . . I don't know, you're certainly not a human being, nor are you beast. I don't know what you are" (Falassi 1980, 43). Under the gaze of others, the girl becomes "it"—both

Ambiguous Bodies and Ambiguous Pronouns 97

"monstrous" and "astonishing." Her body, like a riddle, gets read over and over again.

Hidden behind her body disguise of rags, soot, or animal skins, she works as a domestic servant. Usually she serves as a cook's helper or a cook by requesting the position herself or by following the suggestion of a member of the royal family, a kindly old person, a helpful animal, or a spirit-world being. In Sweden, on the advice of the "wee folk" who live in the mountain, she seeks work as a scullery maid; with their help, she provides delicious meals for all in the palace (Blecher and Blecher 1993, 168–73). In India, her face hidden behind a mask and her gold hair tied tight, she is an expert cook, especially of sweet rice. She follows the advice of an old woman and finds work in the home of a *saukar*, a rich man, with several sons (Ramanujan 1997, 74–79). Sometimes, as in Egypt, she is recognized as a wounded creature and placed, specifically, under the care of the cook: "Mistress cook!" the queen says, "Take this broken-winged soul into your kitchen" (Bushnaq 1986, 196). Similarly, in Palestine, soon after she asks to work in the kitchen "peeling onions and passing things over," everyone says how "happy they [are] to have Sackcloth around"; she stays "in the kitchen under the protection of the cook" (Muhawi and Kanaana 1989, 127–28). Sometimes she works at other domestic, food-related tasks. In Sudan, the royal girl cares for pigeons or geese (Al-Shahi and Moore 1978, 110–18; Hurreiz 1977, 83–85).

After working for years, she begins to remove her unattractive "skin." Dressing in her beautiful clothes and jewelry made with unusual materials, she goes to one or several balls, church services, wedding celebrations, horse races (Pino-Saavedra 1967, 99–103), or feasts; then she puts her "skin" back on. In North Carolina, she cleans the kitchen so well that the prince's mother invites her to the Saturday night dance and offers her clothing to wear (I. Carter 1925, 361–63). In Kentucky, her fairy godmother allows her only thirty minutes in the beautiful dress before she changes the girl back into her donkey skin, but it is enough time for the prince to see her and fall in love (Roberts [1955] 1988, 70–72).[9] She often hides her beautiful clothes in places associated with spirit-world beings and goes back and forth to these places to change her clothing and identity: to a hill with its *huldre* overtones in Norway (Cox 1893, 327) or to an oak in Russian versions (Von Löwis of Menar and Olesch 1959, 47–49).[10]

During this time, she interacts with a young man of high degree who falls in love with her.[11] He tries to discover the identity of this beautiful lady by questioning if she bears any relation to the strange, ugly servant in his household. Often, as in an Afrikaans tale from South Africa, he searches for her when the ring he gave her appears in his own castle, in his soup. Finally he follows the sound of wondrous harp playing to the dungeon, where he finds the beautiful woman, who was also a palace servant, dressed in cliff badger fur (Schmidt 1999, 235).[12]

Often, she and the young man compete with each other through teasing, riddles, contests, and games. Voyeurism and male-to-female cross-dressing also have their places in this section of the tale. In Norway, they race as they ride their horses (Cox 1893, 327). In Scotland, the prince acquires one of her shoes and holds a contest to see whose foot will fit (Campbell [1862] 1969, 226–29, 232–33; see also Bruford and MacDonald [1994] 2007, 64–69, in which the shoe itself "jump[s] on her foot"). In Sudan, he suggests they play *mungala*, a game that resembles chess (Hurreiz 1977, 83–85). Often, as in Italy, the young man turns voyeur, watching the girl undress (Falassi 1980, 42–45). In Palestine, he dresses as a woman so he can go with his mother to the women-only dance and watch the beautiful unknown girl (Muhawi and Kanaana 1989, 125–30). Very often the young man hurls personal, body-identified items of his at the girl: boots or walking sticks, combs, handkerchiefs, or towels. He loses most of the competitions: he cannot solve the riddle, he loses the race, and he sees but does not understand the creature whose body he watches through the peephole. Lovesick, he often takes to his bed.

In one Portuguese version, teasing and violence reach a height during this competition. She takes her wooden dress on and off twice: once in her role as the king's duck herder and later as a prisoner-guest in his palace. When she tells the king she has killed one of his ducks, all he wants to know is the name of the beautiful woman wearing a dress the color of stars whom he saw with the ducks. Wearing her wooden gown, she riddles, "Indeed there was no one else there but myself in disguise" (Pedroso, Monteiro, and Ralston 1882, 68). Even after two more sightings of the beautiful woman, two more dead ducks, and two more riddles, the king does not understand. He refuses to take her to the feast, then asks her what dress she will wear. In return, she asks for a pair of his boots and he throws them at her. When his guards ask the beautiful woman where she is from, she says the land of the boot. He asks the woman in the wooden dress to embroider a pair of shoes for him, and she retorts, "Do I know how to embroider shoes?" Not until he watches her through a keyhole does he understand that the beautiful woman before him and the duck killer dressed in wood are the same person.

During this time, she continues to work, often in the kitchen, while her coworkers and the cook play a special role in her transformations. Sometimes one of her fellow kitchen servants scoffs at her (Bushnaq 1986, 195–96). Usually, though, they appreciate and protect her as the mystery of the disappearing beauty unfolds. In Russia, when the tsar's son asks a servant where the beautiful girl lives, the servant (who knows the girl is also the old woman who stokes the stoves) guards her identity. He offers the tsar's son a place-name riddle instead of revealing her true home: the tsar's own kitchen (Von Löwis of Menar and Olesch 1959, 47–49). Sometimes, the cook takes a special interest in the strange creature who has been placed in the kitchen. In one story from Italy, the cook makes sure the king's son hears the geese who call out that their herder is "lovely" and "perfect for the son of the king." "Your majesty," the cook asks, pointedly, "do the geese always have to make so much noise?" (Falassi 1980, 44). In the Basque country, when the king asks the cook how "content" he is with the new kitchen maid, the cook responds, "Highness, she is a big, big help to me. She understands something about all spices, and I can let her make many dishes on her own that I myself could not make any better." She, in turn, praises the cook for his "kindheartedness" (Karlinger and Laserer 1980, 51). When the time comes for her identity to be known, the cook makes it possible for the king to suspect that the lowly kitchen girl is the beauty he seeks. In one German version, like the Grimms', the cook reveals that the only people in the kitchen who could have put a ring into the king's soup were either the cook or Cinder Blower (Ashliman 1996–2009). Thus, the cook helps her as she shifts back and forth among her bodies, so much so that this figure may be seen as her sympathetic guide, and more; a wise man or woman steeped in the ritual knowledge of the kitchen, that liminal place where civilizing impulses meet the uncivilized and where both foodstuffs and people are transformed.[13]

Finally, she puts aside (or has torn from her) her "skin" disguise for the last time. Even though she stands in her supposed glory, radiant in a dress of the sun or of diamonds, someone—usually the young man—asks the question that never disappears: "Who are you?" "Finally I've found you, love of my heart," the prince says, in Sweden, as he sees her standing in her diamond dress, her rags at her feet. "But who are you really?" he asks (Blecher and Blecher 1993, 173). In Italy, the king's son asks, "Tell me, why did you disguise yourself like this? And why . . . where do you come from . . . who are you?" His mother had lifted the skirt of this girl to marvel at her small feet—everyone had seen the diamond dress under the rags—and the prince rushed forward and ripped away the rags (Falassi 1980, 44).

The question invites her to tell her story. In a powerful act of assertion and identity, she does so. In Italy, she gives a long, detailed report on what she went through, incest and all (Falassi 1980, 44). In India, the young man's mother takes her to an inner chamber, asks questions, and "listen[s] to her strange story" (Ramanujan 1997, 75). The "who are you?" question, however, coming as it does at the very moment of her transformation and well before the wedding, suggests that even though she seems to resume several feminine practices of a conventional royal woman, she trails suspicion. It is this query, especially, that opens the surface of the tale to transgendered undercurrents.

Border Crossers

Sackcloth. Little Stick Figure. Cinder Blower. Louse Coat. Hanchi. Donkey Skin. Ubukawa. Allerleirauh. Well might people be suspicious of her. Throughout the tale, this wandering young woman has been acquiring, wearing, and exchanging disguises. She has lived life in multiple bodies for a long time. Perhaps delight in those multiple bodies with their ambiguous gender lingers. Perhaps she will carry abilities and preferences from those experiences into the palace.

Debates about her suitability are woven throughout. Her foot might fit a magic shoe, and she may be able to cook, but she confounds those who make her fit into one category: Non-human animal or human? Male or female? Her powers extend beyond the natural world: she can hear the advice her dead mother whispers (Cox 1893, 130); shoes, of their own accord, jump onto her feet (Campbell [1862] 1969, 229); and, if she prays, she can make herself disappear (Pino-Saavedra 1967, 99–103). "She's a witch, she's a witch!" some scream (103). A shape-shifter, she is liminal, numinous, betwixt and between. "Border crossers and those living on borders," write Judith Lorber and Lisa Jean Moore of transgendered and intersexed people, "have opened a social dialogue over the power of categories. . . . Multiple genders, sexes, and sexualities show that the conventional categories are not universal or essential" (2006, 162). Having crossed many borders herself, the young woman of the ATU 510B tales opens up a dialogue on categories that never gets resolved, even if a heterosexual wedding concludes the story. The tale explores so many different kinds of physical attractions, liaisons, and appearances that the man-woman wedding can be seen as just one of several possibilities.

Two additional versions of the tale underscore the questing, questioning, subversive nature of this tale complex. At the end of a Portuguese version, after the princess recounts her story of her wooden dress, the king sends "for the little old woman who had given [the princess] the [magic] wand, to come and live in the palace, but she refuse[s] to live there because she [is] a fairy." Earlier, after he learned the identity of the princess by peeping through a keyhole, the king had proclaimed to the princess, "Do not be troubled for you shall marry me! . . . But I wish you first to tell me your history, and why it is that you wear a wooden dress" (Pedroso, Monteiro, and Ralston 1882, 72). The old woman's clear refusal suggests that some do not want to live the forever-after life in a king's palace, with its "who are you?" demands, certainly not those who are from another, otherworldly realm entirely.

Even more suggestive of ATU 510B tales' subversive nature is "Florinda." In this Chilean tale, storytellers seamlessly join the opening sections of the tale type with ones from ATU 514 ("The Shift of Sex"), a story whose heroine changes her gender through a disguise and, then, her sex (see Greenhill and Anderson-Gregoire, forthcoming). The tellers' yeasty combination shows just how related the gender disguises of ATU 510B are to physical sex change. Florinda escapes the incestuous desires of her father: just as he tries to embrace her, she prays to her crucifix and disappears from sight. She dresses as a young man, saddles a horse, and, after a journey, asks for food at a palace. Thus in disguise, she attracts the attention of a king. Here the tale moves away from ATU 510B, as the king wants to be with the "handsome" stranger so much that he marries "him" to his daughter. When Florinda, on the wedding night, tells the princess "I am a girl, a woman just like you," the princess replies, "All the better then. We'll live together like two doves in the world." The king revels in his new son-in-law, all the while "noticing what a beautiful body" he/Florinda has. When Florinda's sex is about to be revealed during a swimming excursion, she is turned into a man by her magical, flying crucifix. Her joy, and that of the princess, comes not from any anticipation of heterosexual lovemaking but from their newfound safety from the king and his court. Florinda's last words praise the power and beauty, not of her new body, but of the crucifix: "I can still see it now flying across the waters" (Pino-Saavedra 1967, 104–8).

By ending with a newly forged heterosexual married couple, the story's surface reflects the Western societal belief that each person has, as Lorber says, "one sex, one sexuality, and one gender, congruent with each other and fixed for life, and that these categories are one of only two sexes, two sexualities, and two genders" (1995, 95). At the same time, "Florinda" offers an in-depth, sympathetic view of the lives and loves of bisexual, transsexual, and transgendered people whose "fluidity of bodies, desires, and social statuses" (95) show the male/female, masculine/feminine worldview to be only a veneer.

ATU 510B is a tale type of immense scope. Like "Bearskin," the Grimms' story of an unemployed soldier who wraps the devil's mantle of rough bear fur around himself, "Allerleirauh" and its international versions ask, What is it to be human? To inhabit multiple "skins"? To further explore gender and gender ambiguity within this complex tale, I turn to an ambiguity on the lexical level of one version: the Grimms' "Allerleirauh." Using my own translation, I offer a rereading of the brothers' 1857 text by exploring the fluid, oscillating, gendered pronouns.[14]

A reading that examines such oscillations shows All Kinds of Fur to be largely responsible for her own transformations and thus contributes to the scholarly conversation about her as an active heroine. Christine Goldberg (1997, 29) sees Allerleirauh as an "active" young woman who "takes charge of her life and bides her time until she is in a position to marry a wealthy, devoted husband." For Hirsch (1986, 166), she is "a particularly female hero." Like Goldberg, Muhawi (2001, 271) contrasts the "passive" Cinderella of ATU 510A with the "active heroine" of ATU 510B. My reading of ATU 510B also argues for the importance of new translations of texts to gender and transgender studies. Above all, this reading makes available a multi-layered discussion of All Kinds of Fur's transformations and her multiple, ambiguous identities.

TRANSFORMATION, IDENTITY, AND GENDERED PRONOUN SHIFTS IN "ALLERLEIRAUH"

Writing in German with its three gendered pronouns (*sie*, she; *es*, it; *er*, he), Jacob and Wilhelm Grimm had the opportunity to make choices about how they wanted to represent men and women in their tales. When it came to their female characters, the brothers took that opportunity. In his study based on a sampling of Grimm tales (exclusive of "Allerleirauh"), Orrin Robinson (2007, 110) provides strong evidence that, from 1819 on, the Grimms established patterns for their use of pronouns: they chose to use either *sie* or *es*, regardless of which pronoun grammatical rules called for, and they shifted pronoun assignment from *sie* to *es* or *es* to *sie* when certain situations of the heroines shifted. Except in a few cases, Robinson writes, the Grimms used *es* (it) to refer to younger, unsexed, good, or nice females, and they used *sie* (she) to refer to older, sexed, and bad or naughty females. Cinderella's stepsisters, for example, are always *sie*, even when words like *Mädchen* (that call for the *es* pronoun) are used. Shifts from *es* to *sie* occur when a young woman becomes sexually mature or the object of sexual desire, marries, or does something "naughty" (111–13). These patterns are unique to the Grimms, Robinson discovered; they appear neither in source materials for the tales nor among the tales edited by their German contemporaries. In the text of "Allerley-Rauch," in Carl Nehrlich's 1798 novel *Schilly*, one of the sources of the Grimms' "Allerleirauh" (Rölleke 1972), no *sie/es* alternation occurs. In the work of one of the Grimms' contemporaries, folktale editor

Ludwig Bechstein ([1845–53] 1983, 183–90), no *sie/es* alternation occurs in his ATU 510B text "Aschenpüster mit der Wünschelgerte" ("Ash-Blower with the Wishing-Wand").[15]

Most *sie/es* pronouns in the 1819–57 texts of "Allerleirauh," however, do not fit the patterns Robinson suggests. Something far more complicated and provocative is happening in this pattern-breaking story with its dizzying numbers of pronoun shifts. Robinson's ideas may contribute to understanding the use of *sie* in the beginning and ending of "Allerleirauh," but the patterns do not apply for most of the tale. Robinson worked with tales involving one or sometimes two pronoun shifts from *es* to *sie* in the entire text, but "Allerleirauh" contains many frequent pronoun shifts. He discusses "slippages" from his pronoun patterns in "Goosegirl," a tale with some affinities to "Allerleirauh," but his suggestions do not hold true for the latter tale. The shifts in "Allerleirauh" from *sie* to *es* cannot be explained, as Robinson suggests, as a return to "innocen[ce]" or "young maidenhood" (2007, 117, 118). Allerleirauh does not return to childhood asexuality; in her mantle of rough furs, she is both sexual and asexual at the same time. She strategically uses asexuality to camouflage her sexual body. Also, I do not see Allerleirauh's sexual desirability, as Robinson's schema would suggest, as the only reason for the use of *sie* to refer to the heroine.

Throughout the first part of the Grimms' text of "Allerleirauh," the king's daughter is referred to only as *sie* (she). However, after she wraps her rough-fur mantle around her, escapes from her father's castle, and is discovered by the hunters of a neighboring king, numerous pronoun shifts begin. From this point in the tale on, the pronouns the Grimms use to refer to All Kinds of Fur switch back and forth between *sie* (she) and *es* (it). This oscillation calls into doubt just who or what All Kinds of Fur is: human and/or non-human animal, young woman and/or asexual child.

Although these pronoun shifts might initially seem to be governed by the grammatical rules of German, many are not. Editorial choice is at work when the Grimms use *sie* (she) at some moments and *es* (it) at others. English translators who use only the feminine pronoun "she" to refer to the heroine deemphasize two vital issues: the oscillating gender designations of the text and All Kinds of Fur's transformations, her shifts from one body to another. To reclaim both issues, I use "she" as well as "it" in my translation of the tale.

Intention is not the issue. Whether or not the Grimms' pronoun shifts were deliberate or systematic, the shifts make the non-human/human issue and the gendered/genderless issue much more transparent. The Grimms' text, I suggest, allows for a reading of complicated, fluid gender positions. I discuss selected sections of the tale to show its fluid, gendered landscape; and I begin with the section about hunters and their dogs, which I number story section 5b (5 refers to the fifth paragraph in the Grimms' 1857 text, *b* refers to the second section of the paragraph that I have divided for ease of discussion). In the Grimms' texts from 1819 through 1857,[16] All Kinds of Fur herself helps set the first gender shift in motion.

As section 5b begins, the king's daughter has fled her father's castle, run into the forest, and fallen asleep in the hollow base of a tree. When the king who owns this forest speaks of the creature his hunters have seen, he uses animal terms in neuter gender: *ein Wild* (a game animal). Here, for the very first time, the young woman, formerly a princess and now something quite other, hears herself referred to not as *sie* (she) but as *es* (it):

1857 TEXT	TRANSLATION
(5b) Sprach der König zu den Jägern: "Seht nach, was dort für ein Wild sich versteckt hat." Die Jäger folgten dem Befehl, und als sie wiederkamen, sprachen sie: "In dem hohlen Baum liegt ein wunderliches Tier, wie wir noch niemals eins gesehen haben; an seiner Haut ist tausenderlei Pelz; es liegt aber und schläft."	(5b) Said the king to his hunters: "Go see what kind of game is hiding there." The hunters followed his command, and when they returned, they said, "In the hollow tree lies a weird animal, the like of which we have never seen before; its skin is a thousand kinds of fur; it is lying there, though, and sleeping."
(5c) Sprach der König: "Seht zu, ob ihr's lebendig fangen könnt, dann bindet's auf den Wagen und nehmt's mit."	(5c) The king said, "See if you can catch it alive. Then tie it down on top of the wagon and take it along."

When the hunters report back to the king, they also use a neuter term for animal (*Tier*) as well as the neuter pronoun *es* (it). In the fifth paragraph of the tale, then, the narrator establishes and intensifies the gender-neutral, non-human animal designation for the king's daughter, now draped in her mantle of fur.

As section 5c continues, the hunters touch the creature. Since her discovery as an attractive young woman is imminent, she speaks, referring to herself as a *Kind* (child):

(5c) Als die Jäger das Mädchen an-faßten, erwachte es voll Schrecken und rief ihnen zu: "Ich bin ein armes Kind, von Vater und Mutter verlassen, erbarmt euch mein und nehmt mich mit."

(5c) When the hunters touched the girl, it awoke terrified and called out to them:[17] "I am a poor child, abandoned by father and mother. Have pity on me and take me with you."

By using the neuter noun (*das*) *Kind*, she declares herself human but hides her sex, gender, and age. Unlike most English translators who use "girl," I translate *Kind* as "child" to show one of the verbal strategies All Kinds of Fur uses to protect herself. My translation also makes clear the young woman's use of language to unsex herself, an act that takes on greater and greater significance as the tale proceeds. My translation and my work with the alternation of *sie/es* have other implications for "Allerleirauh" scholarship. For example, Muhawi (2001, 275), in his essay on Arabic "Cinderella" tales, including ATU 510B, writes that tales such as "Sackcloth" have disguises that belong to the world of culture and, therefore, serve as a "social mask." Allerleirauh's fur mantle disguise, in contrast, belongs to the world of nature and also represents the bestiality of the father; therefore, it cannot serve as a social mask. I suggest, though, that since Allerleirauh requests the mantle herself and then uses it as well as her words (*es* and *das Kind*) to unsex herself, her clothing is just as much a social mask as is a covering of sackcloth. Similarly, Muhawi writes that two Arabic heroines appear, through their disguises, as "members of the opposite sex" and that Allerleirauh's disguise "associates her with the animal world" (271). I argue that Allerleirauh has also changed her human gender to the neuter, not the masculine.

The king's hunters, after hearing the child speak as only a human could, name her *Allerleirauh* (All Kinds of Fur), a name free of gender designation:

(5d) Da sprachen sie: "*Allerlei-rauh*,[18] du bist gut für die Küche, komm nur mit, da kannst du die Asche zusammenkehren."

(5d) Then the hunters said, "All Kinds of Fur, you are just right for the kitchen. Come along, then. You can sweep up the ashes."

Also setzten sie es auf den Wagen und fuhren heim in das königliche Schloß.

So they set it on the wagon and drove it home to the royal castle.

Since *Allerleirauh* combines two adjectives (*allerlei*, all kinds of, and *rauh*, rough, as in fur) and no nouns, German grammar does not designate this name as feminine, masculine, or neuter.[19] No matter what the hunters intend by bestowing such a name, their choice of *Allerleirauh* allows her—and them—to hide her sex and give her the protection she claimed earlier when she called herself "child." The narrator's use of *es* (it) intensifies this protective neutering of All Kinds of Fur; since *Allerleirauh* is a proper name, the narrator could use either *sie* or *es* to refer to this creature wrapped in a mantle of fur. The pronoun shifts and name changes that begin here are tinged with hints of magic, of the transformative power of the spoken word. The folktale, as Muhawi notes, invests "power" in "the speech acts of language" (2001, 279). Words, names, titles, and even pronouns can change a character, both metaphorically and physically, into something other than she was before.

At this point in the tale, a willing game begins; the hunters do not tell the king that All Kinds of Fur is human. Whatever they suspect about the sex or gender of the creature they have discovered they keep secret. Since the king does not hear the hunters speak with her, he does not know that she is human and young. The hunters do, and in the king's presence, they command her *komm nur mit*, gentle words used to urge along a pet or a child. They do not tie her down onto the wagon as the king told them to and as they would usually do with an animal; rather, they "set" her on the wagon. They take her to the one place in the castle that is a space of transformation and magic, overseen by a person of numinous qualities who knows all about animals from the forest—the kitchen.

At the same time, the hunters, the narrator, and All Kinds of Fur herself open a debate about the human condition that will continue: Who and what is she? Non-human animal and/or human? Male and/or female? What is it to be human? With this name, she becomes not just an animal but "all kinds of" (*allerlei*) animals, especially those dangerous animals bearing rough fur and associated with men's hunting parties: fox, wolf, bear, boar. By giving her this name, the hunters send her far away from a human, gendered identity.

In section 5e, the hunters give All Kinds of Fur a place to live and a second proper name, one even more closely associated with the non-human: *Rauhtierchen* (Little Hairy Animal). The narrator, meanwhile, continues to use neuter gender terms for All Kinds of Fur, both with *ihm* and with *es*. Since *Rauhtierchen* is spoken as a proper name here, the narrator could use either *sie* (she) or *es* (it), but *es* is chosen. This choice of *es*, given that the word ends with -*chen*, is reasonable since -*chen* endings generally call for neuter referents.

(5e) Dort wiesen sie ihm ein Ställchen an unter der Treppe, wo kein Tageslicht hinkam, und sagten: "Rauhtierchen, da kannst du wohnen und schlafen."

(5e) There they showed it to a little stall under the stairs where no daylight ever came, and said, "Little Hairy Animal, you can live and sleep there."

Dann ward es in die Küche geschickt, da trug es Holz und Wasser, schürte das Feuer, rupfte das Federvieh, belas das Gemüs, kehrte die Asche und tat alle schlechte Arbeit.

Then it was sent to the kitchen. There it carried wood and water, stoked the fire, plucked the poultry, sorted the vegetables, swept the ashes, and did all of the worst work.

In section 6a, in a major rhetorical move, the narrator shifts to the feminine gender and reveals the female body of All Kinds of Fur. Lamenting the heroine's circumstances, the narrator directly addresses her as *schöne Königstochter* (beautiful king's daughter), thus switching to a feminine noun after the many preceding neuter terms. An exclamation point, rare in this text, calls further attention to the gender shift:

(6a) Da lebte Allerleirauh lange

(6a) All Kinds of Fur lived there

Zeit recht armselig. Ach, du
schöne Königstochter, wie soll's
mit dir noch werden!

quite miserably for a long time.
Alas, you beautiful king's daughter, what will become of you!

Es geschah aber einmal, daß ein
Fest im Schloß gefeiert ward, da
sprach sie zum Koch: "Darf ich ein
wenig hinaufgehen und zusehen?"

Now, one day it happened that a
ball was held in the castle, and she
said to the cook, "May I go upstairs
for a little and look?"

"Beautiful king's daughter" stipulates and intensifies All Kinds of Fur's
sex and gender by broadcasting her female beauty. In naming her noble
rank, the phrase also recalls her relationship to her father, his incestuous
desires, and his attempted possession of her as his wife. At this point in the
1812 text, the brothers Grimm used *Jungfrau* (maiden, virgin) but changed
it in 1819 and onward to the term that clearly names the perpetrator and
his close relationship to his victim: *Königstochter*. English translators of the
1857 edition who use "princess" at this critical juncture in the text (and the
translators of the two most popular anthologies do) deemphasize the incest
motif and the text's subversive question of men's ownership of women.[20]

In sections 6b to 7b, as the tale proceeds through the first ball and its
aftermath, the narrator continues the use of *sie* (she). All Kinds of Fur enters
her stall just off the kitchen, removes her rough-fur mantle, washes, and
clothes herself in the dress of the sun. At the ball, everyone thinks she is
a king's daughter. The king dances with her and she disappears. Back in
her stall, she removes her dress, rubs soot back on her face and hands, and
puts on her mantle. When she starts to sweep the ashes as instructed, the
cook surprises her:

(7b) Als sie nun in die Küche kam
und an ihre Arbeit gehen und die
Asche zusammenkehren wollte,
sprach der Koch: "Laß das gut sein
bis morgen und koche mir da die
Suppe für den König."

(7b) Now, when she came into
the kitchen to resume her work
sweeping up the ashes, the cook
said, "Leave it be until morning,
and instead cook for me the king's
soup."

Cooking soup for the king is a major rite of passage for All Kinds of Fur, an act that signals her transformation from a servant who fetches water, tends ashes, and chops vegetables to one who now assembles all the ingredients and transforms them, over a fire, into a dish literally fit for a king. Cooking also signals her human condition, for, as James Boswell wrote in his journal, "No beast is a cook" (quoted in Symons 1998, xii). Throughout the section that follows the narrator's direct address to the beautiful king's daughter, the narrator continues to refer to All Kinds of Fur as *sie* (she). The narrator's word choice reminds readers that, throughout her days in the kitchen, All Kinds of Fur is both an animal *and* a woman.

When All Kinds of Fur cooks the king's soup and places a gold ring in the bowl (section 7c), the narrator shifts to *es* (it) and continues to use this neutral pronoun through section 9b. Here, as before, the narrator can use either *sie* or *es* after the proper noun *Allerleirauh*. This editorial choice once again links the name *Allerleirauh* with "it" and hides All Kinds of Fur's female sex:

(7c) Da ging der Koch fort, und Allerleirauh kochte die Suppe für den König und kochte eine Brotsuppe, so gut es konnte, und wie sie fertig war, holte es in dem Ställchen seinen goldenen Ring und legte ihn in die Schüssel, in welche die Suppe angerichtet ward.

(7c) Then the cook went away, and All Kinds of Fur cooked the soup for the king, a bread soup, as well as it could. And when the soup was ready, it got from the little stall its gold ring, and laid it in the bowl in which the soup was to be served.

Between section 7c, where she cooks the king's soup for the first time, and section 9b, where All Kinds of Fur prepares for the second ball, the text contains several instances where the use of *es* (it) is especially intensified. In 7f when the cook talks to the king, the cook uses *das Rauhtierchen*, the more animal, less gendered noun, with its neutral diminutive *-chen*. In section 8a, as she comes before the king, she calls herself "child," once again hiding her female sex. As the narrator relates All Kinds of Fur and the king's conversation in sections 8b and 8c, the narrator's repetition of *Antwortete es* (it answered) emphasizes her ambiguous, gender-neutral status.

The narrator continues to use *es* (it) in 9b as All Kinds of Fur transforms herself for the second ball from a creature in a rough-fur mantle into a woman dressed in a silver gown. Directly afterward, though, as she steps into the ballroom in section 9c, the narrator shifts to *sie* (she) and foregrounds All Kinds of Fur's human, female identity:

(9b) Da lief es in sein Ställchen, wusch sich geschwind und nahm aus der Nuß das Kleid, das so silbern war wie der Mond, und tat es an.

(9b) Then, it ran into its little stall, washed quickly, and took out of the nut the dress that was as silver as the moon, and put it on.

(9c) Da ging sie hinauf und glich einer Königstochter, und der König trat ihr entgegen und freute sich, daß er sie wiedersah.

(9c) Then she went up and looked like a king's daughter and the king stepped up to her and was happy to see her again.

From this point in the tale until the end, the gender shifts in the pronouns referring to All Kinds of Fur increase in number, intensity, and propinquity. As the shifts emphasize the complex, fluid, gendered landscape of the tale, they call increased attention to the oscillating feminine/neutral genders and human/non-human animal condition of All Kinds of Fur.

After the second ball, All Kinds of Fur runs from the king, changes, cooks his soup, and puts the gold spinning wheel in the bowl (section 9d). At first the narrator uses feminine pronouns (*sie* and *ihr*), but as All Kinds of Fur wraps herself in her mantle, the narrator calls her (*das*) *Rauhtierchen* (Little Hairy Animal) and shifts to the neuter pronoun:

(9d) Als aber der Tanz zu Ende war, verschwand sie wieder so schnell, daß der König nicht bemerken konnte, wo sie hinging. Sie sprang aber in ihr Ställchen und machte sich wieder zum Rauhtierchen und ging in die Küche, die Brotsuppe zu kochen.

(9d) As soon as the dance ended though, she disappeared again so fast that the king could not notice where she went. She ran however into her little stall and made herself again into the Little Hairy Animal and went into the kitchen to cook the bread soup.

| Als der Koch oben war, holte es das goldene Spinnrad und tat es in die Schüssel. | When the cook was upstairs, it fetched the gold spinning wheel and put it in the bowl. |

The use of *Rauhtierchen* in 9d adds to the gender ambiguity on the lexical level because readers and translators have two choices: they can see *Rauhtierchen* either as a noun or as a proper name. Each choice has implications. If the reader takes the word for the noun "little hairy animal," then *Rauhtierchen* clearly takes neuter pronouns, for in German (*das*) *Tier* is a neuter noun. If the reader sees *Rauhtierchen* as a proper name, then either *sie* or *es* could be used as the related pronoun. In my translation, *Rauhtierchen* is a familiar proper name; the narrator chooses to use the neuter pronoun *es* rather than *sie* and shifts All Kinds of Fur back to her gender-neutral self.

Only a sentence later, as All Kinds of Fur confesses for the second time that she cooked the soup and that she was only good for having boots thrown at her head, the narrator in section 9e calls the heroine *Allerleirauh* and links the name with *sie* this time, shifting to the feminine pronoun. (The narrator paired *Allerleirauh* with *es* in sections 5d and 7c.)

| (9e) Allerleirauh kam da wieder vor den König, aber sie antwortete, daß sie nur dazu wäre, daß ihr die Stiefel an den Kopf geworfen würden und daß sie von dem goldenen Spinnrädchen gar nichts wüßte. | (9e) Then All Kinds of Fur came before the king again, but she answered that she was only good for having boots thrown at her head,[21] and that she knew nothing at all about the gold spinning wheel. |

Immediately after the use of *sie* for *Allerleirauh* in 9e, the cook uses a feminine noun and then switches to neuter nouns to refer to All Kinds of Fur: the cook declares her *eine Hexe* (a witch),[22] then calls her *Rauhtierchen*, all in the space of one sentence in section 10a. Indeed, the cook always uses the latter more familiar, endearing, family-like name, never *Allerleirauh*:

| (10a) Als der König zum drittenmal ein Fest anstellte, da ging es nicht anders als die vorigen Male. | (10a) When the king held a ball for the third time, it went no different from the earlier times except that |

Der Koch sprach zwar: "Du bist eine Hexe, Rauhtierchen, und tust immer was in die Suppe, davon sie so gut wird und dem König besser schmeckt als was ich koche"; doch weil es so bat, so ließ er es auf die bestimmte Zeit hingehen.

the cook said, "You are a witch, Little Hairy Animal, and you always put something in the soup that makes it get so good that it tastes better to the king than what I cook." But because it begged so much, he let it go up at the given time.

(10b) Nun zog es ein Kleid an, das wie die Sterne glänzte, und trat damit in den Saal.

(10b) Now it put on a dress that shimmered like the stars and, wearing it, stepped into the ball-room.

These increasingly close shifts and juxtapositions in gendered words from section 9b highlight the final gender shift that occurs as section 10c begins.

At the third ball, the king secretly places a ring on All Kinds of Fur's finger. The narrator refers to All Kinds of Fur not just as a woman but as *Jungfrau* (maiden), invoking both virginity and the most revered virgin of all: the Virgin Mary. A repeated chorus of *sie* follows *Jungfrau*, pronouncing over and over again this beautiful maiden's female sex and feminine gender:

(10c) Der König tanzte wieder mit der schönen Jungfrau und meinte, daß sie noch niemals so schön gewesen wäre. Und während er tanzte, steckte er ihr, ohne daß sie es merkte, einen goldenen Ring an den Finger.

(10c) The king danced again with the beautiful maiden and thought that she had never been so beautiful. And while he danced, he put on her finger, without her noticing, a gold ring.

Throughout the remainder of the story, All Kinds of Fur remains *sie* (she) as the king discovers her human, female identity, and she and he betroth themselves to each other.

The intensified use of feminine, gender-specific words ends the complex alternation of *sie* (she) and *es* (it). In the tale's concluding moments, the repetition of "maiden," "she," "beautiful," and "her" effectively attempts to seal off and contain the gender ambiguity of bodies, clothes, and pronouns that had come before. These gendered words seek to reinscribe the text with "the binary framework [of] both sex and gender," what Judith Butler calls "regulatory fictions" ([1990] 1999, 33).

The transformative shifts among ambiguous bodies and ambiguous pronouns, however, constitute the alluring, central actions of "Allerleirauh" ("All Kinds of Fur"). All Kinds of Fur wraps herself in the rough-fur mantle, places three gowns and three tiny gold treasures in a nutshell, and flees from her father. As she journeys, she hides her female self behind rough furs and the word camouflage of *das Kind*. Others help her, either inadvertently or on purpose, by calling her *Allerleirauh* and *Rauhtierchen* and by alternating *sie* with *es*—not using just *sie* alone. The gendered words that close the tale, however, can neither regulate nor cordon off the compelling visions of life in the alternative landscape of the tale's interior. Those visions remain vibrant long after the wedding fades from memory.

"Allerleirauh," with its many ambiguities, is one of those "cultural configurations of gender confusion [that] operate as sites for intervention, exposure, and displacement" of the "reified framework" of the masculine/feminine binary (Butler [1990] 1999, 31). In "Allerleirauh," the disguises of skins and words suggest that delineations of gender and sex are themselves disguises, social constructions, and, in Muhawi's words, "social masks" (2001, 278). Skins and words, the tale suggests, can be changed and blended seemingly at will. But the cost is high; one needs a gown of stars in a midnight sky, a mantle from a piece of every animal's fur, and just the right words.

NOTES

Heartfelt thanks to my tutor and cotranslator Irmgard Wagner. Thanks also to Joan N. Radner, Eileen B. Sypher, John Burt Foster Jr., Susan Gordon, Ruth Bottigheimer, and my graduate research assistants Shawn Flanagan, Jennifer Spitulnik-Hughes, and Paulina Guerrero.

1. The last (1857) of the Grimms' seven published versions is more ambiguous than the first (1812). The 1812 version says the princess's bridegroom gave her the three treasures while she was living in her father's kingdom. No such bridegroom appears in the former, which does not name the giver.

2. I write from the perspective where a young woman marries a man who is not her father for two main reasons. First, most people in my audiences and classes imagine the story thus. Most of all, though, like incest survivors and many other women, I am personally more interested in the journey of a young woman away from a threatening situation and toward another, more fulfilling life where she makes her own choices, sexual and otherwise. My discussion of ambiguous bodies and ambiguous pronouns, though, applies to both perspectives.

3. I have included a few ATU 510B* ("The Princess in the Chest") tales because they share many motifs with ATU 510.

4. The story examples that I attribute to one country are meant to be illustrative only, and not exhaustive. When I write "in Scotland," for example, I do not mean this motif occurs in Scotland alone or that it is the sole Scottish version.

5. All German translations by Yocom with Wagner, unless otherwise noted.

6. Translation from Russian by John Burt Foster Jr.

7. By calling herself *Esaua* and later *Jacobina* she offers the king a hint. See the story of Jacob and Esau in Genesis 27:1–40 of the Bible.

8. An *Afreet* is a demon from the *djinn* world.

9. In this tale there is no incestuous request but, rather, its replacement; her father wants her to marry an ugly old king in Faraway Land.

10. For information on the *huldre* or hidden people, see Kvideland and Sehmsdorf (1988).

11. In some versions, especially those where the young man falls ill, the young woman interacts with his mother. For example, see the Chilean tale where the mother refuses to allow Little Stick Figure to make tortillas for the sick young gentleman (Pino-Saavedra 1967, 99–103).

12. Schmidt summarizes a tale found in Grobbelaar (1981, 675) in which there is no incestuous request but, rather, its replacement. Her father wants her to marry an old king, and she is already in love with a young king. According to Schmidt (1991, 87–95), most South African ATU 510B versions begin with this replacement motif or with the opening section of ATU 923 "Love Like Salt."

13. Space does not allow for a full discussion of the role of the cook, his/her relationship with All Kinds of Fur, and the power of the domestic space of the kitchen. In an article in progress, I detail these connections, their implications for "Allerleirauh," and the role of the cook in other tales and literary works.

14. In his work with tales told in Arabic, Ibrahim Muhawi has also explored the significance of pronoun shifts. He discusses how the language of "Sackcloth," a Palestinian ATU 510B version, establishes "a masculine identity for the heroine. Once she dons her sackcloth, this transformation is effected through the latent power of language in creating character and action through narrative. Arabic as we know is characterized by the use of grammatical gender: in "Sackcloth" the teller deploys this characteristic of language iconically, relying on the deictic power of nouns and pronouns to create reference and a masculine gender for the heroine. Till the unraveling at the end, the teller refers to Sackcloth only by means of masculine pronouns, or by the appellation *Abu l-Lababīb* (Sackcloth-Man)" (2001, 279).

15. Instead, Bechstein establishes a pattern of language usage that tells readers that, without a doubt, *Aschenpüster* (Ash-Blower), in her crow-skin disguise, is a young woman who has magically changed her shape (*Gestalt*) to that of a boy. Bechstein avoids the neuter gender (he uses no neuter pronouns to refer to Ash-Blower) and places the feminine and masculine forms of words in clearly different grammatical positions. When he uses nouns and their modifying adjectives (both descriptive and possessive) to refer to her (with her crow-skin disguise and boy's shape), he uses their masculine form. When he uses pronouns to refer to her (with the identical costume and form), he uses their feminine mode (with one understandable exception). Also, the Grimms' 1819 text and all subsequent texts have many more *sie/es* alternations and more neuter references (*Kind*/child) than their first version of 1812.

16. I am using the following texts: for 1810/1812 (Grimm 1975); for 1819 (Grimm [1982] 1993); for 1837 (Grimm [1985] 2007); for 1857 (Grimm 1984).

17. I translate *es* as "it" and not *sie*, as is standard in German, because the Grimms sometimes use *sie* to refer to (*das*) *Mädchen*. See "Aschenputtel," as Robinson (2007) points out.

18. At this point in the German-language edition of the 1857 text I use, edited by Rölleke (1984), *Allerleirauh* appears in italics. It is the first time the name appears in the tale.

19. *Rauch* and its variant *rauh* in the time of the Grimms meant *behaart* (hairy; Kluge [1883] 1960, 586). It also denoted and denotes today, without disparagement, the rough, coarse fur of bear or fox (not sleek deer fur, for example), especially in compound words such as *Rauchwerk* and *Ruchwerk* that referred to a furrier's *Werk* (work [neuter]) or *Ware* (goods [feminine]) (586). Words for fur that might also affect which gender the Grimms and others use when referring to the *rauh* of *Allerleirauh* are masculine and neuter: *der Pelz* (warm, thick fur, refers to clothing) and *das Fell* (fur, skin on a living animal).

20. See the widely used translations of Jack Zipes (2002b, 240) and Margaret

Hunt (1884). The Grimms used *Prinzessin* (princess), a French loanword, several times in their 1812 edition, but by 1819 they used the German *Königstochter*. See also Tatar (1987, 31).

21. For examples of the connection between footwear and human sexuality, see German proverbs that feature boots and shoes (Wander [1867–80] 1964).

22. The Grimms could have had the cook say *ein Hexchen*, a gender-neutral noun available in their Hessian dialect. Similarly, in Swabia, people used the neuter cognate *ein Hexle* to refer to tricky little girls and, in Swiss Allemanic, *ein Hexli*. The Grimms used the feminine *eine Hexe* instead (conversations with Irmgard Wagner, May 2009).

REVISING REWRITINGS

5

A Desire for Death

The Grimms' Sleeping Beauty
in *The Bloody Chamber*

KIMBERLY J. LAU

Sleeping Beauty (ATU 410) is the quintessential Grimms girl.

Deep in slumber, she is nothing but a pretty face, a supple body there for the gazing, there for the taking. She is passive, yielding, available, and—of course—silent, enchantingly incapable of speaking her mind, much less voicing any resistance to the hero's advances. Ruth Bottigheimer (1986) has carefully documented the Grimms' bias for silent girls and women, the brothers' tendency to diminish female voices in *Kinder- und Hausmärchen*, particularly by overwriting female speech through their own edit(orializ)ing practices, altering the agency of women's words by casting them in the passive voice of narrators and limiting the range of verbs used to characterize women's speech acts. For Little Brier Rose, the Grimms' sleeping beauty, direct and active speech is confined to childhood, to the time when the princess still has the freedom of movement, the ability to roam the castle, to follow her curiosity in exploration; during one such investigation, she comes across an old woman spinning in a tower and asks her what the spindle is, her only direct speech act in the entire story.

While exegetically it is the slighted fairy's curse and the prick of Sleeping Beauty's finger that put her to sleep, in the Grimms' ideological narrative it is also this act of asking, combining as it does both curiosity and speech, that ushers in the princess's century of sleep. So critical is her silence to upholding the social structure that in the Grimms' version the princess's falling into sleep brings with it sleep for the entire community. Her straightforward act of asking disturbs the underpinnings of her social world, and it is not until she wakes—silently—to the hero's kiss and to her rightfully passive place beside him that the inhabitants of the castle return to life, immediately resuming their normative roles as if there had been no interruption.

Marking the transition from child to adult, sleep transforms the young girl into the perfect woman—passive, silent, compliant, and sexually available. Little Brier Rose's womanly silence is particularly striking and especially socially significant when compared with Charles Perrault's Sleeping Beauty, whose awakening is preordained and not dependent on the hero's kiss and whose slumber is solitary as opposed to social. In Perrault's 1697 "The Sleeping Beauty in the Wood," Sleeping Beauty says to the approaching hero, "Is it you, my prince? . . . You have kept me waiting a long time!" (A. Carter 1977, 64). Up to this point, the two versions are fairly closely aligned, but the princess's awakening signals their dramatic departure. In Perrault's version, Sleeping Beauty engages the hero in conversation: "He was more tongue-tied than she, because she had had plenty of time to dream of what she would say to him" (66).[1] Little Brier Rose, in contrast, awakens to the hero's kiss and simply "look[s] at him fondly" (Zipes 1987, 189) before they descend from the tower and their "wedding . . . [is] celebrated in great splendor" (189).

Even more than her silence, Little Brier Rose's deathlike passivity is her most becoming feature, as it is for all of the princesses in the "Sleeping Beauty" tales. Beyond the reaches of a common waking, the sleeping beauties offer up the necrophiliac desire for the beautiful corpse, the erotic fascination with dead women. In their deathlike repose, they arouse an irresistible longing in the men who come across them. Even the Grimms' relatively chaste version hints at the sexual attraction of the beautiful, corpse-like woman: "There she lay, and her beauty was so marvelous that he could not take his eyes off her. Then he leaned over and gave her a kiss" (Zipes 1987, 189). More explicit is Giambattista Basile's 1634–36 version in which the traveling king's "gathering the fruits of love" results in the birth of twins to Talia, the sleeping beauty, who fails to wake even in childbirth: "The King called to her, thinking she was asleep; but since nothing he did or said brought her back to her senses, and being on fire with love, he carried her to a couch and, having gathered the fruits of love, left her lying there" (Hallett and Karasek 2002, 21).[2] In Basile's version, "Sun, Moon, and Talia," the king's having sex with Talia despite his inability to wake her foregrounds the necrophiliac fantasy implicit in the "Sleeping Beauty" fairy tales, though subsequent versions such as Perrault's "La Belle au Bois Dormant" and the Grimms' "Little Brier Rose" tend to shy away from such frank references to the hero's sexual acts with the sleeping princess. Nonetheless, the eroticization of the deathlike princess lurks beneath the surface of Sleeping Beauty's seemingly straightforward embodiment of the perfectly passive woman, especially in the Grimms' version where Little Brier Rose remains silent even after she wakes.

Angela Carter interrupts the confining legacy of this Sleeping Beauty tradition with her own tale, "The Lady of the House of Love," a doubly told intertextual tale and metanarrative detailing the burden of this fairy-tale legacy,[3] the articulatory power of popular narrative generally, and the ways in which they extend oppressive cultural constructions of woman. Simultaneously a "Sleeping Beauty" tale and a gothic vampire story, "The Lady of the House of Love" is an intricately mirrored pair of narrative traditions. Neither a simple retelling of "Sleeping Beauty" through the trope of the vampire nor a retelling of the vampire tale through the idiom of "Sleeping Beauty," Carter's "The Lady of the House of Love" brings to life the two narrative legacies through the figure of the somnambulist vampire Countess, caught like her ancestral sleeping beauties and her vampire forebears in the liminal state between sleeping and waking, between life and death, between fairy tale and metanarrative.

In "The Lady of the House of Love," Carter details the lonely nights of the "young" vampire Countess, the sole "living" descendant of Nosferatu, who lives with a mute serving woman in a decaying castle above an abandoned village in Romania. Longing for an escape from her predestined life, the vampire Countess passes much of her time with a deck of tarot cards, forever hoping for an alternative future, an alternative life. This desire is satisfied when an English soldier, on leave and cycling through the forests of Romania, accepts the serving woman's invitation to dine at the castle. As the vampire Countess prepares to seduce—and feast on—the soldier, she fumbles the ritual and, in the process, accidentally cuts her finger on a splinter of glass. Kissing her bleeding wound, the soldier thus frees her from her liminal state, helping her instead to a permanent death.

More than simply resisting and revising the patriarchal inheritance and narrative authority of the "Sleeping Beauty" tales, popularized through the canonical works of Basile, Perrault, the Grimms, and Disney, Carter's vampire Countess is a shadow princess forever haunting these dominant versions of the tale even as she seeks to break the stronghold of their cultural spell and its deathly consequences for women.

"THE LADY OF THE HOUSE OF LOVE": AN INTERTEXTUAL TALE

Carter's long-standing interest in fairy tales is well known, and her translation of Perrault's tales, her Virago collections, and her own inspired retellings attest to her extensive knowledge of the classic tales as well as to her insightful and sharp critique of them (see, e.g., A. Carter 1983; Roemer and Bacchilega 2001; Sage 2001; Jordan 1992). In addition, Carter's (1979b) critical monograph, *The Sadeian Woman*, and her longer fiction highlight her lifelong interest in the deeply intimate relationship between sexual desire and power, a relationship wrapped up with the fairy tale's lasting success. Carter has famously described herself as being in the "demythologizing business" (1983, 25) and her work as "putting new wine in old bottles" (24), and it is precisely this intricate intertextual practice that allows her somnambulist vampire Countess to travel through the "Sleeping Beauty" tales, leaving her ghostly resonance as she goes. At the same time, Carter's recurring fascinations, her repeated images, her regular allusions all yield to an individual intertextuality as well, to her practice of putting even her own wine into a number of different bottles. Amid the vast intertextual richness of her work, Carter returns most frequently to the sleeping beauties, the female vampires, and the living dolls, alluring somnambulists who make their way through both her fiction and criticism and who lay bare the fantasy of necrophilia that drives the dominant cultural investment in women's passivity so perfectly exemplified by the Grimms' "Little Brier Rose" (see, e.g., Sage 2001, 72, 76; Sceats 2001; Mikkonen 2001; Wisker 1997; Peng 2004).[4] Carter's enduring interest in living dolls and female vampires anticipates Sue Ellen Case's well-known theorization of the female vampire's powerful ability to disrupt hegemonic gender ontologies. Case sees in the figure of the vampire an "identification with the insult, the taking on of the transgressive" constitutive of a queer theory and a queer desire, "which seeks the living dead, producing a slippage at the ontological base and seducing through a gender inversion above" (1991, 2, 3). Carter's fascination with the feminine living dead likewise celebrates the potential for slippage at the center of cultural constructions of gender, a slippage she exploits throughout her fiction.

While Carter often casts these compelling somnambulists individually in her fairy tales and novels, she conflates the sleeping beauty and the female vampire in "The Lady of the House of Love" in order to make explicit their essential interconnectedness. Embodying both traditions, the beautiful somnambulist vampire is both Sade's masochistic Justine and his sadistic Juliette, the sisters who offer up the only possible cultural signifiers for woman in their refracted images. Even more, Carter locates in Sade's potentially radical and transformative pornography exactly this conflation:[5] "We see how the chaste kiss of the sentimental lover differs only in degree from the vampirish love-bite that draws blood" (1979b, 24–25). As both sadist and masochist, both "death and the maiden" (1979a, 93), Carter's beautiful somnambulist, her vampire Countess, bears all the weight of her narrative ancestors, the weight of the cultural desires for Sleeping Beauty's seeming innocence as well as the dark seduction and deadly sexuality of the female vampire stories, and through such entwined ancestral legacies she exposes the fairy tale's grim underbelly.

As an intertextual tale, "The Lady of the House of Love" obviously depends on its patriarchal antecedents to provoke a discomfiting recognition. While Carter has a translator's familiarity with Perrault's fairy tales and certainly gestures to his and Basile's versions of "Sleeping Beauty," "The Lady of the House of Love" seems to find its richest intertext in the Grimms' "Little Brier Rose," the version with the most passive heroine. Like the castles belonging to these first sleeping beauties, the one belonging to the beautiful somnambulist is abandoned and surrounded by roses that have "grown up into a huge, spiked wall that incarcerates her in the castle of her inheritance" (95). Even in invoking the same imagery, Carter's slight shift in purpose is significant: here, the "spiked wall" *incarcerates* the Countess whereas the other thickets *protect* their sleeping princesses. As Carter's hero follows the mute crone from the village to the mansion, the literal sensuality of the Countess's roses—their scent, size, shape—overwhelm him and intimate the dangerous sexuality awaiting him:

> A great, intoxicated surge of the heavy scent of red roses blew into his face as soon as they left the village, inducing a sensuous vertigo; a blast of rich, faintly corrupt sweetness strong enough, almost, to fell him. Too many roses. Too many roses bloomed on enormous thickets that lined the path, thickets bristling with thorns, and the flowers themselves were almost too luxuriant, their huge congregations of plush petals somehow obscene in their excess, their whorled, tightly budded cores outrageous in their implications. (98)

Carter's elaboration of the "spiked wall" as full of "too many roses [blooming] on enormous thickets" calls to mind the Grimms' description of the thicket surrounding Little Brier Rose's castle on the day the successful prince comes to wake her; whereas Perrault's thorny bramble simply opens to the prince after the one-hundred-year spell, the Grimms' previously dangerous hedge is in full bloom: "When the prince approached the brier hedge, he found nothing but beautiful flowers that opened of their own accord, let him through, and then closed again like a hedge" (Zipes 1987, 188). In establishing a particularly strong intertextual relationship between her story and the Grimms' "Little Brier Rose," Carter fully exploits the sexual imagery and clear metaphoric innuendo of the rose in the Grimms' fairy tale. The sexual symbolism of the rose *as* the sleeping princess is none too subtle in the Grimms' tale; not only is she named Little Brier Rose, but the willing opening up of the protective thorn hedge full of blooming roses also makes explicit such symbolic meanings. Yet Carter exaggerates the sexual symbolism, indeed almost fully translates it ("their huge congregations of plush petals somehow obscene in their excess, their whorled, tightly budded cores outrageous in their implications" [1979a, 98]) in order to draw out the intoxicating and dangerous sexuality of both her own heroine as well as the Grimms' more passive and, thus, perhaps more alluring counterpart.

Carter further extends the symbolism of the rose beyond the opening thicket, beyond the heteronormative sexual meanings implicit in the Grimms' roses. For Carter, the rose is much more literally the Countess's sexuality and her life, a magical and haunting souvenir of her enduring (cultural) legacy and the deadly consequences of embracing the double fantasy of this female character as both passive sexual object and active sexual subject. When the hero wakes in the morning (after the vampire Countess has been freed from her somnambulist existence), he finds only "a lace négligé lightly soiled with blood, as it might be from a woman's menses, and a rose that must have come from the fierce bushes nodding through the window" (1979a, 106). The rose is, of course, more than just a flower come through the window as the departed Countess's "voice-over" makes clear: "And I leave you as a souvenir the dark fanged rose I plucked from between my thighs, like a flower laid on a grave" (107). No ordinary flower but a fanged rose (a *vagina dentata*, potent symbol of the fear of women's sexuality), the hero's souvenir of his night with the Countess survives, though barely, his journey from Romania to Britain, where he "resurrects" it in a glass of water until his "spartan quarters brimmed with the reeling odour of a glowing, velvet, monstrous flower whose petals had regained all their former bloom and elasticity, their corrupt, brilliant, baleful splendour" (107–8). Like Nosferatu's plague-infested rats, the Countess's rose travels from east to west and portends the widespread death of hundreds of thousands of young men, its scent lingering through the barracks on the eve of the hero's regiment's departure for France during World War I. Carter's roses are heady, intoxicating, and dangerous in their sensuality, their promise of death, and, as such, they force us to reimagine the seeming simplicity of the Grimms' roses, "nothing but beautiful flowers," nothing but the innocent Little Brier Rose.

Just as Carter gives the Grimms' rose fangs, so too does she equip her sleeping beauty: "She has no mouth with which to kiss, no hands with which to caress, only the fangs and talons of a beast of prey" (1979a, 104). While the vampire Countess might have the fangs and talons of a predatory animal, she is of course much more than a simple "beast of prey," her desire for "fresh meat" driven by sexual desire as well.[6] Even as a little girl, when she could be satisfied feasting on smaller animals, "she bit into their necks with a nauseated voluptuousness" (96). The beautiful somnambulist's "nauseated voluptuousness" reveals her simultaneous enculturation and her animal instinct, her internalized reluctance to fully succumb to her sensual gratification. As she grows older, both her reluctance and her desire deepen: "But now she is a woman, she must have men. . . . She sinks her teeth into the [rabbit's] neck where an artery throbs with fear; she will drop the deflated skin from which she has extracted all the nourishment with a small cry of both pain and disgust. And it is the same with the shepherd boys and gipsy lads" (96). In the vampire Countess's need for men, in her sexually charged but ambivalent ravishing of them ("It is dinner time. It is bed-time" [104]), Carter elaborates women's animal drives, women's dreams of sexual freedom, only to thwart them by raising the specter of Sade's Juliette. Like Juliette, the vampire Countess is confined by her social context, by the patriarchal culture that leaves no space for her as an autonomous sexual being, and Carter's description of Sade's "great women" might as well apply to the Countess as well:

> A free woman in an unfree society will be a monster. Her freedom will be a condition of personal privilege that deprives those on which she exercises it of her own freedom. The most extreme kind of this deprivation is murder. These women murder.
>
> The sexual behavior of these women, like that of their men, is a mirror of their inhumanity. (27)

Carter has been controversial among feminist critics and literary scholars for precisely this type of complexity (see, e.g., Jordan 1992; Peng 2004; Sage 2001; L. Tucker 1998); the Countess's expression of her animal drives, her seeming sexual autonomy and agency, are reduced to murder and monstrosity, the marks of her inhumanity. She is not an easy feminist heroine following her animal drives, luxuriating in her sexuality. Rather, she is dangerous because of the society that limits her, and Carter plays up the Countess's monstrosity by aligning her with the cannibalistic giant in "Jack and the Beanstalk." Transitioning from a description of the ritual tidying that follows the Countess's deadly seductions to the arrival of the hero, Carter offers two verses from the "Jack and the Beanstalk" nursery rhyme: "Fee fie fo fum / I smell the blood of an Englishman" (1979a, 96). Both the Countess and the giant are made monstrous by their insatiable, murderous appetites.

And yet, the vampire Countess is not just an inhuman monster; like her more traditional fairy tale ancestors, she is also superlative in her beauty:

"She is so beautiful she is unnatural; her beauty is an abnormality, a deformity, for none of her features exhibit any of those touching imperfections that reconcile us to the imperfection of the human condition" (1979a, 94). The heroine's perfect and unnatural beauty highlights the multiple ways in which she—as vampire, as fairy tale princess, as "a free woman in an unfree society"—exceeds "the human condition." Even more, she is simultaneously the idealized passive sleeping princess, and, like her fairy tale counterparts, she too has a special resting place: "In the centre [of her bedroom] is an elaborate catafalque, in ebony, surrounded by long candles in enormous silver candlesticks. In a white lace négligé stained a little with blood, the Countess climbs up on her catafalque at dawn each morning and lies down in an open coffin" (94). Though the Grimms' Little Brier Rose simply "fell down upon the bed that was standing there" (Zipes 1987, 187), Perrault's and Basile's sleeping beauties are laid to rest in decorative splendor, as if for display and burial. In Perrault's tale, the princess sleeps "on a bed covered with gold and silver embroidery" (A. Carter 1977, 61), and in Basile's tale she is laid out "upon a velvet chair under an embroidered canopy" (Hallett and Karasek 2002, 21). The image of the beautiful sleeping princess, on view as if in death, poised for the taking, satisfies the dark fantasy of necrophilia, and the Countess, at rest in her open coffin dressed only in her white negligee, makes this association most explicit.

As is the case for the fairy-tale sleeping beauties, the Countess's childlike innocence only heightens the allure. However, unlike her more traditional fairy-tale counterparts whose passivity is their greatest attraction, she is much more clearly *both* the beautiful and innocent child and the seductive and dangerous whore: "He saw how beautiful and how very young the bedizened scarecrow was, and he thought of a child dressing up in her mother's clothes. . . . Her huge dark eyes almost broke his heart with their waiflike, lost look; yet he was disturbed, almost repelled, by her extraordinarily fleshy mouth, a mouth with wide, full, prominent lips of a vibrant purplish-crimson, a morbid mouth. Even—but he put the thought away from him immediately—a whore's mouth" (A. Carter 1979a, 100–101). Sexual fantasies of pedophilia and necrophilia, so clearly entangled at the heart of the "Sleeping Beauty" tales, thus come to the fore in Carter's portrait of the vampire Countess. Even the naive and virginal hero makes the connection upon entering the Countess's bedroom: "His colonel, an old goat with jaded appetites, had given him the visiting card of a brothel in Paris where, the satyr assured him, ten *louis* would buy just such a lugubrious bedroom, with a naked girl upon a coffin; offstage, the brothel pianist played the *Dies Irae* on a harmonium and, amidst all the perfumes of the embalming parlour, the customer took his necrophiliac pleasure of a pretended corpse" (105).[7] Carter further underscores the significance of the Countess's boudoir as brothel, the primal scene in which necrophiliac fantasies might be enacted, through the very title of her story, "The Lady of the House of Love," invoking as it does a common name for a brothel.[8]

Carter's earlier reference to the Countess's suite as "Juliet's tomb" (1979a, 100) is thus a particularly apt foreshadowing of what the bedroom promises: the vampire Countess embodies both Romeo's Juliet, the virginal and seemingly dead lover, an early sleeping beauty whose eternal waiting the Countess shares ("I've always been ready for you; I've been waiting for you in my wedding dress" [103]), and Sade's Juliette, the sexually aggressive libertine. As such, the Countess's suite—"Juliet's tomb," her "macabre bedroom" (105), "the Countess's larder" (96)—provides a perfect setting for Carter's tale, a different type of bloody chamber in which the sleeping beauty and the vampire seductress cannot be separated, where love and death are forever linked.

For Carter, the twinning of the two figures only reinforces the double limits on women's subjectivity given the dominant cultural representations of woman. Consequently, the hero's kiss—his instinctive act of love, his kissing the cut on her finger from the splintered glass of her shattered dark eyeglasses—only momentarily frees her from the liminality of her somnambulism. As Carter makes clear, for the Countess as well as for her more traditional Sleeping Beauty ancestors, "the end of exile is the end of being" (1979a, 106). The supposedly liberating kiss is not the harbinger of an alternative sexual freedom of the type Carter celebrates in *The Sadeian Woman* but rather a certain death; it is the symbol of fairy-tale love, a kiss that leads only to a conventional happily ever after, for Carter more of a happily never after. The fatality of the hero's kiss underscores the eternal liminality of women's position in a male-dominated society—caught forever between virgin and whore, between dead and deadening. Deadened in her current state by her lack of agency, the Countess's only escape is mortal death, for

Carter a more satisfying option than the equally deadening future the hero imagines for her: "We shall take her to Zurich, to a clinic; she will be treated for nervous hysteria. Then to an eye specialist, for her photophobia, and to a dentist to put her teeth into better shape. Any competent manicurist will deal with her claws. We shall turn her into the lovely girl she is; I shall cure her of all these nightmares" (107).

Fairy-tale love—foretold by the Countess's tarot cards, enacted in the kiss, projected into the future by the hero—is the death of female animal drive, the death of female sexual desire, not the love that Carter believes to be a possible impetus to complete freedom. In *The Sadeian Woman*, Carter's critical intertext to *The Bloody Chamber*, she suggests that love might have a redemptive quality, that it might in fact be the only possible way of achieving women's emancipation on all levels: "Only the possibility of love could awake the libertine to perfect, immaculate terror. It is in this holy terror of love that we find, in both men and women themselves, the source of all opposition to the emancipation of women" (1979b, 150). However, as Carter's vampiric sleeping beauty learns, this love is not the love of fairy tales, and female animal drives and sexual desires cannot be autonomous when circumscribed by the pornographic fantasies of a male-dominated culture, compelled as it were by numerous ancestral legacies. Thus, in "The Lady of the House of Love" Carter exposes the misplaced cultural longing for and faith in a fairy-tale love, a romanticized love exemplified by the Grimms' immediate transition from the princess's waking and gazing up at her rescuer to their marriage and happily ever after. For Carter, women are better off dead than dying a slow death in the stifling happily ever after of fairy tales where the happily ever after necessarily depends on the heroine's passivity and compliance, the killing off of her desire and sexual agency.[9]

"The Lady of the House of Love": A Metanarrative

If *The Bloody Chamber* is "a book of stories about fairy stories" (A. Carter 1983, 25), "The Lady of the House of Love" is perhaps the exemplar of Carter's meta-storytelling. Running alongside her intertextual tale, Carter's metanarrative suggests that the fairy tale is itself a cultural legacy that contributes to the deadly strictures on women's subjectivity and sexual agency. From such a metanarrative perspective, Carter's explicit vamp(ir)ing of "Sleeping Beauty" draws out the eternal power of Sleeping Beauty's fairy-tale legacy, its power to incarcerate the heroine within its tradition, forever upholding the desirable, corpse-like woman at the center of the tale.

Within this context, the gothic vampire narrative is foundational to Carter's metanarrative critique precisely because "the timeless Gothic eternity of the vampires, for whom all is as it has always been and will be, whose cards always fall in the same pattern" (1979a, 97) captures the timelessness of Sleeping Beauty's story, its constant return to the desire for a deathly, deadly sexuality. As a vampire, the beautiful somnambulist Countess is characterized by her never-ending life, by her being a "system of repetitions . . . a closed circuit" (93), by her frequent possession by ancestors whose very nature drives her to seek out fresh meat, fresh men. Her story is preordained and unfolds in its infinite repetition each night. She is narrative incarnate. As such, she and her story necessarily exceed their exegetical limits. Through her story, the Countess is at once a sleeping beauty and a story about the fairy tale "Sleeping Beauty"; the narrative and the metanarrative are as permanently entwined as Sleeping Beauty and the vampire Countess. Thus, when Carter describes the beautiful somnambulist as "helplessly perpetuat[ing] her ancestral crimes" (93), she calls to mind both the crimes of the Countess's vampire forebears and the crimes of Sleeping Beauty's patriarchal ancestors, the tales of Basile, Perrault, the Grimms, and Disney.

Throughout "The Lady of the House of Love," Carter cultivates the oppressive and tragic weight of such an ancestral burden: the Countess is unable to resist her voracious hunger ("All claws and teeth, she strikes, she gorges; but nothing can console her for the ghastliness of her condition, nothing" [1979a, 95]); she is incapable of dealing a different set of tarot cards ("The Tarot always shows the same configuration: always she turns up La Papesse, La Mort, La Tour Abolie, wisdom, death, dissolution" [93]); she is defenseless against possession by ancestral spirits ("She does not possess herself; her ancestors sometimes come and peer out of the windows of her eyes and that is very frightening" [103]). The Countess's own "horrible reluctance for the role" (95), combined with her uneasy complicity in it, her futile imaginings of alternative possibilities, only compounds the oppressive nature of her inheritance: "She loathes the food she eats; she would have liked to take the rabbits home with her, feed them on lettuce, pet them and make them a nest in her red-and-black chinoiserie escritoire, but hunger always overcomes her" (96). She dreams of similar alternatives for the "shepherd boys and gipsy lads" who come to her as well: "A certain desolate stillness of her eyes indicates she is inconsolable. She would like to caress their lean brown cheeks and stroke their ragged hair" (96). Enacting the script of her patriarchal (narrative) inheritance, the Countess—"Nosferatu's sanguinary rosebud" (103)—is compelled by her ancestors, by the extent of their legacy as well as by their ongoing presence. In this way, she perfectly embodies the fairy-tale tradition even as Carter's metanarrative strategy challenges it, a point Case underscores in what could be a direct commentary on the Countess's "vampirish love-bite" (A. Carter 1979b, 25): "What the dominant discourse represents as an emptying out, a draining away, in contrast to the impregnating kiss of the heterosexual, becomes an activism in representation" (Case 1991, 15).

Implicit in the Countess's life as narrative are questions of agency and alternatives that drive both the intertextual tale and the metanarrative, and Carter twice asks, "Can a bird sing only the song it knows or can it learn a new song?" (1979a, 93, 103). It is a question asked through a metaphor with multiple referents—the Countess, the author, our gendered social scripts—and "The Lady of the House of Love" suggests the answers might be tightly entangled. For instance, just as the Countess permits her ancestors to possess her, to "peer out the windows of her eyes," Carter invites other narrative legacies—Sleeping Beauty's fairy tale, Nosferatu's legend—to momentarily possess her heroine and thus her story. As the Countess wonders at the slim possibility of an alternative ending for the hero as well as for herself, an alternative borne of her desire and the extraordinary presence of *Les Amoureux* among the tarot cards, she is nonetheless compelled to follow her regular rituals of seduction, the social niceties demanded of her gender and her class, the act she has performed innumerable times before—"attend[ing] to the coffee-making," "offer[ing] him a sugar biscuit from a Limoges plate," and "keep[ing] up a front of inconsequential chatter in French" (102, 103). In the case of the hero, however, the social ritual of seduction, narrated in the third-person omniscient, is continually interrupted by the internal script of the Countess's infinite story:

> I do not mean to hurt you. I shall wait for you in my bride's dress in the dark.
> The bridegroom is come, he will go into the chamber which has been prepared for him.
> I am condemned to solitude and dark; I do not mean to hurt you.
> I will be very gentle. (103)

> Embraces, kisses; your golden head, of a lion, although I have never seen a lion, only imagined one, of the sun, even if I've only seen the picture of the sun on the Tarot card, your golden head of the lover whom I dreamed would one day free me, this head will fall back, its eyes roll upwards in a spasm you will mistake for that of love and not death. The bridegroom bleeds on my inverted marriage bed. (105)

Narrated in the future tense, the Countess's script succumbs to what has always come before. Both the Countess's and the hero's actions are simultaneously foretold and circumscribed by her narrative legacy, inspired not by their own power but by the weight of the narratives that lock them in place.

The Countess's story has its own overdeterminative power, and despite her longing for a way out of the "perpetual repetition of [her forebears'] passions, . . . she only knows of one kind of consummation" (A. Carter 1979a, 103). During the tale's extended scene of seduction, Carter encourages the Countess's compulsive narrative to repeatedly disrupt the story she is telling, and the continual emergence of the Countess's story amid her own highlights its power, the enduring grip of the social scripts we inherit, the cultural legacies that maintain the seeming inevitability of our "nature," our identities, our gendering.

It is only when the Countess "has fumbled the ritual"—when she acts, when she *feels*—that her story "is no longer inexorable" (A. Carter 1979a, 105). The Countess's feelings for the hero, the unprecedented welling up of her tears at the thought of their fatal consummation, is the deviation from the script that breaks the spell of the narrative. In opening herself to the frightful possibility of love, she herself is responsible for setting in motion the events that ultimately free her, her tears doing as much to liberate her as the hero's tender kissing of her bleeding finger. In the Countess's resistance to the overwhelming force of her narrative inheritance, Carter seems to suggest that there is always a potential for agency, for the subject as well as for the author of a fairy tale with an enduring patriarchal ancestry, but acting on that potential is no small feat. Rather, it requires embracing the type of love that threatens the libertines, that threatens the patriarchal order.

For the Countess, altering the script results in both freedom and death, an escape from the eternal oppression of her history and her social context, an escape from the oppressive compulsion to act on her animal drives and sexual desires, desires defined and limited by the male-dominated society that renders them foreign to her. For Carter, as author of a fairy tale with a strong patriarchal genealogy, revising the script opens up Sleeping Beauty's story even as it sustains its intertextual counterparts in order to make explicit the doubled meanings of "fairy tale," the double work such stories accomplish as both popular romance and cultural fiction that we too often (mis)take for reality. As metanarrative, "The Lady of the House of Love" argues for the possibility of another song, another tale, though not an entirely new one. In this "stor[y] about fairy stories," Carter (1983, 25) details the weight of the fairy-tale tradition, a weight surprisingly easy to bear but nearly impossible to cast aside, as the Countess demonstrates. Even more, for Carter, both men and women are complicit in the fairy tale's enduring appeal, in the lasting power of its ancestral hauntings.

Knowing Fear, Knowing Love

In keeping with the traditional "Sleeping Beauty" tales, "The Lady of the House of Love" also ends with the heroine waking to love. For Carter's sleeping beauty, however, it is not the hero's love that awakens the Countess but rather her own; she is freed by her love for another, not by the hero's fairy tale love for her. While the legacy of "Sleeping Beauty" encourages us to see the hero's innocent kiss as awakening the Countess from her somnambulist existence, it is actually the Countess's "improvisation" in the scripted ritual that prompts the "unexpected, mundane noise of breaking glass [that] breaks the wicked spell in the room, entirely" (1979a, 106). In the Countess's awakening to life and thus to death, in escaping the liminality of her simultaneously masochistic and sadistic being, she approaches the redemptive love Carter describes in *The Sadeian Woman*, the love that strikes fear among libertines because of its potential to overturn the dominant order, to bring about the true "emancipation of women."

Throughout "The Lady of the House of Love," Carter is careful to emphasize the hero's inability to know fear and, therefore, his inability to know this love. He is a virgin, unknowing, rational. He "does not yet know what there is to be afraid of . . . he cannot feel terror," and it is precisely "[t]his lack of imagination that gives his heroism to the hero" (A. Carter 1979a, 104). Limited by his inability to feel terror, by his lack of imagination (for Carter, the sure characterization of all traditional fairy-tale heroes), the hero simply cannot know the terrifying but liberating love the Countess approaches; he can offer nothing but a fairy-tale love, a love that promises only another death in his desire to whisk her away to Zurich, to make her over into "the lovely girl she is" (107).

With "The Lady of the House of Love," Carter simultaneously exposes the dark allure of the Sleeping Beauty tales—particularly the Grimms' version with its especially passive, deathlike princess—and the cultural power of the patriarchal narrative legacy of which they are a part. Freed by her own love from the eternal imprisonment of this narrative tradition, the Countess's only option is a literal death because for her there is simply no alternative; there is not yet an outside, not yet an escape into a true freedom, only the deadly, deadening confines of a sexist society. Through the Countess's desire for death, her desire to escape the erotic, necrophiliac impulses of the "Sleeping Beauty" tradition, Carter highlights the doubly grim attraction of the Grimms' "Little Brier Rose," the cultural desire for the literal and the metaphoric dead woman. In the end, Carter and the Countess might share fleeting moments of freedom, but the Grimms' erotic fascination with the beautiful corpse endures.

At the same time, through its intertextual richness, "The Lady of the House of Love" offers a glimpse of another knowing, a queer knowing in which the vampire Countess and Sleeping Beauty might find a more productive disidentification that allows them to survive the cultural confines of heteronormativity even as they literally perish within its exegetical strictures.[10] The moment when Carter's vampire Countess awakens to death is also the moment she joins her ancestral sleeping beauties in narrative eternity, forever provoking the uncanny recognitions that bring them together to challenge the compulsive heterosexuality of their patriarchal lineages, enacting what Case sees as the inherently oppositional nature of queer discourse in the "trope" of the lesbian, the way "'she' is the wounding, desiring, transgressive position that weds, through sex, an unnatural being. 'She' is that bride. 'She' is the fanged lover who breaks the ontological sac" (1991, 8). While Carter's "stories about fairy stories" are not about lesbian sexuality as defined by the hegemonic, the vampire Countess reminds us that Carter certainly revels in "queer" portrayals of gender, love, and sex, particularly portrayals whose "vampirish love-bite" pierces the fairy-tale love that facilitates the patriarchal investment in a pornographic culture.

NOTES

1. Perrault's version continues through a series of trials prompted by the prince's ogre mother's attempts to eat Sleeping Beauty and their children.

2. The version of Basile's "Sun, Moon, and Talia" in Martin Hallett and Barbara Karasek's (2002) *Folk and Fairy Tales* is reprinted from *The Pentamerone of Giambattista Basile*, translated by Benedeto Croce and edited by N. M. Penzer in 1932. In Basile's version, Talia eventually wakes when one of the twins accidentally removes the splinter from her finger while seeking to suckle and finding her finger instead of her breast. The tale continues much as Perrault's version after Talia's awakening, though the antagonist is the king's wife, not his ogre-mother.

3. By "intertextual" I mean the process by which a text consciously references another text in order to comment on it.

4. For example, tracing the intertextual references to Sleeping Beauty as well as to the tales of E. T. A. Hoffmann in Carter's novel *The Infernal Desire Machines of Doctor Hoffmann*, Kai Mikkonen (2001, 176) underscores the necrophiliac impulses that structure the plot and drive both of the main characters: Desiderio "makes love to this 'beautiful somnambulist' when she is sleeping, then goes to see pictures of sleeping beauties in peep show machines the following morning, and is finally charged with the murder of this fairy tale-like woman," while Doctor Hoffman embalms his dead wife and keeps her in his castle, his "love for a corpse . . . another instance of necrophilia."

5. Even though Carter sees in Sade a potential for moral pornography, he ultimately fails to deliver on that full potential because he never breaks free of the male-dominated society. For Carter (1979b, 116–32, 150), this is particularly evident in his limited view of the mother in *Philosophy in the Boudoir* and his ultimate fear of the redemptive power of love.

6. In *The Sadeian Woman* Carter (1979b, 137–39) distinguishes between meat and flesh by emphasizing their differences in relation to sensuality. In this case, Carter inverts the more common cultural practice of rendering women's flesh as meat in a move consistent with her characterization of the hero in terms more traditionally reserved for fairy-tale princesses (e.g., "he has the special quality of virginity, most and least ambiguous of states: ignorance, yet at the same time, power in potentia" (1979a, 97)). In general, Carter's characterization of the hero as naive and virginal serves to highlight the predatory qualities of the Countess.

7. In her radio play *Vampirella*, a precursor to "The Lady of the House of Love" (Crofts 2003, 27–28), Carter (1976) makes explicit the sexual *and* marital desire for a corpse. The character Henri Blot explains to a judge his reason for taking corpses from the cemetery for his personal pleasures: "Corpses don't nag and never want

new dresses. They never waste all day at the hairdressers, nor talk for hours to their girl-friends on the telephone. They never complain if you stay out at your club; the dinner won't get cold if it's never been put in the oven. Chaste, thrifty—why, they never spend a penny on themselves! and endlessly accommodating. They never want to come themselves, nor demand of a man any of those beastly sophistications—blowing in the ears, nibbling at the nipples, tickling of the clit—that are so onerous to a man of passion. Doesn't it make your mouth water? Husbands, let me recommend the last word in conjugal bliss—a corpse."

8. See Katherine A. Hagopian (2007) for an additional interpretation of the "House of Love" as relating to the story of Eros/Psyche in Apuleius's tale.

9. For Carter, the killing off of women's sexual desire and agency is especially clear as women become mothers; in *The Sadeian Woman*, Carter argues that it is in Sade's refusal to grant Eugenie's mother any pleasure that his conservatism and limitations as a possible moral pornographer are most evident. Thus, for Carter, fairy-tale love and marriage are especially deadly in a sexist society because they imply motherhood and the death of sexual desire and pleasure.

10. "Disidentification" is José Muñoz's (1999, 4) term for the "survival strategies" that allow for a complex (re)engagement with dominant interpellations.

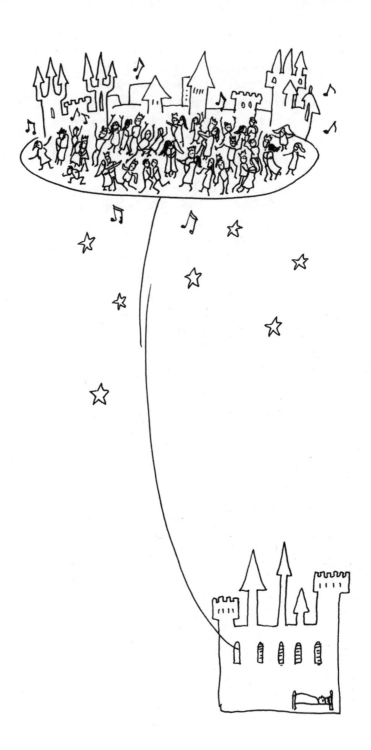

6

Happily Ever After...
According to Our Tastes

Jeanette Winterson's "Twelve Dancing Princesses" and Queer Possibility

JENNIFER ORME

Jeanette Winterson's *Sexing the Cherry* (1989) is a complex text that shifts between multiple narrators of parallel and interrelated stories. Its tellers include monstrous women and dreamy but intrepid explorers. One of the latter, Jordan, discovers that it also contains twelve well-known dancing princesses who have stories of their own to tell. Before he sets out on his voyages, Jordan recalls his discovery "that my own life was written invisibly, was squashed between the facts, was flying without me like the Twelve Dancing Princesses who shot from their window every night and returned home every morning with torn dresses and worn-out slippers and remembered nothing" (Winterson 1989, 2). In an effort to find and understand this other life, Jordan sets out to recount the journeys that his discovery sent him on: "Not the ones I made, but the ones I might have made, or perhaps did make in some other place or time" (2). Early in his travels, Jordan glimpses a dancer from afar. He immediately falls in love with her, and from that point on one of his goals is to find her. After visiting many people in fantastic cities and towns, including a "pen of prostitutes" who are literally interchangeable with the nuns who live in a nearby convent,

Jordan arrives at the home of the Twelve Dancing Princesses. "Thinking that one dancer might well know another and that a dozen of them must surely know one," he knocks on their door (44).

All of the sisters but one are living together again since their marriages to the princes of the traditional tale have ended, and they welcome Jordan into their home.[1] During his visit, the princesses each tell him the stories of their lives *after* the supposed "happily ever after" of their wedding day. The eldest sister, whose current beloved, a mermaid, has accepted and gobbled Jordan's offering of herrings, quickly recounts her version of the "The Story of the Twelve Dancing Princesses" (ATU 306, "The Danced Out Shoes").[2] She ends this brief summary on a surprising note: "And as it says [we] lived happily ever after. We did, but not with our husbands" (Winterson 1989, 48).[3] Each sister then tells of her less than happily ever after with her prince and how she returned to her sisters. Six princesses kill their husbands; four abandon them to their own fates. The fifth sister tells Jordan a version of "Rapunzel" (ATU 310, "The Maiden in the Tower") in which, as the girl's lover, she is cast as the witch of the piece by Rapunzel's family. Rapunzel is captured and carted off to her own imposed "happily ever after" by a prince in drag. In the final lines of her tale, the fifth princess incidentally reveals that hers is the only husband to live with the women. His presence in the house of the dancing princesses does not compromise its status as an all-female enclave however, because the first time she kissed him, her husband turned into a frog (52).

Much later in Jordan's narrative he will finally meet Fortunata, the dancer he has been seeking and the youngest of the Twelve Dancing Princesses. Fortunata will tell Jordan her version of the events of the tale of the sisters, proving that she remembers very well her time in the world in the sky, where she and her sisters danced their shoes to pieces. Fortunata's clear memories of the floating city and the time she and her sisters spent there challenge Jordan's personal interpretation of the tale as one about forgotten or missed aspects of one's life that one must spy out "like a jealous father" (Winterson 1989, 2). Her version also challenges other versions of ATU 306, including the versions most familiar to English-language readers—the Grimms' "The Worn-Out Dancing Shoes" (KHM 133) and Andrew Lang's "The Twelve Dancing Princesses." The tales recounted by the sisters extend the story beyond the traditional endings of their pre-texts. They also exceed critical interpretations of the ultimate meaning of the tale. Where psychoanalytic approaches have read it as a tale about "sexual temptation" (Cashdan 1999, 33), more feminist-inflected readings have seen it as "a story about patriarchal control and the duplicity of women" (Morrison 2003, 107). In the mouths of Fortunata and her sisters, ATU 306 becomes a multilayered and polyphonous tale of resistance to heteronormative marriage and, perhaps, an example of a queer fairy tale.

The twelve sisters escape nightly to another world to dance until their shoes are worn through. In the traditional tales, they descend into a netherworld arrived at via a secret stair beneath the eldest princess's bed, approached through forests of silver, gold, and diamonds and followed by a short sail across a lake to a ball populated by enchanted princes. Fortunata's version recalls, but differs in significant ways from, the Grimms' or Lang's. In it, the princesses lie *on top* of their beds waiting to be pulled through their bedroom window and into the ether by the gravitational pull of a floating city. This metropolis is populated by people who, rather than walking to get from point to point, dance in points of light. Like their Grimm sisters, these princesses are found out by a man, one of many set to the task by their father, the king. In the Grimms' version, this man is a poor wounded soldier, and in Lang's version, he is an ethereal but humble gardener, but in Fortunata's tale, he is the youngest prince.

A "cunning fellow," like his literary predecessors, he pretends to drink the sleeping draught the princesses serve him and makes himself invisible in order to spy on the princesses and report back to their father. In each version, once he has reported to the king of his daughters' nocturnal forays, the spy is rewarded with the hand in marriage of his princess of choice. The kindly poor soldier in the Grimms' tale gallantly chooses the eldest sister, for, he says, "I am no longer young." The tale ends with the promotion of the lowly spy to husband of a princess and heir to a kingdom, and the princesses' dancing partners in the netherworld are "compelled to remain under a curse for as many nights as they had danced with the princesses" (Zipes 2002b, 435). In Lang and Winterson, all of the princesses find themselves betrothed at the end of the story. Lang's gardener has fallen in love with the youngest princess and asks for her hand, while her sisters each choose a husband from the enchanted dancing princes of the underworld. In the rather less romantic version told by Fortunata, the prince has eleven brothers and each is assigned a sister to marry. These cunning princes ensure the presence of the princesses at the mass wedding by chaining their ankles (Winterson 1989, 111). But where other versions end with a wedding, the tale of Fortunata and her sisters is not finished and instead branches off into many more. When Jordan meets them, the princesses have shed their husbands and taken the responsibility upon themselves for telling their own stories to explain what happened to them after the so-called happily ever after of the wedding ceremony.

In a twist of narrative logic consistent with the eccentric temporal structure of *Sexing the Cherry* as a whole, Winterson first has eleven of the princesses recount the stories of their married lives and then sends Jordan back on his journeys for some time before he finally meets Fortunata, who relates the version of "The Story of the Twelve Dancing Princesses" glossed above. She also tells the tale of her own escape from the forced marriage and how she came to live as a dance instructor on an isolated island. Winterson significantly changes the traditional narrative by reversing the floating city for the underground realm; extending events past the wedding day; giving voice to the princesses, who narrate their own versions of events; allowing for contradictory accounts between the sisters; and making the text open-ended.

The combination of these narrative changes, in conjunction with the multiple desires voiced within this version, have always seemed to me to be particularly queer. In fact, in my teaching of this text and in earlier readings of it, I have boldly claimed that "The Story of the Twelve Dancing Princesses" in *Sexing the Cherry* queers the fairy-tale genre. These transgressive sisters resist patriarchal parental control, subvert normative ideals of heterosexual marriage, and refuse to account or apologize for their actions in pursuing their desires. But I should have known that—even though I am on their side—they would not simply allow me to make of them what I will. As I have been struggling to make them fit into logical arguments about queer representation, fairy-tale narrative structuration, multivocality, and the proliferation of desires, I have discovered that my desire to claim some kind of inherent queerness for "The Story of the Twelve Dancing Princesses" was being continually frustrated. In fact it may be a futile pursuit, and perhaps not so desirable after all.

Que(e)ries

As I wrestled with the princesses I began to ask myself, what makes me believe in this queerness? Where does it reside and how can I justify my bold declaration in relation to the princesses and their effect on the fairy tale? Is it merely the presence of same-sex desire of some of the princesses? Is it the fact that Jeanette Winterson is a self-identified lesbian and is often labeled by those engaged in critiquing her work as a queer postmodern writer? Why not just say the "The Story of the Twelve Dancing Princesses" is postmodern with a lesbian twist? Certainly the postmodernity of much contemporary fairy-tale fiction has been well explored and established within fairy-tale studies (see especially Bacchilega 1997; Harries 2001; Smith 2007; Makinen 2008; Tiffin 2009). But queer subjectivity has not been as deeply investigated in fairy-tale studies.[4]

Appearances of the princesses in other contemporary adult literature and film are few, and although they turn up in the poetry of Anne Sexton and Stevie Smith and often in literature and visual media for children, the princesses are less popular characters for revision than the likes of Little Red Riding Hood, Cinderella, Beauty and her Beast or even Bluebeard and his wives, who appear in short-story collections by Angela Carter (1979a), Emma Donoghue (1997), Francesca Lia Block (2000), and Nalo Hopkinson (2001). As a result of their reticence to emerge in contemporary revisions—other than in work on Winterson—critical literary essays on ATU 306 in contemporary literature are also few and far between.[5]

The critical responses to Winterson come from different theoretical and methodological positions but usually include relatively brief discussions of the fairy tale in *Sexing the Cherry*. In their examinations of the fairy tale in Winterson's work, critics like Laura Doan (1994), Paulina Palmer (1999,

2004), Jago Morrison (2003, 2006), Paul Smith (2007), and Merja Makinen (2008) have tended to focus on the fairy tale in *Oranges Are Not the Only Fruit* or to only engage with "The Story of the Twelve Dancing Princesses" in passing, within larger discussions of Winterson and her use of fairy tales as a postmodern, feminist, and/or lesbian writer.

Doan and Palmer both approach Winterson from lesbian-feminist perspectives that have been important to my thinking about "The Story of the Twelve Dancing Princesses" as queer fairy tale. Palmer recognizes that "lesbianism does not enjoy a privileged position in the novel but is treated as one of a number of transgressive sexualities, including homosexuality, bisexuality and sadomasochism" (1999, 49). Although Palmer notes that Dog Woman, Jordan's mother and narrator of other sections of the text, "merits the term 'queer,'" her own examination of the fairy tale in Winterson does privilege lesbianism over the other transgressive sexualities she identifies in the text (51).

Similarly, Doan argues that the proliferation of these non-normative sexualities in both "The Story of the Twelve Dancing Princesses" and *Sexing the Cherry* as a whole permits Winterson to envision "a social order that would permit the breakdown of oppositions . . . call appearances into question and, through the disruption of normative gender relations, reveal them as artificial and arbitrary constructions" (1994, 150). Recalling Judith Butler's ([1990] 1999, 1993) troubling of normative gender relations, which has been central to the emergence of queer theory, Doan appears to be moving toward a queer reading. Butler ([1990] 1999) suggests that the insistence on the instability of the identity category "lesbian" can be put to political use to also destabilize hegemonic discourses about gender and sexuality. Doan, however, chooses to focus on only one sister's tale and what she reads as the failure of lesbian "parody or imitation [of the heterosexual institution of marriage] as an effective way to undermine normative gender ideology" (1994, 151). Because she looks at only one of the marriages represented by the princesses, she fails to see how the proliferation of multiple transgressive desires—both lesbian and non-lesbian—combine to successfully undermine both the institution of marriage and normative gender ideologies.

For Palmer and Doan, *Sexing the Cherry* is primarily a lesbian feminist text, and they focus their short discussions of "The Story of the Twelve Dancing Princesses" on the two lesbian tales in the cycle: the fifth sister's

"Rapunzel" tale and the seventh sister's revelation that "the man [she] had married was a woman" (Winterson 1989, 54). In choosing to privilege some tales over others, Palmer and Doan ignore queer possibility in the embedded section and *Sexing the Cherry* as a whole. Similarly, but coming from a position within fairy-tale studies, in her otherwise astute examination of Winterson and fairy-tale fiction, Merja Makinen's brief discussion of "The Story of the Twelve Dancing Princesses" seems to reduce the tale cycle to a critique of the institution of marriage. Makinen argues "that marriage is not an institution that can promise happiness and that phallocentric society denigrates women and persecutes lesbians is as much as can be gleaned from the tales. The refusal to make grand generalizations appears deliberate" (2008, 172). While I agree that the refusal to generalize about desire and marriage is deliberate, I think that there is more to be gleaned from the princesses' narrations.

It is not so much the representation of non-normative desires in and of themselves, though they are very important, but the ways in which multiple desires in "The Story of the Twelve Dancing Princesses" can exist as siblings, none more "natural," "normal," or "acceptable" than any other, that is key to a queer perspective. At no point do the tales reaffirm heterosexuality as the norm that tolerates the "other" of difference. Rather, because each sister's tale is so unique, "The Story of the Twelve Dancing Princesses" works as a heteroglossic proliferation of desires. Even the princesses who wish that their (male) husbands would love them ultimately reject as impossible the romanticized notion of straight wedded bliss. The eldest provides a clue as to why her own and her sisters' marriages did not "work out." In describing Fortunata to Jordan, she says, "She didn't burn in secret with a passion she could not express; she shone" (Winterson 1989, 61). Coming as it does after a comparison of the rest of the sisters to Fortunata, the negative construction of this sentence ("She didn't . . .") suggests that the contrastive statement "we did" is absent but implied. In reading the eldest sister's evaluation of their different fates in this way, it is not the institution of marriage that is the sole culprit of female unhappiness; the princesses must take some responsibility for their failure to shine with their own passions. The eleven princesses' acceptance of the fairy-tale wedding as the inevitable end to their stories and therefore lives as passionate dancers is contrasted to Fortunata's refusal and decision to follow her desires beyond the tale.

Eve Kosofsky Sedgwick has claimed that "*The relation of gay* [or queer] *studies to debates on the literary canon is, and had best be, tortuous*" (1990, 48; emphasis in original).[6] It would seem that what is precisely meant by "queer" in relation to literary and other cultural productions continues to be, if not exactly tortuous, at least troublesome. Sedgwick stresses the importance of not setting fixed boundaries for queer texts. Critical work from a queer perspective tends to "share a relaxed, unseparatist hypothesis of the much to be gained by refraining from a priori oppositions between queer texts (or authors) and non-queer ones, or female ones and male" (1997, 1). Sedgwick implies that some texts are ontologically queer—that is, some texts simply *are* queer—though she refrains from saying how one is to recognize this inherent queerness.

Paradoxically, the indefinability, the shifty instability of the term *queer* is one of its few stable aspects. As Sedgwick finds, *queer* can refer to "the open mesh of possibilities, gaps, overlaps, dissonances and resonances, lapses and excesses of meaning when the constituent elements of anyone's gender, of anyone's sexuality aren't made (or *can't be* made) to signify monolithically" (1993, 8; emphasis in original). Sedgwick does not necessarily define queer identity by same-sex or bisexual orientation because "there are important senses in which 'queer' can signify only when attached to the first person" (9). For Annamarie Jagose, Sedgwick's "provocative suggestion . . . emphasises the extent to which queer refers to self-identification rather than to empirical observations of other people's characteristics" (1996, 97). However, if queer can only signify in the first person, recognizing a queer text (or proclaiming a text to be queer) based on "empirical observations" of its thematic or other characteristics becomes problematic. It also raises questions about Sedgwick's other claims about "queer texts (or authors) and non-queer ones" quoted previously (1997, 1).

The issue of self-identification and external identification is an important challenge for unpacking my troubles with Winterson's use of the fairy tale. It would seem to become even more difficult in view of her own resistance to being labeled as a "lesbian" or "queer" author and in light of her later work, about which Jago Morrison argues, "In her latest writing especially, Winterson's indebtedness to [a] Christian sensibility forces us into a new kind of reading, almost completely foreclosing the lesbian feminist Winterson we have enjoyed and admired" (2006, 170). Morrison goes on to note the paradoxical position for "critics and fans alike" who are "guarding and conserving an institution of queer postmodernism, whilst at the same time, at a side window, the writer herself seems to be engaged in an escape attempt" (171). So I find that like Morrison, I must grapple with "writer Jeanette Winterson, on the one hand, and the polymorphous cultural institution 'Jeanette Winterson' on the other" (170).

My struggles with the paradoxes, contradictions, and instability when dealing with terminology that, like Winterson and her princesses, seems always to be slipping out through a window just as I approach, have been alleviated somewhat by Alexander Doty's discussions of the term *queer*. Doty provides a list of the ways in which the term has been used in relation to cinematic and literary texts. Of the descriptions he provides, the last is most relevant to my pursuits. Queer, he says, has been used "to describe those aspects of spectatorship, cultural readership, production, and textual coding that seem to establish spaces not described by, or contained within, straight, gay, lesbian, bisexual, transsexual, or transgendered understandings and categorizations of gender and sexuality—this is a more radical understanding of queer, as queerness here is something apart from established gender and sexuality categories" (2000, 7).

As I began working through these problems, I came to believe that it is not so much that this version of the well-known fairy tale *is* queer—that is, it does not possess queerness as an ontological trait. Rather, my identification of queerness is actually an identification of a type of reading practice that I produce when encountering it. This practice is less important in relation to either my or Winterson's gendered or sexual identity but is borne out of a space that will not be settled with/by one kind of understanding of gender and sexuality. That is, for me, the princesses and their multiple desires and modes of articulation in "The Story of the Twelve Dancing Princesses" invite or encourage queer reading—but I cannot presume that they demand it from other readers. I am attempting here to articulate the queerness of this text, or the possibility of queerness, rather than, more narrowly, its representation of lesbian desire. In doing so, I am making a political move of identification with and celebration of resistance to normative desires and expected forms of articulation in the fairy-tale genre, especially as it is embodied in the Grimms, whose institutional relationship to us now is not as brothers but authoritative grandfathers.

At this point in my journey with the princesses, I tend to agree with Doty that "any text is always already *potentially* queer," and like him, "I'd like to see queer discourses and practices as being less about co-opting and 'making' things queer . . . and more about discussing how things are, or *might be understood* as, queer" (2000, 2; my emphasis). What Doty rejects in the idea of "queering" as a verb is that "it implies taking a thing that is straight and doing something to it" (2). That is, rather than subjecting an intrinsically straight text to various circumlocutions, stretchings, shakings up, and turnings over in order to *make* it queer, Doty suggests that beginning with the assumption that all texts are always already potentially queer frees one to explore how the *possibility* of queerness occupies the text. In addition to the representation of multiple desires, I believe that queer potential or possibility may reside in the narrative structures and forms of narration that disrupt what Elizabeth Wanning Harries (2001) calls the "compact" fairy-tale form as exemplified in the tales of the Grimms and other literary fairy-tale "grandfathers" such as Charles Perrault and Andrew Lang.[7]

"Sexing the Narrative"

Although the relevance of gender and sexuality to the structure of a text is still controversial, I believe, following Susan Lanser and Ruth Page, that attention to gender and sexuality will afford important information about how texts work. Lanser (1986) first raised the issue of the possibility of a "feminist narratology," that is, the consideration of gender as relevant to the study of the formal and structural aspects of narrative, in the mid-1980s. Until that point, critics had generally viewed narratology as a wholly objective methodology for the study of universal narrative traits, and thus questions of gender were precluded from narratological discussion because they were not related to the formal elements of the text. Lanser later began to theorize the possibility of sexuality as also relevant to narratology. She argues that *Written on the Body*, another of Winterson's texts, "points to sexual aspects of narrative that are 'proper' to narratology even in its classical sense" (1995, 85). More recently, in her essay on the controversy, consequences, and developments of Lanser's original proposal, Ruth Page (2007) hints at the ways in which queer theory may also invigorate postclassical narratological methodologies. For my part, I feel that the potential queerness of a text will be borne out in the form as well as the content; in other words, I suspect that the queerness I am attempting to identify in *Sexing the Cherry* and other contemporary fairy-tale fiction, such as Emma Donoghue's *Kissing the Witch* or even some of the tales in Angela Carter's *The Bloody Chamber*, will also be found in their poetics.

While Lanser argues for "sexing the narrative" in relation to the gender and sexual identity of narrators, I would like to provisionally suggest that other narrational aspects may inform queer readings. The shifting of narrative voice from princess to princess, the openness of the embedded tale, and the deferrals, interruptions, and disruptions to the order in which the events of the princesses' lives are told are cues to the narrative techniques that may also queer this particular extended fairy tale.

Each story is presented with minimal or no obvious narrational mediation or apparent evaluation by Jordan. In this way, even when they do not narrate them themselves, the princesses' stories are truly their own and rest on their narrative authority, rather than on the "simple but powerful narrative strategy that stands as one of the narrative rules for fairy-tale production: an external or impersonal narrator whose straightforward statements carry no explicit mark of human perspective" (Bacchilega 1997, 34). Most, but not all, of the princesses narrate their own tales within the embedded chapter. The fifth recounting, for example, is narrated in the first person by a princess who addresses Jordan, and possibly the reader, at the beginning of her recitation: "You may have heard of Rapunzel," she begins (Winterson 1989, 52). She also responds to Jordan's unrecorded questions:

My own husband?
Oh well, the first time I kissed him he turned into a frog.
There he is, just by your foot. His name's Anton. (52)

Others seem to employ free direct thought, expressing their inner thoughts and feelings unmediated by obvious narrational control or comment and directed inward rather than to Jordan as narratee. The tales of the second and third princesses are narrated at one remove by Jordan who presents the tales as direct discourse, indicated by tags such as "she said" or simply the appearance of quotation marks at the beginning and ending of each paragraph. The complex use of multiple types of narrative discourse both between stories and within single stories contributes to the polyphony of the tale-telling situation. Each princess has not only her own story and her own desires but her own voice and her own way of telling.

The structure of the embedded tales told by the sisters early in Jordan's voyages at first appears to be radically open-ended. Each sister tells her tale, but the final sister is absent; thus "The Story of the Twelve Dancing Princesses" is actually "The Stories of the Eleven Dancing Princesses." Jordan's eventual discovery of Fortunata seems to promise closure to the tale, but even this move is not so simple. Although the revelation of Fortunata's tale is delayed in Jordan's narrative until long after he has left the home of her sisters, it cannot be totally dissociated from the original setting. Nor can it be said to offer complete closure to the many adventures of the sisters. Fortunata returns to the tale from a different direction and places on it her own narrative logic.

THE FORTUNES OF FORTUNATA

The events of Fortunata's story begin after the well-known adventures of the princesses nightly dancing expeditions but before the sisters are married. She describes the days with her sisters just before the wedding when they worked together to build a garden and then a church out of ice and snow. The "basic color triad" of white, red, and black recur often in this telling, thus intertextually recalling both specific fairy tales (such as "Snow White," ATU 709) and the fairy-tale genre more generally into her narrative (Vaz da Silva 2008). She concludes this part of her tale with the sisters' wedding and her escape from her fiancé: "At the last possible moment I pushed him aside and ran out of the church through the crowds of guests" (Winterson 1989, 105). In just a few more lines, she details her journey across the seas to open the dancing school on the island where she and Jordan are talking.

The return to the "The Story of the Twelve Dancing Princesses" destabilizes the structure of the fairy tale. Coming as it does at such a distance in the text from the embedded tales of the princesses, Fortunata's turn as narrator disorders the action of the tale of the princesses' story. Her tale repeats but also contradicts parts of the tale as it has been narrated so far. While at first it seems the earlier embedded tale cycle will be left open-ended by omitting one princess's tale and thereby refusing closure in preference for openness, this return to the missing sister, rather than providing a tidy conclusion, adds further layers and complications. Not only does Fortunata's turn as tale-teller challenge Jordan's remembered version of the tale, it raises questions about the story she shares with her sisters. When Jordan tells her that the tale her sisters told of her fantastic escape was different from her recounting, she laughs and asks, "How could such a thing be possible?" Jordan counters that the floating city to which the princesses escaped each night could not exist either, to which she replies, "Are there not such places?" (Winterson 1989, 106). Before Fortunata continues her tale with a history of the floating city, a narrative vignette titled "Lies 8" interrupts Jordan's narration of his meeting with Fortunata and her embedded narration of her own tale.[8] This digression provides metanarrational commentary on memory and truth in storytelling. It is only a few lines long, but it suggests that the value of storytelling is not the sustained and incontrovertible mimetic relation of facts but a different kind of truth because "what we have told you is true, although it is not" (106). As a storyteller, Fortunata challenges but does not discount alternative versions of her tale. On the contrary, her questions trouble the notion of the possibility of the existence of any one authoritative version of any tale; therefore, her own metanarrational questions about the veracity of the versions Jordan is familiar with trouble but do not detract from the narrative authority of her sisters.

Fortunata then goes on to recite the history of the floating city, stopping for metanarrational commentary at one point in order to prove the veracity of her tale in spite of its fantastic nature: "Now I have told you the history of the city, which is a logical one, each piece fitting into the other without strain. Sure that you must believe something so credible I will continue with the story" (Winterson 1989, 108–9). She goes on to relate an extended version of not ATU 306 but "The Story of the Twelve Dancing Princesses."

"Twelve Dancing Princesses" and Queer Possibility 153

That is, as a character-narrator Fortunata's focus is on the adventures of the princesses in the floating city rather than on the trials and tribulations of the male "hero." Her story comes full circle at the end. Having reached the point at which she began—the day of the wedding—she abruptly stops: "And the rest you know" (112). The recursive structure would seem to indicate that the radical openness I have argued for is in fact a closed circuit. The ending of Fortunata's tale seems to bring us back to the tales of each of the sisters, the ones we already know. But the narrative breaks, created by the contradictions between the eldest sister's version of the tale and Fortunata's and by the interruption of the vignette that breaks the fairy-tale frame and reinforces the impossibility of language to faithfully reproduce reality, preclude tidy closure. The relationships between each section of the telling of the tale suggest that, just as Jordan (and the reader) did not really know the "true" tale of "The Story of the Twelve Dancing Princesses" when he first met the princesses, he still does not and never will—nor will the reader.

Winterson does more to the fairy tale in *Sexing the Cherry* than a mere revision of the story of the princesses' nightly pursuit of their own pleasures and desires. The princesses are central to the larger context of Jordan's search for himself, his beloved, and his desire to become a hero in *Sexing the Cherry*. Winterson (2008) herself hints at the centrality of this fairy tale on her website: "The narrative moves through time, but also operates outside it. At the centre of the book are the stories of the Twelve Dancing Princesses. . . . The stories aren't just parachuted in there, they are integral to the whole. . . . That is, they tell us something we need to know to interpret the book." The stories of the princesses are not just central to the book; their influence and presence radiate outward, forward, and backward within the text. Thus the delineation of the multiple desires they reveal, the subversions, reversals, and troubles they cause in terms of sexual and gender representation, are key to a queer understanding of *Sexing the Cherry*. In addition, the radical open-endedness caused by the youngest sister's absence from the initial tale-telling situation, her reappearance later in the novel, and her alternate version of "The Story of the Twelve Dancing Princesses" disrupt the possibility of teleological reading and ultimate closure of the fairy tale's structure.

Certainly, "The Worn-Out Dancing Shoes" is one of the few fairy tales in the Grimms' collection in which the female protagonists escape severe punishment for their transgressions of heteropatriarchy. Where other wayward women have their eyes pecked out by birds ("Cinderella," KHM 21, ATU 510A), have millstones dropped on their heads ("The Juniper Tree," KHM 47, ATU 720), or are forced to dance to death in red-hot shoes ("Snow White," KHM 53), the princesses are let off without a specific punishment. While Hayley Thomas does not agree with D. L. Ashliman's argument that the princesses "pay nothing" for their transgressions, or that the eldest sister "loses nothing" in marrying the poor soldier (Thomas 1999, 178), she concurs with Ashliman that in "The Worn-Out Dancing Shoes" "the end of the tale does manage to avoid the cloud of degradation which has inevitably surrounded other immodest women, even if its teleological impulse demands the usurpation of her/their powers" (179). Thomas highlights the princesses' nightly subversion of the "fairy-tale happily-ever-after teleology" and how the princesses "manage to frustrate male interference in their acts of self-assertion." But she is also careful to note the transitory nature of this female resistance to heteropatriarchy by prudently including qualifiers in her discussion of the power the princesses are able to assert. Theirs is a "partially successful bid" in which they "initially manage" to hoodwink their father the king and "for a time" are able to protect their secret from prying patriarchal eyes (171). In *Sexing the Cherry*, however, after the wedding, the princesses return to their initial resistance to masculine control of their lives and bodies by leaving their husbands, and their bids become more fully successful through the creation of an all-female community where they are able to live free of male control.

However, many of the princesses have had to leave their husbands and their homes under one form of duress or another. The fifth sister and her lover are persecuted by her lover's family and eventually the lover is taken away. The seventh sister, who reveals that "the man I had married was a woman," kills this female husband before "they" can catch and burn her. (Winterson 1989, 54). The tragic consequences of the incursion of society into these lives point to the continued struggle and difficulty of creating a queer life freely and without hindrance from a hegemonic heteronormative world in which marriage and childbearing are presumed to be a woman's primary and most natural desires. On the contrary, the fact that the sisters come to live together in a house away from society and free from childrearing underscores not only the support provided by a sorority of women but also its necessity for safety.

Even those princesses who accepted and desired marriage, who loved or wanted to be loved by their (male) husbands, come to live in the castle with their sisters when their marriages end. But if, as Makinen says, "marriage becomes the allegory for the tower in which the dancing princesses are confined by patriarchal power," they are still, in a way, confined within their new home with their sisters (2008, 171). Their stories suggest that at least a few of the sisters are living primarily through their memories rather than, like Fortunata, finding new lives to live and dancing on their own terms. The individual stories the sisters tell from within the isolation of the home they have created together hint at the many struggles of queer existence. Far from finding a utopian free-for-all, these queer sisters live with the memories of the dangers they have survived and sacrifices they have made in order to gain their freedom.

PRINCESSES, PROSTITUTES, AND NUNS

Michael Mendelson argues that "The Worn-Out Dancing Shoes" is one of the very few stories in *Kinder- und Hausmärchen* that features female cooperation in opposition to the "career märchen" of the male-centered tales in the *KHM*. However, he also remarks that the sisters in the Grimms' version are undifferentiated and that "the princesses are not exactly a positive social force, since their collective dalliance leads to the beheading of many suitors," although he immediately acknowledges that "in truth, their deviance is forced upon them by a father who would control their lives and passions" (1997, 117). Fortunata and her sisters do work collaboratively to defy their controlling father. The first time they find themselves pulled toward the floating city they hold "a council amongst [them]selves" and vote unanimously to "open [them]selves to whatever might happen" (Winterson 1989, 110). And although they are initially destined to be separated by marriage to the princes, they work together to build the church of ice in which they are to be wed (105). But cooperation as a form of defiance in Winterson's multivoiced text is not limited to the princesses.

Early on in his search for his beloved dancer, Jordan discovers a house of prostitutes that is owned by a rich but not very clever or observant man. These women are shut away from the world; they are kept by the rich man for his pleasure and the pleasure of his male friends. The prostitutes like Jordan and tell him to return to them, but for his safety, they urge him to dress as a woman. During his time with the women, Jordan learns that they are not as isolated or as victimized as he might have thought. Like the princesses in Grimm, the prostitutes escape from the rich man's house every night by descending below the house where there is a stream. Its current brings them past the nearby Convent of the Holy Mother where "it was the custom of the nuns to keep watch over the stream through the night, and any of the women seen shooting past the convent vault was immediately fished out in a great shrimping net by the nun on duty." In this way, the clever prostitutes, as well as the nuns and other women of the area, are able to completely hoodwink the rich man: "He did not know it but this selfish man, to whom life was just another commodity, had financed the futures of thousands of women. . . . He had also, singlehanded, paid for the convent's renowned stock of fine wine and any number of altarpieces" (Winterson 1989, 28).

While the portrayal of supportive separatist women's communities and the stupidity, villainy, and/or perversion of many of the male characters in *Sexing the Cherry* can and has been read as merely a kind of lesbian man-hating counter sexism (see, for example, Roessner 2002, 120), Makinen reads it "as a story of female escape from patriarchal inscriptions, rewriting the traditional marital closure through eleven narratives that confound heterosexual marriage, unmasking its cruelty to those forced to live within its confines. The happiness of those brave enough to escape cultural expectations to live otherwise, with women or mermaids . . . reinforces the point" (2008, 171). The collective communities that the prostitutes, nuns, and the princesses create are spaces of freedom from patriarchal sexual oppression. The literal "free flow" of women between the house and the convent allows for sorority and mutually beneficial social structures that subvert patriarchal strictures on women's bodies, minds, movements, and labor. These diverse groups of women work cooperatively and independently, creating cultures in which women support and love each other in spaces that might otherwise be assumed to be inimical to them because of their isolation from larger society and from men in particular. Yet these women are not man-haters; they each welcome Jordan as a fellow or even as an honorary sister and freely show him the ways in which they exploit the structures and institutions that are meant to contain them.

In *Sexing the Cherry* the prostitutes', nuns', and princesses' separate societies recall the literary tradition of separatist feminist utopias, where the female characters believe that the only way to escape patriarchy is for women to create completely separate societies in which men are absent or their presence is minimal and controlled by matriarchy.[9] However, Dog Woman's grotesque life on the margins of society, and the cities that Jordan visits, such as the city of floating words, the city where love is a plague, or the city without floors where Jordan first sees Fortunata, indicate that separatism is not the only option, or even the best option for all women. The movement of women between the house and the convent suggests that all-female enclaves not only are potential spaces of respite from heteropatriarchy but they can also become prisons themselves. The prostitutes' eventual wholesale abandonment of the rich man's house to create lives independent of the institutions of prostitution or religion and their thefts from the man who kept them suggest that it is economic freedom that permits these women to create new lives and sustain themselves as subjects in mixed gendered society. The multiple desires of female characters in *Sexing the Cherry* exceed any one social paradigm of either heterosexual marriage or lesbian feminist separatism, and the multiple societies women live in and deal with indicate that a claim for *Sexing the Cherry* as primarily a lesbian feminist text significantly limits it to subscribing to a single overarching desire or solution to women's desires.

In Winterson's "The Story of the Twelve Dancing Princesses," the princesses are not recouped into heteropatriarchy but remain with their sisters. Like the prostitutes and the nuns, they are free from the judgmental eyes and limiting social controls of hegemonic society outside their walls. Although Fortunata has been an object of Jordan's desire since he first saw her early in the narrative, she does not fall in love with him or allow him to "rescue" her from her solitude. Rather than immediately accepting the man who "discovers" her and assumes possession over her, Fortunata tells Jordan her own story and that she learned to "dance alone, for its own sake and for hers" (Winterson 1989, 112). She will not be the agent through which Jordan achieves his dream of becoming a hero.

Like the feminist interventions and revisions of fairy tales that came before *Sexing the Cherry* and since, the stories of the princesses reflect back on their pre-texts. Once having met *these* princesses, one cannot go back to "The Worn-Out Dancing Shoes" and read it in the same way again. Winterson is certainly not alone in raising questions about how the voiceless heroines of traditional fairy tales may have felt about their fates. Her princesses belong to a larger sorority of revisioned fairy-tale heroines in poetry, fiction, and film. Winterson's version of "The Story of the Twelve Dancing Princesses" does "do something" to the fairy tale as a genre; it makes, if not probable, at least possible, serious inquiry into the queer aspects hidden behind the omniscient narrational voice within "classic" tales by opening spaces for queer voices and queer choices.

NOTES

1. Along with Vanessa Joosen (2011), I employ the term *traditional* in relation to fairy-tale pre-texts in order to avoid the implication of "highest quality" associated with the terms *classic* or *classical*. For further discussion of the implications of terminology and intertextual relations in fairy-tale texts, see Joosen (2011, 9–11).

2. See also Pauline Greenhill, Anita Best, and Emilie Anderson-Grégoire's consideration in chapter 8 of "Peg Bearskin" and related tales, some of which, like "Kate Crackernuts," incorporate ATU 306.

3. My own brief summary of ATU 306 runs as follows: a king discovers that, although they have been locked in their room every night, every morning his daughters are found exhausted and with their shoes entirely worn through. He puts out a call for a man to discover what is happening to his daughters, promising marriage to the successful investigator and death to those who fail. An old soldier (or a young prince) hears about the opportunity and discovers that the princesses drug the investigators, causing all before him to fail in their task. Armed with this information and the ability to become invisible, the man follows the princesses to an underground realm where they dance all night with enchanted princes. When they all return in the morning, he goes to the king and informs on the sisters. He is offered the kingdom and his choice of sisters to marry and, if he happens to have brothers, each of them gains a princess as well.

4. Essays by Santiago Solis (2007), Pauline Greenhill (2008), Martine Hennard Dutheil de la Rochère (2009), and of course this volume, however, show that this is beginning to change.

5. A recent essay by Sidney Eve Matrix on Stanley Kubrick's *Eyes Wide Shut* is an exception. Matrix demonstrates the ways in which the film transforms ATU 306 for a contemporary big-budget Hollywood production. She produces a reading of the tale and the film that "reveals each to be a story about the enigma of female desire, the difficulties of domesticity, and the challenge of marital fidelity for both genders" (2010, 179).

6. Eve Kosofsky Sedgwick lists "radical faeries," "fantasists," and "storytellers" among the many possible identities that "queers" may choose as self-descriptors at different times (1993, 8).

7. Harries (2001) contrasts "compact" tales to the more "complex" literary tales as exemplified by the French *conteuses* who employed artful language, irony, and sophisticated wordplay in their work but also used intricate narrative framing techniques to explore social issues that affect women.

8. As the numerical title of the vignette suggests, "Lies 8" is one of a number of digressions or interruptions that appear during Jordan's narrations in *Sexing the Cherry*.

9. For further discussion of the complexities of feminist separatist utopias see Libby Falk Jones and Sara Webster Goodwin's (1990) anthology *Feminism, Utopia, and Narrative*.

7

The Lost Sister

Lesbian Eroticism and Female Empowerment
in "Snow White and Rose Red"

ANDREW J. FRIEDENTHAL

Over the many years since Wilhelm and Jacob Grimm first collected and published *Kinder- und Hausmärchen* (*Children's and Household Tales*), several of their tales have become European and North American classics, adapted to myriad media forms. For example, the Walt Disney Company's success can be attributed to a great extent to their fairy tale animated films (Zipes 1995b). Indeed, a fairy tale served as the subject for Walt Disney's very first film, the animated short *Little Red Riding Hood* (1922),[1] as well as for his first feature, *Snow White and the Seven Dwarfs* (1937). The latter film has ensured the character Snow White's endurance in popular culture and imagination. Yet Rose Red, her sister from the Grimms' tale "Snow White and Rose Red" (ATU 426, "The Two Girls, the Bear, and the Dwarf," Zipes 2002b, 475–80), may be unfamiliar to most who know Snow White well. Receding to the background, Rose Red has a much lower public profile, despite the sisters' loyal, loving, ostensibly equal relationship in their tale.[2]

Through close comparisons of the Grimm and Disney versions of "Snow White" (ATU 709) and "Snow White and Rose Red," and an examination of contemporary reinterpretations of the latter, I tease out subtle themes of lesbianism and female sexual empowerment in ATU 426, comparing its subversiveness to the more heteronormative ATU 709.[3] The seeming

banishment of Rose Red from public consciousness may reflect centuries-old cultural taboos against both lesbianism and free expression of female sexuality, taboos that her story, and thus her very presence, threatens to unleash. This potential, I argue, finds relatively free expression in recent adaptations that play with and nuance the narrative's queer possibilities.

THE GRIMMS' TALE

In the Grimms' "Snow White and Rose Red," two sisters live in a cottage with their poor widowed mother. The girls "looked like the rosebushes" growing in the garden—one which "bore white roses and the other red." Snow White is "more quiet and gentle than Rose Red" who enjoys running around outside, surrounded by nature (Zipes 2002b, 475). Rose Red is thus figured from the story's very outset, in comparison with her sister, as wilder and less domestic. Her free-spirited, untamed ways may seem dangerous in the context of a patriarchal society that idealizes feminine "docility, gentleness, and good temper," in which "good-temper and meekness are . . . regularly associated with beauty, and ill-temper with ugliness" (Lieberman 1972, 385).

Snow White and Rose Red's adventures begin one cold night, while the family of three gather around the hearth in their cottage. Suddenly, they hear a knock at the door. They let their visitor, a black bear, sleep by their fire every night for the whole winter, becoming "so accustomed to him that they never bolted the door until their black playmate had arrived" (Zipes 2002b, 477). The bear becomes the girls' playmate, but when spring comes, he leaves the house to guard his hidden treasure from dwarfs. Later, as the two girls run errands for their mother, they find themselves again and again bumping into a dwarf who has the strange habit of getting his beard trapped in strange places—the cleft of a tree, a fishing line, an eagle's talons. In order to save him, the girls cut off pieces of his beard. Each time, he expresses anger, rather than gratitude, for their help: "Uncouth slobs! How could you cut off a piece of my fine beard? Good riddance to you!" (479). When he threatens the girls, the bear appears from out of the forest and kills the dwarf with a single swipe of his massive paw, after which he turns into a handsome prince. He explains that the evil dwarf had cast a spell on him, turning him into a bear, and that with the dwarf's death he is released from that curse. Having regained his human form, the prince marries Snow White while his brother marries Rose Red, and the sisters, princes, and widow all live happily ever after.

"Snow White and Rose Red" deals with many of the archetypes found in better-known Grimm tales, concerning societal roles accorded to individuals based on age, sex, gender, class, and so on (see, e.g., Holbek 1987). Virginia Walker and Mary E. Lunz's study of schoolchildren's reactions to fairy-tale imagery examines these shared archetypes' roles in ATU 426 as well as in the broader corpus of the Grimms' work. They see the basic conflict in "Snow White and Rose Red" revolving around the lack of a masculine element/entity at the story's opening, which when added restores psychic balance. The feminine household triad of Snow White, Rose Red, and their widowed mother gains an element of masculinity with the intrusion of the bear, unwanted at first but ultimately accepted and even welcomed, literally joining with the girls via marriage. This union "is the completion of the tale and symbolizes the most important psychic process, the restoration of unity or wholeness to the self, accomplished by the unity of the masculine and the feminine aspects of the personality, creating psychic balance" (Walker and Lunz 1976, 96–97).

This process of coming to balance, concluding when the sisters release the bear/prince ("the positive state of the animus") from his imprisonment in animal form by the dwarf ("the negative animus"), leads to a kind of self-reintegration prefigured and symbolized throughout by the rose, arguably the tale's central metaphor. A dual-natured symbolic vehicle, white and red, the rose represents both wholeness (due to its spherical nature) and femininity (as a "vessel-like flower"). The sisters are tied metaphorically and by name to the roses, which are agents of transformation from (one-sided) femininity to wholeness. These flower symbols quite literally come to full bloom at the tale's conclusion as the two rosebushes are transplanted to the palace: "The marriage of the two sisters to the two Princes offers the promise of wholeness suggested by the symbol of the rose in the beginning of the fairy tale" (Walker and Lunz 1976, 97).

This analysis assumes that the white and red roses, and thus the White and Red sisters, are fundamentally the same and their color differences only superficial. Yet the meanings of the hues engage the tale's symbolism and

semantics. Snow White, associated with the color of cleanliness and innocence, of inexperience and childhood, is, literally, pure in essence. Rose Red,
in contrast, is named for the color of blood and passion. Her name invokes
a stain on the whiteness, the menstruation that signals a girl's blooming,
and the awakening of her sexuality as she becomes a woman and loses her
innocence to sexual, hormonal desires (see Heather 1948). While the girls'
story affirms their common qualities—"they were more pious and kind,
more hardworking and diligent than any other two children in the world"
(Zipes 2002b, 475)—their names discriminate between them. One sister
receives a pure, clean slate, cleared of all wrongdoing and sexual knowledge, while the other has the sins of womanhood thrust upon her. The link
with heteronormativity in this color scheme is introduced when the bear
arrives, and his connection with Snow White, who "was very sad about his
departure," emphasizes her orientation toward heterosexual desire (477).

Throughout the story, from the opening emphasis on Snow White's quiet
gentility to the happy ending of marriage(s), Rose Red plays a secondary role.
It is Snow White who sees the foreshadowing "gold glimmering through
the fur" when the bear leaves at the end of the winter, who first thinks to
cut the dwarf's beard in order to free him, and who ultimately marries
the prince (Zipes 2002b, 477). Rose Red, on the other hand, becomes her
sister's sidekick, even to the point of her marriage at the story's end to the
prince's hitherto unmentioned brother (480).

Sadly for Rose, her plight as second fiddle within the tale reflects her current standing in popular culture. Snow White is best known as a character
from a *different* story, one featuring a wicked stepmother, seven dwarfs, and a
poisoned apple, rather than one about two sisters, a bear, and a single dwarf.
Rose Red features only as the bad sister, the whore to Snow White's virgin,
as the sisters act out a contrast between purity and—often sexual—cor-
ruption. Why must Rose Red live in Snow White's shadow? Can it be only
coincidental that the innocent persecuted heroine (see Bacchilega 1993; S.
S. Jones 1993), "Snow White," instantiates the heteronormative moments
that constantly reassert patriarchy, while Snow White and Rose Red's narrative is riddled with the serious societal transgression of female sexual
empowerment and, even more troubling, sisterly homoeroticism?

A Transgressive Reading of Rose Red /
A Heteronormative Reading of Snow White

Though the Grimms' "Snow White and Rose Red" may lack overt expression of incestuous lesbianism, the entire tale centers on a series of queer images and symbols. The main figurative element of the tale suggests a subtle sexuality—the two sisters are associated with two rosebushes, one white and one red, in front of their widowed mother's house (Zipes 2002b, 475). The rosebushes, with their thorns, recall other fairy-tale pricking objects, especially the needles associated with the fabric that ultimately results from spinning, an activity that Snow White and Rose Red themselves engage in as a part of their everyday lives.[4] Sharp items serve as recurring motifs in the Grimms' tales concerning young ingenue females. The act of pricking may invoke the penetrating male penis, or it may symbolize stimulation of the blood flow that results from menstruation, the blooming of womanhood, and, ultimately, female sexuality. A widow living in a lonely cottage with two daughters named after thorny rosebushes suggests a simmering sexuality at work in the heart of a home characterized initially by the absence of male figures. From the very beginning, then, a queer dynamic manifests in this story.

As ATU 426 continues, the sexuality moves from the blossoming girls in the cottage and out into the world. The girls often wander alone together in the forest gathering "*red* berries," emphasizing the menstrual/sexual connotation to their activities (Zipes 2002b, 476; my emphasis). Their "sisterly" love for each other often finds physical expression: they "loved each other so much that they always held hands whenever they were out"; they swear never to leave each other as long as they live; and they sometimes "would lie down next to each other on the moss and sleep until morning came." Their mother recognizes their closeness, telling them that "whatever one of you has, remember to share it with the other" (476). The sisters' actions and their symbolism suggest an equal division of sexual knowledge and growth and explain the sudden appearance of a second prince for Rose Red at the story's end, when by implication they (separately) share sexual experience with their husbands. The atmosphere of sisterly affection taken into the physical realm permeates the tale, until the entrance of the bear. As the heterosexual romantic interest for Snow White (despite the potential unruliness of interspecific human-bear love), he offers a preternaturally powerful representative of heteronormative society invading the cottage.

When the sisters leave the cottage to play in the physical realm of the woods, fecundity and fertility surround them—a hare eating a cabbage leaf from their hands, a roe grazing by their side, a stag leaping about them, and so on. So in tune with the natural world and its rhythms are they that a (super)natural figure saves their lives when they sleep at the edge of a cliff one night. In the morning, "a beautiful child in a white, glistening garment" saves them from falling, a figure their mother assures them was "the angel who watches over good children" (Zipes 2002b, 476). The natural world in which the girls are enmeshed even follows them home, first in the form of a lamb and a dove who listen to stories with them at night and ultimately and most significantly in the figure of the bear.

Once the bear enters the household and is accepted as a well-meaning figure rather than a dangerous one, the girls' interaction with him becomes overwhelmingly physical. He displays his masculine power by stretching his large body by the fire and growling "to show how content and comfortable he was," and Snow White and Rose Red literally crawl all over him: "They tugged his fur with their hands, planted their feet upon his back and rolled him over, or they took a hazel switch and hit him." When this violence becomes too rough, the bear cries out, "Snow White, Rose Red, / would you beat your suitor dead?" (Zipes 2002b, 477). The girls' intensely playful, active, equal participation in this primitive flirtation with the bear creates a sensual tension he identifies by declaring himself their "suitor." As a flirtation between human and animal, this relationship, in its playfulness at the tale's beginning and ultimate consummation at the tale's end, is a queering in and of itself, if not a homoerotic one.

The sisters differentiate their romantic desire for the kind of powerful masculinity embodied by the bear through their complete *lack* of desire for the tale's contrasting masculine figure. The dwarf, small in stature and decrepitly old, is a "little fellow" with an "old, withered face and a beard that was snow white and a yard long." Rose Red calls him "little man" (Zipes 2002b, 477–78). He is distinguished from the bear's large, powerful, and youthful physique and, later, from the prince, "a handsome man clad completely in gold" (480). The girls, attracted to the physicality of the bear/prince, demonstrate sensual desire in a way that the passive Snow White, in her solo tale, never does. In "Snow White and Rose Red," the sexual interest and interactions—both queer and straight—derive from a *female* source.

Note the contrast here with the Grimms' "Snow White." Its protagonist not only lacks any sexual initiative or affectionate relationship with women, but her own stepmother tries to kill her out of envy for her beauty. Just as the White sister is lauded for her beauty in "Snow White and Rose Red," so too in "Snow White," she is "the fairest of all" and is compared with her jealous stepmother rather than her loving sister (Zipes 2002b, 181). The queen's envy of her stepdaughter's appearance drives the narrative, making Snow White's beauty her defining characteristic. Snow White, in fact, rarely *does* anything; her beauty is primarily what lets her survive. Instructed by the queen to kill Snow White, the hunter takes pity on her "since she was so beautiful"; a fact also immediately noted by the dwarfs in whose cottage Snow White takes refuge (182). They see Snow White as "a beautiful child" (183). The prince whose actions ultimately save Snow White from a deathlike state is also obsessed with her beauty and physical appearance, saying, "I can't go on living without being able to *see* Snow White" (188; my emphasis). Snow White's few and rare actions are located in the traditionally feminine realm of home and hearth. In order to stay with the dwarfs, she promises to "keep house . . . cook, make the beds, wash, sew, and knit, and . . . keep everything neat and orderly" (183–84). Yet these same domestic proclivities ultimately put her in danger of the queen's machinations. She gets taken in by the promises of "staylaces in all kinds of colors," a comb that "pleased her so much that she let herself be carried away and opened the door," and, most destructively, an enticing apple, twice described specifically as "beautiful" (184–86). This apple that nearly kills Snow White shows beauty as a double-edged sword that initially destroys but then saves her.

The masculine realm of work and the men practicing it serve purely as a saving grace to Snow White. The huntsman helps the girl to escape by engaging directly in his trade, killing a boar and using its lungs and liver "as proof that the child was dead" (Zipes 2002b, 182). The dwarfs, hardworking men who "searched in the mountains for minerals with their picks and shovels," offer safe haven for Snow White. Protectively, they tell her, "Beware of your stepmother! . . . She'll soon know that you're here. Don't let anybody in!" (184). When the queen first deceives Snow White, the dwarfs again caution her, "Beware, don't let anyone in when we're not with you!" The second time, they warn her "to be on her guard and not open the door for anyone" (185). With each volley from Snow White's stepmother, the cottage's realm of masculine protection, depending on the dwarfs' labor as miners, is endangered when the daughter allows its breach due to a desire for feminine wares.

The dwarfs' warnings unattended, Snow White apparently dies, and they decide to keep her in "a transparent coffin so that she could be seen from all sides" rather than to bury her (Zipes 2002b, 187). This action, once again influenced by the girl's beauty, ultimately leads to her salvation, as it allows the prince to become enamored of her. Before he can possess the coffin, however, the prince and the dwarfs must engage in another quintessentially masculine practice—bargaining and negotiating prices for goods and for women (see Rubin 1975). He asks, "Let me have the coffin, and I'll pay you whatever you want," to which they reply, "We won't give it up for all the gold in the world." The love-struck prince then somewhat pathetically begs, "Then give it to me as a gift," and the dwarfs take pity on him. The prince then "ordered his servants to carry the coffin on their shoulders, but they stumbled over some shrubs, and the jolt caused the poisoned piece of apple that Snow White had bitten off to be released from her throat" (188). With the apple gone, Snow White returns to life, marries the prince, and enacts revenge on her stepmother. Yet at no time does she express any desire for the prince or indeed for any man. Snow White's resurrection, marriage, and denouement are enabled by the masculine bargain between the dwarfs and the prince, as well as by the *prince's* wants, rather than by any desire or action of her own. Her apparent lack of initiative and sexuality alike starkly contrast with "Snow White and Rose Red," wherein the White sister's marriage arises from clearly expressed mutual desire.

The Walt Disney animated movie *Snow White and the Seven Dwarfs* takes this dichotomy of female beauty versus male work even further. The storybook montage that opens the film lists beauty as Snow White's defining characteristic. As in the Grimms' tale, her loveliness, coupled with naive innocence and kindness to animals, changes the hunter's heart and keeps him from killing her and causes the dwarfs to become enamored. When she first arrives at the dwarfs' cottage, she cleans it while singing a song about her housework; the dwarfs also sing about their toil as miners. The film's songs, then, invoke the contrasting fields of masculine and feminine jobs.

The songs also serve to hypersexualize Snow White. In the opening moments of the film, she sings to herself about her wishes for a man to love. Her hope is granted in the form of a prince who shows up and sings a duet with her. Having escaped from the castle and now living with the dwarfs, she longs to be rescued by him and find true love:

> Someday my prince will come
> Someday we'll meet again
> And away to his castle we'll go
> To be happy forever I know.

This song, reprised at the film's end as the prince and Snow White literally walk off into the sunset toward a glowing castle, reminds the audience that Snow White's destiny is fulfilled. Her prince has indeed come.

The romantic series of events in the Disney film contrasts sharply with the Grimm tale, where the servants' (accidental) jostling of the coffin knocks free the apple in Snow White's throat. Perhaps taking a page from the Grimms' tale "Brier Rose" (ATU 410),[5] Disney ends the story with a kiss from the prince awakening Snow White (see Zipes 2002b, 171–74). Their relationship's sexual undertones are subdued, but their heteronormative longing for each other (explicitly expressed through song) allows them both to find a happy ending in each other's arms.

Snow White's beauty and femininity are her primary attraction for all the males in the film, but the wicked queen, consumed with jealousy, sets out to destroy them, and her. In the Grimms' version, the stepmother costumes herself in disguise as an "old peddler woman" (Zipes 2002b, 184). In the film, she casts a magic spell so that she appears as an "old hag." Unlike Snow White, the queen has supernatural power and active capabilities, yet neither is a virtue for her as it is for the male characters. Snow White is "killed," in both the film and the tale, by an apple, given to her by a temptress. The evil queen evokes the danger of female empowerment associated with Eve in the Garden of Eden.[6] An aged, powerful figure, the queen of Disney's film is destroyed while engaged in physically potent labor (attempting to dislodge a boulder to crush the dwarfs who chase her from their cottage after she has "killed" Snow White), literally struck down by the forces of the universe, in the form of a bolt of lightning. In *Snow White*, a woman who is too powerful and active must be destroyed by the hand of fate.

Again, this perspective contrasts with "Snow White and Rose Red," where the girls perform the story's primary actions. First described not only as beautiful but also as "more hardworking and diligent than any other two children in the world" (Zipes 2002b, 475), the sisters initiate interaction with the bear (encouraged by their mother); they take care of and play with him; they go to the woods both to frolic and to run errands for their mother; and, most important, they take direct, physical action in the narrative by snipping the dwarf's beard, saving him from being trapped while simultaneously emasculating him, symbolized by the loss of his (facial) hair (see Synnott 1987). Their play with the bear, rather than demurely feminine, is characterized by (tom)boyish enthusiasm and horseplay. Furthermore, through their errands for their mother, they perform actual physical work and labor. Without a male figure in the household, they do "masculine" chores, such as "gather[ing] firewood" and "catch[ing] some fish for dinner" (Zipes 2002b, 477–79). Thus, when compared with the weak, passive Snow White of the film and solo tale, noted solely for her beauty, the sisters of "Snow White and Rose Red" are active and adventurous and perform quite outside the bounds of the patriarchal ideal for well-behaved, demure girls. Similarly, while the Snow White of her own story is overabundantly demarcated as heterosexual, the sisters of the shared tale are queered. Perhaps it is no coincidence, then, that contemporary culture favors the more conventional tale of Snow White, sans Rose Red and sans homoerotic overtones.

Intimate Friendships

In "Snow White and Rose Red," the sisters' relationship of intense intimacy lends the tale an air of homoeroticism. As Martha Vicinus points out, sororal and homoerotic relationships are linked: "Women frequently referred to each other as 'sister,' the most egalitarian relationship they had in a nuclear family. . . . The widespread use of the sororal metaphor may have been a cover for something more intimate" (2004, xxvi). This intimacy between women is commensurate with the lesbianism in Renaissance literature that Valerie Traub describes as "a representational image, a rhetorical figure, a discursive effect, rather than a stable epistemological or historical category. It is employed as an exceptionally compressed and admittedly inadequate rubric for a wide, and sometimes conflicting, range of affective and erotic desires, practices, and affiliations, which have taken different historical forms and accrued varied historical meanings" (2002, 15). Such "intimate friendships" have been explored by Carroll Smith-Rosenberg (1985) and Lillian Faderman (1981). The relationships that these scholars examine include a full spectrum of both filial and friendship bonds, often expressed idiomatically in a heavily romanticized way.

Smith-Rosenberg (1985) examines the world of nineteenth-century women's relationships as recorded, not in public documentation, but rather in their private letters and diaries. Women wrote about the joy they shared in each other's company and the despair they felt when isolated from one another (63). The intimacy, and eroticism, of these relationships must not be overlooked, as the women's support networks commingled with desire for more emotional and sensual sorts of love (73). Smith-Rosenberg also indicates that these relationships led to an alienation from males, so that marriage caused "a girl's traumatic removal from her mother and her mother's network . . . [and] adjustment to a husband, who, because he was male, came to marriage with both a different world view and vastly different experiences" (69). Arguably, in "Snow White and Rose Red," the encounter with the masculine brings about just such a life-altering occurrence for the two sisters.

Lillian Faderman, in examining Victorian society, suggests that its culture actually condoned romantic friendships and notes that only twentieth-century mores cause this kind of relationship "to be perceived as a refinement of the sexual impulse, . . . in many other centuries romantic love and sexual impulse were often considered unrelated" (1981, 16). Lisa Moore, however, disagrees, arguing that these intimate/romantic friendships were seen as taboo, and that they could be understood as either sexual or romantic by female friends (1997, 8). Her account of lesbianism in the British novel emphasizes the conflict between eighteenth-century fears of the dangers of female homosexuality and contemporary accounts that approved of such relationships so long as they were exemplars of chastity. As her study's title, *Dangerous Intimacies*, indicates, Moore finds that such lesbian relationships held great risk to heteronormative society. Just as lesbianism, viewed as dangerous, was repressed in Victorian culture, so too was the sexually problematic "Snow White and Rose Red" marginalized, giving way to the heteronormative "Snow White."

Nevertheless, Rose Red has not disappeared completely; rather, her name, figure, and character are used from time to time to highlight the virgin/whore dichotomy that her original tale prefigures. More modern figurations of Rose Red demonstrate how contemporary writers interpret her and use this dichotomy as a kind of shorthand to explore diverse expressions of femininity.

MODERN REPRESENTATIONS OF ROSE RED

Dan Andreasen's sumptuously illustrated children's book adaptation of "Snow White and Rose Red," titled *Rose Red and the Bear Prince*, is described as being "adapted from 'Snow White and Rose Red' by the Brothers Grimm" (2000, 4). This revision, though, as the title implies, completely leaves out Snow White. It becomes the story of "a poor widow and her only child, Rose Red," who is not only "as lovely as the roses on the rosebush that grew near the garden gate" but also "as sharp as the thorns." The daughter's Snow

White–like lack of sisterly companionship is, indeed, specifically noted: "Though she had no other children to play with, [Rose Red] was never lonely. There was the forest to explore, and all the forest animals were her friends. Rose Red was so kind that the animals were not afraid of her, and as for Rose Red—well, she was afraid of nothing" (6).

Other than the lack of a Snow White to be her counterpart and the fact that Rose Red cuts off the dwarf's beard, mustache, and hair, rather than just three parts of his beard (possibly to facilitate variation in the illustrations), Andreasen's adaptation is quite faithful to the Grimms' original. It follows that story right down to the transplanting of the rosebush from the mother's garden to their castle home at the end: "Rose Red and the bear prince planted it outside their window, and every year it bore the finest red roses in the land" (Andreasen 2000, 30). In this story, Rose Red herself remains wild and undomesticated, more allied with the animals of the forest than with the home and hearth of her mother. This "wildness" is even further accentuated in this version by the fact that she goes into the woods all alone, without a sister to accompany her.

Of course, Snow White's absence from Andreasen's narrative cannot be overlooked. Producing this book in a Western context in which the Disney version of Snow White has attained classic, iconic status (the book was published over sixty years after the premiere of the movie), Andreasen *needs* to remove Snow White in order for the story to be about Rose Red. Snow White's absence from the book takes away any misapprehension that the story will be about Snow White and the seven dwarfs. But it also allows Andreasen to retell this narrative on its own strengths and merits, rather than trading on its associations with the more famous story of a Snow White who, despite having the same name, is an entirely different character from Rose Red's sister. In the context of this children's book, Rose Red's story can only be told by entirely deleting the potentially dominating figure of Snow White. Yet her absence also overdetermines the narrative's heterosexual focus.

A more adult yet equally overdetermined use of Snow White and Rose Red's tale makes direct reference to the differences between the two sisters, using both names for their associated imagery. Ed McBain's novel *Snow White and Rose Red* is not a retelling of the Grimms' fairy tale but a contemporary story that uses the original, and its dichotomy between the two sisters, as a metaphor. The names represent the vacillations in the mental state of protagonist Sarah Whittaker, whose initials are by no means coincidental. However, when, in an exchange near the end of the book, narrator Matthew Hope calls her "Snow White," she reacts forcefully and negatively: "'Oh no,' she said, 'no, my dear, it's Rose Red, didn't you know? Rose *Red!*' she screamed and came at me with the knife. I had never known such brute strength in my life" (1985, 230). McBain knowingly plays with the differentiation between Snow White and Rose Red, which posits the former as gentle and the latter as a thoroughly dangerous woman.

The novel's final chapter, composed mainly as a stream-of-conscious narrative from Whittaker's point of view, relates how the daughter discovers and murders her father's mistress. She first learns of her father's affair when overhearing his erotic phone call with his mistress. This moment is responsible for violating the chaste, virginal status she possessed as a self-described Snow White: "I was wearing white that day, Snow White was, a white dress and white sandals and white lace-trimmed bikini panties, inadvertently and surprisingly damp as I listened to this illicit conversation" (McBain 1985, 235). This sexuality and death of innocence becomes directly tied to the color red: "I stood aghast, as well I might have, such obscenities falling upon my maiden ears, oh the horror. Snow White blushes, actually feels the rush of blood red to her maiden cheeks" (234). The white-as-virgin/red-as-whore symbolism and the intimate connection between the two become even more direct within the flow of Whittaker's somewhat delusional monologue when she confronts her father's mistress, noting, "She is barefoot, Rose Red in her bright red wrapper, and her hair is wet, she is fresh from her *toilette*, my father's whore, his Rose Red whore in her scarlet dress and golden tresses, hair like mine, blonde like mine" (242). These similarities between daughter and mistress invoke the incestuous and queered father/daughter relationships in other tales discussed in this volume, including "Princess Mouseskin" (see chapter 10) and "Donkeyskin" (ATU 510B, "Peau d'Asne," also "Allerleirauh"; see chapter 4).

McBain's adult take on the images (if not the tale) of Snow White and Rose Red, along with the overshadowing of Rose Red by Snow White, is further addressed in writer/creator Bill Willingham's comic book *Fables*. The series portrays traditional fairy tales and folktales with a twist: all the characters live in modern-day New York, having been driven out of their homelands by an evil "Adversary." Although Snow White and the Big Bad

Wolf (now the sheriff of Fabletown) are the main protagonists of the first few storylines, Rose Red, Snow White's younger sister, becomes a crucial secondary character. In *Fables*, she is depicted as "the last of the dedicated party fiends. She's the *original* wild child" (2002a, 13).[7] The very first storyline of the series, "Legends in Exile," revolves around one such "wild" act. Rose Red fakes her own murder so she and her boyfriend, Jack of the Tales (a composite of famous Jacks from various stories and nursery rhymes) can enjoy the dowry she received from secretly getting engaged to the wife-murdering Bluebeard, without ever having to marry him.

The second storyline, "Animal Farm," reveals even more of Willingham's characterization of Rose Red. She and Snow White take a vacation to the upstate farm community where the non-human "Fables" (as all the fairy tale/folktale characters are called) are forced to live. The sisters arrive just in time to encounter an armed uprising. Rose Red seemingly joins the rebellion, which Snow White eventually quashes. As Rose Red is put under arrest, she tellingly states, "It seems I was a bad girl again" (2002c, 21). However, the story later reveals that Rose was working against the revolutionaries, buying Snow White enough time to create a plan of escape. When the girls finally confront each other on this issue, Rose eloquently states her predicament, a metafictional accounting of the place she holds in the contemporary world:

> The Mundys [ordinary humans] adore you by the millions. By the hundreds of millions! They keep making their godawful animated movies and writing their endless children's stories about you. So you can't die! They'll never let you! But who remembers me? Not one in a million of them! It used to be Snow White and Rose Red. Now it's just Snow White, period. All alone! No sister needed or desired, thank you so very much. . . . When we were young, back in the cabin, we pledged we'd be together forever. You and me against the world . . . remember? But the moment your pretty prince charming came along, you rode off with him, without so much as a backward glance. . . . You're still the popular one and I'm fed up with living in your shadow. (18–20)

After boldly stating her case, Rose finally gets her due—she is put in charge of the restructured and rebuilt upstate farm, where her character (and her own internal strength and self-confidence) develops over the course of the series.

Rose Red's Predicament

Unlike in the world of *Fables*, in European and North American cultures, Rose Red has never had a chance to prove herself or to grow as a person and a character beyond her initial portrayal as the whore to Snow White's virgin. Thus *Fables* offers an extreme exception to a general pattern—Rose Red is silenced by the very fact that she is the symbolic representation of a dangerous, active woman, a femme fatale to Snow White's innocent persecuted heroine. Though periodically invoked to express the danger of a sexualized woman and female-dominant spaces (as in Walker and Lunz's [1976] analysis), Rose Red is for the most part restrained, ignored, and forgotten in contemporary culture. The overshadowed Rose Red takes the Grimm tales' silenced woman (see Bottigheimer 1986) a step further; Rose is the silenced and *forgotten* woman.

As Ruth Bottigheimer posits about such female characters, "To the extent that these tales corroborated and codified the values of the society in which they appeared, they reinforced them powerfully, symbolizing and codifying the status quo and serving as paradigms for powerlessness" (1987, 130). Rose Red and her sister, however, are by no means silent within their own story; they are active and passionate girls with a frighteningly close intimacy that borders on queer. Thus, the status quo of not only patriarchy but also heteronormativity is maintained and reinforced through the silencing, overshadowing, and disregarding of the sisters' tale. By forgetting Rose Red, twenty-first-century culture forgets its own dark secrets and desires.

Notes

1. See "Little Red Riding Hood," *The Encyclopedia of Disney Animated Shorts*, http://www.disneyshorts.org/years/1922/littleredridinghood.html.

2. For example, the Internet Movie Data Base (IMDB) lists at least seventy film characters called "Snow White" (http://www.imdb.com/character/ch0026716/), while no "Rose Reds" can be found (http://www.imdb.com/find?s=ch&q=rose+red).

3. To avoid confusion, the Grimms' tales will be referred to as "Snow White and Rose Red" and "Snow White," while the Disney movie will be referred to as *Snow White and the Seven Dwarfs*, or shortened to *Snow White*.

4. "Then they sat down at the hearth, and their mother put on her glasses and read aloud from a large book, while the two girls sat and spun while they listened" (Zipes 2002b, 476).

5. Disney would later also make this story into a feature-length animated movie retitled *Sleeping Beauty*.

6. Furthermore, in the movie, Snow White is specifically tempted by the apple so as to further engage in "women's work": the queen/hag tells her, "It's apple pies that make the men folks' mouths water."

7. Rose's "wildness" is further accentuated when Willingham actually raises the issues of lesbianism and incest, though he shies away from approaching it directly or making it a full part of Snow White and Rose Red's story. Take the following exchange, for example:

> *Snow White:* Relax. It's big enough for two, and it's not like we haven't shared a bed before.
>
> *Rose Red:* That was in days long past, and I've since grown out of the habit of sleeping with girls—except for once every year or so, as a special birthday present for Jack.
>
> *Snow White:* Please spare me the sordid details of your social life.
>
> *Rose Red:* Relax, sis. You're safe from me. Even if I could get beyond the incest thing, you're not my type. (Willingham 2002b, 20)

QUEERING THE TALES

8

Queering Gender

Transformations in "Peg Bearskin," "La Poiluse," and Related Tales

PAULINE GREENHILL, ANITA BEST,

AND EMILIE ANDERSON-GRÉGOIRE

The repertoire of traditional folktales, including the Grimms' versions, is replete with transformations, particularly of non-human creatures into men or women (and sometimes vice versa) (see appendix 1). They include both genders. That is, for all the swans who (re)turn into lovely maidens and thus become appropriate sexual partners for male heroes, there are frogs, snakes, crayfish, generic beasts, and even donkey's heads appear who seek and eventually realize their true form as handsome men. Transmutations are generally unidirectional from animal to human; few traditional tales permanently change princesses into swans or princes into frogs.

Also in transformative mode, clothing switches make suitable consorts for princes of otherwise unattractive females like All Kinds of Fur and Cinderella. Such characters speak to Joan Rivière's (1929) famous notion of womanliness—especially femininity—as masquerade and perhaps also suggest Judith Butler's ([1990] 1999, 1993) concept of gender as performative and thus discursively constructed. Other tales, like "Puss in Boots" (ATU 545B), give unlikely peasant heroes access to the trappings of wealth, including rich clothing, so that they can win the heart and hand of a socially superior woman. These narratives of male transformation demonstrate the importance of class in considering men's social locations, but also suggest that in the fairy-tale universe, social identities other than gender can be enacted performatively.

Mature women fairy-tale characters generally have the knowledge to understand transformations. The husband in "East of the Sun and West of the Moon" (ATU 425A; "The Iron Stove" in the Grimms), a bear during the day and a handsome man at night, neither knows how to effect the alteration to his true form nor is he capable of actually making it so. Only the woman has sufficient magical understanding and the practical sense to fix the situation to their mutual satisfaction. The fairy-tale world often gives women such capabilities and powers. And yet the corporeal beautification of actual humans seems, in tradition, to be entirely concerned with female figures. For Peg Bearskin and La Poiluse (ATU 327B/328/711), and for their relative Tatterhood (ATU 711), change is somatic. Face and body alter to fit the position to which women are expected to aspire in patriarchy, as wives to princes. In related tales like "Kate Crackernuts" (ATU 306/711) the heroine may already be beautiful, but she acts to enable the transformation of another woman to a more acceptable form (see table 1). Yet no traditional tale involves an already-human male becoming more physically attractive so he can marry the female character.[1] For beast-men (who may or may not be ugly but are always inhuman), appearance is "an obstacle to be overcome . . . a relatively short-lived mishap which can be cured by a woman's love" (Henein 1989, 45). But "very rarely are heroes persuaded to love ugly women" (47).[2]

In contrast, literary and popular fairy tales have played more extensively with reversals of such conventions.[3] Perhaps most familiar now, thanks to film versions of the story, is William Steig's *Shrek* (1990), which allows love to triumph when a princess becomes an ogre to match the form and nature of her male counterpart. That is, the primary female character becomes arguably less attractive, not more so, though she thus better fits her partner. Perhaps even more transgressive is a theatrical version of "Peg Bearskin" in *Jack-Five-Oh*, written by Andy Jones and Philip Dinn (n.d.) and based on a telling by Elizabeth Brewer originally of Clattice Harbour, Placentia Bay, Newfoundland, to collector Harold Healey on November 5, 1976 (see Halpert and Widdowson 1996, 215–29; Dinn and Jones 2003). It offers a transformation that remains heterosexually oriented yet queers the narra-

Table 1—sequence

	327B/328/711	711	327B/328	306/711
ATU #	Peg Bearskin/La Poiluse	Tatterhood, etc.	Muncimeg, etc.	Kate Crackernuts
Title				
Distinction between girls	interdiction—one ugly	interdiction—one ugly	one different	one magically disfigured
Home	girls leave it	trolls invade it	girls leave it	girls leave it
Encounter	with giant/witch, etc.	with trolls	with giant/witch, etc.	with king
Trials/impossible tasks	three		three	disenchants sister/King's son
Reward	king's sons for sisters	king's son for self	king's son or gold	king's sons for sisters
Transformation	of ugly girl	of ugly girl		

tive by reversing conventional heterosexist presumptions. In this story, the prince is the character who transforms—not Peg herself. His makeover is indicated in the stage directions thus:

> **Narrator (Elizabeth Brewer):** The prince . . . wished for Peg to be beautiful.
> (*. . . We hear Peg's voice offstage. . . .*)
> **Peg:** Do you like me now?
> **Peg's Husband Prince** (*Still with his face away from us*): You are the most beautiful woman that water ever wet or the sun ever shined on.
> (*Peg enters now; we see that she has not changed a bit.*)
> **Peg:** And of course you are as good lookin' as ever my darlin'.
> (*He turns to reveal that he is as covered in hair and is as warty as Peg. They kiss sweetly and romantically.*)[4]

The two become more physically similar, in that each equally diverts from conventional notions of human beauty. Yet the idea that men should transform to become more fitting partners for women, rather than vice versa, departs from heterosexist norms.

In another example of role reversal, combined with a refusal to conduct an animal-to-human transformation, an extremely popular cultural narrative, usually disseminated on the Internet, criticizes the expectation that conventional marriage must be women's ultimate goal:

> Once upon a time,
> In a land far away,
> A beautiful, independent,
> Self-assured princess
> Happened upon a frog as she sat
> On the shores of an unpolluted pond
> In a verdant meadow near her castle.
> The frog hopped into the Princess's lap
> And said: Elegant Lady,
> I was once a handsome Prince,
> Until an evil witch cast a spell on me.
> One kiss from you, however,

And I will turn back
Into the dapper, young Prince that I am
And then, my sweet, we can marry
And set up housekeeping
In yon castle with my mother,
Where you can prepare my meals,
Clean my clothes, bear my children,
And forever feel grateful and happy doing so.
That night, dining on a supper of lightly sautéed frogs legs
Seasoned in a white wine and onion cream sauce,
She chuckled to herself and thought:
I don't fucking think so.[5]

This brief satire queers women's desires by transmuting popular Freudian and other symbolic interpretations holding that the original tale refers to women's initial disgust with, but eventual acceptance of, male genitalia, symbolized by the frog (see, e.g., Falassi 1980, 39–41). Simultaneously referencing the Grimm tales' familiar interest in cannibalism and implicating Rosalind Coward's (1985) ideas about the relationships between food and sex,[6] the new version suggests that good food is by far superior to a bad marriage.[7]

The protagonist of "Peg Bearskin" may not be a classic ballbuster like the princess in the Internet text. Nor does her name evoke for contemporary readers, as does Kate *Crackernuts*, female dominance over males.[8] Yet Peg remains unconcerned about and unaffected by female conventions. She does not care about dresses and appearances, though she is practical and knows that her sisters do, and so she marries them off, while working on transforming her own circumstances. Peg literally and figuratively controls male and female characters alike. She is quite unlike the almost invariably passive young fairy-tale ingenues understood by Euro–North American audiences as prototypical: Sleeping Beauty, whose greatest achievement is passing out for one hundred years (see chapter 5 of this volume); Rapunzel, who sits on her hands in her high tower until she gets kicked out by her foster mother (the evil, active witch); and, of course, wonderful, industrious Snow White (an unpaid domestic keeping house for seven men), dead! and revived by a prince's necrophilia.

But, as many feminist theorists have pointed out, these women do not present the whole fairy-tale picture, nor do these passive characters accurately represent the countless fairy-tale heroines who take destiny into their own hands with strength, courage, and creativity. These include clever Gretel, who pushes a cannibalistic witch into her own stove and so rescues her brother as well as herself; the protagonist of ATU 425A who, having lost her magical husband, sets out to get him back; Donkeyskin, who leaves home to escape the advances of her incestuous father and ends up marrying a prince (see chapter 4 of this volume); and even Cinderella, the oppressed stepdaughter who actively overcomes all adversity with her perseverance and demonstrates her clear moral superiority over her lazy and cruel stepsisters. All these good, active heroines share a common locus for their intrepid actions, the domestic setting: Gretel murders in the kitchen; Donkeyskin conveys proof of her identity by means of a baked cake; the heroine in "East of the Sun" regains her husband by washing his shirt; and Cinderella slaves away at the hearth, thus earning her status as the chosen one.

Feminists have criticized the symbolic and actual relegation of Euro–North American women to the domestic, private sphere, along with the concomitant association of men with public locations and activities. Though problematic as a simple binary distinction—for example, wealthy white women are expected to venture outside to shop and working-class women of color to leave their homes in search of employment—the public/private dichotomy helps to clarify such sexist conventions as the idea that women should remain "barefoot, pregnant, and in the kitchen" (see Green 2000). Thus, fairy-tale women who leave the traditional domestic milieu often become gender benders. The roster of characters who do so includes Peg, Tatterhood, and Kate Crackernuts, but also Molly Whuppie and Mutsmag (ATU 327B/328). Rather than recognizing, as the heroines themselves do, that sometimes acting in another gendered cultural realm is simply the best course of action, particularly for female characters, folklorists have too often cast their actions as fundamentally male. For example, in the tale type indices, ATU 327B has been called "The Brothers and the Ogre," and ATU 328, "The Boy Steals the Ogre's Treasure." Such titles suggest that the main protagonist must be male, despite counterexamples including Molly, Mutsmag, Peg, and others.[9]

Here one of Torborg Lundell's (1983) critiques of the Aarne-Thompson version of the tale type index (Aarne 1961)—the presumption that the generic protagonist is male—appears to be reproduced in the Uther revision. However, we contend that this is by no means a simple error but may in fact represent a more fundamental understanding of gender. That is, women who abandon the domestic realm can indeed revoke sex/gender's conventional expectations. As Gayle Rubin's groundbreaking study argues, the fundament of sex difference is not genitalia but work role:[10] "The division of labor by sex can . . . be seen as a 'taboo': a taboo against the sameness of men and women, a taboo dividing the sexes into mutually exclusive categories, a taboo that exacerbates the biological differences between the sexes and therefore *creates* gender" (1975, 178; emphasis in original). Understanding sexual difference thus requires perceiving gendered work roles and locations, elements subject to genderfuck in the tales we consider here.[11]

Of the types incorporated in the complex tale and related versions we discuss here, only ATU 306 ("The Danced-Out Shoes") appears in the Grimms—and it is not actually part of the "Peg Bearskin"/"La Poiluse" narratives. A few physically unruly young Grimm heroines ultimately triumph (in the heteroconventional sense of winning a prince), including All Kinds of Fur (as Margaret Yocom discusses in chapter 4) and Princess Mouseskin (as Joy Fairfield discusses in chapter 10). But physically and psychologically unruly women like Frau Trude (discussed by Kay Turner in chapter 11) usually manifest as crones, and ugly but admirable young heroines seem entirely absent. Of course the very purpose of *Transgressive Tales* undermines the idea that univocally patriarchal, straight readings of the Grimms cover the entire territory of their works—Cristina Bacchilega, Joy Fairfield, Kevin Goldstein, Jeana Jorgensen, and Catherine Tosenberger all argue that, contra straight readings, many seemingly conventional Grimm women actually manifest queer personas and eccentric femininities. Thus

"Peg Bearskin" and "La Poiluse" stand tellingly outside the Grimms' oeuvre at the same time as they shed light on its particular qualities.

Our exploration, opening with the Brewer and Jones and Dinn versions of "Peg Bearskin," also refers to other versions and close relatives of this tale published in English and French. As we show, many compilers and theorists have presumed feminist leanings in the characters of Tatterhood, Kate Crackernuts, Mutsmag, Molly Whuppie, and their ilk. But we also look at ways that most versions queer heterosexuality itself, as they focus "on mismatches between sex, gender, and desire . . . demonstrating the impossibility of any 'natural' sexuality . . . [and calling] into question even such apparently unproblematic terms as 'man' or 'woman'" (Jagose 1996, 3). Such variances include the figure of the tomboy, a girl or woman who chooses both self-presentation and work/play more conventionally associated with men than with women or "an extended childhood period of female masculinity" (Halberstam 1999, 155). Though tomboy-like figures appear cross-culturally (see, e.g., Abate 2008a, 2008b, xxii–xxiii; McEwen 1997; Fajardo 2008), their Euro–North American characteristics include several that are true of Peg, Tatterhood, Mutsmag, and Kate, such as dressing as a man/boy; preferring boy's/men's toys, work, and activities; resembling a boy/man; wishing to be a boy/man; and being loud and/or boisterous (see Burn, O'Neil, and Nederend 1996, 422). We extend our analysis to suggest that these tales may encode an embodied sex change from male to female—transsex.[12] As Cressida Heyes explains,

"Trans-" terms capture various kinds of sex and gender crossing, and various levels of permanence to these transitions: from medical technologies that transform sexed bodies, to cross-dressing, to passing, . . . to being legible as one's birth sex but with a "contradictory" gender inflection. For some, the adjective "transsexed" captures the specific project of changing one's sexed body through surgery and hormones, while for others it more broadly describes a distinctive form of narrative. "Transgendered" might describe any project of gender crossing or blending that eschews medical interventions, or the term might be used as a catch-all that includes anyone who disturbs established understandings of gender dichotomy or its mapping to sexual dimorphism. (2000, 170)

Thus, we understand these characters as instantiating various forms of transsex and transgender.

Many Stories, One Main Character

"Peg Bearskin" and "La Poiluse" (ATU 327B/328/711)

A woman who has been married but has no children meets an old man who tells her to eat two berries ("one as sweet as molasses one as sweet as sugar") but not the third ("as bitter as gall"). She ignores the interdiction and gives birth to three girls, "two as pretty as ever the sun shined on" and the other "big, hairy, an' ugly," Peg, whom "nobody liked" (Halpert and Widdowson 1996, 215). Her sisters leave home to try to escape her, but Peg follows. When the three need to find a place to stay for the night, Peg asks for a room, but the old woman in the house says she only has space for two. Peg "didn't make no matter about herself. She said she didn't care where her [bed] was. So she got some place for her two sisters" (216). Peg lies on the floor and notices that the old woman puts caps on the heads of her two daughters, sleeping in the same room as Peg's sisters. Peg re-places the caps on her sisters' heads. The old woman then kills her own children instead of Peg's sisters. The three escape.

Peg decides to meet the king and requests that his eldest son marry her eldest sister, offering in return "a 'canter [i.e., *decanter*] that could never be empted [emptied]" and asking only for a "handful o' pepper" (Halpert and Widdowson 1996, 216). She returns to the old woman's house. When the old woman brings the 'canter, Peg throws the handful of pepper and absconds amid the coughs and sneezes, taking the object back to the king. Her eldest sister and the eldest prince are married. In a similar request, the middle prince is obtained in exchange for "a lantern that can show a half-a-mile light" using a handful of salt. When Peg makes the soup too salty, the old woman sends "the girl" to get water, leaving the lantern for Peg, who steals it.

Finally, Peg asks for the youngest son for herself, and the king "didn't like that one bit."[13] But she promises to bring "a horse that can go ten times swifter than a cannonball, [with] a golden bell from every hair on his mane." She asks for a saw and a knife. She meets the old woman, who recognizes

Peg as the one who was "the cause of me killin' me two daughters. You stole me 'canter . . . that never could be empted and ya stole me lantern that could show a half-mile light." She asks Peg, "If I did that to you what would you do to me?" Peg replies, "I'd take ye an' I'd put ye in a bag. . . . I'd take you away to the side o' the road. . . . I'd pick hazel rods an' I'd beat ya till you'd miaow like a cat, bark like a dog, an' your bones would rattle like crockery ware" (Halpert and Widdowson 1996, 217). When the old woman puts Peg in the bag and goes into the woods to pick the hazel rods, Peg cuts herself out of the bag, puts the old woman's cat, dog, and crockery in the bag, and steals the horse. When the old woman finds out, she follows on a horse "who could go ALMOST as fast" (218). Peg crosses a bridge first and saws it so that it gives way and the old woman falls in the river.[14]

The marriage of Peg and the youngest prince follows. The prince is unhappy, and Peg tells him to burn her. Peg gives him a half ring and tells him, "If you ever gets another half'll fit that . . . that would be who'll be your wife." He does so "an' she went up the chimley in flames" (Halpert and Widdowson 1996, 218). Later "the beautifullest lady that ever the sun shined on" (219) appears at the door and shows him the matching ring half to identify herself as Peg (see table 1).

In the remarkably similar French version collected by Germain Lemieux from Warren, Ontario, teller Joseph Prud'homme on March 24, 1963, a third daughter, born because her mother violates an interdiction, is called La Poiluse (Bristles) because of skin "couverte de poil, comme un chien" (1978, 183; covered in bristles, like a dog). She develops quickly and becomes a strong, hardworking giant. Her sisters head for town to get work, and La Poiluse follows. They are too timid to ask for work at the castle, but "La Poiluse avait plus d'audace et plus d'assurance" (184; La Poiluse had more audacity and self-assurance). She gets work in the stables for herself and housework for her sisters, "à condition qu'elles ne soient pas Poiluses comme toi" (184; on condition that they're not bristly like you). La Poiluse does the work of ten stable hands.[15]

She meets the king and offers to make him a cake—he has never tasted better and wants to move her to the kitchen, but she refuses. When the royal troops cannot repel an attack, La Poiluse successfully goes into battle armed only with a long fork from the stable. The king holds a banquet and offers to marry La Poiluse. Instead she asks him to build a wood pyre, to chain her on top of it, and to burn her. "Le roi eut beau prier, insister, se lamenter et pleurer" (Lemieux 1978, 186; In vain the king prayed, insisted, bemoaned, and cried), but he does as she asks. When all is burned, La Poiluse appears as a woman "plus belles que toutes celles qu'il avait vue auparavant" (186; more beautiful than anyone he had ever seen). La Poiluse says that if the king wants to marry her now, she will accept. Another banquet celebrates their wedding (see table 1).

Peg and La Poiluse have strong, practical good sense. They know they cannot succeed in their role as a prince or king's wife without becoming more feminized. They accept their new position as princess or queen on their own terms, enforcing their husband's compliance with their directions. The true seers in the narrative—other characters constantly misrecognize and misconstrue—Peg and La Poiluse remain conscious of how the world works. Irish versions further masculinize this tale's protagonist with a red beard (Halpert and Widdowson 1996, 223). A mother's first two daughters, blessed by an "old travelling woman," are born beautiful. On a third visit from the same traveling woman, "the woman of the house was very short with her, and the old woman was not pleased at all. 'Your child will be a daughter, and she will be ugly. And ugly she will stay until some young man marries her for herself and not for her appearance.' Well, God bless the mark, when the third child was born she had a head of red hair, and a beard of the same colour growing on her face" (Danaher 1990, 103). This character, Máirín Rua, like Peg and La Poiluse, endures scurvy treatment from her sisters, defeats a giant, succeeds at impossible tasks, and marries a prince. "And as soon as the young prince turned to Máirín Rua, wasn't the hair gone from her face, and wasn't she even more beautiful-looking than either of her handsome sisters" (107). This narrative, then, involves somatic transformation—transsex. The primary character begins as apparently female but with male physical attributes and proficiency and interest in men's work—sometime exclusively, sometimes in combination with equal skill in female domains. However, she ends as an apparently unequivocal bio-female, though the tales do not specify what work she will do in future.

"Tatterhood" (ATU 711)

Stith Thompson argues that "this story is popular in Norway and Iceland, and seems to be quite unknown elsewhere" (1946, 96). However, Hans-Jörg Uther's updated tale type index cites Latvian, Swedish, Scottish, Irish, English, Spanish, Portuguese, Flemish, Turkish, English Canadian, French Canadian, and Spanish American as well as Norwegian and Icelandic instances of what he calls "The Beautiful and Ugly Twinsisters," some of which may be composite forms like "Peg Bearskin" and "Kate Crackernuts." He notes that the tale sometimes combines with ATU 306, "The Danced-Out Shoes" (a link we discuss below; see also Jennifer Orme's analysis in chapter 6) and ATU 708, "The Wonder Child" (Uther 2004, 2:386). He does not discuss the Peg Bearskin/La Poiluse/Máirín Rua links to ATU 327B/328 (see table 1).

"Tatterhood" and its versions have attracted no more than passing mention by folktale scholars. It is included in Daniela Perco's consideration of "Cinderella"-type plots about "the trials and situations that 'girls' must confront in order to become integral members of society" (1993, 73) when she refers to "a ragamuffin, a 'Tatterhood'" (80; see also Muller 1984). It is unclear whether Perco intended to include ATU 711, though evidently for that named character, as for Cinderella and her ilk, "dress and appearance, which initially function as symbolic markers of the heroine's sexual maturity, serve her well to safeguard her integrity once she has left the paternal household" (Perco 1993, 81–82). Perco understands such characters as being on "a quest for personal autonomy: the woman leaves her paternal home . . . takes . . . risks . . . takes care of herself by working and chooses her companion and future life" (82). With many other theorists (e.g., Girardot 1977), she posits the tales she considers—ones with young female protagonists—as narratives of initiation.[16]

Ethel Johnston Phelps named after "Tatterhood" a collection of retold tales she identifies as feminist.[17] She notes that "active heroines are not common among the folk tales that survived by finding their way into print. . . . The overwhelming majority of these tales present males as heroes, with girls and women in minor or subservient roles; or they feature young women . . . who passively await their fate" (1978, xv). In contrast, she argues, "'Tatterhood' . . . deals with the themes of individuality and nonconformity . . . the story of an unconventional young personage, disdainful of approval, of expected behavior, of pretty clothes" (163), a turning from more conventional fairy tales with the youngest, prettiest ingenue as heroine. While a beautiful sister appears in most versions of "Tatterhood," in many, she is not the main, eponymous protagonist. Though Tatterhood might then appear as the counterpart of Cinderella's ugly stepsisters, as heroine and ultimate victor she better resembles Cinderella herself.[18]

Obviously, the characters, personalities, and physical appearances of Peg and La Poiluse link them to Tatterhood, who also shares their marvelous birth. Her mother, the queen, is instructed to choose from two flowers, "one fair and one ugly. The fair one you must eat, the ugly one you must let stand; but mind you don't forget the last."[19] Predictably, the mother ignores the interdiction. Her first twin, Tatterhood, is born with a "wooden spoon in her hand, and rode upon a goat; loathly and ugly she was" (Dasent 1906, 268), named "because she was always so ugly and ragged, and because she had a hood which hung about her ears in tatters." Subsequently, the queen gives birth to "another girl, who was so fair and sweet, no one had ever set eyes on such a lovely child" (269).

Tatterhood drives invading trolls from the house. Though she instructs the queen (mother) to keep the door shut during this process, her beautiful twin peeks out and "POP! up came an old witch, and whipped off her head, and stuck a calf's head on her shoulders instead" (Dasent 1906, 270). Tatterhood sails away with her sister, steals the head back, and replaces it. A king falls in love with the sister, but Tatterhood will agree to their marriage only if she herself can have the king's son. The king eventually gives in, though "to look at [the prince], it was more like going to a burial than a wedding." Coached by Tatterhood, the prince asks, "Why do you ride on that ugly goat?" (272). Tatterhood responds that it is a grand horse, and it becomes one. He asks, "Why do you ride with that ugly spoon?" (273), and she replies that "it's the loveliest silver wand a bride ever bore," which it, too, becomes.[20] The prince is finally instructed to ask about her face, which then becomes "so lovely, he thought there never was so lovely a woman in all the world" (274).

Tatterhood trades in her domestic woman's implement (the spoon), which she uses like a club or sword (Muller 1984, 16, 24) in a fantastic genderfuck clash/merging of domestic/military, fe/male, for the sleek, dainty, silver wand. The wooden spoon, like Tatterhood herself, is rough, aggressive (beating off trolls, witches, and ogres), and unlovely. Thus, though clearly a woman's tool, it occupies an in-between space when wielded as a defensive weapon. But more implications arise than only the transition from androgynous (tomboy) to female, butch to femme, male to female. In the change from common wood to precious silver, from the symbol of domestic labor to one of sovereignty, Tatterhood's transformation, like that of many young male characters, is about status. Though born to a queen, she is unacceptable as royalty until she settles on a more culture-compliant gender identity—or perhaps, until she realizes, transforms, or transgenders into her desired gender identity.

"Molly Whuppie" and "Mutsmag" (ATU 327B/328)

Peg and La Poiluse's ogre/giant killing link them to Molly Whuppie and Mutsmag; so, by implication, does Tatterhood's troll vanquishing (see table 1). As previously suggested, though the tale type's denomination as "The Brothers and the Ogre" and "The Boy Steals the Ogre's Treasure" presume that the main character is male, Molly herself tricks the evil figures—sometimes ogres or giants; sometimes male, sometimes female, sometimes both. She is another unfeminine character who defeats difficult adversaries and solves complicated problems outside the domestic context. In one Appalachian version,[21] a dying widow gives her other daughters costly inheritances, but the youngest, Muncimeg, gets only "her old pocket penknife and a gold ring" (Roberts 1974, 229), which later prove to be invaluable. Her two sisters, going out to seek their fortune, try to keep Muncimeg from following them but eventually must give in. They encounter a giant and his wife, who decide to kill the three girls while they sleep. Clever Muncimeg tricks the monster into slaying his own three daughters using the cap-switching ploy that works for Peg. She escapes with her sisters, eventually coming into the service of a king who sends her on three tasks against the giant. "What would you give me?" As a reward, Muncimeg asks for marriage into the royal family for each of the girls: "I'll give you my oldest son for the oldest girl if one of you will go to that old giant's house and drownd [*sic*] his old lady" (230). The king gives his sons in succession to her sisters and finally to Muncimeg in return for (impossible) tasks, which she accomplishes using her mother's gifts.[22] Here, the king's sons become commodities traded for a service; marriage into royalty and elevation of status in exchange for a brave deed. In other versions of the story (e.g., Davenport 1992), the heroine is paid not with a husband but with gold, underlining the structural objectification of the king's sons in other versions.

Tina L. Hanlon shares with other feminist writers a concern with "the quest for tales that provide contemporary children with more positive female role models than the heroines in the best-known fairy tales." She recommends "retelling selections from older collections of European folktales, searching the folk heritage of other cultural traditions for lesser known heroines, and adapting or satirizing old stories to highlight the strengths of female characters" (2000, 225). She locates Mutsmag as one of several "Appalachian heroines who appear as strong and self-reliant as many of their more familiar male counterparts and European ancestors" (226). Her name in German directly denominates her character—*mut* is "courage" and *magd* is "maid." Though not explicitly ugly, as "Mutzmag" this character is interpreted in Tom Davenport's film version (1992, apparently closely based on Chase 1948, 40–50) as less feminine than her sisters and less concerned than they with girly appearances.[23] Though she begins as a tomboy, at the end she is a much feminized but still independent and apparently unmarried woman. Her transformation in this version is clearly class- and gender-inflected. Like the peasant or working-class girls in other stories who marry princes, Mutsmag comes up in the world, but she does so without resorting to a heterosexual relationship.

These figures "are female counterparts of Jack and other giant killers" (Hanlon 2000, 236). In some Appalachian versions, "Mutsmag, who is never a passive victim, a braggart, or a disloyal sister, is freed from the concerns other heroines have about competing with or getting revenge on their sisters" (237). But the fairy-tale sister/heroines we discuss here are altruistic protectors of the other girls in their families, not their rivals. Kate Crackernuts and Peg also repay scurvy treatment from their sisters not only by saving them from giants/ogres, male or female, but also by finding them appropriate places for their style and role in their own society, which often includes getting them quality husbands.[24] They understand that being outside social expectations can mean being unable to survive. They recognize that individuals need community, so they work on being inside it in their own terms.

Kate Crackernuts (ATU 306/711)

The tale type numbers of "Mutsmag" and "Kate Crackernuts" suggest they are unrelated, and yet they have similarities other than their common presence in anthologies of feminist retellings of fairy tales.[25] They also both appear in Maria Tatar's *The Annotated Classic Fairy Tales* (2002, 229–33), though one might suspect that editor's feminist sensibility more than the tale's representativeness—or any strictly classic status—suggested it as a candidate for inclusion therein.[26] Specifically, each heroine faces difficult or impossible tasks outside the domestic locus and conquers them with wit and perseverance. We argue that Kate's disenchantment of her sister and the prince are functional equivalents of Molly/Mutsmag's tricking of the giants/ogres. They are obstacles the heroine must overcome in order to get her reward. Thus the links between these stories and their common connections with ATU 711 and its combination versions are structurally and semiotically manifested (see table 1).

Kate Crackernuts sometimes attracts her stepmother's jealousy because her stepsister is less beautiful (K. Briggs 1970, 344–46). Alternatively, when Kate's sister, Anne, is better looking, *she* attracts the jealousy (Tatar 2002). In all versions, however, the two stepsisters are close friends. The more beautiful sister magically loses her head, which is replaced with that of a sheep (though in some versions the two characters become confused, and it appears that Kate is the one who loses her head, though she still disenchants her sister). The two girls go to seek their fortune and ask for lodging at a king's castle. "This is granted on condition that Kate sits up all night to watch the king's sick son" (Robertson 1890, 200). She does so in return for a peck of silver, following him into a fairy hill where he is forced to dance all night.

The next night she demands a peck of gold, gathers nuts as she follows the prince, and uses them to distract a fairy baby whose wand "would make Kate's sick sister as bonnie as ever she was" (Tatar 2002, 232). On the final night, Kate agrees to watch the prince in exchange for marrying him. She again gathers nuts, which she uses to get a "birdie" from the baby, three bites of which "would make the sick prince as well as ever he was" (233). The prince's brother marries Kate's stepsister.

ARE YOU A BOY OR ARE YOU A GIRL?

We have introduced four folktale types/combinations whose heroines, we argue, are more or less identical. All act forcefully, usually in explicitly male-identified ways. Our opening characters, Peg and La Poiluse, along with Tatterhood and the ugly sister in "Kate Crackernuts," physically transform from a masculinized to a feminized character and, concomitantly, from ugly to beautiful. Molly/Mutsmag's makeover is more subtle, perhaps even more conventional, but no less a result of her own feats in taking charge of her life and those of her sisters. We now turn to a consideration of what these transformations might mean in the queer and trans terms we introduced at this chapter's opening. We recognize that for the traditional cultures in which these stories circulated, a frail and helpless woman would not survive. Then, as now, only wealth and privilege would make feminine weakness and incompetence viable, let alone sexy. As we noted before, the dichotomy of public/private is similarly a class-based distinction. Thus, our comments here refer to possible current understandings and Euro–North American middle- and upper-class presumptions about gender distinctions.

As D. L. Ashliman comments (an observation all the contributors to this collection would enthusiastically echo), "The household fairy tale—told primarily by women—provides a vehicle for the expression of forbidden desires" (1986, 196). Nevertheless, for female tellers, even narrating stories focusing on strong male main characters can lead to suspicions of gender inappropriateness; "Cáit O'Sullivan's grandmother admonished her against telling hero tales by saying, 'You'll be making a tomboy of yourself by telling them stories'" (Harvey 1989, 120). Brave heroes in fairy tales often get rewarded with the hand of a princess. Princes, in contrast, are not generally handed out as prizes, and yet *winning* the hand of a prince—for a protagonist and often also for her sister(s)—is a common thread running through these stories. The role reversals suggested are highlighted in observations by fairy-tale critics. For example, the penknife—Mutsmag's inheritance and the means by which she accomplishes her goals—is a "down-home equivalent of the weapon heroic men are given to display their strength and defend themselves"; and the "scene in which Mutsmag uses her ingenuity and the knife to recover the king's horse . . . also puts Mutsmag in control of a powerful male symbol" (Hanlon 2000, 237). One narrator begins Mutsmag's story thus: "There was something in that girl that made her want adventure as much as any man" (239). Mutsmag and Molly, if not others, appear never to be anything but female, though the repeated comparisons to their male counterparts heavily reinforce that they are the exception, not the rule, as women. Though tomboys, not girly girls, they are still unequivocally female.

Michelle Ann Abate argues that literary tomboys have long "disrupted the rigid dichotomy separating 'good' and 'bad' female conduct" (2008a, xi). Tomboys, however, can be complexly gendered; though they "may defy the boundaries between heterosexuality and homosexuality, . . . they often reinforce the ones between masculinity and femininity" (xvii).[27] For example, the requirement that a girl or woman be identified as a tom*boy* underlines that she is a type of *boy*, not a type of *girl*. Louise Westling draws attention to "a fear that to be female and to dare to achieve is to venture into dangerous territory, to violate one's gender, to become a kind of freak. The girl who insists on following her ambitions almost inevitably pays the price of shame and guilt as an adult; she must live with a troubled sense of herself as a woman because she has abandoned the familiar boundaries of her gender" (1996, 157). Judith Halberstam concurs that tomboys are "punished . . . where and when . . . [they manifest] extreme male identification (taking a boy's name or refusing girl clothing of any type) and . . . extend beyond childhood and into adolescence" (1999, 155, see also 156). Karin Quimby suggests that the tomboy's "queer dilemma" may explain why so many tomboy tales resolve (as do most of the traditional narratives we discuss) into more conventional narratives:

> The demand that the tomboy exchange her overalls for a dress to signal her availability for heterosexual romance is a clear attempt to "order"

her "precarious" gender development into an acceptable heterosexual narrative framework. It is precisely because the tomboy's plot always threatens to "turn queer" that it arouses so much anxiety at a certain pubescent point. . . . As a result, strategies for containing the tomboy's queer energies are not in short supply. (2003, 2)

The primary characters in these tales, after passing through their tomboy phase, could be seen as set securely on the road to hegemonic femininity—if they have not already arrived there. But Abate points out that "theories of narrative desire often fail to recognize the narrative middle as more than a space that delays, through sometimes perverse subplots, the ultimate climax. But it is more accurate to say that this middle space traces the movement and trajectory of the tomboy or queer girl's plot" (2008a, 4; see also Elliott 1998).[28]

Though tomboyism could be dismissed as no more than "a very common phase through which little girls would pass on their way to the safe harbor of domestic femininity" (O'Brien 1979, 354), a queer reading of these tales follows Abate's suggestion. Attending not to their more compliant ends but to their disruptive middles shows how Peg, La Poiluse, and their sister characters destabilize gender binaries by doing and being both female and male. PJ McGann argues that "out of tomboy as gender misfit arises an incipient gender warrior" (1999, 122). There may be an even more extensive relation between gender transformation and tomboys. Abate (2008a, 231–32; see also 2008b) points out that the fourth edition of the American Psychiatric Association's *Diagnostic and Statistical Manual of Mental Disorders* describes girls with "gender identity disorder" (GID)—the precursor to transgender and sometimes transsex—in ways that closely approximate the traditional notion of the tomboy. Indeed, one study found "highly increased incidence of tomboyism" among intersex children (Baker 1980, 84, see also 87–89, 95–96).[29]

All these characters are tomboys, but the protagonists of tales explicitly incorporating ATU 711 may also represent transsex. Consider the beginning of the narrative action: the multiplication of the sisters—one or two beautiful ones and an ugly, hairy, beastly one in "Peg Bearskin," "La Poiluse," "Máirín Rua," and "Tatterhood." The beautiful ones result from following instructions, eating the sweet berry or the beautiful flower, while the ugly one comes instead from failure or ignoring an interdiction. They are opposites that emerge from opposite actions: disobedience rather than compliance. Following this binary thinking, that which is opposite to female is male; the beautiful sisters are unequivocally female, and, therefore, arguably their "sister" is male.[30]

Further, the characters' hairiness often manifests in male forms—both Máirín Rua and Tatterhood have beards. And whether riding about on a goat, tricking a giant, driving out trolls, or going to war, these boy/girls are extreme examples—at the very least—of Mutsmag/Molly's masculine behavior. In most versions, as already suggested, they act primarily outside the female domain. They are the bold, clever, resourceful ones, instantiated most obviously in La Poiluse, who is exceptionally strong, works in the forest and in the stable, and wins a war through physical prowess. Like some others, however, these male to female transsexuals experience themselves in female terms despite masculine appearance and action. Their femininity, at first inexpressible, ultimately may become nothing more than a masquerade when located exclusively in their change of appearance.

In some versions of "Kate Crackernuts," the heroine is the more beautiful and her sister, stepsister, or bosom friend is less so, occasioning someone else's jealousy. But even when the other sister is apparently more beautiful, she transforms into an animal-headed woman, whose sister must cure her.[31] The literal or figurative twinning of the sisters serves a similar symbolic function to that of the mirror in other tales. It marks a point on the lesbian continuum where similarity and eroticism meet;[32] that is, both mirror and sister/friend twinning produce two bodies/images that reflect each other but also reference the sometimes erotic pleasures that can be found in seeing oneself in another. Though the attraction between the two (or three) main female characters is not necessarily based on exact physical interchangeability, in "Kate Crackernuts," it references similarities of spirit and character—though of course Kate remains the bold and active sister.[33]

Thus, actual bodily alteration is not the true test of a transsex character in this group of fairy tales. Instead, they exemplify what we call the "transgender imagination," the conceptualization that a person—self or other—is or could be of a different sex or gender than they appear. This semiotic expression appears in a variety of other forms of traditional culture, including ballads (see Greenhill, forthcoming). Despite the fact that Tatterhood, La Poiluse, and Peg, for example, seem female, other characters fail to see them in that mode and put them to work in places where women are not supposed to be. Even Mutsmag is excluded from socializing with her sisters. All these trans girls/boys imagine themselves beyond appearances and conventions. Each voluntarily repudiates the passive qualities expected of her sex, given her social class, by choosing to become an active agent in her own and others' lives.

We argue that these texts reference sex and gender crossing alike. Some characters (Mutsmag and Kate, for example) are legible as—and seem to pass as—their desired female sex/gender, though they act in nonstereotypical ways and locations. Others, initially less successful at performing the physical feminine, particularly Peg and Tatterhood, fail to pass initially as "normal" women, but ultimately transform/transsex, and are then read not only as women, but as beautiful ones. For some, transformation is affected by a literal ordeal by fire (see chapter 11); for a few, marriage changes them into women.[34] Again, we return to the theatrical version of "Peg Bearskin" with which we opened this chapter. Heterosexuality becomes queered, particularly by joining in marriage two, at least initially, male-associated characters (through their work as well as their physicality). Alternatively, and even more realistically given the sources of these narratives, we could see the prince (especially in "Peg") as female-identified (in terms of class), upper-class feminized. Both revoke gender expectations; the prince by marrying someone it appears he should not be marrying—not femme enough, not beautiful enough—and the male-to-female character by reversing the expectations for her birth gender (ambiguously male) *as well as* for her gender of choice (female). She enacts the former in her hairy, physically imposing embodiment and in her work outside female domains. La Poiluse, for example, works in the forest, then the stable, then the kitchen, then the battlefield. A less gender-predictable series might be difficult to imagine! The story's finish does not narrate what will happen to her. It concludes, "Quant à moi, s'ils ne sont pas heureux, je n'y suis pour rien" (Lemieux 1978, 186; As far as I'm concerned, if they aren't happy, it has nothing to do with me).

Though most of these tales offer formulaic conclusions, the traditional formulae are by no means as unequivocal as the conventional "And they all lived happily ever after." Joseph Jacobs's version of "Molly Whuppie" concludes, "So Molly took the ring to the king, and she was married to his youngest son, and she never saw the giant again" ([1898] 1967, 130). "Tatterhood" also ends in the middle of the action, without specifying what actually happens to the two characters: "There was no end to the fun; and if you make haste and run to the King's palace, I dare say you'll find there's still a drop of the bridal ale left for you" (Dasent 1906, 274). This figure makes the audience, more than the tale characters, a final focus—returning the job of interpretation of what will happen to the person who hears or reads. The recorded version of "Peg Bearskin" simply concludes, "An' the two halves [of the ring] went together. So—that was his wife, then" (Halpert and Widdowson 1996, 219).

Few folktales have been examined using a transgender or queer lens, even when, like the hero/heroine of "The Shift of Sex" (ATU 514; see Greenhill and Anderson-Grégoire, forthcoming), a character literally and explicitly changes sex. Yet these stories remain as meaningful for those who do not understand their sex/gender in conventional ways, as they are for those who do. Further, the binary of male/female, as indicated above, is a social construction better associated with class and wealth than with sex/gender per se, so that the fairy tales themselves embody queries about what it is that makes a person (conventionally) male or female. In these tales, attaining a desired persona results from acting as both female and male. The stories discussed in this chapter may offer slightly more subtle manifestations than in "The Shift of Sex," but they equally exemplify not only queer but also transgender and transsex in traditional fairy tales.

NOTES

1. A possible exception is "Ricky of the Tuft," a version of ATU 711 in which the protagonist bestows intelligence on the beautiful princess, and she, in turn, makes him handsome. However, in Perrault's version, "some people assert that this was not the work of fairy enchantment, but that love alone brought about the transformation. They say that the princess, as she mused upon her lover's constancy, upon his good sense, and his many admirable qualities of heart and head, grew blind to the deformity of his body and the ugliness of his face; that his humpback seemed no more than was natural in a man who could make the courtliest of bows, and that the dreadful limp which had formerly distressed her now betokened nothing more

than a certain diffidence and charming deference of manner. They say further that she found his eyes shine all the brighter for their squint, and that this defect in them was to her but a sign of passionate love; while his great red nose she found naught but martial and heroic" (Ashliman 1996–2011). For another translation, see Zipes (1989, 56). We rest our case!

2. Grooms are rarely pleased with their less-than-lovely brides.

3. Ballads have male and female shape-shifters such as "Tam Lin" (see Hixon 2004) and "Kemp Owyne," respectively. An English tale parallel to the latter, published by Joseph Jacobs as "The Laidly Worm of Spindleston Heugh" and "The Lambton Worm," has a main female character who is a dragon during the day and a beautiful woman at night. Usually contextualized within heterosexual relationships, women shape shifters in folktales and ballads pick men who give them the freedom to choose their own preferred form (see Heiner 1998–2011, http://www .surlalunefairytales.com/authors/jacobs.html).

4. We are grateful for permission from Andy Jones and Philip Dinn to reproduce this section of their play.

5. For further discussion of this text, see Preston (2004).

6. As Maria Tatar succinctly puts it, the Grimm brothers' selection of wonder tales revels in "murder, mutilation, cannibalism, infanticide, and incest" (1987, 3).

7. Links between food and sex are familiar in psychological interpretations of folktales, including "Tatterhood." According to Bengt Holbek, Franz Riflin (the psychiatrist and colleague of Carl Jung) "actually refers to the eating of flowers in the Norwegian version of AT 711 as a documentation of his view that eating symbolizes sexual intercourse" (1987, 632).

8. Thanks to our colleague Joe Goodwin for pointing out this aspect of Kate's name and persona.

9. Linda Dégh's *Story-Telling in a Hungarian Peasant Community* includes a tale called "Zsuska and the Devil," which she identifies as AT 328. She points out that "The international index does not indicate the female version of the tale which is very popular in Hungary" (1989, 317).

10. Consider, for example, any Two-Spirit First Nations individual anthropologists misnamed "berdache." Though born with male genitals, she is nevertheless female, which she demonstrates not only by wearing women's clothing but most crucially by doing female work. As discussed by Will Roscoe (1991), among others, individuals in this role are also frequently associated with special social, spiritual, and/or magical powers—not unlike Peg, Kate, Tatterhood, Mutsmag, and so on.

11. Jacqueline N. Zita defines genderfuck as "tampering with the codes of sex identity by mixing male and female, masculine and feminine, man and woman

signifiers on one body" (1992, 120), to which we would add the imagination and/ or representation of such acts.

12. Though some transpersons prefer "transexual," we have chosen to use the term most often employed in Stryker and Whittle's (2006) programmatic, ground-breaking reader.

13. As D. L. Ashliman suggests for this kind of character, "It is not her acceptance of traditional values, but rather her violent assertion of sexual independence, that brings her satisfaction" (1986, 194).

14. I thank Martin Lovelace for pointing out that traditionally Newfoundlanders did not learn to swim; falling into the icy Atlantic meant near-certain death in any case.

15. Neither Peg nor La Poiluse judges their weaker femmey sisters; they recognize their circumstances and help them out. In the fairy-tale world they create, there is room for all kinds of sex/gender forms.

16. For another type of initiation, see Kay Turner's discussion of "Frau Trude" in chapter 11.

17. Feminist or women-centered retellings of fairy tales often include versions of "Molly Whuppie," "Mutsmag," "Tatterhood," "Kate Crackernuts," et al. (e.g., Barchers 1990), probably because they seem to instantiate some of the androgyny, capability, and dynamism that second-wave feminism appreciated in women.

18. Note, however, the class differences between Cinderella/Tatterhood and Peg/ La Poiluse.

19. Hodne (1984, 155) cites six versions from Norway.

20. For all its associations with the kitchen and therefore with the stereotyped female domain, the only instances of spoons noted in the list of motifs included in Uther's (2004) index involve men employing the spoons to mischievous ends: ATU 1449*, "The Stingy Hostess and the Inn"; 1565*, "The Big Cake"; and 1842C*, "The Clergyman's Nights."

21. For more Appalachian versions of this tale, see Hanlon (2008). In a tale from Aberdeenshire, though, the distinction between the three sisters is simply in terms of age, though the youngest, Mally Whuppie, "was very clever" (K. Briggs 1970, 401).

22. Roberts notes that "many of these tales are proving hard to classify, even for the indexers, because of the number of children involved. In them one to three girls, a girl and a boy . . . , or one to three boys . . . set out to seek their fortunes and unwittingly stay all night with a giant" (1974, 363).

23. Even the illustrations appear to have influenced Davenport's vision. For discussions of the film, see Charney (1993), Davenport (1993), and Hanlon (2008).

24. Hanlon (2000) also notes that magical actions are absent from Appalachian

versions. Perhaps we have here a parallel with the transformation of traditional ballads from supernatural to naturalistic when they come to the United States (Abrahams and Foss 1968).

25. Indeed, Alison Lurie's (1980) collection of "forgotten folktales" and Rosemary Minard's (1975) feminist retellings include both "Molly Whuppie" and "Kate Crackernuts."

26. That anthology includes a few other traditional narratives arguably less popular in Euro–North America, but most, like "Little Red Riding Hood," "Cinderella," "Beauty and the Beast," "Jack and the Beanstalk," and "Puss in Boots," are very familiar.

27. We caution that there is a danger here of conflating sex/gender identity with sexual orientation. A sense of male embodiment for a female-sexed individual does not necessarily mean a sexual orientation toward females (see Castendyk 1992).

28. Queerly, Quimby reads *Little Women* as resolving into the "classic oedipal drama (in which the girl gets 'Papa' in getting a husband)" (2003, 11). We note this narrative trajectory's centrality to "Peau d'Asne" (ATU 510B), discussed by Margaret Yocom in chapter 4.

29. Intersex individuals have genitalia that cannot be easily identified as falling within a male-only/female-only binary.

30. Note that many transsexuals do not understand their sex/gender as fluid or betwixt and between but instead as the direct opposite of the one assigned to them.

31. Being too beautiful attracts the evil eye; even praising children exposes them to jealousy and negative reaction. See also the sister cure in "Fitcher's Bird," as discussed by Greenhill (2008).

32. The lesbian continuum, as theorized by Adrienne Rich ([1980] 1993), allows for a range of women-centered positions which may or may not involve genital sexual relations between women.

33. D. L. Ashliman might characterize Peg's and her counterparts' roles as "symbolic sex-role reversals": "There is a large group of fantasy tales, well represented in the Grimms' collection as well as other folklore sources, in which [gender role norms are] reversed; tales in which it is not the man who reforms his self-willed bride, but rather the woman who transforms her bridegroom—normally one selected for her by her father—into a person of her liking" (1986, 193).

34. Since, until recently, marriage between two men could not be socially or legally contemplated, marriage effectively renders one partner female.

9

The True (False) Bride and the False (True) Bridegroom

"Fitcher's Bird" and Gendered Virtue and Villainy

CATHERINE TOSENBERGER

The Grimms' version of "Fitcher's Bird" (KHM 46) is one of the strangest in the collection, a dark tale of violence that proceeds with the relentless logic of a nightmare. Its gruesomeness ensured that it never achieved widespread popularity with a public insistent that fairy tales were only for children, but the story has recently enjoyed a burst of attention from writers, artists, and scholars attracted by its resourceful heroine and her clever escape from the serial killer who wishes to marry her. While Marina Warner claims that "Fitcher's Bird," the best-known example of ATU 311 ("Rescue by the Sister"), "feels . . . like a rummage bag of scraps for the making of a patchwork quilt" (1994, 255), the story is striking in its symbolic coherence. "Fitcher's Bird" invokes and undermines the male gaze and performative femininity through a series of visual set pieces that haunt the imagination: the basin of blood, the skull bedecked with jewels, the girl shivering under her disguise of feathers. Like the constructed quilt, far from being a random assemblage of motifs, these images pack an emotional punch by concretizing the tensions operating within the tale.

When I first encountered "Fitcher's Bird" as a teenager, I was fascinated and disturbed by its renunciation of heterosexual marriage, which subverted the expectations I had of both fairy tales and of my own future. Unlike the fairy tales most of us in Euro-dominated North America grow up with, this story ends not with a wedding but with a joyous escape from marriage.[1] The heroine is no romantic lover waiting for her prince to come but is, instead, a witch, a thief, a trickster, a survivor. But more than that: not only does the heroine defy cultural and narrative expectations of women, but the tale as a whole embeds the construction of the heroine's virtue and her antagonist's villainy in a series of parodic exaggerations and overt transgressions of normative gender roles. The heroine skillfully manipulates images of true and false brides in order to subvert patriarchal authority. She uses assumptions about normative femininity—in particular, the demands for women to be obedient, subservient, beautiful, and, especially, silent[2]—to systematically unman the villain, thus destroying his power over her.

The story begins when Fitcher, an evil wizard, disguises himself as a beggar and kidnaps a beautiful young girl from her home. He brings her to his castle, where he hands her a key and an egg. She may not go through the door the key opens and must keep the egg with her always. Of course, she opens the door and discovers a basin full of the dismembered corpses of Fitcher's victims; horrified, she drops the egg, which is then indelibly stained with blood. When Fitcher sees the egg, he kills her. He then returns to her house and kidnaps the second sister, and it goes exactly the same with her. With the third sister, however, Fitcher meets his match: she is "clever and sly" and hides the egg before she uses the key (Tatar 2004a, 204). When she discovers the basin, she reassembles her sisters' bodies, returning them to life, and hides them in the castle. When Fitcher returns and sees the unblemished egg, he proposes marriage; she agrees, but only if he will take her parents a bushel of gold. She hides her sisters in the basket, covers them with gold, and warns Fitcher not to rest along the way. After he leaves, she decorates a skull with jewels and places it in the attic window; when Fitcher turns to look back, he waves at the skull, thinking it his bride. When he wishes to rest, the sisters call out, "I can see you! Get a move on!" Back at the castle, the heroine disguises herself as a bird and flees through the forest. After tense encounters with first the wedding guests and then Fitcher himself (wherein she assures them, "From the attic window, [the bride] is staring down at you" [205]), she makes it home. Her sisters, meanwhile, have raised the alarm. Their brothers arrive, lock Fitcher and all his guests in the castle, and set it on fire, thus destroying the villain and his works.

This story bears obvious similarities to the far more famous "Bluebeard" (ATU 312). Understandably, then, most of the scholarship on "Fitcher's Bird" has folded the story into a discussion of that tale. Nearly every recent critic of "Bluebeard" stories has remarked on the tendency of this group of tales, especially literary versions, to focus on the crimes of the wife rather than the husband—or, as Cristina Bacchilega puts it, their "explicit condemnation of the heroine's curiosity, but total silence on the ethics of the husband's serial murders" (1997, 106). Maria Tatar (2004b, 61–63), Jack Zipes (2006b, 193–94), Marina Warner (1994, 244–47), and Bacchilega (1997, 105) all discuss the ways in which the heroine has been equated with those other famously disobedient women, Eve and Pandora. This equation does not stop with the tales; critics, especially the psychoanalytically inclined such as Bruno Bettelheim (1976) and Alan Dundes (1993),[3] reproduce the tale's morality when they proclaim that the heroine's transgression is sexual infidelity, a stance Tatar calls "willfully wrong-headed" (2004b, 20).

Charles Perrault's 1697 version of the story is by far the most famous and lends itself well to misogynistic finger wagging, both academic and otherwise. Zipes argues that Perrault's "Bluebeard" was probably cobbled together from a variety of motifs floating around in French folk narrative and was "created to play a role in the debate about the civilizing process, masculine domination, and the proper roles of men and women during the time of Louis XIV's reign" (2006b, 158). In the Perrault "Bluebeard," the heroine is excoriated throughout for her greed, silliness, and curiosity and is only rescued by her brothers when she repents for her disobedience. Tatar (2004b, 24) even points out that Perrault is at pains to claim Bluebeard's cruelty as highly unusual for husbands, while framing the heroine's vice of curiosity as, sadly, all too common among women. Bluebeard's outrageousness lies neither in his demand of absolute obedience nor in his assumption of the role of judge and jury over his wife's alleged indiscretions; rather, Bluebeard's crime is that he is too cruel in enforcing his God-given rights.

This upholding of patriarchal authority is reinforced by the Grimms' "The Virgin Mary's Child" (KHM 3; ATU 710), a tale that bears a striking structural similarity to "Bluebeard" stories. In this tale, the Virgin Mary forbids a young girl from entering a room. The girl disobeys and is confronted with the splendor of the Trinity; unable to resist, she reaches out to touch the light, thus turning her finger gold. When the girl refuses to admit her disobedience, Mary throws her out, renders her mute, and continues to torment the girl until she finally admits her wrongdoing. As Tatar remarks, "That the Virgin Mary could slip with ease into the functional slot occupied by Bluebeard is telling and does much to explain why it became easy for rewriters and critics of the tale type to let Bluebeard off the hook" (1987, 169). This similarity in tale structure suggests that Bluebeard, like the Virgin Mary, is a legitimate—indeed, divine—authority who has the right to demand obedience from inferiors and to exact punishment for disobedience. Bluebeard merely wishes to ensure that his wife displays the proper feminine virtue of obedience to authority, and, like the Virgin Mary, he forces her silence as punishment. While Bluebeard's method of punishment is far more permanent than the Virgin Mary's, the logic is identical: both castigate the lack of one feminine virtue (obedience) by enforcing another (silence).

However, other folkloric examples of "Bluebeard"-related tales are not nearly as consistent in their condemnation of the heroine. As Zipes remarks, "The fairy tales about Bluebeard take different forms that range from legitimation and justification of male power to exposure of the faulty premises and condemnation of male power" (2006b, 193). ATU 311 stories, as a group, almost always foreground both the villain's overt evil and the heroine's cleverness. Perrault's Bluebeard is an ordinary mortal man marked only by the unusual color of his facial hair; Nicholas Ruddick (2004, 348) claims that this can be read as a sign of "unnatural masculinity," but the fact remains that Bluebeard's powers are merely an extreme interpretation of the powers ordinary men had over their wives. On the other hand, the villains in many ATU 311 tales are obvious monsters—a troll, a giant, the devil himself—who kidnap their victims by force or treachery. Fitcher, an evil sorcerer, actively disguises himself as a harmless beggar to get close enough to work his magic on his victims. Likewise, the heroines of ATU 311 stories are actually celebrated for their ingenuity; in contradistinction to the behavior expected from most women, their cunning and duplicity are what enable them to survive.[4]

I argue that it is vitally important not to subsume ATU 311 tales in general, and "Fitcher's Bird" in particular, under discussions of "Bluebeard," because the tales differ so radically in their assignations of virtue and villainy; "Bluebeard" reinforces patriarchal authority, while "Fitcher's Bird" undermines it, recasting Bluebeard's wife's vices of curiosity and disobedience into virtues and pairing them with cleverness as necessary traits for survival. While most ATU 311 tales feature clever heroines, the heroine of "Fitcher's Bird" is unusually so. As E. Sidney Hartland (1885, 201) notes, "Fitcher's Bird" is unique in that the heroine both escapes under her own steam *and* creates a false bride; moreover, "Fitcher's Bird" is, according to Stith Thompson (1966, 545), the only example of motif C913I.I, "Bloody egg as sign of disobedience"—the bloody egg, as opposed to the bloody key in "Bluebeard," is of enormous symbolic resonance, as I will show.

Indeed, Bacchilega argues for a shift in the emphasis of readings of this family of tales: "If the 'Forbidden Chamber' rather than the 'Bloody Key' is treated as the tale's central motif, then 'Bluebeard' is no longer primarily about the consequences of failing a test—will the heroine be able to control her curiosity?—but about a process of initiation which *requires* opening the forbidden chamber" (1997, 107). In "Fitcher's Bird," there is no clearer illustration that the heroine has undergone this "process of initiation" than the fact that after she enters the forbidden chamber she strips Fitcher of his power and is able to use it to raise her sisters from the dead. The story is a symbolically cohesive narrative of a wised-up heroine systematically unmanning a villain who represents an ultimate goal of patriarchal authority; the power of life and death over women. Pauline Greenhill, the only scholar as of yet to have focused extensively on "Fitcher's Bird" as distinct from "Bluebeard," describes the heroine's triumph as a result of her "series of queer actions, eroticized, tabooed, perverse, and women-centered" (2008, 156). Each of the heroine's "queer actions" relies on a simultaneous exaggeration and subversion of normative femininity designed to throw Fitcher off her track so she can escape him.

Understanding the "Forbidden Chamber" as the central motif of "Bluebeard"-type stories also highlights an important structural distinction between "Bluebeard" and "Fitcher's Bird." While both tales involve a penetration to the heart of the castle, "Bluebeard" keeps the action close; the heroine does not escape from Bluebeard's domain but is saved only by the penetration of further masculine authority, in the form of her brothers, into the castle. Her entry into Bluebeard's secret room comes nearly at the end of her story. In "Fitcher's Bird," however, the heroine's entry to the forbidden room is just the beginning: she is not captured and then rescued but instead is a rescuer, springing herself and her sisters free from the castle. This move is mirrored in the structure of the story: the climax of "Bluebeard" takes place at the heart of his castle, in the seat of patriarchal authority; "Fitcher's Bird," like other ATU 311 tales, devotes as much narrative space to the escape of the heroine and her sisters from the physical confines of the castle, with the most intense encounter between heroine and villain taking place in the woods.

There is another salient distinction between "Bluebeard" and "Fitcher's Bird"; the entirety of "Fitcher's Bird" takes place before the heroine marries, while "Bluebeard" describes the plight of an already-married woman. Ruddick, discussing the heroine of "Fitcher's Bird," points out that "she uses the power she has gained over the wizard to destroy him *before* the wedding ceremony—after which he would have regained power over her by law rather than by magic" (2004, 352; emphasis in original). Bluebeard is not a supernatural monster; as the heroine's lawfully wedded husband, he does not *need* to be in order to enforce his wishes and commit his crimes. Only his blue beard signals that there is anything whatsoever wrong with him. Fitcher's position is more precarious, as he does not yet legally "own" the heroine. In this way, the heroine's escape is not just a subversion but a *dodge* that highlights the power of husbands over wives. She knows that once he catches her, there is nothing she can do, so her only chance is to find Fitcher a more suitable bride: death.

In this chapter, I focus on and explore this combination of motifs that are unique to "Fitcher's Bird": the egg deception, which is really a falsified true bride test, and the heroine's construction of multiple false brides in order to effect her escape. The egg test and false positive is a funhouse mirror of similar true bride tests in other tales. Unlike, say, Aschenputtel's (ATU 510A) evil stepsisters, who mutilate their feet in order to fit into the shoe and pass the bride test, in "Fitcher's Bird," cheating the bride test is a heroic strategy. In contradistinction to most "true bride/false bride" tales, the false brides in ATU 311 stories are not villainous obstacles to the heroine's happiness but necessary deceptions performed by the heroine herself to ensure, not her "fairy tale ending," but her very survival.

"Fitcher's Bird" has an unusually diverse and evocative series of "false brides": the skull in the window, which most closely resembles ATU 311's other constructed false brides; the heroine's sisters, concealed in the basket; and finally, the heroine herself, decked out in honey and feathers. Greenhill has perceptively discussed the heroine's facility at replicating herself in a variety of "avatars," who "speak for the heroine, and can allow her to be in two places at once, giving her alibis for her true actions. Yet each knows more about Fitcher than he does about her—or about himself" (2008, 158). I would like to extend Greenhill's argument to discuss the ways in which the heroine's "avatars"—both human and animal—serve not just as alibis and spectacles for Fitcher's benefit but also as dark mirrors of Fitcher himself. The heroine, deceptively playing the "true bride," sets up a series of false brides that reveal both her canny perception of what Fitcher wants for her and Fitcher's own true face.

The unmanning of Fitcher begins with the heroine's defeat of his egg test. By circumventing his trick, she acquires his power: by controlling the egg, "a queasy female symbol" (Marina Warner 1994, 255), she controls her sexual autonomy—particularly her fertility. With the egg, she also acquires the power to put her sisters back together and to raise them from the dead—thus, control of the egg means control over life itself, a reversal of Fitcher's death-dealing powers. She does not simply repair Fitcher's violent dismemberment of her sisters but claims his power for herself. Instead of the threat of involuntary dismemberment, she can voluntarily separate her identity into the avatars who can save her. Her mastery of the egg is what enables her transbiologically to transform, to hatch into Fitcher's bird.

Significantly, she acquires this mastery through deception; unlike other attempts to falsify the results of a true bride test—as in "Aschenputtel"—the heroine of "Fitcher's Bird" actually succeeds in beating the system. Unlike her sisters, she refuses to accede to Fitcher's demand that she keep the egg with her at all times; prefiguring her false bride tricks, she removes the egg from her person and hides it someplace safe before entering the forbidden chamber. If we read the egg as a symbol of female sexuality and fertility, this is the heroine's assertion that she will not allow male desire to reduce her to a sexual object or to control her fertility but will don or doff her sexuality and fertility as she sees fit. This refusal to allow Fitcher to define her is the necessary first step, if she is to enter the forbidden chamber and emerge unscathed.

Once within the chamber, she does not spill the egg; she subverts the gender role Fitcher is counting on her to play. Her use of the egg moves from subversion of gendered expectations into outright parody of the same; the pristine, unbloodied egg embodies the virtues expected of women, namely, ignorance and its cousin chastity.[5] Moreover, it neatly illustrates the transfer of power—the heroine's deceptive presentation of the clean egg mirrors Fitcher's deceptive presentation of himself as a harmless beggar. This hoists Fitcher on his own petard; the egg test designed to prove women's duplicity is defeated by a woman whose duplicity outpaces that of the deviser of the test.

The heroine's theft of Fitcher's power links her with the witches of witch-hunt propaganda who robbed men of their potency, both metaphoric and literal. It is worth noting that the Grimms call Fitcher a "Hexenmeister" (1971, 257), usually translated as "sorcerer" (Zipes 2002b, 155; Ashliman 1996–2011) or "wizard" (Manheim 1977, 158; Tatar 2004a, 202). However, in certain contexts, "Hexenmeister" also means "witch master"—one who detects witches and turns them over for punishment (Ellis 2004, 40). "Fitcher's Bird" thus complicates gendered constructions of witchcraft by valorizing the heroine's underhanded acquisition of male power; the story then compounds this by inflicting the traditional continental European punishment for witchcraft, death by burning, on Fitcher himself.

It is a common trope of antiwitchcraft propaganda that female witches are, above all things, devoted to robbing men, and men's institutions, of their power; it is no accident that roughly 80 percent of the known victims of the European witch hunts were female (Bever 2002, 956). Whether by desecrating the symbols of the patriarchal church, disturbing the sanctity of the patriarchal family, or, at its most laughably literal, robbing men of their penises,[6] the witch steals power from the males to whom it rightfully belongs. As Steven T. Katz puts it, "Women are anathematized and cast as witches because of the enduring grotesque fears they generate in respect of their putative abilities to control men and thereby coerce, for their own ends, male-dominated Christian society" (1994, 435).

The heroine can "unfix the limits of her own body," just as a witch can (Purkiss 1996, 125)—her deception of Fitcher involves creating the illusion that she is not where she is. She colludes with other women, her sisters, to deceive and overthrow male authority, just like a witches' coven. More overtly, she not only siphons off Fitcher's power but uses it to work her own magic spell: the resurrection of her sisters. This is not merely powerful magic; in Christian mythology, the ability to raise the dead is reserved for God alone. The heroine claims for herself powers that are reserved for patriarchal authority and uses them to overthrow that authority. The heroine thus defies not only normative femininity but also Christianity itself. Even more terrifying, she conceals her power behind a mask—multiple masks—of feigned feminine virtue in the form of a clean white egg. She becomes Fitcher's mirror image; a magic-worker who uses her stolen power to deceive. However, her work operates in the service of life, not death.

With this first act, the egg deception, she drains Fitcher of his magical power. However, it is not enough; she must continue to unman him, and finally destroy him, if she is to be safe. She therefore uses his assumptions of her as a controllable totality—an unbroken egg—to conceal her manifestations of multiple selves, in the form of the false brides.

The motif of the false bride is common in a number of folk narratives. The usual fairy-tale pattern is that a villainous woman deceives the husband by displacing the rightful bride, against the wishes of both bride and groom. Examples of this can be found in ATU 403 ("The White Bride and the Black Bride"), 408 ("The Love of Three Oranges"), 425 ("The Search for the Lost Husband"), 450 ("Little Brother, Little Sister"), and 533 ("The Goosegirl"). Nicole Belmont and Brunhilde Biebuyck have connected this form of the false bride motif with rural French wedding customs that involve hiding the bride and dressing up the bride's friends; "The 'donors of women' (the future bride's relatives and friends) express and play out their reticence toward the 'takers of women' (the future husband's kinship group and friends)" (1983, 186). Belmont and Biebuyck link the wedding rituals to ATU 403 stories; however, this is not necessarily an easy fit. In ATU 403 tales, the false bride is, as in most fairy tales, a villainous figure who seeks to replace the bride—unlike the false brides in the wedding ritual, who protect the bride and test the groom. Indeed, "Fitcher's Bird" scans more easily onto the wedding ritual; the heroine's sisters pose as the bride to fool Fitcher, and the heroine herself "expresses her reticence"—to say the least—toward the would-be bridegroom and his friends. It is worth noting that at the end of the story, it is not just Fitcher who is destroyed but also his wedding guests.

While the villainous false bride is very common in fairy tales, a false bride can also, as in the wedding ritual, function as the heroine's ally. In a "bedtrick" plot, the heroine herself arranges or constructs a false bride to deceive her intended. This deception may be in order to seduce an unwilling man (as in Shakespeare's *All's Well That Ends Well*), to hide the fact that the bride is not a virgin, or to escape the unwanted attentions of a villainous suitor. Wendy Doniger argues that bedtrick stories complicate Western notions of a unified identity: "Since parts of the person masquerade as other parts, to fragment the sexual identity is to open the way to a liberating infinity of possibilities, of selves, rather than to a constricting totality" (2000, 11). In stories where the bedtrick functions as an escape from a villain, that "infinity of possibilities" is liberating in the most literal way; by creating avatars of herself, the heroine achieves freedom. Moreover, the trick would not work unless the villain assumes that she is a single, unified entity, a totality that he can control; this fantasy of wholeness and unity underpins essentialist constructions of gender and sexuality. While the heroine of "Fitcher's Bird" does not pull an actual bedtrick, her construction of three false brides reproduces the structural logic of one.

The role of the first false bride is filled by the heroine's sisters, concealed in a basket and carried home by Fitcher: "He sat down to rest a while, but within moments one of the girls cried out from the basket: 'I'm looking out my little window, and I see that you're resting. Get a move on!'" (Tatar

2004a, 206). As in a bedtrick, the heroine uses another woman—in this case, two women whom she has herself reconstructed—to stand in for herself. Fitcher, "an expert in the art of division" (Tatar 2004b, 121), has violently dismembered the sisters; the heroine has reassembled and revived them with the power she has stolen from Fitcher and, significantly, restored their voices. The sisters—in contradistinction not just to other false brides but also to most same-sex siblings in fairy tales who act as antagonists—function as the heroine's avatars; they carry out her orders to Fitcher by driving him onward. There is something sexually suggestive in the description of the journey; the women ride on top, and they exhaust him so much that "the sweat began to pour down his forehead" (Tatar 2004a, 206).

A woman on top, barking orders, never allowing him to rest until she is satisfied—this is the misogynist nightmare of woman as shrew and succubus, and continues the unmanning of Fitcher that began with the heroine's defeat of the egg test. Moreover, this trick relies on collusion between women to defeat male sexual designs; Bacchilega locates the heroine's triumph over death not just in her bravery and mental acumen but in her "strong community ties" (1997, 110). Greenhill goes a step further and argues that the tale "present[s] *only* close female-female relationships as positive and supportive" (2008, 150; my emphasis). Fitcher, like patriarchy itself, dismembers women's bodies and destroys women's voices; the heroine defeats him by literally putting women back together and restoring their voices.[7]

If the first false bride is an invisible voice, the second false bride is a silent spectacle: "She took a skull with grinning teeth, crowned it with jewels and a garland of flowers, carried it upstairs, and set it down in an attic window, facing to the outside" (Tatar 2004a, 206). A favorite with illustrators, this is perhaps the most haunting, evocative image in the entire story. Fittingly, this trick invokes sight rather than sound; while the sisters' shouted orders play into patriarchal hatred of women's voices, the decorated skull turns patriarchal fantasy—the male gaze—against Fitcher.[8] This avatar of the heroine bears the closest resemblance to a traditional bedtrick. While the trick does not actually take place in a bed, the skull substitution illuminates Fitcher's true desires, which are ultimately necrophiliac. The heroine escapes Fitcher's bed by substituting a false bride who perfectly embodies Fitcher's fantasy: a bride as beautiful, obedient, and silent as the grave. Doniger remarks that a bedtrick requires the victim's self-delusion in order to work (2000, 8);

by catering to Fitcher's fantasy of a beautiful bride decorated in jewels and flowers who has obediently "swept the house all the way through" (Tatar 2004a, 206), the heroine parodies expectations of traditional femininity to lull him into a sense of complacency. Bedtrick victims, reproducing the logic of patriarchy, cannot tell the difference between one woman and another; the heroine of "Fitcher's Bird" has so undermined Fitcher's authority—to see, to name, to judge—that "he can't tell the difference between what looks like a woman and what actually is a woman" (Greenhill 2008, 161–62).

By using a souvenir of Fitcher's earlier murders,[9] the heroine creates not merely a fantasy spectacle for his benefit but also a reflection of his own true face; as a bridegroom, he brings only death, and therefore his true bride *is* death. The skull is truly "a bride in his own image" (Tatar 2004a, 206). By fragmenting herself, by using a skull to create her own "self-portrait" (Greenhill 2008, 161), the heroine leaves death behind in Fitcher's house, as a promise and a warning; his attempt to wed her will mean his destruction. The skull in wedding finery is a remnant of his past, a mirror of his present, and a prophecy of his future.

The third false bride, the Fitcher's bird disguise, is the most ambitious and dangerous deception; Fitcher can see and hear not just a fragment of the heroine but the heroine herself. As Tatar observes, "Her real art emerges in performance" (2004b, 122). Like a drag performer, the heroine self-consciously shakes up conventional notions of distinction. Fitcher, unable to conceive of a multiplicity that is not violent dismemberment, does not recognize in the speaking bird his true/false bride—he is the ideal victim of a bedtrick, because he deludes himself into believing that he is capable of ferreting out all deception on the part of women. The heroine utilizes the fairy tale's allowance of slippage between animal and human—here, the ability of animals in fairy tales to talk—as a conscious strategy. Rarely are fairy-tale characters more than startled by a talking animal, and most simply take eloquent beasts as no more surprising than chatty humans. Because of this, the heroine is able to convey the necessary information to Fitcher—namely, that she is at home, preparing for her upcoming nuptials. The heroine's choice of a bird costume, out of all the disguises available to her, marks the culmination of her first deception: the egg. Like the clean egg, Fitcher's bird appears to be an unsullied being of the natural world but is really an artifice. The Grimms, in their annotations for the story, attempt to link the bird disguise to two historical instances of women being tarred and feathered. However, this does not make much sense, as in both those cases the women had the bird "disguise" inflicted on them by others—and in the second case, the woman in question "had permitted herself to speak in disrespectful terms of the King" (Hunt 1884), so it was clearly a punishment for speaking out against patriarchal authority. The heroine of "Fitcher's Bird" assumes the disguise herself in order to escape patriarchal authority.

But this connection to tarring and feathering as a punishment does further reinforce the heroine's complex use of gender expectations to deceive her would-be husband—she in her tarred/honeyed-and-feathered state, the punished and degraded woman, is the opposite of what Fitcher has been led to believe about her by the egg trick, the sisters in the basket, and the skull in the window. However, everyone in the story responds to her not as a punished woman, but as a *bird*; first the wedding guests, then Fitcher, address her as "Fitcher's bird." By disguising herself as a bird, she is able to fly away.

The previous false brides have laid her alibis, but in order to escape, she must tell Fitcher one last lie to reestablish herself—or, rather, the skull in the window—as his true bride. Moreover, she must succeed in fooling both his eyes and ears simultaneously; he must not see her under the feathers, and he must not question the veracity of her song, where she sings that "[The bride] has swept the house all the way through, / And from the attic window, she's staring down at you" (Tatar 2004a, 205). All three false brides (the sisters, the skull, the bird's song) establish that Fitcher's true bride is at home where she should be, preparing for the wedding—and keeping an eye on her husband. But the heroine has so thoroughly undermined Fitcher's authority that, as Greenhill remarks, "when the youngest sister does watch him, as Fitcher's Bird, he doesn't recognize the fact. This reverses and subverts the patriarchal gaze, which is supposed to be directed by and from the male toward and against the female, not vice versa" (2008, 158).

Every one of the heroine's deceptions is an exercise in misdirection, all leading Fitcher to believe that she has been safely contained: the egg tells Fitcher that she has not been where she should not be, and the false brides claim that she is where she should be. But "Fitcher's Bird" is a tale about crossing boundaries and getting away with it; the heroine trespasses in the forbidden room, siphons off the power—both literally and figuratively—from her male antagonist, and, finally, blurs the distinction between the human and animal body.

The central narrative of "Fitcher's Bird" is one of tricking patriarchy out of its power and using that power to literally "re-member" and raise one's sisters from the dead—a striking metaphor for feminist scholarship. I have spent years studying this story and my own emotional reactions to it; eventually, I decided I wanted to mark on my skin what this story has meant to me. For my tattoo, I could have chosen the decorated skull. Yet, like most women, I chafe under the expectation to become a beautiful, grinning skeleton. Further, "decorated skull" is one of the stock tattoo images, and I wanted something unique. So I took a copy of "Fitcher's Bird" to the artist and asked that he read the story and draw me something. What he drew was a lovely minimalist depiction of the heroine in her bird costume; she is drawn as a swan, the wing cupping her body. I loved the interplay of concealment and revelation, the lie that tells the truth. The heroine of "Fitcher's Bird" transgresses normative gender roles, refuses conventional heterosexual marriage, collapses the categories of heroine and witch, forges an alliance with other women, and turns the fears and fantasies of the patriarchy against it. In the end, "Fitcher's Bird" is no bride at all but a "thing with feathers" (Tatar 2004b, 122) who flies into a story of her own devising, a story of liberation; as a queer, feminist scholar, I look at her and see my own face.

NOTES

1. It is no accident that "wedding" is the final function in Vladimir Propp's system (1968, 63–64).

2. Ruth Bottigheimer (1986, 116), discussing the attitudes about gender in the German-speaking realms when the Grimms were active and how these attitudes affected their editing of the fairy tales, notes that "silence as a positive feminine attribute had gained wide acceptance" by the 1830s, with the 1860s–70s as the high point.

3. See Tatar (1987, 161).

4. For a related tale type, ATU 955 stories (such as "The Robber Bridegroom" and "Mr. Fox") likewise celebrate the heroine's ingenuity at outwitting a murderous fiancé.

5. This is most amply illustrated by Chaucer's Virginia, in "The Physician's Tale," who is so innocent she is not even aware that she is a virgin. For a more detailed discussion of the "epistemology of ignorance" as it relates to women's sexuality, see Nancy Tuana (2004).

6. The famous witch-hunting manual *Malleus Maleficarum* (1486), by Heinrich Kramer and James Sprenger, gives numerous examples. See Walter Stephens (2002) and Edward Bever (2002) for more information on witchcraft and impotence beliefs.

7. See Bottigheimer (1986) on the Grimms' reduction of women's direct speech in the tales.

8. See Greenhill (2008) for an extended discussion of the male gaze in the story.

9. I would like to thank Emilie Anderson-Grégoire for pointing out that the heroine's use of the skull of one of Fitcher's previous victims can be read as an act of revenge by and for the murdered women of Fitcher's house.

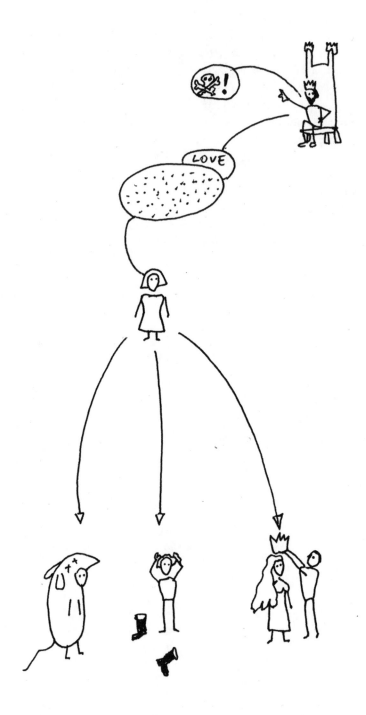

10

Becoming-Mouse,
Becoming-Man

The Sideways Growth
of Princess Mouseskin

JOY BROOKE FAIRFIELD

"Princess Mouseskin" is a fairy tale that appeared in the first edition of the brothers Grimm's collection in 1812 but was removed from the second edition in 1819, ostensibly due to its similarity to a literary French tale published in 1697, Charles Perrault's "Peau d'Âne," or "Donkeyskin" (Zipes 2002b, 744). While "Princess Mouseskin" shares certain motifs with ATU 510B, "Peau d'Asne," the tale is classified as a variant of ATU 923, "Love Like Salt" and could be described most accurately as a combination of the two traditional tale types (Ashliman 1987, 190). The Grimms attribute "Princess Mouseskin" to their close friends, the bourgeois, literate women of the Wild family who may have been influenced by Perrault's written version as well as other more common retellings of these two tale types (Bottigheimer 2009, 48–50). Its reincorporation by Jack Zipes into his 2002 edition, *The Complete Fairy Tales of the Brothers Grimm* (in the "Omitted Tales"), presents the opportunity to revisit this intriguing tale from a contemporary perspective. Viewed in this context, we can read it not just as an empowering success story of a persecuted daughter but as a subtle and haunting vision of a queer child growing not *up* but *sideways*, expanding into and claiming as her own new territories of subjective, embodied experience. This chapter focuses first on the character of Princess Mouseskin as a queer child ejected from her family of origin and second on the repeated performances of incomplete becoming that she stages on her own body over the course of her adventures, including becoming mouse, becoming man, and becoming king. Within the short tale, the heroine repeatedly enacts not total but *partial* transformations of self across lines of gender and species differentiation, inviting a methodological approach to the tale that utilizes queer and transgender theory.

The story begins when a king, curious about who loves him the most, challenges his three daughters to describe their filial devotion. The first says her love is larger than the whole kingdom, the second declares that she loves him more than all the jewels in the world, and the third attests earnestly that she loves him more than salt. Unhappy with the latter answer, he sends his youngest daughter to the forest to be put to death. However, the servant ordered to kill her instead spares her life and offers to travel with her in exile. She declines his companionship but requests a garment made of a mouse's skin, which he provides. She travels directly to a nearby court where, passing as a man, she becomes servant to the prince. After some time he becomes suspicious of her origins and her twin identities as a woman and princess are revealed. The prince, smitten with her beauty, declares her his bride. The princess's father, who no longer recognizes his daughter, attends the wedding only to find that all his food is served unsalted. When he complains, she reveals her identity, and he finally understands his error. They are reunited in peace.

While the story is not well known, its resemblances to more recognizable cousins render its motifs and characters strangely familiar. The beginning of the tale follows the structure of ATU 923 ("Love Like Salt"), variants of which appear in English, Austrian, and German folktales (Ashliman 1996–2011). The motif of salt as an insufficient measure of filial love can also be found as a subplot in the Grimms' "The Goose Girl at the Spring" (Zipes 2002b, 518). Disinheritance and banishment of a princess due to her inability to describe her love for her father has been etched into the classical canon in Shakespeare's *King Lear*, widely known to have borrowed from the ATU 923 tale type (Dundes 1982, 232). The princess's attempt to find protection and anonymity through donning an animal skin links her to tales like the Grimms' *Allerleirauh* or "All Kinds of Fur" (ATU 510B, discussed by Margaret Yocom in chapter 4), both of which feature a young girl taking flight into the animal realm as an escape from incestuous desire. From a postmodern, queer standpoint, both of these tale types could be reclassified as "daddy stories." Unlike many fairy tales that prioritize the mother-daughter relationship, "daddy stories" place the father-daughter dyad in the foreground, with the mother either dead or mysteriously absent. While ATU 510B tells of paternal overvaluation via incestuous desire, ATU 923 involves paternal undervaluation via exile. The notorious incest-themed tales are rich sites for fairy-tale scholarship and have been approached from many theoretical angles, including psychoanalytic, anthropological, and feminist.[1] Alan Dundes suggests that ATU 923, the exile story, may in fact be a watered-down version of the darker incestuous tale: "The 'love like salt' plot appears to be a weakened form of the folktale in which a 'mad' father tries to marry his own daughter" (1982, 325). Maria Tatar also links the two "daddy story" tale types, noting that in all cases the fathers are "responsible for the flight of their daughters from home into nature. That flight into the woods, with its concomitant degradation of the heroine into a creature of nature, remains the lasting mark of the father's attempted incestuous violation" (1992, 133).

Though its ATU 510B lineage links the story with a long history of sexually vulnerable heroines on the run, "Princess Mouseskin" has no overt incestuous content. This chapter will set aside the question of paternal incest and instead consider this "daddy story" as an example of a young girl internally negotiating her relationship with masculine embodiment and the patriarchal power that seems to flow from male bodies. From the title, we already know that the story concerns questions of size. A mouse is an archetypal figuration of "smallness" in the Western imagination, and a princess is traditionally the smallest person in the royal family. A story involving a mouselike princess is an invitation to consider the effects of the commonly recognized statistical difference in body mass between men and women that results in the figuration of women as "small." We also know from the title that the tale will concern questions of surfaces. A mouse's skin is different from a girl's skin. A girl's skin is different from her father's skin. Is the surface texture of one's body somehow definitional to one's character? Does it determine the power and agency one can hold? This analysis of "Princess Mouseskin" will take as a compass these questions of corporeal size and surface. Rather than focusing on the interpersonal boundary-crossing event of incest, this story—and thus this chapter—provides a meditation on the permeability of intrapersonal boundaries. The concept of incest is, in part, about combining things that shouldn't merge, about disregarding social structural and kinship restrictions. "Princess Mouseskin" is an investigation of different kinds of boundary transgressions and the growth they can enable.

Indeed, size is one of the elements that distinguishes this tale from its sister stories; it is less than one page long. Its concise, mouselike structure performs smallness while simultaneously unfolding ideas of size thematically. Much like the salt metaphor that the princess offers her father, the tale itself could be described as "a meager thing" (Zipes 2002b, 616). Like many small things, the tale moves quite quickly. The narrative crosses latitudes and years in a few short paragraphs; we are surprised to learn at the end of the brief tale that the king thought his daughter "had died a long time ago." How many years of disguised service did the princess give to the neighboring prince before becoming his bride? Her transformations also occur swiftly and without magical justifications, as though any young woman could shed skins as easily as a snake: "She unwrapped the mouseskin and her golden hair streamed down" (616).

While many variants of ATU 510B utilize the motif of animal skin as disguise, "Princess Mouseskin" alone invokes the skin surface and texture as indicative of gender. In other versions of these tale types, the heroine uses her animal-hide garment to pass as a poor woman ("Donkeyskin"), an old woman ("The Goose Girl at the Spring"), or an animal ("All Kinds of Fur"). In all of these stories, any change to the surface of a young woman's skin (or even the concealment of that surface) is immediately linked to social debasement. This decline in status emphasizes the cultural value placed on the texture and appearance of the skin, particularly in young women; any loss of smoothness and regularity results in loss of social prestige. In all variants, the heroine's animal skin disguises her as an entity farther down the hierarchy of social empowerment, thus shrouding her in the safety of anonymity. Her safety is dependent on her self-debasement. However, only in this tale does it also facilitate her self-nomination as a male. Reading this tale in concert with its variants, are we asked to view male skin as a debased version of female skin? Or perhaps we can read her transformation into a male servant—a simultaneous movement downward in class status but upward in then-current gender empowerment—as the first indication that her journey inherently challenges and cuts across traditional delineations of social power structures.

Female to male cross-dressing is uncommon but not unheard of in the Grimms' tales. In "The Twelve Huntsmen" (ATU 884, "The Forsaken Fiancée: Service as Menial") a scorned bride collects eleven look-alikes and equips her former fiancé with a pack of cross-dressed huntsmen. In "The Two King's Children" (also ATU 884, mixed with 313C, "The Girl Helps the Hero Flee"), a powerful young princess on the run momentarily transforms herself into a pastor preaching in the pulpit of her beloved, whom she has transformed into a church. Both of these heroines use their sojourn in men's clothing as a way to regain or retain their betrothed. Victoria Flanagan, in *Into the Closet*, aptly identifies female to male cross-dressing in children's literature as a sometimes-successful play for power in a patriarchal society: "The societal norms that generally govern feminine behavior are temporarily displaced by the masculine disguise, allowing the subjectivities of these heroines to evolve through a dialogic exchange between masculine and feminine subject positions" (2008, 14). Though other motives for cross-dressing exist, this dialogic exchange is an apt way to describe the strategic deployment of cross-dressing in "The Twelve Huntsmen" and "The Two Kings Children." In both stories, women dress as men in order to do things that only men were socially sanctioned to do: preach and hunt. Their sojourns as "men" are strategic efforts to rise temporarily in status and help the heroine "grow up," namely through securing marriage.

Princess Mouseskin, however, begins her tale in flight, seeking refuge rather than a husband and physical safety instead of wedded bliss. Her repeated transformations are not in pursuit of a societal goal or an attempt to rise through an established power structure via gender disguise. Rather, her fugitive status impels her into what Gilles Deleuze and Felix Guattari call "a line of flight," or a movement that cuts through established borders and classifications and, in so doing, encourages the dissolution of recognized territories (1987, 3). Unlike the characters in "The Twelve Huntsmen" and "The Two Kings Children," Princess Mouseskin isn't a cross-dresser in search of the pleasure or power promised by the performance of manhood but a transgender child, defined by Susan Stryker as one whose identities can "cross-over, cut across, move between, or otherwise queer socially constructed sex/gender boundaries" (quoted in Flanagan 2008, 12).

"Sideways growth," a concept formulated by Kathryn Bond Stockton, is a form of personal evolution in which meaning and matter are accumulated laterally. More than a refusal to grow up, growing sideways "questions developmental models based on one's steady progress towards genital maturity" and in doing so destabilizes gender, species, age, and the power structures typically associated with these qualities (2004, 281). Stockton considers sideways growth specifically significant to queer subjects, who often eschew the traditional Western trajectory of school, then work, then marriage, then children. Blessed and cursed to find themselves at the edge of social legibility, queer subjects (and queer families) grow outside of, and in spite of, the reproductive imperative. Sideways growth challenges linear, hierarchical, and filiational models of human development and proposes modes of personal change that are additive rather than serial: perhaps little girls need not give up prior versions of themselves in pursuit of new ones. Stockton challenges us to consider personal growth not as a smoothly unfolding inevitability or the progression through a series of stages but as the accidental and intentional accretion of diverse textures that grow in layers, rubbing their smooth and rough edges against each other.

Sideways growth is a kind of transformation that Deleuze and Guattari might describe as "becoming" (a particular meaning they signal with the use of a hyphen, as in becoming-animal or becoming-woman)—always in motion, yet nonteleological in aim. "To become is not to progress or regress along a series . . . becoming produces nothing other than itself" (1987, 238). Becoming is a process in which a subject enters into association with something (real or imagined) and is changed: mid–sexual act, a couple could be described as not human but "becoming-animal." Singing to herself while doing laundry, a mother might be a "becoming-bird," a young girl riding her horse a "becoming-centaur." Becoming follows the pull of desire, specifically the desire to assemble with, yet rather than consolidating power through this assembling, "becoming" always produces greater diversity of forms and connections between forms. While Deleuze and Guattari deny the possibility of "becoming-man" "because man is the molar entity par excellence" (292), in the context of this fairy tale, becoming-man describes a movement toward trans-identification. Given the great distance between Mouseskin's juvenile female body and the molar entity known as "man," this becoming transports her toward the minoritized state of gender ambiguity, while still presenting new possibilities inside her own subjective experience.

Quoting Marcel Proust, Deleuze and Guattari (1987, 271) describe girls as "fugitive beings," simultaneously the most vulnerable to the exercise of external power, yet also well-equipped to enact powerful self-transformations, often through and on their own flesh. Princess Mouseskin can perhaps be seen not as a fugitive being but as a "fugitive becoming." Forced out of her father's homeland on a line of flight toward the unknown, she must embrace the irregular, unpredictable process of sideways growth and the shifting vision of selfhood it produces.

Princess Mouseskin is the youngest of three unmarried girls in an era when marriage happened as early as possible to secure patrilinear progressions of power and ownership (Lévi-Strauss 1969, 23–27). In short, she is a child. Stockton invites us to consider the claim that "all children are Q." Suspicious of the "all too elastic properties of this word [queer]," she makes no claim regarding their sexual orientation but rather situates children on the whole as a "species of strangeness" that she refers to as "Q," connected to the queer through their similarly nongenerative sexuality (2004, 282). Historically, childhood sexuality and homosexuality have both been known to generate anxiety in dominant culture, and like queer adults, children are often seen as the logical "Other" to the sexually "normal" adult. "Queers, one observes, trail children behind them or alongside them, as if they are wedded, one to another, in unforeseen ways. . . . Scratch a child, you will find a queer" (278). The queer union of homosexuality and childhood has nothing to do with sexual relations but rather reflects their shared status as fugitives from the well-entrenched system of heterosexual relationality and reproduction. Deleuze and Guattari see this childhood queerness manifested as heightened ease with places of transition and "in-betweenness": "Thus girls do not belong to an age-group, sex, order, or kingdom, they slip in everywhere, between orders, acts, ages, sexes" (1987, 277). While her age isn't specified, Princess Mouseskin is likely prepubescent at the tale's beginning. A member of this queer, slippery underclass, she is not gay, but—as Stockton describes all children born into the heteropatriarchy—she is also "not-yet-straight" (2004, 282). When her character is scratched, her queerness is visible.

The pivotal scratch at the beginning of the tale is her father's request that she describe her love: "A king had three daughters, and he wanted to know which one loved him most. So he summoned them to him and began asking" (Zipes 2002b, 616). The king positions himself as a jealous single parent, eclipsing any memory of the girls' absent mother, and demands from his daughters not physical affection but words. Through this maternal substitution and invitation to language, he fulfills the legislative and prohibitive function of the Symbolic Father as depicted by Jacques Lacan in his "Seminar on the Psychoses" (1993, 305–10).[2] Her older sisters have internalized the symbolic order of the father and answer his question diplomatically in terms of real-world commodities; they know how to speak their father's language. Mouseskin, however, responds sensually, using embodied metaphorical figuration to compare her love to salt. Taste is a primal realm of pleasure, and the sense that most closely links the girl to her absent mother whose milk she tasted; unlike her elder sisters, she still speaks her mother tongue. The princess is perhaps too young to understand that sensual pleasures have no place in her widowed father's court. Salt is debased because it is too common; there is too much of it, including its profound availability in the human body. It is the dominant flavor of the body's excretions (sweat, tears, urine, semen), and, as such, has uncontrollable sexual and abject resonances. Salt also conjures up the fleshiness of the human tongue, the strongest muscle in the body proportional to its size and the organ that links language capacity to sense perception. To the youngest princess, love is not about riches or power but about pleasure: the pleasure of the body as well as its tongue-birthed words.

Given the link between father-daughter relationships in Shakespeare's *King Lear* and ATU 923 (Dundes 1982, 232), this same tension between the body and its words arises in the response given by Cordelia, also the youngest of three girls, to King Lear's similar request to describe filial love:

I cannot heave
My heart into my mouth. I love your majesty
According to my bond; nor more nor less. (Shakespeare 1988, 911)

Cordelia confesses that she does not yet know how to use her mouth for the manipulation of others through figurative words, as her sisters can.

Her tongue is used solely for tasting. As their tales prove, both Cordelia and Mouseskin love their fathers dearly, but they are naive. They have not yet learned, as their sisters have, that love is a realm in which women must compete for the attentions of men using the tool of language.

Unlike Cordelia, who refuses to join the game of linguistic flattery, Mouseskin follows her sisters' example and attempts to represent, through use of figuration, her filial love. However, she deploys a metaphor that her father does not understand: "The third said she loved him more than salt" (Zipes 2002b, 616). There are many potentially flattering interpretations of this comparison. Perhaps the princess is particularly fond of salt; young children typically appreciate the flavor even more than their adult counterparts. Or perhaps she sees her father as sharing its many potent qualities: he enhances everything he touches; he has the power to preserve the past; he is necessary for the sustenance of human life; he pervades the human body as well as the natural world. But the king is unable to see these interpretive possibilities and is, instead, "furious that she compared her love for him to such a meager thing" (616). Her metaphor, like her prepubescent body, is too small. Stuck in a narrow worldview dominated by the measurably commodifiable, the king is unable to see through the meagerness of the analog to the love implied by her analogy. The princess is punished for her father's inability to understand her.

Stockton sees metaphor itself as a tool of queering. In the creation of a metaphor, the thing being described is linked with a foreign body through imaginative lines of flight that can cut across categories of size, species, and social significance. Metaphor moves laterally, like dream logic, and linkages made through this kind of figuration often have a materiality and lasting power far beyond the moment of their verbal conjuring. Love and red roses are hard to unlink—they stick together stubbornly in the Euro–North American mind as if conjoined. Stockton refers to this process as "fattening up a concept through the use of a metaphor" (2004, 279). Not only does Mouseskin choose a queer metaphor to describe her love for her father, but she also reveals that she is learning how to use the queer tool of metaphor itself. Fattening up the concept of love and paternity with the concept of salt, her use of metaphor at the beginning of the tale is evidence of the onset of her queer growth, her "growing sideways":

We are going to see that concepts of the queer child demand that we talk in terms of growing sideways. If you think about it, metaphors, in some respects, are themselves a sideways growth. They "grow" meanings ("increase [them] in quantity, size and degree") by putting people and things rather oddly beside themselves. So, when the gospels say, for example, that "Christians are sheep," we compare their features. We put a sheep body next to a Christian and "find" the Christian inside of the sheep, growing, expanding the meaning of a Christian. (2004, 279)

In her metaphor, the princess has put her love for her father beside the image of salt, placing the three signifiers (daughter, father, salt) in a strange clump of unstable, sensual meanings. More than not *understanding* her metaphor or finding it meager, the king is disturbed by the queerness of this particular metaphor and the clump of meaning it generates. He intuits, perhaps correctly, that Mouseskin's meaning-making threatens his power and autonomy.

At the beginning of the tale, the king, seeking a more stable subject position, has requested from his daughters a little ego bolstering. He needs reassurance that he is a good father and ruler, or, in fairy-tale words, that he is big and strong and powerful. His first daughter's comparison situates him in a comfortably geographic relationship to his large landholdings ("she loved him more than the whole kingdom"). His second daughter places him in the safe halls of his immense treasury ("she loved him more than all the jewels and pearls in the world"). Salt, in contrast, is not nearly as comfortable a neighbor. First, grains of salt are "meager," and no self-respecting monarch wants to think of himself as small in size or potency. Moreover, it is also an unstable substance. Salt dissolves in water, where it vanishes, integrating completely with its surroundings. Disappearance and total assimilation are threatening to the body and kingdom of a patriarch, particularly one with no male offspring and thus an uncertain heir. What will happen to the regulated boundaries of his landholdings and treasury (acknowledged by his two elder daughters) if the uncontrollable element of salt is introduced by the youngest? Just as metaphor "moves us across the distance between two separate concepts" (Stockton 2004, 280), salt transports and bridges difference. It has no respect for boundaries and with its negative charge pulls water through semipermeable membranes (through the process of osmosis) in an attempt to create equilibrium. The king's boundaries of body, bounty, and territory brook no such incursions; he is not interested in the radical equilibrium between himself and his daughter that her metaphor suggests.

The young princess's offering is not just insufficient ("meager") but it is also *too much* (fattening, expansive, queer). Salt itself, through interaction with water, fattens up the human body. An excessive amount of salt implies an excess of consumption and carries along resonances of gluttony and insatiability. A small princess should have a voracious appetite neither for salty food nor for her salt-like father. Rather than proving her filial love, her metaphor exposes her inappropriate desire for *more*. Hearkening back to the incest narrative of ATU 510B, we wonder for a moment if the shadow of incestuous desire in "Princess Mouseskin" runs not from father to daughter but from daughter to father: "I want to eat you up," the small girl seems to say, "for you are delicious." Rather than growing up progressively from small to tall, hungry Princess Mouseskin is veering sideways toward inappropriate, incorporative growth. Perhaps he is not afraid that she loves him too little, but rather that she loves him too much. What affect could this love, and indeed this reverse-incestuous desire, have on his body and body politic? While she may be a prepubescent princess, the potential threat she poses to the intact margin of the king's body and kingdom warrants her death sentence. Princess Mouseskin, like many queer children before and after her, is exiled from the family home for the simple act of not fitting in.

As a way of managing this psychic experience of not fitting, Mouseskin seeks out an article of clothing that could not possibly fit: "The princess demanded nothing except a garment made out of a mouse skin. When he fetched it for her, she wrapped herself in the skin" (Zipes 2002b, 616). While it is possible to imagine a small girl successfully wearing a cloak made of the skin of a donkey or even a cat as in other variants, a garment made of a single mouse skin is pure fantasy—or pure metaphor. Stockton describes children as having "a knack for metaphorical substitution, letting one object stand in for another, by means of which they reconceive relationships to time" (2004, 279). In this case, Mouseskin uses this act of substitution (fitting in at home/fitting into a mouse's skin) as a way to reframe her relationship to the temporal experience of growing up. She reconceives the journey to adulthood not as a linear, time-bound progression but as an absorptive, incorporative process that can expand and contract dramatically, like the hide of the mouse, thus destabilizing the boundaries of her skin, species, and gender.

Stockton would describe the princess's sojourn in the mouse's skin as "the interval of animal," during which the child can carve out time for herself wherein normative identities do not yet hold sway: "[The animal] becomes a metaphor—actually a metaphor claimed to be material—where the child can legally hide" (2004, 282). The temporal pause that takes place within the interval of animal resonates with Judith Halberstam's notion of "queer time" in which gays and lesbians who participate in queer subcultural activity expand the period of time prior to long-term partnership and reproduction, an expansion that "facilitates community formation and offers alternative life narratives" (2005, 175).[3] Mouseskin uses the queer time of her interval of animal to hide from her father's paternalistic rage as well as from the amorous intentions of the servant who wishes to follow her into the forest. Her dismissal of his offer of male companionship is a rejection of the heteronormative paradigm, and her request for the animal skin displays her preference for something new, strange, and potentially transformative. She rejects the proposed partnership and instead lingers in this queer time, wrapped in her queer new garment, in search of alternative life narratives.

But wrapping herself in a mouse's skin is a necessarily incomplete transfiguration. Like the Noh mask that reveals the actor's jowls beneath the illusion of the character's visage, the mouse-skin garment reveals at the same time it conceals (Schechner 1985, 6–8). The princess is not attempting to stage a deception but rather ritualistically layering a new, chosen identity on top of her existing self. This layering artfully bypasses the self-fracturing act of rejecting her "old self" in favor of a new one and instead allows her to begin an accumulation of identities. Deleuze and Guattari, like Stockton, also see in children the creative potential for diverting the sequential progress narrative of growing up, specifically through wedding seemingly unrelated entities: "It is as though, independent of the evolution carrying them towards adulthood, there were room in the child for other becomings, unnatural nuptials, outside the programmed body" (1987, 273).

The transition from prepubescent princess to mouselike creature is not an act of magic but of the human will; it is less a transformation than an active "becoming." Mouseskin doesn't subsume her humanity completely but rather engages in "unnatural nuptials" with a creature of the natural world in order to take flight from the programmed body.[4] Deleuze and Guattari describe the "becoming-animal" as between two thresholds of identity, a "fiber stretching from a human to an animal" that, in its very inbetweenness, constitutes a line of flight away from the known (1987, 249). The becoming-animal is active rather than static, composite rather than pure, an assemblage that breaks down the distinction between ontology and imitation: "Becomings-animal are neither dreams nor phantasies. They are perfectly real. But which reality is at issue here? For if becoming-animal does not consist in playing animal or imitating animal, it is clear that the human does not "really" become an animal . . . becoming produces nothing other than itself. What is real is the act of becoming" (238).

In wrapping herself with the mouse's skin, Mouseskin is staging an intervention on her body with her body, not growing up, but growing sideways into a dynamically in-between creature that is none other than herself. Never *being* but always *becoming*, she hovers at the edges of legibility and definability, an embodiment of what Mikhail Bakhtin describes as the grotesque:

> The grotesque body . . . is a body in the act of becoming. It is never finished, never completed; it is continually built, created and builds and creates another body. Moreover, the body swallows the world and is itself swallowed by the world. This is why the essential role belongs to those parts of the grotesque body which outgrows its own self, transgressing its own body, in which it conceives a new, second body: the bowels and the phallus. (1984, 317)

Similar to Deleuze and Guattari's becoming-animal, which "always involves a pack, a band, a population, a peopling" (1987, 239), Bakhtin's grotesque creature is always a multiple. In donning its skin, Princess Mouseskin swallows and is swallowed up by the mouse, creating a double body for herself that grows sideways—at once pregnant and cancerous, natural and unnatural. She has become a clump of mouse qualities and girl qualities, a seemingly undifferentiable mound of meaning, just as her father had feared.

To Bakhtin's list of novel, grotesque becoming-body parts ("the bowels and the phallus"), Mouseskin adds the salt-tasting, word-uttering human tongue that led her into this mess, as well as her little mouse's tail, the queerest of appendages, that now trails the transfigured princess. As a proto-phallus, her new tail presages her impending flight across the gender line, which never constitutes a move toward consolidated, patriarchal power, but rather toward the becoming-grotesque of the world of in-between.

The inside of an animal's hide is an abject cave of blood and fleshiness. Like Little Red Riding Hood swallowed by the wolf, Mouseskin finds herself enclosed in a space, tight but hollow, like the grotto-esque cavern of the womb. Bakhtin describes the image of "a pregnant hag" as the epitome of the grotesque: an intimate proximity of life and death, sexuality and mortification. "It is ambivalent. It is a pregnant death. A death that gives birth" (1984, 25). The princess, having barely escaped her own death, chooses self-enclosure within the recently dead mouse and, in doing so, places life and death uncomfortably close. In pressing the sticky inside of the dead animal's skin against the outside of her live little girl skin, she binds herself—this time literally—to the salty products of the uncontrollable body. Her transformation into this image of the feminine grotesque brings to fruition the queer premonition of boundary dissolution the king felt upon hearing his daughter's salt analogy. But what was a threat to her father is in fact more comfortable for the princess than the familiar, yet oppressive, structures of her childhood home. Like Bakhtin's grotesque, she has outgrown her own self and must conceive within her flesh a new self, the fruit of her unnatural nuptials with an animal's hide. While her father may aspire to a "classical body," described by Mary Russo in her work on the female grotesque as "monumental, static, closed, and sleek, corresponding to the aspirations of bourgeois individualism," the princess is on a quest for a "protruding, extending, secreting body" that is both her own and "connected to the rest of the world" (1994, 63). The princess is a fugitive from her father, but now her body itself attempts to take flight from its program into new ways of becoming.

An old belief, perhaps known to the tellers of this story, holds that a female mouse can become pregnant in the presence of salt without need of male insemination. Recorded in antiquity by Aristotle (1987, 37) and more recently by Jungian psychoanalyst Ernest Jones, this belief was related to a general mapping of salt with fertility and semen.[5] Fattened up on her metaphor of salt and self-impregnated into the mouse's skin, our princess, like this mythological mouse, has no need for a male. She sends the servant back to her father the king and decides to step into these masculine roles—first servant, then king—herself. Mouseskin doesn't want a man; she wants to *be* a man.

The princess's decision to trade her skin for a mouse's skin prefigures her later choice to become a man. The desire to trade skin resonates with the traditional transsexual narrative of wrong embodiment, described by Jay Prosser as "the feeling of sexed body dysphoria profoundly and subjectively experienced" (1998, 69). While some transgender people authentically experience this sense of being in "the wrong skin," it is also a rhetoric that has been used strategically in order to produce a specific psychiatric diagnosis that will facilitate access to the medical interventions desired.[6] Many contemporary trans theorists question the usefulness of the wrong-body narrative as described by Prosser, pointing out that notions of right embodiment and wrong embodiment still subscribe to a binary conception of gender identity, leaving no space in between. Alexis Shotwell suggests an alternate genesis of this "wrong" feeling: "We might feel like we are in the wrong body because there is something wrong with our world" (2009, 63). In forced exile from her homeland, something is clearly wrong with Princess Mouseskin's world. Her desire to "trade skins" arises not from the sensation of being "trapped in a wrong body, of being wrongly encased" (Prosser 1998, 69) but rather from being trapped in the wrong world. Given the options of submitting to the patriarchal system of her homeland or setting out for new worlds wearing new skin, she chooses the latter. She is able to find safety not through "fitting in at home" but through constructing an even more illegible self on which she imposes further exile—first from her species and later from her gender and class.

The description of her transition from becoming-animal to becoming-male is quite concise: "When he [the servant] fetched it for her, she wrapped herself in the skin and went straight to a neighboring king. Once there, she pretended to be a man and asked the king to employ her" (Zipes 2002b, 616). The brevity of this passage echoes the efficiency of poetry, and we peer in vain to see what happens in the space between the sentences. It is possible to assume that the mouse-skin garment magically transforms her aspect into that of a man (and indeed, the Grimms' stories are full of magic cloaks).[7] However, there is no textual evidence of magic, and, in fact, the story does not claim that she takes on the physical appearance of a man at all, but rather the behavior of one: she "pretends." Here Princess Mouseskin participates in Judith Butler's model of gender as performance rather than core identity or set of attributes, recognizing that "gender is always a doing" ([1990] 1999, 33). The mouse's skin does not transform her but acts as costume, one that enables her to "do" the male gender. While she was previously girl-becoming-mouse, now she is girl-becoming-mouse-doing-man.

Butler has been critiqued for making the performance of gender sound more flexible than contemporary culture actually allows. Society is deeply invested in gender performances, and powerful disciplinary systems have been developed to produce the sensation that gender is innate or natural. Because of these various systems, reality rarely permits a subject to simply wake up one morning and decide to stop performing or to completely and forever alter her gender performance. Butler herself advocates not for a gender-free or gender-fluid utopian society but for increased attempts to make "gender trouble" through "the mobilization, subversive confusion, and proliferation of precisely those constitutive categories that seek to keep gender in its place by posturing as the foundational illusions of identity" ([1990] 1999, 44). Like Stockton, Butler calls for a lateral expansion, and crossing over, of categories. Like Deleuze and Guattari, Butler dreams of increased mobilization through hitching rides on lines of flight that take off from known places of gendered performance and flee toward the unknown.

Does Princess Mouseskin actually "pass" as a mouse? Does she actually "pass" as a man? The question of "passing" haunts drag performance and transgender embodiment. Its emphasis, like the wrong-embodiment narrative, is linked to a cultural fear of the in-between and illegible, which is often read as monstrous. In certain social scenarios, failure to pass successfully can result in discrimination or violence against transgender people and cross-dressers. However, the world of fairy tales is a space where the "foundational illusions of identity" are even more illusory (Butler [1990] 1999, 44). According to Flanagan, "this remove from contemporary consensus reality" enables fictional heroines to "use cross-dressing in a metaphoric or strategic way that comments upon the constructedness of gender in the real world occupied by the readers or viewers, as opposed to directly reflecting or recreating this condition" (2008, 15). The ease with which Princess Mouseskin can cross the gender line seems to mock the ease with which she could have been born a boy rather than a girl, emphasizing the arbitrary nature of the power differential that results from distinct gendered embodiment. Our heroine has already demonstrated her knack for "metaphorical substitution" by translating a badly fitting home life to a badly fitting animal hide (Stockton 2004, 279). Here she substitutes the geographic step away from her birth home with a sidelong step away from the identity of her birth gender and in doing so seeks not to pass as male but to annex new latitudes of subjective, embodied experience. A child takes a lock of hair and holds it between her nose and her mouth saying, "Look, I have a mustache." For a queer fairy-tale child who doesn't fit her prescribed gender identity, the brown fur of a field mouse resembles, closely enough, the hirsute secondary sex characteristics of the male to facilitate a successful performance.

This performance of masculinity is her second enactment of incomplete becoming. She is growing sideways into "manhood" with only a furry coat and impersonation skills to disguise her. While this may be another bad fit by traditional standards, the princess is becoming bolder about not fitting in. Her body is becoming a collage of various identities and costumes acquired along her route and assembled into a version of selfhood that surrounds without enclosing her. This loose collection of attributes aligns with a Deleuzean notion of subjectivity, one that eschews the solitary, centered self in favor of a more mobile and intersubjective experience: "A body is not defined by the form that determines it nor as a determinate substance or subject or by the organs it possesses or the functions it fulfills. On a plane of consistency, *a body is defined only by a longitude and a latitude*" (Deleuze and Guattari 1987, 260; emphasis in original). For Deleuze and Guattari, longitudes measure not only geographic space but also the speeds at which they can be crossed, and latitudes measure potential intensities of bodily and emotional experiences. In this system then, a body is something that moves at variable speeds, in many directions, across various territories, following multiple lines of flight. A body is also an assemblage that can touch and be touched by others in variably intense ways. Princess Mouseskin's layered embodiment, combining genders and species, aligns with this notion of selfhood. She refuses to be defined by her organs (her female tongue, her mouselike tail, her lack of male genitalia). Rather, she creates her body and her shifting experience of self by moving through space and pushing outward toward new ways to affect and be affected by others.

The next latitude annexed by the princess after manhood is the space of servanthood. Service is a new affective experience for a princess accustomed to being served by others, but, nevertheless, she is able to slip from being served to becoming-servant in the space of two brief sentences. As the prince's manservant, her main task is to assist him in getting into and out of his boots: "In the evening, whenever she pulled off his boots, he always tossed them at her head" (Zipes 2002b, 616). This ritual is unexplained and somewhat mysterious. Her evening duty as manservant further solidifies her status as male. She is engaging in the "stylized repetition" described by Butler as constitutive of gender, for "the action of gender requires a performance that is repeated" ([1990] 1999, 178). However, the sexual imagery of his foot (a frequent phallic substitute) withdrawing from the empty space of the boot hugged close to her body suggests the ghost of her female anatomy. Is it this gender ambiguity that inspires the prince's anger, resulting in his aggressive desire to throw his boots at her head? Framing this action as a moment of trans panic,[8] we can see his assault on her head—the seat of knowledge and will—as a violent way of enforcing society's demand for a fixed, legible identity.

But the violence of the nightly boot ritual does not convince Mouseskin to submit to a legible identity; if the prince is attempting to "out" her, he fails. More than just ammunition, the boots function as identity-determining objects of bodily adornment. In this story, objects like these mark significant turning points in the plot; the mouse-skin cloak transitions her from girl to man, and the transfer of the prince's crown later transforms her into his wife. These objects change hands swiftly (an indication of the slipperiness of the identities they symbolize) and enact transformation through their exchange. Mouseskin has learned through her use of the cloak that identities are not essential but performed; all one needs is the appropriate outfit. Her repeated tugging at the prince's boots can be read as evidence of her continuing desire for self-fashioning through lateral acquisition of new textures of identity. Perhaps those shiny leather boots would look good with her mouse-skin coat. Perhaps, like manhood, the identity of princehood can be annexed through the strategic use of costume. She pulls at the prince's boots, performing her desire for his identity. Like the king who feared his daughter would swallow him up, the prince thwarts her plan to "walk in his shoes" by throwing his boots at the ambitious, ambiguously gendered creature.

Another identity-determining object is ultimately Mouseskin's undoing. Apparently skilled at passing as a man, she is unable to pass convincingly as a servant. Under suspicion of theft, Mouseskin must justify her ownership of a valuable ring. While she is hungry for new identities, the stigma of "thief" is not one she can bear, and she is forced to reveal her birth identity as a princess. Throughout the tale she audaciously refuses to settle on a fixed version of herself, embarking instead on a journey of expansion through queer, sideways growth. Will this forced revelation compel her to leave the interval of animal and the refuge of queer time? Or can the diverse textures of her assumed selves adhere to the princess as she transforms once again?

Let's return to the text: "She unwrapped the mouseskin, and her golden hair streamed down. As she stepped out of the skin he could see she was beautiful, indeed so beautiful that he immediately took off his crown, put it on her head, and declared her his wife" (Zipes 2002b, 616). Upon seeing her beauty, the prince falls in love with Mouseskin and the seemingly conventional wedding narrative follows. But is it an act of true union or another act of substitution and incorporation? As his servant, Mouseskin took off the prince's boots, the foundation on which he stood. As his wife, she puts on his crown, the symbol of his authority. In ceding to her his heavy crown, still wet and salty with the sweat from his brow, does he crown her queen or, replacing himself with her, crown her king?

The naked princess stands before him as if before a mirror. It is a moment of recognition and desire—he desires her body, sexually, and she desires to have his body, his crown, and his kingdom as her own. Through her journey, she has become skilled at the absorptive, incorporative act of becoming-other. As if in a reversal of Lacan's (1977, 1–7) mirror stage moment, the princess imagines the prince as part of her flesh: a composite, an assemblage, a becoming-one. This is no heteronormative happily ever after. Immediately after declaring her his wife, the prince disappears completely from the tale and is not mentioned again in the final three paragraphs. It is as though she has swallowed him whole like the wolf swallows Red Riding Hood, fattening herself with the metaphor of his manhood. Have they literally become what the wedding ceremony metaphorically describes—one body, one flesh? Does the princess skin him and wear him, exchanging the skin of the mouse for the skin of the prince? Or has she absorbed him into her body like salt absorbs water, performing on him the boundary-dissolving incorporation that once threatened her father?

Not finished with her journey from exiled child to becoming-mouse, to becoming-man, to becoming-king, Princess/King Mouseskin is still hungry for new longitudes and latitudes inside and outside her becoming-body. In the last scene she reunites with her father; as the now-favorite daughter, it is safe to assume she will inherit his kingdom as well, instigating a new phase of sideways growth for our queer child all grown up/out. Will she incorporate her father's body, crown, and land like she absorbed the prince? This final move of swallowing up her own father's kingdom is a geographic enactment of the salt metaphor that set the tale in motion. Through her sideways growth and repeated acts of incomplete becoming, Mouseskin has found a way to reinscribe the formerly restrictive boundaries of her childhood homeland. Far from being a story of a young girl trying to fit in, this is a tale of a trans child expanding latitudinally and longitudinally, outgrowing the very measure of fitting in.

Notes

1. For a small sample, see Goldberg (1997, 28–46); Jorgensen (2008, 27–37); Gilbert (1985, 355–84); and Woodman (1992).

2. The Symbolic Father is a function, rather than an individual, who, in Lacanian psychoanalytic philosophy, triangulates the mother-child relationship, eventually intervening into the imaginary dyad and creating a space into which the symbolic (namely language) can be introduced. The Symbolic Father legislates and prohibits desire and also makes possible normative systems of signification and subject formation.

3. This connection between queer time and the interval of animal was pointed out to me by my colleague at NYU, Aliza Shvarts.

4. Here again we sense a resonance to the incestuous heritage of ATU 510B. Interestingly, an alternate name for the "Peau d'Asne" tale type is "Unnatural Love" (see Ashliman 1987, 108–9). While this story eschews an overt incest plot, the notion of unnatural love is retained in the heroine's merging with the mouse, as well as in the homosexual and sadistic overtones of her violent homosocial relationship with the prince.

5. The profusion of mice on salt-bearing cargo ships was seen as scientific evidence for this theory (see Kurlansky 2002, 2–6).

6. Because access to hormones and surgery has traditionally required medical diagnosis, transgender people seeking such interventions must "accurately describe" symptoms of gender identity dysphoria (GID) as described by the DSM-IV. Information on how to "accurately describe" these symptoms to the medical establishment has been shared between transgender people since the 1970s (see Stryker and Whittle 2006).

7. See Zipes (2002b: "Bearskin," 340; "The Worn-Out Dancing Shoes," 432; and "King of the Golden Mountain," 310).

8. Transpanic is an extension of the controversial gay panic defense, a juridical concept used by defendants in hate crime trials as a way to reduce their sentences. For a good analysis of transphobia and transpanic, see Shelley (2008).

11

Playing with Fire

Transgression as Truth in
Grimms' "Frau Trude"

KAY TURNER

[The fairy tale] is a medium deeply concerned with undoing prejudice.
—Marina Warner, *From the Beast to the Blonde*

For many years I have been inordinately curious about an obscure Grimms' fairy tale called "Frau Trude" (ATU 334). The tale concerns a witch and a girl and how their passionate relationship comes into being despite staunch prohibition. As a story arguing the nature of "truth," it makes numerous direct and indirect claims concerning identity, feeling, sex and gender fluidity, kinship, and being—all within the framework of transgression and transformation, or perhaps better put, transgression *as* transformation.

I make much of this brief tale, one infrequently given scholarly consideration. And yet, as I see it, and as the history of queer studies attests, the very task of queering the Grimms' or any other traditional tales is to seek out the small and little-known story to discover queer possibility in the traces it offers, realizing that, as José Muñoz states, "instead of being clearly available as visible evidence, queerness has instead existed as innuendo, gossip, fleeting moments, and performances" (1996, 6). "Frau Trude" is a model for tracking the traces of queer existence in folklore.

The manifest and various relations between witches and girls in fairy tales, as between old women and young girls generally, have been undertheorized. Yet such attraction is as old as Sappho, who pined for and then penned her desire for lithe Atthis and youthful Anactoria.[1] Fairy-tale scholarship rarely dips a proverbial toe into interpretive waters that might impel readers to take account of attractions, rather than repulsions, between witches and maidens. But in both well-known and obscure tales, girls find themselves drawn consciously toward, or inadvertently encountering, old women in various roles, including witch, sorceress, old woman, very old woman, grandmother, mother, mistress, wise woman, old hag, and stepmother.[2] The old woman/young girl character dyad shapes a complex narrative model of female relationships, some of which beg for queer interpretation. Thus, working through "Frau Trude" leads down a winding path of transgressive wonder to arrive at bolder possibilities for understanding the diversities of desire between older and younger women in other fairy tales.[3]

The Grimms' *Kinder- und Hausmärchen* is filled with a rich assortment of Frau Trude's "sisters." Though it is beyond my scope here, reading "Frau Trude" intertextually with others of its kind would no doubt bear analytical fruit concerning the structural position queer old women occupy in the fairy tale. Whether they are malevolent, like the cannibal in "Hansel and Gretel" (ATU 327A) and the kidnapper of one thousand girls in "Jorinda and Joringle" (ATU 405), or benevolent, like the old woman who hides the girl in "The Robber Bridegroom" (ATU 955) and provides for her in "The Sweet Porridge" (ATU 565), the charisma associated with these female figures emanates from their unusual propensity for agency. Housed in their marginality, abjection, and private nature, they seem to take secret delight in going it alone in those cottages deep in the woods. Frau Trude is among them: an outcast and outlaw living in her self-created house of marvels. But she finds her solitary confinement has lost its allure.

Frau Trude's tale merits reading in its entirety. I use Bettina Hutschek's translation of "Frau Trude," from the version in Hans-Jörg Uther's (1996, 1:216–17) edition of the Grimms' seventh edition of the *KHM*.[4]

There was once a little girl who was very obstinate and willful, and who never obeyed when her elders spoke to her; and so how could she be happy? One day she said to her parents, "I have heard so much of

Frau Trude, that I will go and see her. People say she has a marvelous-looking place and they say there are many weird things in her house, so I became very curious." Her parents, however, forbade her going, saying, "Frau Trude is a wicked old woman, who performs godless deeds, and if you go to see her, you are no longer our child."

The girl, however, did not care about her parents' interdiction and went to Frau Trude's house. When she arrived there, Frau Trude asked her, "Why are you so pale?"

"Ah" replied she, trembling all over her body, "I have frightened myself so with what I have just seen."

"What have you seen?"

"I saw a black man on your steps."

"That was a collier."

"Then I saw a green man."

"That was a hunter."

"Then I saw a blood-red man."

"That was a butcher."

"Oh, Frau Trude, I was most terrified, I peeped through the window, and did not see you, but the devil with a fiery head."

"Oh, ho," she said, "Then you have seen the witch in her proper dress. For you I have long waited, and longed for you, and now you shall give me light." Thus she transformed the girl into a block of wood, and then threw it into the fire. And when it was in full glow, she sat down next to it, warmed herself on it and said, "For once it burns brightly!"

I read certain structural binaries—girl/woman; young/old; youth/age; life/death; human/witch (devil); parents/witch (lover); home/house; blood/non-blood relations; fire/light; and light/dark—as leverage to interpret this short but provocative tale as it marks intergenerational mutual attraction and lesbian seduction, inviting understanding of strategic ways that social and sexual prohibitions may be overcome symbolically and imaginatively. Indebted to a generation of queer and LGBT academics who began broadly theorizing the heterogeneity of sex in the 1980s, I work with "Frau Trude" to invite folklore and fairy-tale scholars to touch queer theory in new ways.[5] Queer scholarship generally accepts postmodern assumptions concerning the contradictory and contingent nature of signs and their systems of representation. I follow medievalist Carolyn Dinshaw, claiming for queer fairy tale analysis what she asserts for a queer history interested in unraveling the multiple meanings of sex (including sex acts, sexual desire, sexual identity, and sexual subjectivity): "Sex . . . is at least in part contingent upon systems of representation, and, as such, is fissured and contradictory. Its meaning or significance cannot definitively be pinned down without exclusivity or reductiveness, and such meanings and significances shift, moreover, with shifts in context and location" (1999, 12). Sounds like the stuff of folklore, doesn't it? But Dinshaw's new twist helps us rethink traditional narrative, suggesting that when queerness touches interpretation, it demonstrates "something disjunctive within unities that are presumed unproblematic, even natural. I speak of the tactile, 'touch,' because I feel queerness work by contiguity and displacement; like metonymy as distinct from metaphor, queerness knocks signifiers loose, ungrounding bodies, making them strange, working in this way to provoke perceptual shifts and subsequent corporeal response in those touched" (151).

There may be no better narrative site for discovering strange, ungrounded bodies and contingent sexual meanings than the fairy-tale genre, which problematizes desire, convened as wish fulfillment set in the realm of enchantment. Operating as a trope for the non-normative (but not necessarily the non-heteronormative), enchantment's liminal state invites speculation along queer lines. Even if many tales hurtle headlong toward normative reunion, marriage, and stability, often the route navigates a topsy-turvy space filled with marvels, magic, and weird encounters that don't simply contradict the "normal" but offer, or at least hint at, alternative possibilities for fulfilling desires that might alter individual destinies. Remarkably, in the case of "Frau Trude," disenchantment never even occurs; rather, the witch's marvelous realm is queered as a new home for the young girl and the old woman.

If sex, desire, and pleasure can signify heterogeneously in the fairy tale, attendant issues of kinship, family, and spousal attachment come to the fore. What narrative room does the genre supply to enlarge our consideration of relational bonds across binary differences of age, status, gender, sex, and even species? The heterogeneity of kinship is the central human problem the fairy tale presents, often queerly construed within the fundamental, if ambivalent and shifting, binary "belonging/exclusion." Certain tales transpose the social and emotional tensions stemming from this division into architectural motifs (see, e.g., Labrie 2009). Two houses oppose each other in the landscape described by "Frau Trude." One, symbolizing conventional belonging, is natal, heteronormative, parental, known; the other is non-kin based, homonormative, single dweller, strange. I seek in this chapter to demonstrate that the distance between them can be bridged by queer desire.

"Frau Trude" presents an especially useful example for exploring the predicament raised by these oppositions because the tale draws force from a considerably more profound one: natural/unnatural, or what Robert McRuer calls the ultimate binary of "who fits/who doesn't" (1997, 143). The tale unmakes this divide's inexorability by different terms of desire and agency. Queering, as a utopian project built with the brick and mortar of failure to comply, privileges the necessity of that which not only does not fit but chooses not to fit. "Frau Trude" offers two "choosey" gals—stubborn, unruly, in a word, perverse—who prove unwilling to belong to anything or anyone but themselves and each other.

ENCOUNTERING "FRAU TRUDE"

My initial encounter with "Frau Trude" occurred in 1998. Invited to teach as a guest professor at the University of Winnipeg by co-editor Pauline Greenhill, I prepared a course called Sexualities, Folklore, and Popular Culture. For a session on folk narrative, I wanted us to study the fairy tale because the feminist scholarship in this area had by that time matured into its own fertile field of reconsiderations and new ideas. Indeed, feminist reimaginings of the Grimms' and other tales had reached an apex of production. Among the rewriters, Irish novelist Emma Donoghue's *Kissing the Witch* proffered an explicitly lesbian take. I vividly remember my first reading of her version of "Rapunzel" in which the sorceress and the long-tressed girl, after much despair, separation, and longing, come back together as lovers in the tale's end (1997, 83–99).

I wondered how Donoghue got there. Did the Grimms' version of the tale embed motifs, functions, or structural oppositions that made such reimagining logical? Bonnie Zimmerman would answer that lesbianism as a way of knowing the world affects how we read literature, that lesbians may willfully "misread" texts, adopting "a perverse strategy of reading" (1993, 139). But what stood out most at the time and has sustained me throughout these Grimm years was Zimmerman's instruction that appropriation through reading perversely requires "hints and possibilities that the author, consciously or not, has strewn in the text" (144). Thus while reading Jack Zipes's (1992) translation of the *KHM* in preparation to teach, I found myself regularly exclaiming my discovery of deeply queer "hints and possibilities." Numerous tales held such requirements, especially lesser-known ones such as "The Three Spinners," "The Star Coins," "The Grave Mound," and, of course, "Frau Trude," which struck me then, as it does now, as the queerest tale of all.

For class, I assigned Kay F. Stone's (1993) feminist rewriting of "Frau Trude" called "The Curious Girl." Comparing the Grimms' original with her adaptation, what a difference a gay makes! With the encouragement and help of my young lesbian students, we interpreted "Frau Trude" as a classic "coming-out story," an adumbration replete with the desire mixed with prohibition and fear that now distinguishes that genre. We found plenty of sex, too. Stone visited our class and I remember the evening's brilliant explosion of ideas as we engaged with her. She conceded that, though she had "lived with" the tale for many years, returning again and again as she rewrote and told it, she had never thought of it in queer sexual terms.

Rather Stone's interest landed in her conviction that the girl was neither destroyed nor punished for being too curious; instead, her inquisitiveness was prized. In Stone's retelling, the girl is transformed into a log, becoming fire, a shower of sparks, a bird, a hare, and a fish. "Through these metamorphoses, she experienced the sacrifice of her ego-self, which . . . gave her even greater power—freedom over herself as a fuller human being" (1993, 298–99), rewarded finally with her own story of self-knowledge and fulfillment. At the essay's close, Stone summarizes the evolution of her relationship to "Frau Trude" with a question equally pertinent to my interpretation: "And I wonder: Is it possible to ignite oneself without being consumed?" (304). Our answers are different, but compatible.[6]

I, too, began to live with "Frau Trude." Years passed and still she nagged, so to speak. My interest waxed and waned and slowly changed. Whereas earlier my interest—like the other Kay's—centered on the girl, later I felt more and more Frau Trude's fire drawing me to her hearth. It seemed she and I had been waiting a long time for each other. I became the curious scholar compelled to meet the witch.

The Tale: Its History, Variants, and Language

Numbered 43 in the *KHM*, "Frau Trude" ("Mistress Trude" or "Mother Trude") conforms to ATU 334, "Household of the Witch." It belongs to the complex of old "devourer tales" (Ranke 1990, 617–18), which also includes 333B, "The Cannibal Godfather (Godmother)," subsumed by Uther under ATU 334 in his recently updated tale type index: "A girl (woman) disregards the warning of friendly animals (parts of her body) and visits her godmother (grandmother) who is a cannibal. The girl sees many gruesome things (e.g., fence of bones, barrel full of blood, and her godmother with an animal's head). When the girl tells her godmother what she has seen she is killed (devoured)" (2004, 1:225).

The Aarne-Thompson synopsis yields less information but more intrigue: "Visit to house of a witch (or other horrible creature). Many gruesome and marvelous happenings. Lucky escape" (Aarne 1961, 125). Demonstrating the longevity of ATU 334's hundreds of variants, Kurt Ranke (1978, 98–100) traces its roots in Eastern Europe, with subsequent migration west from Slavic and Baltic realms—Poland, Lithuania, former Yugoslavia (Bosnia and Serbia)—to eastern Germany. He speculates that ATU 334 evolved from a myth concerning the realm of death, then changed to a macabre, demonic tale, and finally to a somewhat farcical one, happily ending with escape from the ogre. He counts about ninety variants, including thirty-six from Germany alone, where the historic-geographic record demonstrates the story's notable change to its milder version.

In his study devoted to the form and function of gruesome children's tales, Walter Scherf (1987) interprets twenty-seven thematically related types, including AT(U) 334, with "Frau Trude" as an example. To reflect its progressive shift in content from horrific to moderate, he proposes the tale's division into Eastern (334A+) and Western (334B+) European versions of different oikotypes (61–62). Reminiscent of Russian Baba Yaga tales, the descriptively more ghastly Eastern versions feature, for example, a fence strung with human intestines and doorknobs made of hands.[7] Discovering her "true nature"—not woman but ogress—is a pivotal plot device in ATU 334, often intensified through a series of riddle-like questions and answers concerning what the visitor has seen at the witch's house. In numerous variants, the girl (cousin, neighbor woman, sister, rarely a male) encounters frightening figures right before meeting the witch (Ranke 1990, 617). Once inside the house, the formulaic interrogation about these individuals begins. Initially ameliorating, the discourse recalibrates markedly in ATU 334 when the girl states she also saw a horrifying creature, witch, or devil. The ogress identified as such then usually kills her visitor but in "Frau Trude" transforms her.

In older variants typically a horrifying devourer and uncompromising murderer, the witch—or death-woman (*Tödin*)—sometimes possesses a flexible animal head she removes at will, for the purpose of picking lice. This ogress who became Frau Trude changes dramatically as she moves west to Germany. For one thing, she gains a proper name. Likely a description of her nature, it may be derived from *trut* or *drut*, a type of demon well known in the Bavarian-Austrian regions (Uther 1996, 4:88).[8] As the gory, death-driven tale slowly modulates, the marvelous replaces the gruesome until finally "only a fairy tale, moreover for children, remains"; one that "is totally disarmed . . . and trivialized" (Ranke 1978, 99). If Ranke regrets that the German variant has been belittled, I offer a remedy for his woe. Once drained of the explicitly gory and murderous death drive, a different drive, equally potent, replaces it in the tale.

The Grimms' version of "Frau Trude," first published in the 1837 *KHM*, substituted for "Die wunderliche Gasterei" ("The Strange Feast"), the comedic variant of ATU 334, which filled slot 43 in the first two editions. This innocuous tale features a liverwurst escaping from a murderous blood sausage (Zipes 1992, 658–59). Zipes suggests the change happened because

"The Strange Feast" too closely resembled number 42 in the *KHM*, "The Godfather," ATU 332 (738). "Frau Trude" derives from a literary source, Meier Teddy's *Frauentaschenbuch* (1823), a pocket book for women including the poem "Little Cousin and Frau Trude" (see Bolte and Polívka 1913, 377), which the Grimms retold in prose.[9]

According to Uther (1996, 4:88), Wilhelm Grimm conceived a new opening, creating a didactic tale to show children the punishment that results from disobedience to their parents. One wishes to have been present in the editorial chambers when the brothers decided to make the switch from sausage to witch. No doubt, sometime between publishing the volume of notes for the second edition in 1822 and the publication of the third edition of the tales in 1837, one or both read Meier Teddy's little lyric tale and saw in it an opportunity to intensify their project's moral agenda. Moving from meat to *Mädchen* (maiden), from comedy to tragedy, from lucky escape to murder seems to me a profound reflection of the Grimms' desire to solidify their narrative portrayal of social values such as women's silence and obedience. Equally, it might signal their worry over changing mores, including those sexual ones slightly slipping out of closets across Europe, a result of the first prospects of the Enlightenment's individual freedoms.[10]

"Frau Trude" evidences these concerns in its use of language. Though compact, the Grimms' version nonetheless spends a wealth of linguistic currency in direct speech of an intense and ardor-laden kind: argumentative between daughter and parents, then discursive between girl and witch. Though the story begins with a standard "There once was a little girl" followed by description of her obstinate and stubborn ways, the third-person narrator soon gives over the account to the first-person protagonists. Plunged immediately into a tense, dramatic dialogue, the reader first hears the girl's definitive, assertive tone as she demonstrates her desire to go to Frau Trude. Her parents respond by admonishing her and denouncing the Frau. A few lines later, in quick succession, girl and Frau engage with each other in interrogative, reported, expository, and declarative speech modes. Having transformed her visitor into fire, Frau Trude sits down by her bright flame and, speaking to herself/to the girl, declares her satisfaction.

The exceptionally argumentative and chatty girl and the loquacious witch by no means hold to the "silent woman" protocol Ruth Bottigheimer (1986, 116) finds in full swing in Germany by the 1830s, when "Frau Trude" was first published. Bottigheimer's correlation of the Grimm tales' speech patterns, gender hierarchies, and values is suggestive for "Frau Trude." In what she calls the "century of criticism" celebrating "Wilhelm Grimm's shift from indirect speech in the earliest versions of individual tales to direct speech in the later and final versions," she finds, "No critic has asked, 'Who speaks?' or 'Under what circumstances?'" (1987, 52). In contrast, Bottigheimer argues that Wilhelm consciously determined how much speech he would bestow any particular character (53).

Finding "good" girls and women muted or relegated to indirect speech and authority, often male, noted in direct speech, Bottigheimer also discovers that if "sprach" (spoke) too often introduces speech from a woman's mouth, "it usually heralds a bad hat" (1987, 55). That girl and witch both speak directly and constantly suggests Wilhelm's editorial choices in "Frau Trude." He loads the tale with a garrulousness that announces how "bad" he thinks both protagonists are. Again Bottigheimer is suggestive: "Transgressions can be carried out knowingly or unwittingly. Conscious transgressions by girls occur in at least four tales; in two the girls are punished and in two they escape. These two possible outcomes correspond with the good or evil nature of the prohibitor." Bottigheimer says "Frau Trude" exemplifies a knowingly disobedient girl's punishment, foretold in Grimm's rhetorical insertion at the tale's start: "so how could she fare well?" (88). We thank Wilhelm Grimm for filling the tale with direct speech, for thereby inadvertently he raises our awareness of the impassioned relationships between the characters by giving us access to their heightened emotional states (including fascination, anger, resentment, fear, yearning, and contentment) expressed in a range of speech acts.

Reading "Frau Trude" Queerly

Diving deep into the queer possibilities of "Frau Trude," I offer, but certainly don't exhaust, queer understandings from both the girl's and Frau Trude's perspectives. I read certain passages multiply, without contradiction. More decipherment than conventional analysis, much remains to be explored in my approach. I find the girl too knowing and too anxious to leave her past behind, the witch too desirous of warmth and light, the ending too filled with *jouissance*, ardor and contentment, heat and brightness to regard the story simply as a caution against curiosity or a warning against an old woman's nefarious ways. My investigation of "Frau Trude" takes further inspiration from Dinshaw's assignment of impulse and tactility to her work on late medieval England. Following a "queer historical impulse" (1999, 1), she embraces the radical possibilities for making connections between lives in the past and present. In defining a contingent history, she takes seriously the term's root meaning L. *com + tangere*, to touch, as it revises our relation to the disjunctiveness and indeterminateness of queer lives and sexualities. Deliberately celebrating fragmentation, using "new pieces of history," Dinshaw shows that "queers can make new relations, new identifications, new communities with past figures who elude resemblance to us but with whom we can be connected partially by virtue of shared marginality, queer positionality" (39). Of course, fictional figures may provide even wider latitude for connecting past and present, existing only to be touched by and to touch the changing generations who read their stories. In this time, in this place, I touch "Frau Trude" queerly.

For anyone who has gone through the emotionally demanding drill of "coming out" gay or queer, as I have, reading "Frau Trude" retrospectively as an early narrative model of this painful yet exhilarating process is revelatory. Emphasizing a conscious self-recognition of one's homo-identity, postliberation "coming-out" narratives now occupy their own category.[11] Their widespread acceptance as a popular genre, beginning in the 1990s, inspired my Winnipeg class of that era. We discovered all the motifs of the classic coming out narrative in "Frau Trude": forbidden attraction; desire to meet the love object; parental restriction on such desire announced in a threat of disownership; stubborn determination to go, regardless of such threat; feelings of fear and self-doubt manifested in menacing images; encounter with the lover, who simultaneously calms the fear and stokes the fires of passion; and, finally, the transformation—no longer just any girl, but now a glowing gay girl. Reading "Frau Trude" as a coming-out story, our interest focused on the young woman's compulsion, fears, courage, and identity shift. This interpretation dovetailed nicely with Stone's emphasis on the girl's quest for self-knowledge and freedom.[12]

But "Frau Trude" also touches an older, transgressive narrative tradition, alive and well in the nineteenth century and earlier. Our tale aligns nicely with the Sapphic subgenre, those steamy stories of obsession, deviance, desire, and seduction. In these narratives an older woman, schooled in seduction, lures a younger girl willing, in some sense, to learn.[13] Even if positioned as an innocent, the girl, drawn to the seducer, sticks around long enough to be debauched, or at least to gain carnal awareness of her intended debauchment.[14] The older woman figures as what Terry Castle calls "the apparitional lesbian" in her investigation of lesbian spectrality in novels ranging from Denis Diderot's *The Nun* (1797) to Henry James's *The Bostonians* (1886) and Radclyffe Hall's *The Well of Loneliness* (1928): "Western writing over the centuries is from one angle a kind of derealization machine: insert the lesbian and watch her disappear" (1993, 6). Yet Castle maintains that "the very frequency with which the lesbian has been 'apparitionalized' in the Western imagination also testifies to her peculiar cultural power" (7). She is actually "in plain view, mortal and magnificent" (2). In novels, the elder character often holds institutional power—a mother superior, for example—but fairy tales carry the spectral lesbian in the marginalized figure of the witch.[15]

Tension builds in Sapphic stories as the cat-and-mouse game of lure and seduction plays out. This function of transgressive mutual attraction also drives the "Frau Trude" plot, flying in the face of normative prescriptions for relations between young girls and mature women. Neither the girl's desire to go to Frau Trude nor Frau Trude's desire to possess the girl is ultimately interrupted; rather, the plot inexorably draws the two together, promoting their encounter's inevitable climax. Mutual attraction is the tale's turnkey, raising the power of desire against all others. Much of the narrative establishes this mutuality, first from the girl's, then from Frau Trude's, point of view.

We enter the tale at a point of exasperation and bitter argument between parents and daughter. We're not hearing this quarrel for the first time. The willful girl insists on going to see Frau Trude then, attempting to diminish parental concern, rationalizes her desire by claiming her real interest lies not in the older woman but in getting a firsthand look at her "marvelous" house and its "weird" contents. This deflection only serves to alert the reader that "going to" Frau Trude is the girl's real goal.[16] The parents try, of course, to block her, excoriating Frau Trude as "a wicked old woman who performs godless deeds." They are in direct competition with the witch, who appears to have a quite lively reputation. The girl has "heard so much" about her, but from whom? Likely, vicious gossip and innuendo, including suggestions of sodomitical acts, have trailed Frau Trude for some time. Whatever the daughter has heard evidently has not repelled but rather intrigued her. Over time, this feeling has cranked into high gear.

I prefer "intrigued" to Stone's gloss of the girl as "curious" to capture the sense of anxious arousal she manifests. Intrigue is a specific kind of curiosity associated with "arousal of interest," the "fascinating," the compelling, and hidden, often sexual, desires. It also names an illicit love affair (Brown 1993, 1405). Where attraction meets prohibition, something more than conventional cognitive curiosity is at stake. This intrigued girl allows nothing and no one to stand in the way of her fascination with the source of her allure, Frau Trude. The parents sense their daughter's transgressive desire; whatever she wants from the witch is irredeemably contaminating. The monstrous possibility that Frau Trude's "godless" non-normative state might become hers as well can only be addressed through the ultimate parental threat: "if you go to see her, you are no longer our child." Disowned, she loses both her legal and her social-emotional status as blood kin, marked effectively as abnormal, unnatural.

Does she care? No. In this charged moment of disavowal by her parents, the girl senses change in herself; she's already *disavowing* them. She's transforming, even as she will soon be transformed. She heads off. Given numerous warnings and thereby chances to retreat from her mission,[17] inexorably, she proceeds. Despite meeting three frightening male figures on the steps entering the Frau's house, she still goes forward. Looking through the window and seeing the devil, she does not turn back; instead, she enters the house to finally meet her witch. Intrigue and attraction trump prohibition and trepidation every time.

This girl is but one case of the curious, willful maids found in Grimms' tales, from "The Virgin Mary's Child" to "Fitcher's Bird."[18] The sin of knowledge (Eve's error) compounds curiosity with the disorderly impulses of desire and sexuality that spur some fairy-tale girls out into the world beyond interdiction.[19] Yet curiosity remains, as Michel Foucault suggests in his introduction to volume 2 of *The History of Sexuality*, the great stimulus for abjuring propriety to gain the knowledge that sets one free: "As for what motivated me, it is quite simple; . . . It was curiosity—the only kind of curiosity, in any case, that is worth acting upon with a degree of obstinacy: not the curiosity that seeks to assimilate what is proper for one to know, but that which enables one to get free of oneself" (1985, 8).

Fairy-tale curiosity links with inappropriate directives conventionally deemed most disastrous for women: I wish, I want, I will. Fulfilling such self-determining commands requires a determined disobedience. The girl's curiosity demands a decision to disobey her parents and an acceptance that such defiance is tantamount to disownership. Borrowing a phrase from Judith Butler, disobedience is a failure to "repeat loyally" (1993, 220).[20] If, as Butler ([1990] 1999) critically assessed, gender and sexuality norms are never original but are based on citation and repetition, then obedience, the reiteration of the normative, is the hammer of carnal conformity. Wilhelm Grimm may have rewritten "Frau Trude" to emphasize the perils of girls' curiosity and disobedience. But for the queer reader, he unwittingly creates a perfect entrée for identification with a character who, in pursuit of her transgressive desire, declines loyal repetition. Breaking convention, her "failure" sets the girl on her own initiatory journey. As Cristina Bacchilega suggests for "Bluebeard," "Frau Trude" is not a cautionary tale about learning to control curiosity but is about "a process of initiation which *requires* entering the forbidden chamber" (1997, 107). Initiation's goal is revelation: to convert partial knowledge to full. The girl directs her curiosity toward someone she has already "heard so much" about. Something about what she almost knows—or senses—for herself about Frau Trude powers her curiosity and, more important, her shamelessness. Though she eventually feels fear, the girl never expresses a hint of regret or shame for pursuing her desire to know. With non-normative sexual desire at stake, shamelessness propels curiosity's norm-breaking function. Specifically, for "Frau Trude's" girl, driven by a compulsion for "unholy" alliance, shamelessness queers curiosity.

Even so, she is "trembling all over her body" as she stands before the woman for the first time—with fear but also with the anxiety of first encounter and perhaps a modicum of release. Having crossed the threshold, exiled from her natal home, she stands now inside the house of marvels. Frau Trude allays the girl's fear of the figures she has met outside. Soothingly, and perhaps with a faint inflection of flirtation, she says they are not phantoms, just the routine men—collier, hunter, butcher—who assist her in everyday living. The figure the girl saw inside the house, a fiery devil, is no phantom either, but a true manifestation of Frau Trude, who emphatically exclaims, "Then you have seen the witch in her proper dress." Later, I will return to this dramatic self-proclamation of who Frau Trude is; for the interim, I am interested in what she wants. For at this crucial juncture the Frau identifies her witchy nature in the same breath as she unburdens her womanly need: "For you I have long waited, and longed for you" or, as Zipes translates the same passage, "I've been wanting you here and waiting for a long time" (1992, 160). How remarkable. The all-powerful devil-witch has been feeling a very human yearning for her cohort, with the exigencies of her longing made explicit by recourse to romantic convention: the confession of temporal anxiety both in terms of duration (waiting) and emotion (longing). Reading Zipes's and Hutscheck's translations together yields the triumvirate of desire's expression: wanting, waiting, longing.

Witches live in both real (human) and supernatural (magical) time. In her womanly aspect, Frau Trude does not—or cannot—use her otherworldly powers to force the girl to her. As Roland Barthes claimed, "Waiting is an enchantment: I have received *orders not to move*" (1978, 38; emphasis in original).[21] The witch endures such enchantment. She waits, as she must, for the fulfillment of a seduction she no doubt has plotted but cannot complete without the girl's autonomous desire to seek her out. Seduction's game depends on waiting and requires both parties to spend some time getting worked up. The girl's willfulness and Frau Trude's yearning are dynamic emotional forces in this tale, exerting a mutual pull that resolves in their meeting. The story's heightened play of attractions is contingent on Frau Trude and the girl knowing about each other. More than suggesting, the story demonstrates explicitly that they've been circling each others' wagons for awhile. Their proximity lends itself to a relational reading of their encounter. The girl's sense of intrigue concerns her desire to engage Frau

Trude, a specific, named woman, while the witch admits her yen not for any girl but for this particular girl.[22]

From the normative outside, predation haunts homosexual relations in literature, theater, and film as well as in life. Sapphic novels hyperbolize the older woman as a ruthless hunter after young flesh. The witch has fared no better; her predatory compulsions are assumed. From the lesbian inside, however, predation's unidirectional aim is blunted by attention paid to how desires and feelings actually play out. The girl's attraction to the witch negates any presumption of one-sided sexual greed. And Frau Trude, no hunter, stays at home, saddled with yearning and its attendant anticipatory joys and frustrations.

FIRE UP THE FLAMES OF DESIRE AND PASSION

Having waited too long, Frau Trude wastes no time making her move. Immediately following her declaration of need, the witch changes the girl into fire. The converted girl then blazes for the pyro-prone witch, who sits down to warm herself next to this flame she has so long desired. Both protagonists are highly flammable and fire operates as the tale's core symbol. Modernity ended our forebears' need to live daily with open flame as the major humanly controlled source of heat and light. But fire fills the realm of fairy tales, like it did the world of their earlier telling—from hearth to oven, candle to coals, and torch to stake. An essential element, it acted as a force, a tool, and a potent, if ambiguous, symbol representing both creative and destructive forces. Bottigheimer notes that fire in the Grimms' tales ranges in meaning, "as an image of Promethean progress or domestic comfort, as well as a Satanic symbol." In a nod to "Frau Trude," she says "the hearth is where the witch sits" (1987, 25).[23]

Associated in Christian tradition with martyrdom, purification, and transformation as well as evil and damnation, fire, the tale's central motif, grounds "Frau Trude" in familiar religious binaries. The Grimms mark the putatively innocent, if willful, girl's self-martyrdom as well as Frau Trude's satanic manifestation. Attempting to prevent their unblemished child from seeking Frau Trude, the parents indict her and threaten disinheritance, setting the girl on her Grimm highway to hell. At this point the tale burns zealously, fueled by defensiveness, because as the Grimms were only too well aware, protection of a young girl's innocence—of her unknowing-ness—services the perpetuation of family bloodlines, property rights, and economies. Religion stands with the family as a bulwark preventing the realization of young women's wishes and desires.

The Grimms note both the standard sacred/profane and pure/impure binaries, yet the story does not ultimately support the moral divide these oppositions conventionally create. Even if chaste, the girl is not pure. Her willfulness interrupts her trip down the straight path of protected inno-cence, which is the course of parental, religious, and state authority. The Grimms burn her as punishment for her failure to remain exemplary, her refusal to obey. The girl goes to hell. Stained by her perversity, she dies in flames—becoming the fires of hell—and Frau Trude, the satanic force, lives on to revel in the glow. The Grimms' warning at the tale's end provides this equation: play with the fiery devil and you may become the devil's flame. For the brothers, the story concludes with a teleological clunk. The girl gets what she deserves, and the witch, satisfied with capturing her prey, sits at the hearth blazing with her winnings.[24]

A queer approach reads "Frau Trude"'s fires differently, drawing on secular and sexual rather than religious connotations. Associations of fire with pas-sion and love include the fourteenth-century "to inflame with passion" (L. *inflammare*) and "ardor" (L. *ardere*, to burn), referring to the heat of sexual desire (Harper 2001–10). The girl's sense of intrigue and Frau Trude's sense of longing meet in the flames of passion, not damnation. Fire signi-fies their appetite and its means of satisfaction. Frau Trude, the tale's fire marshal, manipulates the meaning and use of fire in service of seduction. Though the girl looks through the window expecting to spy Frau Trude, she says she sees instead "the devil with a fiery head." The woman's retort simultaneously verifies the blazing manifestation as an identity of hers but quashes any direct equation with the satanic. She immediately reroutes the girl's claim; she has instead "seen the witch in her proper dress" or "in all her finery" (Tatar 2004a, 368).

Frau Trude's sartorial metaphor alludes to the red raiment of fire: to see her as she truly is, is to see her "dressed" in her elemental form. Outside the house peeping in, the girl observes only the devil; once inside, she is offered a different interpretation. Frau Trude defines herself as a witch, a kind of magnificently burning woman, whose reference to feminine finery lends a seductive shine to her self-identification. The girl will discover what her compulsion to see Frau Trude suggested: someone quite extraordinary; not a wretched hag, or a slimy ogre, but a woman dressed in finery, queen of her realm, confident in this moment of revealing her truth.

What particular truth does she impart in this dramatic instance of encounter? Frau Trude's associations with fire, witchery, the satanic, the profane, and the godless are suggestive. They point to something the text both conceals and reveals: this witch also can be read as a sodomite, harboring a lesbian desire. Research in related European materials shows the infamous sin against nature bearing a long historical relationship to fire, diabolism, and witchery.[25] But according to Mackensen (1934/1940, 225), Frau Trude's dual nomination as both witch and devil is rare.[26] Yet if it codes her as sodomite (lesbian), Frau Trude's ready substitution of herself from devil and fire to woman and witch makes perfect sense. She exercises a range of sodomitical symbols to announce her intentions. When the girl sees her as fiery devil, she sees Frau Trude as the sodomite symbol she truly represents. Then her declaration as fire-dressed witch doubles the sodomitical symbolism while indexing its humanity. Transferring sign to reality, she becomes the lusty lesbian, the woman who will have what she's waited for, while the girl finds what she's wanted, too.

Momentarily they stand face to face conversing. Their discursive foray concerns the actual, but this is also the moment of *their* truth, revealed by Frau Trude and immediately recognized by the girl. The queer utopian crux of the tale witnesses what Maria Tatar names the "magic [that] happens on the threshold of the forbidden" (2004b, 1). Their truth, to use a worn but worthy cliché, will set them both free. In this singular instant of encounter, they are present and open to each other, their agreement sealed; they enter their own time.

The girl makes no attempt to escape, nor does the witch kill her by throwing her bodily into the fire. Instead, a transformation occurs. Having demonstrated that status change—symbolic and real—can be willfully achieved, Frau Trude touches the girl for the first time, turning her into a block of wood, adequate fuel for the witch's ardor. By first being made into a neutral source of fuel and thence into flame, the girl is not annihilated but, rather, given the elemental condition that makes it possible for her to meet the fiery Frau on mutual, powerfully erotic terms. The girl, too, dons her "proper dress." Yearning for her for too long to simply destroy her, Frau Trude instead gives her a new and highly compatible form. The story's dual flames, which in a conservative reading overdetermine the hellish, queerly provide a point of sexual contact and consummation. Now the girl also lives by burning, for Frau Trude and for herself. Yet she need not only burn. Frau Trude easily could convert the wood block back into girlish form; the Grimms' "The Drummer" (Zipes 1992, 610–11) features just such reverse transformation of a burning log into a maiden at a witch's command. Or perhaps Frau Trude may grant the girl her own capability to change at will.

Putting such speculation aside, in the end, the two effect a merger through an elemental medium. The witch, who plays with and can manifest as fire, transforms the object of her desire into a proper partner. Fire plus fire makes for greater heat and passion, with two desires burning together in the harmony and unity symbolized at the tale's conclusion by the hearth. Erasing differences in human age, station, and history, their passion cannot be acknowledged in the language of human social life, but it can be spoken in flames.

This reading of fire finds consonance with German scholar Elke Liebs's (1993, 128) suggestion that the burning wood, left at the finale "in voller Glut" ("full blaze" or "gleaming"), refers to the widely understood nineteenth-century German symbolism for sexual ripening and first experiences in love. While she does not move to a lesbian interpretation, Liebs, like Stone, leaves the question open as to why the girl blazes exuberantly in the end. Perhaps this gap can be retroactively referred to the contemporary gay colloquialism "flaming" or "to flame," which refers to flamboyant, often excessive transgression of gender, sexuality, and other norms of behavior.[27] Frau Trude's transformation "flames" the girl, ignites her, releasing her own transgressive lesbian desire. Moreover, by remaking the girl in her fiery likeness, the Frau recruits her as protégé. No longer daughter, the girl celebrates her natal disownership by "flaming" for, and with, Frau Trude. Now, as undying homoerotic flame, she carries Frau Trude's line forward into a future we discover here. Judgment on relations between witches and maidens too often damns them as fueled by rapaciousness, resentment, or jealousy, resulting in deceptions and negative transformations.[28] Frau Trude, however, conceives a positive solution to meet her need. Using her powers to free the girl, she perpetuates their passion by ensuring their likeness as fire, not their opposition as ogre/human. The binary that might separate them goes up in flames. The fiery ending is actually a beginning for these two, whose future of transformations lies ahead for them.

The Ontology of "Frau Trude"

Finding Frau Trude's earliest incarnations in the realm of devouring and death synchronizes her story with a greater complex of patriarchally devised narratives inspiring categorical fear and loathing of woman. They include tales of the biblical Eve and Lilith, the apocryphal Mary Magdalene, figures found in pagan antiquity—including those associated with descendents of major Greek goddesses Hecate and Artemis and mythical monsters such as the fire-breathing Chimera—and early European man-eaters and hags.[29] Frau Trude's Freudian counterpart is the phallic mother, fantasmically endowed with both the mother's "breast" and the father's "penis."[30] The complex problematizes the female body, appetite, sex, desire, childbirth, knowledge, and agency and is underwritten in the structural relations its female figures bear to each other, especially in terms of the life/death binary. "Frau Trude"'s early variants fit this narrative model with its reviled protagonist. A strange and estranging female character, living in a house filled with vats of gore and entrails strewn about for decorative effect, her association with misplaced blood; dismembered, disordered flesh; decomposition; and death makes her just one more in a long line of female inverts, perverts, women impossible to convert: witches.

Despite its concision, "Frau Trude" provides a more detailed record than most of the multiple associations to be gleaned from witches in fairy tales. Among the most "undisciplined" of female characters (Greenhill and Tye

1997), she is unclassifiable. Largely due to their age and unmarried, non-reproductive status, witches bespeak the anomalous. They are woman/not woman, a biological and social contradiction arousing fears of pollution and requiring severe castigation, even death. Anomalous women pose a danger to the common rule of what Adrienne Rich ([1980] 1993) termed "compulsory heterosexuality"; thus their association with deviant sexualities comes as no surprise.

However, witches like Frau Trude are not just out of order; amorphous shape-shifters, they are also out of form. The very qualities that marginalize them as subhuman can also lend them superhuman transformative potency. Frau Trude manifests four different personas—woman, witch, devil, and elemental fire—and she can choose to become any one of these momentarily, at will. Theatrical by nature, she plays the drama queen: a masculine devil one moment, a feminine witch the next, but always the "showgirl." She flaunts a transvestite's gift for rendering gender as a form of artifice (see, e.g., Garber 1992). The girl's parents accuse "the wicked old woman" of "performing godless deeds," and certainly, she is a performer par excellence, skilled in questioning the opposition between construction and essence. An icon of "gender trouble," Frau Trude's performances fully execute the witch's anomalous/amorphous status in its ability to destabilize and denaturalize imposed categories of gender completion. As she herself suggests, it's all a matter of "dressing" the part.

Remarkably, her anomalous/amorphous status on the sex/gender/power continuum presents as patriarchy's problem—not hers. Being impossible, she attains her power of doing the impossible and quickly brings her partner up to speed. The girl's transformation into neutered wood, then elemental fire queers her into a powerfully amorphous state, too. Structurally, she moves from determinate gender and social categories to becoming, like Frau Trude, an unclassifiable shape-shifter, a flickering flame.

In interpreting witches, exploring the relationship between normativity, anomaly, and power is critical.[31] But the oppositional power politics of witchery tends to overshadow its less obvious "structures of feeling," Raymond Williams's (1977, 128–35) designation for the affective social content in art and literature that cannot be reduced to other systems. Queer scholars take Williams's lead, modeling affect-centered approaches to non-normative desires, heterogeneous sexualities, and abjection.[32] In their keeping, Frau

Trude's story and others like it beg new questions of a queerer, more intimate kind, exposing suppressed, ignored, or coded links between witchery and lesbianism. How do fairy-tale witches feel? Can we read their emotions as well as their powers? How do they change over time? They seem to take pleasure in being alone, but do they also suffer from loneliness? Are they capable of love as well as desire? Are they a special case of the subject whose evolving consciousness has been obscured by structural bias?

In beginning to answer these complex questions, we see certain emotional intricacies and contradictions of lesbian sexuality and subjectivity writ in the mysteries of Frau Trude's tale. Witches do have feelings, and complex ones at that. The Frau's uncertain future recalls that of the protagonist in novelist Irène Némirovsky's *Fire in the Blood*: "It might be impossible to predict the future, but I believe that certain powerful emotions make themselves felt months, even years, in advance, through a strange quiver in the heart" (2008, 134–35). Having felt that quiver, Frau Trude's desire for the girl provokes new, if uncertain, affective urgencies. She craves, but not the old yearning for flesh to be devoured or for lips to be smacked at the taste of blood. Now she wants the warmth of an overheated girl. Her cravings have altered into longings for sexual relationship and union with another. And along with them have come emotional vulnerabilities and ontological quandaries as well.

Traditionally, ATU 334 resolves in formulaic murder or escape. "Frau Trude" finishes differently, not in determinant action, but in an unresolved mood of contemplation. The flaming frenzy of anticipation and desire modulates, literally and figuratively, to enlightenment, thereby marking the crucial ontological, as different from gendered or sexual, outcomes of our story. Certainly they are wrapped together, but Frau Trude's tale is striking in the degree to which it ultimately resonates with Sue-Ellen Case's proposition that queer theory does its real work "not at the site of gender, but at the site of ontology, to shift the ground of being itself, thus challenging the Platonic parameters of being—the borders of life and death" (1991, 3).

The ontological concerns of "Frau Trude" underscore its profound interest in discovering the truth: who knows it, who doesn't, who wants to know it, who represents it, who can claim it, and, finally, who is absolved by it. Characters pronounce the truth, argue its status, and make its case. The parents think they know the truth about Frau Trude and her godless ways;

they defend the "normal" and "natural." The girl seeks to discover the truth of Frau Trude on her own terms. She wants to "see" the naked truth of this "other" and when she does, she tells Frau Trude the truth of her observation. Their subsequent mutual interrogation tests the truth of the visible until Frau Trude proclaims her truth, dressed in metaphor. Her long-awaited encounter with the girl results in the witch's moment of truth; she "comes out," entrusting the girl with the knowledge of who she really is and what she truly wants. All this stress about the nature of truth finally dissolves at the hearth, that ancient symbol of domestic peace and harmony, and the story finishes with the Frau's distinct pleasure in gaining more light.

Having cried out to the girl right before changing her, "now you shall give me light," she afterward sits next to the blazing essence to warm herself and also to enjoy a pure moment—perhaps the one she has waited for most—of receiving the fire/girl's full gleam. Her delight evident, she philosophizes, with satisfaction, in the final line, "For once it burns brightly!" Having touched, transformed, and set the girl burning, the initial passionate meeting subsides in meditative afterglow. In an observed moment of domestic quietude and contentment, we picture a woman at last brightened by the light of her life. Notably, the Grimms' prototype for "Frau Trude," Meier Teddy's 1823 poem, does not end in the witch's cry for light, only in her desire for warmth. But by partnering with light in Wilhelm Grimm's version, Frau Trude gains a new eminence.

Light, like fire, is old in symbolic meaning, variously associated with soul, spirit, higher mind, new knowledge, and with life itself.[33] This witch, whose long history in the tale world has been defined by darkness, menace, and death, at last sees a glimmer of freedom from her sullied past. As fire, the girl stokes the old woman's passion, but as light she brings what feels like relief. A queer liveliness pervades the story's end. Frau Trude no longer kills what she craves. Instead she keeps it near, treasures it, marries it. Gone are the entrails and blood-filled vats that crammed her home in earlier variants of the tale. Now her house of marvels produces visions and transformations, not corpses, and her distinct yet fluid manifestations as fire, devil, woman, and witch mark her own ambivalent state of becoming. The man-eating sociopath of old is changing her one-dimensional, monstrous, murdering ways. Done with those centuries-old defensive, ogreish shenanigans, she is no longer interested in finality; her teleological darkness has morphed into a desire for ontological brightness, a shift from the determinate, death, to the possible, life. She cries out her need for light eagerly as much as gleefully. The witch herself is transforming, undergoing a process of self-shattering that would free her.

Frau Trude's emotional longing for the girl is critical to this move. Longing and waiting pose different temporal meanings in this story. Waiting tropes seduction and desire, but longing associates with a deeper need for companionship and kinship. Animals, ogres, humans all engage in mating games and stratagems to satisfy base instincts for food and sex. For certain, the witch retains a good bit of all that sordidness. Yet her longing for the girl seems to demonstrate a desire to be better than who she is—or was: not just hungry, not just hormonal. Frau Trude tentatively experiences the warmth of the heartfelt, poised to reap the benefits of light.

As for the girl, her transformation from human to elemental form guarantees a change from gendered mortality to immortal status. Her youthful energy, sexual curiosity, and willfulness converted into fire and bright light, she blazes; she gleams; she is passion and hope all at once. Now she is the symbol of life. The Frau remarks, almost surprised, how brightly the girl's light shines. She implies that it's giving her more than she knew to expect, not only passion and light, but the illumination of life itself. Not a figure of innocence betrayed or moral martyrdom, the gleaming girl ends the story as Frau Trude's redeemer and, by implication, rescuer of a whole class of witches heretofore stranded in the realm of death. She becomes an exemplar of what gay beat poet Harold Norse calls "the fiery force": "Nothing more than the life force as we know it. It is the flame of desire and love, of sex and beauty, of pleasure and joy as we consume and are consumed, as we burn with pleasure and burn out in time" (2003, xix). Of course, neither the girl nor the witch "burn[s] out in time." Living outside mortal constraints in the fiery force of their tale, they perpetuate, for our understanding, their queer ontology of pure flame, pure eroticism, and pure light.

The truth at the core of "Frau Trude" dissolves the potency of prejudices stemming from the "inclusion/exclusion," "who fits/who doesn't" binary. In this tale, truth and transgression walk together to undo any determinate calculation of the fixed or proper meanings of sex, gender, age, feeling, or being, all finally summarized in the meaning of home. The parents work the inclusion/exclusion binary as the calling card of their authority; they want the girl under their roof and they have the right to disown her. Initially, the girl possesses all the trappings of heteronormative familial inclusion, but she chooses to relinquish them. Accepting exclusion from her family to come to Frau Trude, she initiates the possibility of her inclusion in a new relationship.[34] Frau Trude personifies exclusion, as all witches do, and she exploits the fearful power it inspires. But she also endures its loneliness. She chooses the girl to belong to her, so as no longer to feel essentially excluded and alone. Coupled, the two seal a transgressive—and innovative—bond of kinship in *their* house in the woods. Frau Trude and the girl have, in the end, been absorbed into their own self-created "fit" unopposed, consummated but not consumed.

Notes

Special thanks to Jeana Jorgensen for research expertise and Bettina Hutschek and Vanessa Roberts for German translation. Additional thanks to Ann Cvetkovich and Mary Sanger for reading early drafts and providing useful critique. I owe a debt of gratitude to the women in my 1998 University of Winnipeg seminar, especially Nathalie Cohen. With them, I first explored my queer interpretation of "Frau Trude." In Winnipeg I also began using the tools of structural analysis to unlock queer possibilities in fairy tales (see K. Turner [2009]). I continue refining queer fairy-tale analysis with my NYU Performance Studies Department students, four of whom wrote essays for this book.

1. See Grahn (1985), DeJean (1989), and DuBois (1995).

2. Fairy-tale scholarship on issues of sexual jealousy, oedipal rivalry, and the history of the genre open possibilities for my work here, e.g., Tatar (2003), McGlathery (1991), S. Jones ([1995] 2002), Marina Warner (1994), and Bacchilega (1997).

3. Including "The Three Spinners" (ATU 501), "Mother Holle" (ATU 480), "Jorinda and Joringle" (ATU 405), "Rapunzel" (ATU 310), and "The Sweet Porridge" (ATU 565), among others. See Kevin Goldstein's discussion of the wise woman and the princess in "The Goose Girl at the Spring" in chapter 2.

4. Unless otherwise noted, quotations from the tale rely on Bettina Hutschek's English translation of "Frau Trude," made exclusively for the purpose of this essay, from Uther's (1996) complete *KHM*, based on Grimms' (1857) seventh and final edition. Additionally, I refer to translations by Magoun and Krappe (1960), Zipes (1992), and Tatar (2004a).

5. In addition to works cited throughout, see Boswell (1981), Dolan (1987), Wil-

liams (1989), Sedgwick (1990, 1993), Haraway (1991), Nestle (1992), Lorde ([1981] 1993), Case (1993), Michael Warner (1993), de Lauretis (1984, 1994), Grosz (1994), Kennedy and Davis (1994), Stockton (1994, 2009), Doty (1993, 1995), Halberstam (1995, 1998), Lamos (1995), Probyn (1995, 1999), Martin (1996), Glasgow (1997), Munt (1998), Muñoz (1999), White (1999), P. B. Harper (2000), Nealon (2001), Jagose (1996), Edelman (2004), and Freccero (2006). Except Solis (2007), Greenhill (2008), and Orme (2010), little is published in LGBTQ fairy-tale interpretation, but see Greenhill's (1995, 1997) work on same-sex possibilities in balladry.

6. See Stone (2004, 2008). I thank Kay for her many insights into "Frau Trude."

7. Tatar notes the three male figures in "Frau Trude" are "probably kinsmen of the three horsemen that the Russian folklore heroine meets in tales about the witch Baba Yaga" (2004a, 368).

8. Bolte and Polívka (1913, 377) cite Jacob Grimm ([1835] 1854, 394) on the etymological relationship between witches and *trudes*.

9. See Scherf (1987, 270–71) for the complete text of Meier Teddy's 1823 version of "Frau Trude."

10. See Zipes (1988a, 2002a, 2006a) and Bottigheimer (1986, 1987), among others, for historical, biographical, and analytical resources on how the Grimms conceived the tales' use to consolidate and spread nineteenth-century bourgeois values. Indeed, Zipes states that "the genre as an institution operates to safeguard basic male interests and conventions" (1988a, 59). Yet women resisted, for example in the *Kaffeter*, a literary salon active in 1840s Berlin, whose members wrote fairy tales and fairy-tale plays presenting "heroines who found happiness in being educated and single rather than married and brain dead" (Jarvis 1993, 106). Such evidence of a feminist libratory mood does not implicate a homosexual analog, but the German historical record includes, for example, the 1671 account of trader Gretta, who possessed a masculine affect and pursued young girls (Vicinus 1993, 437), and the eighteenth century's Catherine Linck, who passed as a man, fashioning a dildo from leather and pigs' bladders, married a woman, and was eventually executed for her crime (Rupp 1996, 155). Progressively, Germany felt the presence of lesbians in its social midst. By the late nineteenth century, Berlin, Hamburg, and other urban centers were becoming havens for them (Vicinus 1993, 444).

11. Julia Penelope and Susan J. Wolfe's ([1980] 1989) *The Original Coming Out Stories* was among the first collections, influencing those that followed. Also see Plummer's (1995) analysis of the characteristics and meanings of the new genre.

12. Nathalie Cohen (1998, 4) analyzed "Frau Trude" by way of Victor Turner's ([1964] 1972) theory of liminality and initiation, finding that by "coming out" the girl comes to her "queer sexual awakening."

13. An early example is Margaret Cavendish's "The Convent of Pleasure" (1668). Emma Donoghue's *Passions between Women: British Lesbian Culture, 1668–1801* (1993) provides an exemplary catalog of authors, male and female, and printed sources (chapbooks, serializations, novels, and plays) that encouraged dissemination of Sapphic narratives in Britain. Donoghue covers roughly the same period as folklorist Dianne Dugaw ([1989] 1996), who treats the theme of female transvestism in the English popular ballad. Also see Moore (1997) on the Sapphic history of the British novel. The subgenre continued to thrive for centuries into the era of my own lesbian tutelage with films such as *The Killing of Sister George* (Robert Aldrich, 1968) and the German cult favorite *Mädchen in Uniform* (Leontine Sagan, 1931).

14. Sedgwick's queer take on Diderot's *The Nun* (1797) unmasks the privilege of the young novice Suzanne's innocence. Her state of ignorance and passivity, "pure unknowing," opposes the epistemological impurity of the seducing, older Mother Superior. However, Sedgwick amply demonstrates Suzanne's opposition as mediated by her "vibrant willfulness" and selfishness (1993, 31). Suzanne knows more than a conventional reading aimed at preserving the tension of the opposition allows: "Is it any wonder that, far from passively *lacking* the knowledge that what is going on constitutes 'sexuality,' she actively and lustily *repels* it?" (38; emphasis in original).

15. A lingering problem in lesbian and queer studies revolves around the issue of lesbian invisibility/visibility in the past. Retrieval of characters from the past depends on derivation from the modern lesbian whereby, as Jagose maintains, "the historical subject is rendered in terms that are not her own" (2002, 23). Jagose prefers a reading of "lesbian" characters in Dickens and James as perverse, pre-sexological, anticipatory figures, designations that could equally be assigned to Frau Trude and the girl.

16. While described by the Grimms as a "little girl," her defiant attitude, prevarications, claims, and actions weigh against the conventional diminutive. Likely she is a teen and certainly pubescent. When they have family and school support, some teens currently "come out" successfully at twelve to fourteen years (see Denizet-Lewis 2009).

17. See Stone (1993, 297).

18. While I describe her as "intrigued," she exemplifies "curiosity," used by the Grimms in their tales and by fairy-tale scholars as a standard description of girls and women seeking forbidden knowledge (see Bacchilega 1997; Tatar 2003, 165–70; 2004; Greenhill 2008).

19. Bottigheimer suggests the Grimms understood Eve as the first sinner, deserving punishment for "misusing her voice in speaking with the serpent" (1987, 170). Tatar marks the connection between Eve's disobedience and that of curious

girls in her discussion of the Grimms' "The Virgin Mary's Child" (1992, 26–29). Referring to the Eve story, Renfroe (2001) discusses initiation and disobedience in Carter's "The Bloody Chamber" (1979a).

20. Butler locates subversive possibility in a "repetition that fails to repeat loyally" the identities assigned by systems of power (1993, 220).

21. Barthes's chapter "Waiting" in *A Lover's Discourse* inspired my understanding of Frau Trude's state of longing for the girl. Another relevant passage is "the other comes here where I am waiting, here where I have already created him/her. And if the other does not come, I hallucinate the other: waiting is a delirium" (1978, 39).

22. Though the witch may be a stranger (see, e.g., McGlathery 1991, 116) encountered by chance or by getting lost, she may also live locally: right next door, as in "Rapunzel," or not too far off, as in "Frau Trude." Few fairy-tale witches have names, and though hers signals her as archetype (witch = *trude*, see note 9), it also identifies her as a knowable individual.

23. See Bachelard ([1938] 1964) on the history of fire, its use in alchemy, its purification aspects, and its use as a sexual symbol. The dissident radical lesbian theologian Mary Daly theorizes the power of elemental female fire, defining "pyrosophy" as women's "impassioned wisdom" and "pyromancy" as women's ancient practice of divination by fire or flame (1984, 187). For fire symbolism in general, see Matthews (1986, 75–77, "Fire") and Hall (1979, 121–22, "Fire").

24. If burning to death in "Frau Trude" equals being devoured in early versions of ATU 334 (Scherf 1987, 47), the ogress of old is up to her usual tricks. In a conventional reading, only her murderous means change, from primitive cannibalism to Christian-friendly conflagration.

25. For associations of diabolism and sodomy in medieval England, see Dinshaw (1999). Conner illuminates the historical linkings of faggot, bundle of sticks, fire, heretic, and homosexual (1993, 177–78) and the old Germanic terms *"ergi, argr, and scratta,* which weave together the concepts of gender variance, homoeroticism, and the practice of magic" (178, also 163–66). The witch-hunter's manual *Malleus Maleficarum* (1486) or *Der Hexenhammer* (*The Hammer of Witches*) denounces women's carnality, pronouncing it the source of her demonic temptations, including having sex with the devil and recruiting innocent women to his service (see MacKay 2006). German witchcraft historiography demonstrates the entanglements of gender, homoeroticism, diabolism, and witchery (see Durrant 2007, 154–60; Roper 1994, 2004; Clark 1999); on demonic conspiracy and rumor, see Frankfurter (2006). Bottigheimer discusses the Grimms' participation in and contribution to nineteenth-century Germany's medieval revival in which library and archival materials were used as sources for images of Eve's sin and for values such as the silencing

of women (1987, 167–72). Though old, associations between homosexuality and diabolism are sadly also new; a February 2010 sermon preached in Philadelphia by Martin Luther King Jr.'s daughter, Bernice King, referred to gay attractions as "the work of the devil" and to gay persons, in their seductiveness, as "sly like the devil" (Lorna Reid, personal communication).

26. Mackensen argues that this duality does not push the tale's lineage back before the seventeenth century when the identity of witches and devils was more pronounced (1934/1940, 225). Nevertheless, the Frau Trude figure recalls long-standing historic links between witchery, devilry, and sodomy (previously discussed) and associations of devilry with old women. Jungian analyst Marie-Louise von Franz (1995, 126) discusses the devil's grandmother and Marina Warner describes medieval portrayals of the devil's own "wrinkled female dugs—his perversion blazoned on his chest as breasts that have lost their true purpose of nursing" (1994, 47). She equates this image of infertility with a "perverted dimension of the natural, [that] becomes transgressive in itself, open to derision as well as fear" (47–48).

27. "Flaming," meaning negatively conspicuous, referred in the late eighteenth and early nineteenth centuries to sexually flagrant wenches. Its use as slang to describe obvious homosexuals came into vogue in the 1970s, but the term retains a longer association with unrepressed transgressive behaviors (see Harper 2001–10).

28. On the fateful relations between fairy-tale hags/witches and young characters, see Bettelheim (1976), Tatar (2003) on female oedipal conflicts and the rivalrous mother figure split into good and evil, and McGlathery (1991, 115–22) on the witch/old woman's resentments and jealousies and her need to thwart the budding desires of young girls. See also Lyndal Roper (2004) on envy and old women in German witchcraft history.

29. The abundant feminist literature treating this complex includes Vance (1984), Rubin (1975), MacCormack and Strathern (1980), Sanday (1981), Daly (1978, 1984), Eisler (1995), Okpewho (1998), Doniger (1999), Felman (1975), Irigaray (1985), Friedman (1987), Schneider (1997), Radner (1993), Hollis, Pershing, Young (1993), Marina Warner (1994), and Bottigheimer (2004).

30. See Marcia Ian's (1993) critique of the Freudian phallic mother and Kay Turner (2010) on witch figures as maverick phallic mothers, exemplified by Frau Trude.

31. Mary Douglas (1973, 136–44) discusses social and symbolic boundaries between inside/outside and their power to enforce conformity. Witchcraft historiography on the subject provides especially relevant background for reading "Frau Trude." See Robin Briggs (1996), Deborah Willis (1995), Purkiss (1996), Rowlands (2003), Davies and de Blécourt (2004), and Toivo (2008). See also Isidore Okpewho's (1998) feminist analysis of contemporary African folk narratives featuring marginalized but magical old women.

32. For affect-centered queer theoretical approaches, see Dinshaw (1999), Nealon (2001), Cvetkovich (2003), Eng and Kazanjian (2003), Sedgwick (2003), Muñoz (2009), and Stockton (2009).

33. Light symbolism is old and culturally widespread (see Matthews 1986, "light" and "lamp"). Judeo-Christian symbolism contrasts light (good) and darkness (evil), as in "The light of the righteous shines brightly, but the lamp of the wicked is snuffed out" (Proverbs 13:9). Bachelard ([1938] 1964, 106) suggests that fire is idealized as love when transformed into light.

34. "Frau Trude," along with other tales wherein needs and desires are met in creative, non-normative kinship arrangements or marriages, problematizes Bengt Holbek's (1987) normative conclusion that the fairy tale attempts to resolve three main binary tensions, youth/adults; male/female; low status/high status. On lesbian, gay, and queer kinship theory, see Weston (1991), Edelman (2004), Kay Turner (2009), and Eng (2010).

BEYOND THE GRIMMS

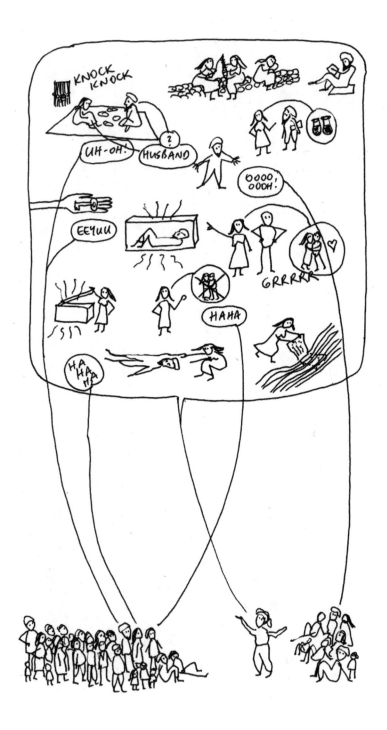

12

Destroying Patriarchy to Save It

Safdár Tawakkolí's Afghan Boxwoman

MARGARET A. MILLS

Women tricksters, systematic rule-breakers and rule-benders by the standards of everyday behavior, are very popular and pervasive figures in Islamic popular literature and tradition in general (see Mills 1999, 2000a, 2000b, 2001). They are abundantly represented in the over 450 hours of narratives in Afghan Persian (Dari) language I have been able to record from 1974 through the present. The idea that women are tricksters by nature is reinforced by such Persian expressions as "She's a real daughter of Eve!" used to comment on some contemporary woman's devious behavior. Women tricksters are said to be "seven steps ahead of the devil himself," but this raises a question pertinent to the story below and others. If women can outsmart the devil, that master of perversity, what is their trickery in service of? Suggesting some answers to that question also addresses the question of what queer is or what is available for queering in this and other tales of tricky women emerging from, indeed flourishing in, patriarchal traditions. Reluctant to police the readings of this tale by imposing a unitary analytic frame as preface, I endeavor to call attention to aspects of this performance and its context to illustrate the range of possible readings of it. Notes to the translation itself also point to moments in the story when things may be seen as queer, or queerable. Further, readers are invited to ignore these notes ad lib and draw their own que(e)ries.

This story as told lies outside the canon of Grimm-style fairy tales. It contains no magic; rather, it fits in international tale typology as a humorous tale (*schwankmärchen*). A performance text from a certain place and time, this translation is not canonical, though the tale as a type is by no means unknown. Ulrich Marzolph's (1984) typology of Persian tales lists it as *1351B, a tale divergent from the Aarne-Thompson-Uther folktale type index but clearly belonging to the genre, and Marzolph cites other variants in Arabic and Kurdish. Richard Burton (n.d., 172–79) in his notes to the *1001 Nights* mentions a number of thematically related published tales (some of them collected from oral performance) of women trapping unwanted suitors in boxes, from Somadeva's eleventh-century Sanskrit *Kathasaritsagara* (Tawney 1928) to Giovanni Boccaccio's *Decameron* (McWilliams 1995) and George Dasent's *Popular Tales from the Norse* (1859). The tale is offered here more specifically for what it reveals the Grimms' canonized collection to lack: fresh ironies and transgressive moves at play in a particular performance context. It is important for such readings to maintain (as the Grimms' own work and most Grimm scholarship does not) the distinction Katharine Galloway Young (1987) made in folk narrative analysis between story realm (the setting of the tellers' performance) and tale world (the world within the tale). The contemporary study of performed narratives has worked the rich ground between those two loci of meaning.

The Grimms deserve credit for pioneering the notation of the identity of the teller of particular tales. Yet their editorial and ideological priorities stunted that development in their textual practice, while creating a canon that, rich as it is, unduly constrains nonspecialist readers' notions of the flexibility and mobility of folktale texts. Close verbatim translations of performances, when they are possible, open up possibilities for alternative readings through the rich narrative texture (stylistics) and audience responses that are unavailable from canonical literary texts. They offer linguistic and paralinguistic nuances that can make ironies and indeterminacies available to tellers and listeners. Performers of canonical tales, of course, reinsert such performance features and sometimes get accused of hijacking the canon as a result. This volume presents excellent examples of the fruits and joys of such interpretive hijacking and illustrates the need to inhabit and thus reanimate canonical texts, not to be bound by canonization or typologization that yields overly defined, summarized plots and fixed texts around which commentators can only circle and hover.

The variant I present in translation here, of the cluster of stories I am calling after its heroine, "The Boxwoman," was performed by a renowned twentieth-century Afghan male storyteller, Safdár Tavakkolí, for two or three male listeners.[1] The performance is thus informal and intimate in style, with frequent audience comments. My translation preserves the informality of idiomatic expressions and the audience comments, which are of interest for a couple of reasons. It is always illuminating to know what an audience familiar with the stories laughs at. Laughter tracks delight but also insta-bility of meanings and attitudes at play, especially unease. A good deal of the laughter and commentary in this telling is the nervous, even rueful laughter of men reflecting on powers of women that should be controlled by patriarchal norms but are not. Although this monaural recording leaves all the audience comments equally off mic, making it hard to distinguish among speakers, it seems that besides folklorist Ravshan Rahmoní, who invites Safdár to tell his story, there is at least one other audience member speaking on the tape, and probably two.[2] One in particular functions almost as a collaborator, interjecting comments that complete or enlarge slightly on what Safdár himself is saying. This is not simple interruption; in most cases Safdár has paused just slightly at the point where the eager listener puts in his "two cents," so the comments are a kind of audience prompt; "Yes, we get it, we understand." It seemed to me from the overall pattern of comments that this listener considered himself a friend of Safdár's and knew his storytelling. He perhaps even knew and relished this very story from prior performance, judging by his intensified collaborative commen-tary during the climactic scene when the heroine drags the unconscious and befouled mullah from the chest where she has hidden him.

Rahmoní kindly offered me use of his recording in support of a book proj-ect concerning women tricksters in Afghan oral tradition. I was particularly grateful to him for access to a recording made with an all-male audience, the better to understand how Afghan men interpret and enjoy these tales of transgressive women. Islamic literary representations of women tricksters, written almost exclusively by men, tend to be overtly misogynistic; women tricksters are greedy (for sex, wealth, food, or just action) and antisocial.[3]

Afghan Dari oral tradition, if not Muslim oral tradition in general, appeared to me to be more even-handed. The successful woman trickster is not simply antisocial but often, as in the story below, strategically exploiting and exposing the hypocrisy of male would-be authorities. Safdár's obvious relish for this woman hero's display of control over men, especially over a pretentious and misbehaving mullah, and the obvious enjoyment his all-male audience takes from her tricks, reveal the woman trickster at her most virtuosic as an intriguingly polyvalent figure. She wields sexuality; she is not ruled by sexual desire as the negative Muslim literary stereotype of women would have it. Although she can easily subvert and evade male attempts to control her, the total impact of her deeds is not always antisocial, rather she may protect the interests of males who are not themselves exploitative hypocrites. The putative authority and power of patriarchy are pretty well shredded in the course of such a prosocial woman trickster's exploits, but in the end she also protects at least the public appearance of male-centered values. In the story at hand, she wrests authority in the household from her husband through masterful, if playful and highly risky, manipulation of a wager, but, in the process, she also refuses to cuckold him and stringently punishes a would-be seducer.

The misbehaving representative of patriarchy in this story is the would-be mullah, intellectually unqualified,[4] venal, vain, and self-serving. Although anticlerical humor undoubtedly went down particularly well in the determinedly secular context of Marxist-sanctioned public performance during the Soviet occupation of Afghanistan, anticlerical humor was already abundant in Afghan storytelling before the wars began. It survives today even though, or perhaps because, sincere adherence to Islam itself is something most Afghans would probably still deem necessary to a morally functioning society, of which they currently mourn the loss. While Safdár is not at all concerned with portraying his heroine as religiously motivated, it is a delicious moment when, in the end, the heroine forces the erring mullah to take a binding oath by the legendary Nasúh, himself a repentant transgressor of women's privacy.[5]

One observation by Safdár, repeated twice, does seem to index the particular conditions of the Soviet years in Afghanistan. At two different points, remarking on women's supreme power to outsmart men, he says emphatically, "Women *today*, in these times . . . ," perhaps referring to the real progress aspired to by and for women under the Afghan Marxist regime in which women, in cities at least, entered the education system and public workplaces in unprecedented numbers, and gender equality was strongly promoted in the Marxist-controlled press.

However many details of local Afghan color, culture, and politics Safdár invokes to embellish his performance of the boxwoman's story (as I like to think of her), he is working with an international tale type or motif that has traveled widely, as indicated above. Marilyn Jurich (1998, 20–21, 34–35) discusses a tale from India collected by Maeve Stokes (1879, 216–23), also appearing in the *1001 Nights* as translated and annotated with reference to still other variants in Indic and Islamic classical literature by Richard Burton (n.d., 172) and titled by him "The Lady and Her Five Suitors." In it, a woman deals with a whole series of would-be seducers by locking them into stacked trunks or cupboards as they each arrive and successively interrupt the encounter with the previously arrived seducer. In the *1001 Nights* version, the heroine, trying to get her lover (whom she calls her brother) out of prison, has approached a series of officials of increasing rank, all of whom proposition her. Having incarcerated all four in locked sections of a specially constructed cupboard (as well as the carpenter who made the cupboard, who also propositioned her), she leaves town with her lover and the would-be seducers are left trapped for three days, each befouling the one below him before they are discovered and released.

Although the motif of befouling common to this and Safdár's story works differently (paralytic fear is not an issue in the *1001 Nights* tale, though near-death is),[6] the symbolic weight is perhaps similar; the aggressive adult sexual predators are immobilized in a female-controlled enclosure and robbed of normal adult bodily control. By virtue of such infantilization, perhaps they are returned to a less than comfortable womb. Perhaps, too, and queerly enough at a deeper level, infantile fantasy, a desire to return to the womb, to be released from the demands and controls of adult consciousness, lurks repressed in these listeners' laughter. Doubtless none of these listeners would consciously own up to such a desire, but if it is there, it illustrates yet another possible form of "trans"-ness in tales, transparturence, travel across not the divide of death (which is explicit enough in the heroine's comments in our tale) but the divide of birth to preconscious (and indeed pregendered) existence.

Also, as in Safdár's tale, the trickster heroine in other boxwoman stories acts against male abusers of authority to protect not only her own sexual self-determination but also the interests of her man: her husband in Stokes's story and Safdár's and, more transgressively, her lover in the *1001 Nights* version. It merits further reflection that it is men telling, and obviously enjoying, this story about a woman demonstrating her ability to trap and humiliate men, subverting the intentions of both a would-be exploiter (the "mullah" in this case) and her husband, whose legitimate role within this patriarchal society would include having ultimate authority in his household. The very fact that she and her husband can plausibly wager over who shall exercise dominance could be taken several ways, as encouraged by queer theory. Among the simultaneous possibilities are the following: (1) that this male audience is far from sure that patriarchal domestic authority is a "done deal" in their own world; (2) that the couple portrayed is not heteronorma-tively patriarchal but exceptionally egalitarian (and as affectionate as they are playful); (3) that this husband is a bit of a weakling or a dupe, while the wife is the clever one and acts as his protector as well as his manipulator; (4) that the listeners identify collectively with the husband as vulnerable to female manipulation; and/or (5) that they experience some titillation when the heroine's seductive behavior is described, even while they take their distance and laugh at the mullah who falls for it.

Feminist writers on folktales (e.g., Jurich 1999) tend to assume, reason-ably, that women's tales told by and to women will provide the mother lode of antipatriarchal, subversive acts and viewpoints. This male storyteller and his listeners appear to enjoy female exploits that clearly undermine patriarchal authority at home even though the trickster preserves her own chastity and thus her own and her husband's honor. One stratum of male listeners' enjoyment may be, as Afsaneh Najmabadi (1999) argues, that these stories (and more especially tales of women tricksters who *are* out for illicit sex or other selfish pleasures) serve to distance men from women categorically, supporting homosocial and heterophobic social values and practices. In the ample assortment of Afghan stories like this one, how-ever, in which a woman trickster wards off and punishes a more powerful male's attempts to exploit her lower-status self and her man, there is also an element of class, as discussed by Turner and Greenhill in the introduc-tion to this volume. Part of male enjoyment is in the class-based appeal of the underdog trickster, which cuts across gender identity. Heterophobia need not exclude class-based identification, for both effects seem to be at play: comic horror at the woman's virtuosity *and* solidarity with her and her husband against those who threaten the underdog's honor and the sanctity of the home. The pretentious would-be author/mullah's defeat constitutes Safdár's punch line: "That's the story of the mullah writing his book." Yet as I suggest, a third, much queerer and much more deeply buried source of male pleasure could be a fantastic relief from male responsibility in the mullah's horridly amusing trip back to unconsciousness (or preconsciousness) in the womb/box.

This is also perhaps a place to reflect that the Afghan home is specifically the women's realm, with male authority only attempting to control it from without. Domestic space in the tale world is not the space of secluded control of females, as patriarchal values would idealize it, but of female control and subversive activities. This makes the trickster woman's sphere of action a poor fit with, and I think a direct challenge to, Michel de Certeau's (1980, 1984) classic theoretical dichotomy distinguishing strategy (the position of the dominant, involving the control of territory and advance planning) from tactics (the reactive/resistant position of the dominated, opportunistic actions in physical domains they do not control). In this case and others, the woman trickster reactively and opportunistically maneuvers her adversary onto turf that she does control, domestic space (and time), where he becomes just a tool in her larger scheme to dominate her husband, one that unfolds through her advance planning toward larger goals. It seems to me that male laughter in this and similar stories hinges in general on the instability of patriarchy, of apparent dominance and real power, both in male/male and female/male relations.

Are we then disappointed that the bottom line here, the end point of this story, seems to celebrate, or at least support, the appearance of heteronormative monogamy? There was a great deal of fun in getting there. Further, this hetero seems not so normal, departing as it does in oblique ways from the Afghan patriarchal ideal and its twin, misogynist stereotype of female perversity. And as Lévi-Strauss taught us and Turner and Greenhill remind us in this volume's introduction, the linearity of plots is only apparent; a tale's "goods to think (with)" continue to resonate in its orchestral array of ironies, possibilities, and mixed motives, which remain deliciously and perpetually unresolved. Also unresolved is this (admittedly female and non-Afghan) reader's capacity to decipher with accuracy multiple layers of Afghan male humorous engagement, conscious and not. In that sense, this reading of mine remains an exercise in xeno-ethnography, trying to understand other genders' potential for narrative queerness, in cultural contexts other than my own, unlike other authors in this collection who demonstrate through their own readings, with both authority and creativity, extended possibilities for women inhabiting the stories they tell or read.

"Women's Tricks"

Ravshan: What are you going to tell about, Nephew?[7]

Safdár: There was this guy, he'd read a few pages, bits of a book, and he thought to himself, "Now, by God, I've gotten an education, I'm a mullah,[8] after all! [*Laughs.*] Come on, then, a book—I'll write a book—all the mullahs, the theologians,[9] have written a book. I'm going to write one, too! [*Laughs, listeners laugh. Audience member: "I'll get some profit off it!"*] I'll just get some pages together, put 50–60 blank pages together and bind them up."[10] He thought some more, and wrote a title on the cover, *Wiles of Women or Women's Tricks,*[11] as if to say, "I'm collecting women's tricks." [*Audience member: "Yeah . . ."*]

OK? He wrote that and then went and wrote some more, went and threw it all together, there—wherever—whatever alley he'd wander through, whatever neighborhood, wherever. He got about half his book filled. [*Audience member: "Yeah."*] So he came along to Qala Sháida, or Kárteh Sakhí, or maybe Dashti Bárchí, to those places.[12] He went to Dashti Bárchí, just around there, where there were a few women sitting around on the wall between two fields,[13] doing some work. Two or three of them were busy spinning with drop spindles, one was stitching something.

So right there he spreads out his handkerchief to sit on, gets out his book, his pen and ink, and gets busy watching these women and writing, watching and writing.

One of the women was a little quicker, and she whispered, "Oh, my dear, that mullah guy—he's watching us and writing in his book, watching and writing, he's up to no good." [*Audience: "Yeah, he's writing poetry about us."*]

"He's making up poems about us or he's doing some magic spells, what's he up to?"

Another one said, "No, he's writing something about us, writing down what we do, then looking some more."

So OK, he shut his book, finished writing, shut the book. The woman who'd said, "He's watching us and writing things down," she calls out, says, "Mullah, you wrote something down, by God! And you were watching us, writing, watching and writing—tell the truth! What did you write in that book of yours?!"

"Nothing."

"No, tell the truth!"

He said, "Go on, don't worry about it."

She said, "No, tell the truth, what you've got there! You're no innocent! If you don't tell the truth, I'm going to tell the guys in Hajji's family."[14] [*Laughter.*]

So she forced him to tell, and he said, "I'm writing about women's tricks." [*Audience: "Uh-oh! Uh-oh!" Laughter.*]

"What do you know about women's tricks?" she said, "What do you know, that you can talk about women's tricks?"

"Well, I've got women's tricks right in my pocket! I know *you've* got this kind of tricks, and that one has that kind of tricks, and that other one has that other kind—this kind of tactics and tricks, that other one has that other kinds of skills and arts [*another audience member: "Yeah!"*], short women are like this, tall ones are like that, the tan-colored ones are like so and the pale ones are like so and the yellowish ones are like so"[15]—he makes like a list, there—

"OK, fine," she said. "You must be tired, worn out, come on, let's go to my house so I can give you some tea."[16] [*Second audience member: "Yeah!"*]

They go off together. He follows her to the house, and she immediately lays out seat cushions for him, and oo-oo—she makes a big fuss all around him, makes him some tea right away, and puts the pots of food on to cook, starts to cook him a pot of rice. And it's lunch time—she knows, "My husband Jacob will be along now."

Now she had a wager going with her husband, they'd broken a wishbone together,[17] and they wagered for who would have the "say," the authority in the house. Well, she brings a pitcher of water for the mullah to wash his hands, and she washes his hands for him, and spreads the cloth for the food. And she puts the chain on the front door. She locks the door, and washes her own hands, and sits down with the mullah.[18] Starts to eat. The mullah takes a bite, and she takes a bite,[19] and with the second bite, she makes up a mouthful with her fingers and holds it close to the mullah's mouth. And the mullah has gotten a devil up his ass—mullahs get the devil in them really fast, you know?! [*Audience member: "Mullahs get hot!" Laughing.*] Mullahs get hot! Right away he took that mouthful out of her hand. [*Audience member: "Yeah—"*] When he takes that mouthful. [*Second audience member: "He gets hot!"*] Yeah, right, he gets hot—and he's just *quivering.* [*Audience member: "So he eats a little more . . ." Laughing.*] *Right* away he makes *her* up a mouthful. [*Audience member: "Yeah, yeah, yeah!"*] He makes up a mouthful and holds it out for her. She leans forward and takes it. [*Audience member: "Yeah—"*] Just when she takes it, there's a knock at the door. [*Audience member: "Ooohh!"*] The door's locked, there's a knocking on the door, "Hurry up, how come you've locked the door right at lunch time?!"

The mullah says, "Who's that?"

"My husband—" [*Audience member: "Ooohh!"*]

[*Whispering*] "God curse you, your husband's come home, where are you going to put me?!! With me here in the house, your husband here, and the door locked—when he sees me here, won't he make a scene? This isn't some empty *dasht,* it's Dashti Bárchí!"[20] [*Laughter.*]

She said, "It's OK, don't panic!" She'd told him before, "Go on, don't get mixed up with women's tricks. [*Audience member: "Yeah—"*] You'll get killed at the hands of some stupid woman!" The mullah had said to himself, "What has she got for tricks? What does *she* know?"

So she said, "Don't panic. I can hide you in this trunk. I'll open it up right now"—a great big wooden trunk, like they used to have. [*Audience member: "Yeah."*] She opens the lid and stuffs the mullah into the trunk, and her husband's yelling and yelling, "How long till you open this door?!!"—while she gets the trunk locked up and tucks away the key. [*Quietly.*] She went and opened the door, and when she opened it, her husband is yelling, "Bastard,[21] you locked the door right at lunch time, no matter how I yelled, how come you didn't answer the door?!!"

"Sit down, don't yell, it's OK—swallow your anger—"[22] [*Audience member:*

"*Yeah.*"] This guy looks around and sees the food all spread out on the cloth, with the tray of rice and the guest cushions and pillows all laid out, and he says, "Who did you spread all this out for?"

"Sit down and I'll tell you the story," she said, "Now I—maybe ten years ago, I had a boyfriend, when I was still in my father's house, before I came to you—after I came to *your* house I didn't see him at all, I couldn't, but today by chance he turned up, and he said, 'Today you've really stuck a thorn in my peace [of mind],' this guy said that, 'By God, a thorn all of my life—no one else has gotten to me this way, in all my life! After all these years, it's just like ten years ago!' [*Laughter.*] Today, by chance, he appeared right in front of this house, so I brought him in and [*mumbling*] until just now I've been making a little love with him. . . . [*Audience laughing.*] I locked the door, I said, 'He'll eat some food, and after that I'll pass a little time, make a little love with him.' We said, 'Let's eat a little, then sit and enjoy ourselves a little.' So there we were, with the food, and I made up a bite and put it in his mouth, and he made up a bite and put it in my mouth, and then you knocked on the door. You knocked on the door, so I put him in the trunk [*laughs*] and locked it, and that made me late opening the door."

"What are you saying, you bastard?!"

"By God, it's true! I'm telling the truth!" [*Laughter.*]

And the mullah—this guy—the mullah, right there, now, his ass is beginning to stink [*laughs*], he's losing it altogether, right then he fouled his pants, and inside the trunk it starts to stink. In his heart he's thinking "By God, it's really true what she said before, she's going to get me killed, and after *this* it'll be a bad death—"

So this guy, the husband, is good and mad, he's in a rage. [*Audience member: "Furious—"*] "Bastard, you've hidden him in this trunk?!" He *jumps* for the key, but before he can grab it, she [*holds it out*], says, "Here, take the key! Open the trunk, he's inside it!"

Just as he takes the key [*smiles*], she says, "Ha!! I remembered, you forgot!" [*Audience member: "Eeyuuu!"*] "Ohh, curses on your father!" [*Audience member: "Eeyuuu!"*] "Shame on you, shame! [*Laughter.*] At the hands of a woman's art! Shame, shame, shame!" [*Audience member: "What a tactic!"*] He threw down the key, and he says, "Now look, you used *these* tactics, all this just for the sake of that wager—to have the 'say' in this house?! Look what you came up with, to put it over on me!"

She said, "Well, OK, guys are just so foolish—you just don't have the tricks. [*Laughter.*] We couldn't do it if you weren't so foolish, so simple!" [*Laughter.*]

It's true, men get taken in by women's tricks right away—[*Audience member: "Ahhh!"*] They trick men really easily—with all their tricks and tactics, forget it! [*Audience member: "They've got their tricks and tactics!" Second audience member: "And then women—"*] And women *these* days, in these times! [*Both laughing.*] Women can trick the devil himself! [*Claps once. Audience member: "Yeah, yeah!"*]

So she said, "You believed it all—is it logical, would a logical mind believe that if I *had* a boyfriend, I'd bring him home, and be with him [*Audience member: "Eating—"*] like that, going after pleasure and love and fooling around, and do all these things, then hide him in a trunk and lock it, and then sit here and *tell* you the whole story? Woo, are you simple! The point is, I won the wager, so do you give up, or not?"

He said, "I give up, I give up, I give up already! [*Laughing. Audience member: "Come on, let's eat!"*] I submit, you've got the 'say' in this house, come on, let's eat!"

She washes his hands,[23] sits him down, and says, "There, now, I laid you out a seat cushion, propped up your pillow [*audience laughter*], and brought this food that was all cooked, laid it out on the tray, but you didn't come. I waited for a while, then I latched the door, I said, 'Let's not have anyone else show up—'[24] Then I took one bite from your side, and one bite from mine, pretending I was eating with you—'I'm eating with Mamdali's dad.'[25] [*Laughter.*] Since you didn't come, I started, then you knocked on the door, and by the time I got the door open, it was later still—Sit down, let's eat!"

So the guy sat down and ate with her, together, had some tea—she buttered him up, till finally, "Go on, back to work, now!" She sent the guy off to work, went out to see him off, to make sure he's *go-o-ne* [*audience member: "Got on the bus and left—"*] off to his work, anyway. Got on the bus at the bus stop, and the bus left, he was gone. [*Audience member: "Then she comes back—"*]

She comes back. [*Both laugh.*] Picked up the key. [*Laughter.*] Opened the box lid, and the box is stinking! [*Laughs*] Like anything! She doesn't lean over that box! [*Laughing. Audience member: "Ohh, look at the mullah!"*] And the mullah—he's out like a light. Nothing. [*Audience member: "She drags him by the feet*—"] "Mullah, get up!" Nothing, nothing! "Are you dead? Since when—last year?"[26]

Well, she drags him out—drags him out, splashes some water on his face, gives him something sweet to drink, till he comes to [*laughter*], and he's messed himself all *over* his pants—he's so under her sway, just so totally under her sway, that he's just at her mercy. She said, "OK, are you going to write about women's tricks any more, or not?"

He said, "No, I'm done with women's tricks."

She said, "No, that's not enough. It's not enough, your just saying 'I'm done with women's tricks.' First," she said, "you draw a line with your nose, in front of me!"[27]

"OK," he said to her, "I'll draw a line with my nose," and he draws a *good* line with his nose, on the ground, with his *nose* like that, and says, "I drew a line with my nose!"

Then she said, "Let's go down by the stream."[28] She takes him to the stream, and takes his book, and washes the ink off all its pages, down over his head, and throws the book in the water, then says, "Now—do you repent?"

He said, "I repent, the repentance of Nesú![29] That I'll never even *mention* women's tricks again! By my earlobes![30] I repent of it, right here!"

She said, "Go on, then." She said, "Look, I brought you to the point of death and I saved your life. [*Audience member: "And I also won the thing, the wager*—"] And on the other hand, I won the wager. But if I'd been some *stupid* woman, I *would* have gotten you killed! Go on, then, leave this stuff alone."

So there, she washed away the mullah's book over his own head, made him repent, and made it a way, you know, to win the control in her own house. [*Audience member: "That's what women are like!"*] Women are like that, you know? Women these days are that clever—that's the story of the mullah writing his book.

NOTES

Jalil Ahmad Osmani, for transcription aid and comments, and Ulrich Marzolph, for commentaries and references, are thanked profoundly for their contributions to this discussion. Any errors of translation or interpretation remain my own.

1. Safdár Tawakkolí's performance of two tales about woman tricksters, the first

of which is translated here, was tape recorded by the Tajikistani folklorist Ravshan Rahmoní while he was stationed in Kabul during the Soviet occupation of Afghanistan in the 1980s, working as a translator for Russian-speaking instructors at the national technical university. In his free time, with his own resources, he was able to record a number of performances by local storytellers, many of which he has since published in the volume titled *Afsánaháyi Darí* (Rahmoní 1995).

Of Safdár Tawakkolí, the storyteller, Rahmoní (1995, 40) wrote that in the early 1980s he was a well-known poet, singer, raconteur, and performer of oral traditional narratives, born in Yak Aulang district, Bámiyán Province, and educated through the sixth grade. A Shi'a Hazara, Tawakkolí belongs to a much-abused religious and ethnic minority in Afghanistan. According to the anthropologist S. Akhtar Mousavi, of the Afghan Ministry of Higher Education (personal communication) he survived later upheavals of the almost thirty years since this performance, including mass killing of Hazara men in his own home of Yak Aulang by Taliban. I have not yet been able to meet him.

2. By the year 2000 when Rahmoní shared this recording with me, he no longer had detailed information about the identities of those present in the audience.

3. For a telling example, see Marzolph (2006, 236–55).

4. It is also strangely gratifying to me that he is a failed ethnographer. His pretentious project is essentially to write an ethnography of women's tricks, informed, it appears, by the descriptive theories of medieval physiognomy whereby different women's (and men's) personalities are reflected in their physical appearance. The mullah's pretentions should caution all of us ethnographers about attempting to "write up" with contemporary theoretical flourishes the "subaltern" and her devices, *pace* James Scott in *Weapons of the Weak* (1985) and other works.

5. See note 29 on Nasúh's legend, as developed in Muslim religious literature.

6. The motif of the man who aspires to observe and know all women's tricks likewise belongs to the tale version with only one box and one lover.

7. Literally, "Uncle's dear," a friendly form of address to a junior male nonrelative. Rahmoní, the academic, seems to be asserting, in a friendly form, some mild status hierarchy over Safdár. Safdár may well be getting his own back rather directly with his description of the intellectual pretensions of the "educated" mullah. *Caveat emptor*. The story was told by Safdár Tawakkolí to Rahmoní and friends, Kabul, Afghanistan, mid-1980s.

8. Islamic clergyman, approximately like a rabbi in authority.

9. *Mujtáhed*, the term refers to Shi'a clergy who have achieved a formal level of expertise sufficient to establish their authority to interpret scripture. This category for clergy is not used in Sunni Islam.

10. He plans to have a blank book made up of a certain size, which he can then fill up to create a manuscript.

11. The title, *Heylát un-Nisá yá Makrát un-Nisá*, is in Arabic, making the subject and writer sound more scholarly to Persian speakers.

12. These are all well-known neighborhoods around Kabul with substantial Shi'a populations.

13. Irrigated agricultural fields are separated by low walls or dikes that retain water when the fields are irrigated. Some are wide enough to be used as footpaths.

14. A threat that she will get the neighborhood strong man's retainers to take him, a stranger, in hand.

15. The idea that physical appearance reveals character was a well-represented physiognomic theory down to early modern times in Europe as well.

16. "Will you drink tea with me?" is a generic "line" inviting sexual contact.

17. When Afghans break a wishbone together they do not make wishes but simply agree to compete for something. From the point of breaking the wishbone together, if either party gives the other one anything, the receiver has to say, "I remember [the wager]." If he or she forgets to say the formula, the giver of the object wins the wager.

18. In formal hospitality a host or hostess does not sit down to eat with guests but remains standing to serve the guest(s) unless he or she is well above them in status. Sitting down to eat together, especially for a woman with a man, is an intimate or seductive act.

19. They are eating with their hands in traditional fashion from a common platter of food, perhaps with side dishes, laid out on an eating cloth between them as they sit on the floor.

20. A *dasht* is open country, mostly flat, with brush and grass. The storyteller plays on the name of the now built-up Kabul neighborhood, invoking its former status as open ground. The mullah worries that the husband will call in reinforcements, or simply that the neighbors will know.

21. "Bastard," a standard epithet used for men or women, simultaneously insults her parents and implies that she is socially worthless.

22. This is a conciliating phrase but it also admonishes him to be even tempered in a society where losing one's temper causes one to lose face. Self-control is a quality meriting respect. Thus her ability to cause her husband to lose his composure, with what follows, also compromises his authority.

23. Offering a basin and ewer of water, a polite service to guests or superiors.

24. As a prudent housewife, avoiding the possibility of a guest dropping in who would then need to be fed the prepared lunch out of politeness.

25. Politely referring to him by their son's name. Direct use of a spouse's personal name is rude.

26. Because of the smell. Loss of control of the bowels, whether farting or defecating, is as hilarious as it is socially disastrous. Pakistani folklorist Adam Nayyar (personal communication) opined that because release of the bowels is a common event in death, the abundant regional humor over the loss of bowel control and consequent loss of social status is psychologically charged by fears of death.

27. A gesture of complete repentance and obedience extracted from misbehaving children, who are compelled to get down on all fours, rear in the air, and draw a line on the ground with their noses.

28. This scene could be inside the house compound or outside. Where piped water is not available, a traditional house of sufficient size would, if possible, have a small water channel running through its courtyard, tapping off a nearby communal water channel.

29. According to legend, Nesú (Arabic Nasúh) was an effeminate-looking man with prurient sexual interest in women who grew his hair long and masqueraded as a woman in order to get a job in a women's bath house giving massages and body scrubs. He became highly successful, until one day one of his regular clients, a princess, lost a valuable jewel in the bath. When all the workers were about to be strip-searched to find the jewel, Nesú went into one of the private rooms, prayed fervently and repented, weeping, promising to give up his evil ways as he had tried and failed to do repeatedly in the past. At the point when his name was called for the search, a shout went up that the jewel had been found. God had accepted Nesú's fervent prayer and his vow, which he kept henceforth, immediately refusing to massage the princess as she then requested and never again working in the women's baths. The story is told by Jaláluddín Rúmí in the *Mathnawi* (Nicholson 1933/1934, bk. 5). Rúmí tells that Nasúh had asked a holy man to pray for him to succeed at repentance, and that this terrifying event was the answer to his prayer. Commentators have pointed out that the term *taubeh-i nasúh* as used in the Arabic of the Koran (sura 66, "The Forbidding," verse 8) simply means a sincere, permanent repentance and has no reference to this legend. Interestingly, with regard to this particular story's theme and context, the whole sura (chapter) admonishes the Prophet to control his wives better though the expression is not so narrowly themed in colloquial use. Rúmí himself seems to have attached the word as a personal name to a legend that appears in earlier writings without a named protagonist. "Nasúh's repentance" is used as a phrase for any such sincere, binding oath of repentance foreswearing immoral behavior; but here it is particularly fitting as the mullah swears off an unnatural interest in the private affairs of women. Jalil Ahmad Osmani (personal

communication), commenting on the expression, attributed the whole tale to the Koran. It seems likely the storyteller and other Afghans, like Osmani, would consider it a religious story.

30. Grabbing one's earlobes with both hands is a gesture for oath taking.

13

"The Grave Mound"

A Queer Adaptation

ELLIOT GORDON MERCER

The Grimm brothers' "The Grave Mound" is a short, moralistic tale that includes socioeconomic struggles, divine intervention, and non-normative homosocial bonding as a means of promoting the Christian values of forgiveness, charity, honesty, power against evil, and companionship. It opens with a vivid description of great wealth and vibrant prosperity. The riches belong to a single person, a lone farmer, initially portrayed as commendable for amassing the rewards of maintaining a smart and steadfast work ethic; he has a plentitude of food, property, good health, a successful business, and well-cared for livestock. The richness of this man's life may appear noble and praiseworthy, yet a quick plot twist early in the tale reverses the audience's view of the wealthy farmer. It is this plot change that first posits a moralistic lesson on the nature of worldly possessions. While the farmer is viewing his riches, an unknown voice begins to speak from an undisclosed location, putting into question the Christian ethics of the farmer's life. This disembodied voice can be read more literally as the voice of God, or another omniscient figure who has been able to both observe and assess the farmer's existence. Alternatively, this voice could represent popular opinion in the farmer's region, and the message he hears could be his realization of the collective "talk of the town." In either case, the farmer is asked to account for his deeds and provide examples of how he has used his prosperity to forward the Christian messages of charity, love, and faithfulness to those who surround him. In this conversation the farmer is not given a voice himself; instead, his heart speaks. It unabashedly discloses the truth, announcing that he has not followed the words of God and instead spent his time indulging the cardinal sins of luxury, greed, and pride. Speaking from the heart, the farmer acknowledges his selfishness.

Cast as a sinner, the farmer, not immediately punished for his un-Christian behavior, is instead left alone with his realization and the opportunity to repent. Embedding this message of opportunity for atonement into the tale shows the audience that they, too, have time to account for their wrongdoings and a chance to return to the teachings of the church. Soon a poor man comes to the farmer's door begging for a loan of food to feed his children. Righting his ways, the farmer gifts twice the amount of food the poor man requests in exchange for a favor: the poor man is to watch over the farmer's grave for three nights after his burial. Three nights of watch is symbolic of the period between the burial and resurrection of Christ.[1] In choosing this number of nights for protection, the farmer soon suggests that he wants his body and soul to be guarded until the time has come for his ascension to heaven.

Having quickly changed his ways and prepared for his death, the farmer dies and the poor man sets out to fulfill his promise to watch over the grave. Two nights go by without event, but on the third night he encounters a figure standing alongside the churchyard wall: a lonely paid-off soldier. Waiting through the night, these men encounter the devil, who has come to collect the sinful soul of the rich farmer. Together, the two use trickery to fend off the devil until dawn while cunningly extorting great amounts of gold from him in the process.

The tale concludes with a change in domestic arrangements for the two men. The poor man offers to split the devil's gold between the two and presumably part ways, but the soldier renounces his share, instructing the poor farmer to have it given to the poor. After announcing his rejection of his half of the gold, the soldier states that he will come to the poor farmer's cottage and they will live together "for as long as God permits." Ending their tale in this way, the Grimms suggest that these two socially marginal men commit to join together for the rest of their lives. Since the farmer has a collection of children, though there is no mention of a wife, by choosing to enter into cohabitation the pair not only appear to commit to spending the rest of their lives together as domestic partners but also to forge a new family unit consisting of two fathers and the children they will raise. It is this creation of an obviously homosocial and arguably homosexual bond between the two men that inspired my reworking of this tale.

In this adaptation of "The Grave Mound," I have similarly drawn from the Grimms' themes of abundant wealth, divine intervention, and non-normative homosocial/homosexual bonding. However, I have replaced the Christian thematic of the original tale with a message of social and political support between members of the LGBTQ community. I have moved the story's setting from a rural one to present-day New York City and substituted the tale's characters with new personae who fit the mold of the Grimms' originals but are notably modernized. The rich farmer becomes a selfish, greedy drag queen who has only used her performance talents to serve her own needs, never hosting a charity benefit or appearing for free at a community event. The poor farmer is represented by a young, inexperienced drag queen down on her luck. The paid-off soldier has been transformed into an old transvestite prostitute searching aimlessly for companionship. And the devil has been reinterpreted as a corrupt financier viciously capitalizing on the current subprime lending debacle.

As the Grimms edited their collection of fairy tales for various editions they not only highlighted numerous Christian references but also reconstructed the tales to be appropriate as educational material (Zipes 2002b). Through this process the tales came to be seen as teaching tools that could be used to instill what the Grimms thought was proper to learn. My adaptation of this tale's more general Christian moralism to express the social power and political potential of the LGBTQ community comes at a time when LGBTQ activism is at a crucial point in both American and global history. With LGBTQ communities currently fighting for both social and legal equality, LGBTQ civil rights have become a popular source of national debate. Same-sex marriage laws, civil union benefits, domestic partnership rights, equal opportunity employment, adoption restrictions, and hate crime legislation are not only contested informally in public discourse but have recently become the topics of congressional rulings, Supreme Court hearings, statewide elections, and lawsuits nationally covered by the media. My adaptation of this tale presents my optimistic belief in what can be taught and believed within the LGBTQ community, the idea that the continued development of social bonding and collective community support will deliver the outcome the Grimms give to their two protagonists: the ability for a same sex couple to announce a public union, cohabit by choice, raise a family, and live with both financial security and legal protection, all while being free from bias, persecution, and extortion.

One day a rich drag queen stood in her West Village townhouse and looked over her many closets and makeup cases. The lipstick sparkled vigorously, and the sequins dangled abundantly from the gowns. The feather boas of the previous year still lay in such large piles in the loft that the rafters could barely support them. Then she went into her storage unit to look at the well-teased wigs, the fat purses, and the glistening tiaras. Finally she returned to her townhouse and took a look at the pink plastic Caboodles in which she kept her money. As she was standing there surveying her wealth she suddenly heard a loud knocking. However, it was not a knocking at the door of her room but the door of her heart. It opened up, and although she expected to hear it sing out Taylor Dayne's "Tell It to My Heart" or Celine Dion's "My Heart Will Go On," she instead heard a voice that said to her, "Have you done good things with all this for your LGBTQ kindred? Have you been aware of the needs of the hags? Have you shared your rhinestone pumps with the less fortunate? Have you been satisfied with your fabulousness, or have you always demanded even more pizzazz?"

Her heart did not hesitate with the answer: "Oh, girl, I've been hard and pitiless and have never done good things for my kindred. If a poor person came my way, I turned my eyes from him. I haven't cared about others but have only thought about increasing my wardrobe. Even if everything under the sky had become mine, it would still not have been enough for me."

Upon hearing this answer, the rich drag queen was greatly horrified. Her knees began to tremble in their nylons and she had to sit down on her leopard-print chaise lounge. Once again she heard a knocking, but this time it was a knocking at the door to her townhouse. It was her neighbor, a poor drag queen, who had numerous gowns and could no longer afford to dry-clean them. I know, the poor drag queen thought, my neighbor is rich, but she is just as hard as she is rich. I don't believe she'll help me, but my gowns are screaming for a washing, so I'll have to take the risk. Then she said to the rich drag queen, "You don't readily give away things that belong to you, but I stand before you as one who can barely keep her wig above water. My gowns are filthy; lend me four of your own."

The rich drag queen looked at her for a long time. Then the first sunbeam of kindness began to melt part of the ice of greediness. "I won't lend you four gowns," she responded, "instead I'll give you eight as a gift, but there is one condition you must fulfill."

"What must I do?" the poor drag queen asked.

"When I'm dead, you're to watch over my townhouse for three nights."

The poor drag queen felt very uneasy when she heard the proposition. However, she would have consented to anything because of her terrible situation. So she agreed to do it and carried the gowns home with her.

It was as though the rich drag queen had foreseen what was going to happen, for she suddenly dropped dead three days later. Nobody knew exactly how this had come to pass, but no one cared because they were too busy drinking, cruising, and preparing their outfits for the upcoming tea dance. When she was buried, the poor drag queen remembered her promise. She would have liked to have been released from it so she could watch the new Beyoncé concert on DVD, but she thought, She treated you kindly, and you were able to look fabulous at the Donna Summer lip-sync contest in her gown. And even if that hadn't happened, you gave your promise and you must keep it.

At nightfall she went into the West Village and sat at the top of the townhouse's steps. Everything was quiet. Only the moon was shining over the townhouse, and at times a drunken lesbian flew by on her way home from a piano bar and screeched her doleful sounds. When the sun rose, the poor drag queen went home unharmed, and the second night passed just as peacefully as the first. On the third night she felt especially afraid.

It seemed to her that something was going to happen. When she arrived at the townhouse, she noticed another queen on the corner whom she had never seen before. She was no longer young, had scars on her face, and her eyes darted around sharply and fervidly. She was wrapped completely in an old mink coat, and only her large rhinestone pumps were visible.

"What are you looking for here?" the poor drag queen asked her. "Aren't you afraid of being out here, or are you planning on restaging 'Memory' from CATS?"

"I'm not looking for anything, honey," she answered, "and please, dear, if I do start to sing Andrew Lloyd Webber, strangle me with my boa. I'm just a young queen who set out to be a pageant star, but who tried in vain and still won a socialite's daughter as a hag and great wealth along with her. However, I've always remained poor. I'm nothing but a washed up tranny and want to spend the night here because I don't have any other shelter."

"If you've no man to attend," said the poor drag queen, "then stay with me and help me guard the townhouse."

"Keeping guard is a hot muscle stud's business," she replied. "But, lord knows how long it's been since I've been able to wrangle in one of those, so I guess it's just up to the two of us. Whatever we encounter here, twink or bear, let that be our common lot."

The poor drag queen agreed, and they sat down together on the steps and lit up some menthols, which they puffed through long cigarette holders as they pretended to look like Audrey Hepburn. Everything remained quiet until midnight. Then suddenly a shrill whistling could be heard in the air, and the two watchwomen became aware of the presence of the Evil One, who strikingly resembled a banker and stood in full life before them. "Be gone, you scoundrels," he bellowed at them. "The outfits and accessories lying in that townhouse are mine. They were purchased on credit, and having not been paid off they are slated to be repossessed. I'm here to fetch them, so if you don't turn and leave, I'll twist your boas and wring your wigs."

"Sir with the red tie" the washed-up queen said, "You're not my leather daddy. I don't need to obey you, and I've yet to learn how to fear middle-aged tricks. So move on, for we're going to remain sitting here."

The collections agent thought, Gold is the best way to trap these two meddlers. So he used a sweeter tune and asked very confidentially whether or not they would like to have a big bag of gold sequins that they could take with them.

"That's worth considering," the washed-up queen answered, "but just one bag of sequins is not of much use to us. We couldn't even cover one Britney Spears outfit with that. If you give us enough sequins as will go into one of my Jimmy Choos, we'll clear out and retreat."

"I don't have enough gold with me," the credit broker said, "but I'll get it. There's a good friend of mine at WaMu who's a moneychanger in the Financial District. He'll gladly advance me the gold."

After the devil had disappeared, the washed-up queen took off her left pump and said, "Just wait, we'll soon be leading him around by a leash. Give me your nail file, my friend." Then she cut off the toe of the shoe and tucked the pump under her arm in the clump of feathers on the edge of a large purse half bedazzled with rhinestones. "That's just right," she said. "Now let the girl return."

The two queens sat down and waited. It was not long before the credit broker came, carrying a small sack of gold sequins in his hand. "Just pour it in there," the washed-up queen said and raised her shoe a little in the air, "but that won't be enough."

The creditor emptied the sack. The gold sequins fell through and the pump remained empty.

"Stupid creditor," exclaimed the queen. "Didn't I tell you right off? Now turn around and fetch some more."

The credit broker shook his head, left, and came back after an hour with a much larger sack under his arm.

"Just fill it up," the queen cried out, "but I doubt the shoe will become full."

The gold sequins jingled as they dropped into the pump, but the shoe remained empty. The creditor peered into the heel himself with glaring eyes and convinced himself of the truth.

"The bunions of your feet are ridiculously large," he cried out, and made a wry face.

"Do you think," replied the queen, "that I have a cloven foot like yours? Since when have you been so stingy? See to it that you get more gold sequins; otherwise, you can forget about our deal."

The demon toddled off once again. This time he stayed away longer than before, and when he finally appeared, he was panting due to the weight of the pack he was carrying on his shoulders. He poured the gold sequins into the shoe, which remained just as empty as before. Then he became furious and wanted to tear the pump from the queen's hand, but just at that moment the first ray of the rising sun burst from the sky, and the evil creditor ran away shrieking loudly. The townhouse full of gowns and accessories had been saved.

The poor drag queen wanted to divide the sequins, but the washed-up queen said, "Give my share to ACT UP. I'll move in with you in this townhouse, and together we'll live quietly and peacefully with what's left over of the gold, hosting brunches as long as God permits."

NOTES

1. Thanks to Rodney Leonard (2009) for drawing my attention to the Christian symbolism of the number three as it appears within this tale, specifically in connection to the resurrection of Christ.

APPENDIX
Trans and Drag in Traditional Folktales

All tales types listed are from Uther (2004, vol. 1). Page numbers are given in parentheses.

ANIMAL TRANS

302	The Ogre's (Devil's) Heart in the Egg (180–81)
313	The Magic Flight (194–96)
313E*	The Sister's Flight (197–98)
314	Goldener (previously The Youth Transformed to a Horse) (198–200)
316	The Nix of the Mill-Pond (203–4)
318	The Faithless Wife (205–6)
325	The Magician and His Pupil (207–8)
369	The Youth on a Quest for His Lost Father (231)
400	The Man on a Quest for His Lost Wife (231–33)
402	The Animal Bride (234–36)
402*	The Princess Who Scorned an Unloved Suitor (236)
402A*	The Princess Transformed into a Toad (236)
403	The Black and the White Bride (236–38)
405	Jorinde and Joringel (239)
408	The Three Oranges (241–43)
409	The Girl as Wolf (243)
409A	The Girl as Goat (243–44)
409A*	The Girl as Snake (244)
411	The King and the Lamia (246)
413	The Stolen Clothing (247)
425A	The Animal as Bridegroom (248–50)
425B	Son of the Witch (250–52)

750K* The Lost Genitalia (402; partial)

750K** Wishing the Cat to be a Prince (402)

751A The Farmwife is Changed into a Woodpecker (402–3)

753* Christ (God) Turns a Thief into an Ass (409)

761 The Cruel Rich Man as the Devil's Horse (421–22)

780C The Tell-Tale Calf's Head (440; partial)

782 Midas and the Donkey's Ears (441; partial)

798 Woman Created from a Monkey's Tail (444–45; partial)

824 The Devil Lets the Man See His Wife's Unfaithfulness (462–63)

856 The Man with Four Wives (484)

871 Princess and Ogress (491)

ANIMAL DRAG

311 Rescue by the Sister (191–92)

333 Little Red Riding Hood (224–25)

510B Peau d'Asne (295–96)

810B* The Youth Sold to the Devil (452)

936* The Golden Mountain (579–80)

BIO TRANS

403C The Substituted Bride (238)

407 The Girl as Flower (240–41)

408 The Three Oranges (241–43)

425M The Snake as Bridegroom (255)

GENDER DRAG

514 The Shift of Sex (301–2)

514** A Young Woman Disguised as a Man is Wooed by the Queen (302–3)

570A The Princess and the Magic Shell (340–41)

875D The Clever Young Woman at the End of the Journey (498)

875D* The Prince's Seven Wise Teachers (500)

880 A Man Boasts of His Wife (502–3)

881 Oft-Proved Fidelity (503–4)

881A The Abandoned Bride Disguised as a Man (504–5)

882 The Wager on the Wife's Chastity (505–6)

883A The Innocent Slandered Maiden (506–7)

884 The Forsaken Fiancée: Service as Menial (508–9)

Sex Change

Others

CONTRIBUTORS

Emilie Anderson-Grégoire is a student at the University of Winnipeg and a fairy-tale aficionada.

Cristina Bacchilega teaches fairy tales and their adaptations, folklore and literature, and cultural studies at the University of Hawai'i at Mānoa. Her publications include *Postmodern Fairy Tales: Gender and Narrative Strategies*; *Angela Carter and the Fairy Tale* (co-edited); and *Legendary Hawai'i and the Politics of Place: Tradition, Translation, and Tourism*. With Donatella Izzo and Bryan Kamaoli Kuwada, Bacchilega co-edited "Sustaining Hawaiian Sovereignty," a special issue of *Anglistica*, an online journal of international interdisciplinary studies (2011). Her current work focuses on the poetics and politics of twenty-first-century fairy-tale adaptations. She claims her collection of "frogs" has almost nothing to do with the Grimms.

Anita Best was born on the island of Merasheen in Placentia Bay on Newfoundland's south coast the year before Newfoundland joined Canada. Anita performs the traditional songs and stories from her childhood, building a marvelous bridge between old-time and contemporary Newfoundland song-making and storytelling traditions. She has received several honors for her work in collecting and disseminating Newfoundland folklore, including the Marius Barbeau Award from the Folklore Studies Association of Canada, an honorary doctorate from Memorial University, and Member of the Order of Canada.

Joy Brooke Fairfield is a PhD student in drama at Stanford University. She has undergraduate and master's degrees in performance studies from Harvard and New York University, respectively, and her current research focuses on intimate spectatorship and the queerness of creative collaboration. In addition, Joy is a San Francisco–based theater director specializing in new play development and ensemble-generated work with a highly visual, movement-based, queer sensibility.

Andrew J. Friedenthal is a doctoral candidate in American studies at the University of Texas at Austin. His research interests include comic books, theme parks, immersive environments, tourism, and escapist entertainment. In his small amounts of spare time, he is a playwright and a competitive karaoke performer.

Kevin Goldstein is a doctoral candidate in comparative literature at New York University. His research interests include the literature of the Americas, oral poetics and mnemonics, disability studies, and cognitive approaches to literature. His dissertation project concerns the influence of late-onset blindness on the work of several writers, including Jorge Luis Borges, María Josefa Mujía, William H. Prescott, and John Milton.

Pauline Greenhill is professor of women's and gender studies at the University of Winnipeg, Manitoba, Canada. Her most recent books are *Make the Night Hideous: Four English-Canadian Charivaris, 1881–1940* (University of Toronto Press, 2010); *Fairy Tale Films: Visions of Ambiguity* (co-edited with Sidney Eve Matrix, Utah State University Press); and *Encyclopedia of Women's Folklore and Folklife* (co-edited with Liz Locke and Theresa Vaughan, Greenwood Press, 2009). She devotes her spare time to documenting the many miracles enacted by the relics of her late, great kitty, Bobbie, to ensure her prompt beatification.

Bettina Hutschek is a visual artist who lives and works in Berlin and Malta. She studied fine arts, art history, and philosophy in Florence, Augsburg, Berlin, Barcelona, and Leipzig and spent one year as visiting scholar at Tisch School of the Arts, New York University. Today she uses fragments of different realities to examine the possibilities of knowledge transfer—that is, to tell stories.

Jeana Jorgensen defended her dissertation on gender and the body in European fairy tales at Indiana University in March 2012. She has published articles in *Marvels & Tales* and other folklore journals. Her research interests include narrative, feminist theory, dance, body art, and the digital humanities.

Kimberly J. Lau is professor of literature at the University of California, Santa Cruz. She is the author of *Body Language: Sisters in Shape, Black Women's Fitness, and Feminist Identity Politics* (Temple University Press, 2011); *New Age Capitalism: Making*

Money East of Eden (University of Pennsylvania Press, 2000); and numerous articles on fairy tales and folklore.

Elliot Gordon Mercer is a professional arts administrator, dramaturg, and performance historian. He attended the Idyllwild Arts Academy, graduated summa cum laude from St. Mary's College of California, and received an MA in performance studies at New York University. Elliot's research focuses on performance adaptation as well as the documentation and reconstruction of historic performances.

Margaret A. Mills is professor of Near Eastern languages and cultures at Ohio State University. She specializes in the popular culture of the Persian-speaking world. Her books include *Conversations with Davlat Khalav: Oral Narratives from Tajikistan* (with Ravshan Rahmoní, Humanity Press, 2000); *Rhetorics and Politics in Afghan Traditional Storytelling* (University of Pennsylvania Press, 1991); and *Gender, Genre and Power in South Asian Expressive Traditions* (co-edited with Arjun Appadurai and Frank J. Korom, University of Pennsylvania Press, 1991).

Jennifer Orme's work has appeared in *Beyond Adaptation: Essays on Radical Transformation of Original Works* and in *Marvels & Tales: Journal of Fairy-Tale Studies*, where she is also the assistant review editor. Her current research project is called "Fair(l)y Queer: Intersections between Fairy-Tale Studies, Queer and Narrative Theories."

Catherine Tosenberger is an assistant professor of English at the University of Winnipeg, where she is attached to the Centre for Research in Young People's Texts and Cultures. Her research interests include fandom studies, pornography and erotica, adolescent culture, and folklore.

Kay Turner is director of folk arts, Brooklyn Arts Council, and adjunct professor, Performance Studies Department, New York University, where she teaches courses on oral narrative, fairy tale in performance, gender, and queer theory. Among her publications are *Beautiful Necessity: The Art and Meaning of Women's Altars* (Thames and Hudson) and "September 11 and the Burden of the Ephemeral" published in *Western Folklore* in 2009. Turner remains dedicated to her own queerly conceived artistic pursuits: she released her song "Do the Baby Jesus" in 2010; presented the live, collaborative work "When Gertrude (Stein) Met Susan (Sontag)" at Dixon Place Theater in Manhattan in 2010; and curated "HomoHome" with David Kolwyck in 2006 at Cinders Gallery in Brooklyn. Can *Frau Trude: The Musical* be too far behind?

Margaret R. Yocom is codirector of the Folklore Studies Program and associate professor of English at George Mason University. She specializes in oral narrative and storytelling, material culture, family folklore, and gender studies. Her work on folktales includes her essay "Exuberance in Control: The Dialogue of Ideas in the Tales and Fan Towers of Woodsman William Richard of Phillips, Maine" in *Northeast Folklore: Essays in Honor of Edward D. Ives* (2000) and *Ugiuvangmiut Quliapyuit: King Island Tales* (assistant editor, 1988).

REFERENCES

Aarne, Antti. 1961. *The Types of the Folktale: A Classification and Bibliography*. Translated by Stith Thompson. 2nd rev. ed. Helsinki: Suomalainen Tiedeakatemia/ FF Communications.

Abate, Michelle Ann. 2008a. *Tomboys: A Literary and Cultural History*. Philadelphia: Temple University Press.

———. 2008b. "Trans/Forming Girlhood: Transgenderism, the Tomboy Formula, and Gender Identity Disorder in Sharon Dennis Wyeth's *Tomboy Trouble*." *Lion and the Unicorn* 38 (1):40–60.

Abrahams, Roger D., and George Foss. 1968. *Anglo-American Folksong Style*. Englewood Cliffs, NJ: Prentice-Hall.

Afanas'ev, A. N. (1861) 1985. *Narodnye russkie skazki A. N. Afanas'eva v trekh tomakh*. 3 vols. Moscow: Izdatel'stvo Nauka.

Al-Shahi, Ahmed, and F. C. T. Moore, eds. and trans. 1978. *Wisdom from the Nile: A Collection of Folk-Stories from Northern and Central Sudan*. Oxford: Clarendon Press.

Andreasen, Dan. 2000. *Rose Red and the Bear Prince*. New York: HarperCollins.

Anzieu, Didier. 1989. *The Skin Ego: A Psychoanalytic Approach to the Self*. Translated by Chris Turner. New Haven: Yale University Press.

Aristotle. 1987. *Aristotle's History of Animals: In Ten Books*. Whitefish: Kessinger Press.

Ashliman, D. L. 1986. "Symbolic Sex-Role Reversals in the Grimms' Fairy Tales." In *Forms of the Fantastic: Selected Essays from the Third International Conference on the Fantastic in Literature and Film*, edited by Jan Hokenson and Howard D. Pearce, 193–98. Westport, CT: Greenwood Press.

———. 1987. *A Guide to Folktales in the English Language*. New York: Greenwood Press.

———, ed. 1996–2011. *Folklore and Mythology Electronic Texts*. http://www.pitt .edu/~dash/folktexts.html.

Atwood, Margaret. 1993. *The Robber Bride*. New York: Doubleday.

Austin, J. L. 1962. *How to Do Things with Words*. Oxford: Clarendon Press.

Bacchilega, Cristina. 1993. "An Introduction to the 'Innocent Persecuted Heroine' Fairy Tale." *Western Folklore* 52 (1): 1–12.

———. 1997. *Postmodern Fairy Tales: Gender and Narrative Strategies*. Philadelphia: University of Pennsylvania Press.

Bachelard, Gaston. (1938) 1964. *The Psychoanalysis of Fire*. Translated by Alan C. M. Ross. Boston: Beacon Press.

Baker, Susan W. 1980. "Biological Influences on Human Sex and Gender." *Signs* 6 (1): 80–96.

Bakhtin, Mikhail. 1984. *Rabelais and His World*. Bloomington: Indiana University Press.

Barchers, Suzanne I. 1990. *Wise Women: Folk and Fairy Tales from around the World*. Englewood, CO: Libraries Unlimited.

Barthes, Roland. 1974. *S/Z*. Translated by Richard Miller. New York: Hill and Wang.

———. 1978. *A Lover's Discourse: Fragments*. Translated by Richard Howard. New York: Hill and Wang.

Bear, Bethany Joy. 2009. "Struggling Sisters and Failing Spells: Re-Engendering Fairy Tale Heroism in Pegg Kerr's *The Wild Swans*." In *Fairy Tales Reimagined: Essays on New Retellings*, edited by Susan Redington Bobby, 44–57. Jefferson, NC: McFarland.

Bechstein, Ludwig. (1845–53) 1983. *Deutsche Märchen und Sagen*. Berlin: Aufbau-Verlag.

Belmont, Nicole, and Brunhilde Biebuyck. 1983. "Myth and Folklore in Connection with AT 403 and 713." *Journal of Folklore Research* 20 (2/3): 185–96.

Ben-Moshe, Gomer, and Michele Klein. 2008. "Wise Women: Perhaps It's Time for the Knesset to Strengthen Midwifery as an Autonomous Profession." *Jerusalem Post*, September 11.

Benjamin, Walter. 1968. "The Storyteller." In *Illuminations: Essays and Reflections*, edited by Hannah Arendt, 83–111. New York: Harcourt, Brace.

Bernheimer, Kate. 2006. "This Rapturous Form." *Marvels & Tales: Journal of Fairy-Tale Studies* 20 (1): 67–83.

Berger, René, and R. Scott Walker. 1989. "Re-Enactment and Simulation: Toward a Synthesis of What Type?" *Diogenes* 37 (1): 1–22.

Bersani, Leo. 1996. *Homos*. Cambridge, MA: Harvard University Press.

———. 2009. *Is the Rectum a Grave? and Other Essays*. Chicago: University of Chicago Press.

Bettelheim, Bruno. 1976. *The Uses of Enchantment: The Meaning and Importance of Fairy Tales*. New York: Knopf.

Bever, Edward. 2002. "Witchcraft, Female Aggression, and Power in the Early Modern Community." *Journal of Social History* 35 (4): 955–88.

Blecher, Lone Thygesen, and George Blecher, eds. 1993. *Swedish Folktales and Legends.* Minneapolis: University of Minnesota Press.

Bloch, R. Howard. 2004. "The Wolf in the Dog: Animal Fables and State Formation." *differences: A Journal of Feminist Cultural Studies* 15 (1): 69–83.

Block, Francesca Lia. 2000. *The Rose and the Beast: Fairy Tales Retold.* New York: HarperCollins.

Bolte, Johannes, and Georg Polívka. 1913. *Anmerkungen zu den Kinder- und Hausmärchen der Brüder Grimm.* Vol. 1. Leipzig: Dieterich'sche Verlagsbuohhandlung Theodor Weicher.

———. 1915. *Anmerkungen zu den Kinder- und Hausmärchen der Brüder Grimm.* Vol. 2. Leipzig: Dieterich'sohe Verlagsbuohhandlung Theodor Weicher.

Boswell, John. 1981. *Christianity, Social Tolerance, and Homosexuality.* Chicago: University of Chicago Press.

Bottigheimer, Ruth B. 1986. "Silenced Women in the Grimms' Tales: The 'Fit' between Fairy Tales and Society in Their Historical Context." In *Fairy Tales and Society: Illusion, Alllusion, and Paradigm,* edited by Ruth B. Bottigheimer, 53–74. Philadelphia: University of Pennsylvania Press.

———. 1987. *Grimms' Bad Girls and Bold Boys: The Moral and Social Vision of the Tales.* New Haven: Yale University Press.

———. 1996. "Kluge Else." In *Enzyklopädie des Märchens* 8:11–16. Berlin: Walter de Gruyter.

———. 2004. "Fertility Control and the Birth of the Modern European Fairy Tale Heroine." In *Fairy Tales and Feminism,* edited by Donald Haase, 37–51. Detroit: Wayne State University Press.

———. 2009. Fairy Tales: A New History. New York: SUNY Press.

Braidotti, Rosi. 2009. "Animals, Anomalies and Inorganic Others." *PMLA* 124 (2): 526–32.

Briggs, Katherine. 1970. *A Dictionary of British Folk-Tales in the English Language.* Vol. 1, pt. A, *Folk Narratives.* London: Routledge/Kegan Paul.

Briggs, Robin. 1996. *Witches and Neighbors: The Social and Cultural Context of European Witchcraft.* New York: Viking Press.

Brown, Lesley, ed. 1993. *The New Shorter Oxford English Dictionary.* Vol. 1, *A–M.* New York: Oxford University Press.

Bruford, Alan, and Donald A. MacDonald, eds. (1994) 2007. *Scottish Traditional Tales.* Edinburgh: Birlinn.

Burn, Shawn Meghan, A. Kathleen O'Neil, and Shirley Nederend. 1996. "Childhood Tomboyism and Adult Androgyny." *Sex Roles* 34 (5/6): 419–28.

Burton, Richard. 1997. *The Arabian Nights.* New York: Modern Library.

———. n.d. *The Book of the Thousand Nights and a Night*. Vol. 6. Bassorah edition. Burton Club Private Subscription.

Bushnaq, Inea, ed. 1986. *Arab Folktales*. New York: Pantheon.

Butler, Judith. (1990) 1999. *Gender Trouble: Feminism and the Subversion of Identity*. New York: Routledge.

———. 1993. *Bodies That Matter: On the Discursive Limits of "Sex."* New York: Routledge.

———. 1997. *Excitable Speech: A Politics of the Performative*. New York: Routledge.

———. 2000. *Antigone's Claim: Kinship between Life and Death*. New York: Columbia University Press.

———. 2004. *Undoing Gender*. New York: Routledge.

Byatt, A. S. 1998. *The Djinn in the Nightingale's Eye*. London: Vintage.

Campbell, J. F. (1862) 1969. *Popular Tales of the West Highlands, Orally Collected*. Translated by J. F. Campbell. 4 vols. Detroit: Singing Tree Press.

Carter, Angela. 1976. *Vampirella*. Radio 4 Original Broadcast, July 20.

———, trans. 1977. *The Fairy Tales of Charles Perrault*. New York: Avon Books.

———. 1979a. *The Bloody Chamber*. New York: Penguin Books.

———. 1979b. *The Sadeian Woman: An Exercise in Cultural History*. London: Virago.

———. 1983. "Notes from the Front Line." In *Critical Essays on Angela Carter*, edited by Lindsey Tucker, 24–30. New York: G. K. Hall.

———, ed. 1990. *The Virago Book of Fairy Tales*. Illustrated by Corinna Sargood. London: Virago Press.

Carter, Isabel Gordon. 1925. "Mountain White Folk-Lore: Tales from the Southern Blue Ridge." *Journal of American Folklore* 38 (148): 340–74.

Case, Sue Ellen. 1991. "Tracking the Vampire." *differences: A Journal of Feminist Cultural Studies* 3 (2): 1–20.

———. 1993. "Toward a Butch-Femme Aesthetic." In *The Gay and Lesbian Studies Reader*, edited by Henry Abelove, Michèle Aina Barale, and David M. Halperin, 294–306. New York: Routledge.

Cashdan, Sheldon. 1999. *The Witch Must Die: The Hidden Meaning of Fairy Tales*. New York: Basic Books.

Castendyk, Stephanie. 1992. "A Psychoanalytic Account for Lesbianism." *Feminist Review* 42 (Autumn): 67–81.

Castle, Terry. 1993. *The Apparitional Lesbian: Female Homosexuality and Modern Culture*. New York: Columbia University Press.

Certeau, Michel de. 1980. "On the Oppositional Practices of Everyday Life." *Social Text* 3:3–43.

———. 1984. *The Practice of Everyday Life*. Translated by Steven Rendall. Berkeley:

University of California Press.

Chase, Richard. 1948. *Grandfather Tales*. Boston: Houghton Mifflin.

Charney, Sappho. 1993. "No Chalkmark on the Mantel." In *The Antic Art: Enhancing Children's Literary Experiences through Film and Video*, edited by Lucy Rollin, 39–46. Fort Atkinson, WI: Highsmith.

Cixous, Hélène. 1981. "The Laugh of the Medusa." Translated by Keith Cohen and Paula Cohen. *Signs* 1 (4): 875–93.

Clark, Stuart. 1999. *Thinking with Demons: The Idea of Witchcraft in Early Modern Europe*. New York: Oxford University Press.

Clouston, William Alexander. 1888. *The Book of Noodles: Stories of Simpletons; or, Fools and Their Follies*. London: Elliot Stock.

Cohen, Nathalie. 1998. "The Queering of a Tale: Reinterpreting Mistress Trude." Unpublished term paper, University of Winnipeg.

Conner, Randy P. 1993. *Blossom of Bone: Reclaiming the Connections between Homoeroticism and the Sacred*. New York: HarperCollins.

Coward, Rosalind. 1985. *Female Desires: How They Are Sought, Bought and Packaged*. New York: Grove Press.

Cox, Marian Roalfe. 1893. *Cinderella: Three Hundred and Forty-Five Variants of Cinderella, Catskin, and Cap O' Rushes*. London: Folklore Society.

Crofts, Charlotte. 2003. *"Anagrams of Desire": Angela Carter's Writing for Radio, Film, and Television*. Manchester: Manchester University Press.

Cvetkovich, Ann. 1998. "Untouchability and Vulnerability: Stone Butchness as Emotional Style." In *Butch/Femme: Inside Lesbian Gender*, edited by Sally R. Munt, 159–69. London: Cassell.

———. 2003. *An Archive of Feelings: Trauma, Sexuality, and Lesbian Public Cultures*. Durham, NC: Duke University Press.

Daly, Mary. 1978. *Gyn/Ecology: The Metaethics of Radical Feminism*. Boston: Beacon Press.

———. 1984. *Pure Lust: Elemental Feminist Philosophy*. Boston: Beacon Press.

Danaher, Kevin. 1990. *Folktales of the Irish Countryside*. Cork: Mercier Press.

Dasent, George Webbe. 1859. *Popular Tales from the Norse*. Edinburgh: Edmonston and Douglas.

———. 1906. *A Collection of Popular Tales from the Norse and North German*. London: Norroena Society.

Davenport, Tom. 1992. *Mutzmag: An Appalachian Folktale*. Delaplane, VA: Davenport Films.

———. 1993. "Media Literacy for the Future: Advice to Beginning Filmmakers." In *The Antic Art: Enhancing Children's Literary Experiences through Film and Video*, edited by Lucy Rollin, 195–203. Fort Atkinson, WI: Highsmith.

Davies, Owen, and Wilhelm de Blécourt, eds. 2004. *Beyond the Witch Trials: Witchcraft and Magic in Enlightenment Europe*. Manchester: Manchester University Press.

De Caro, Frank, and Rosan Augusta Jordan. 2004. *Re-Situating Folklore: Folk Contexts and Twentieth-Century Literature and Art*. Knoxville: University of Tennessee Press.

Dégh, Linda. 1989. *Story-Telling in a Hungarian Peasant Community*. Bloomington: Indiana University Press.

DeJean, Joan. 1989. *Fictions of Sappho, 1546–1937*. Chicago: University of Chicago Press.

De Lauretis, Teresa. 1984. *Alice Doesn't: Feminism, Semiotics, Cinema*. Bloomington: Indiana University Press

———. 1994. *The Practice of Love: Lesbian Sexuality and Perverse Desire*. Bloomington: Indiana University Press.

Deleuze, Gilles, and Felix Guattari. 1987. *A Thousand Plateaus: Capitalism and Schizophrenia*. Minneapolis: University of Minnesota Press.

Denizet-Lewis, Benoit. 2009. "Coming Out in Middle School." *New York Times Magazine*, September 27, 36–41, 52–55.

Dinn, Philip, and Andy Jones. 2003. *Peg Bearskin*. St. John's, NL: Running the Goat.

Dinshaw, Carolyn. 1999. *Getting Medieval: Sexualities and Communities, Pre- and Postmodern*. Durham, NC: Duke University Press.

Dinshaw, Carolyn, Lee Edelman, Roderick A. Ferguson, Carla Freccero, Elizabeth Freeman, Judith Halberstam, Annamarie Jagose, Christopher Nealon, and Nguyen Tan Hoang. 2007. "Theorizing Queer Temporalities: A Roundtable Discussion." In "Queer Temporalities," edited by Elizabeth Freeman. Special issue, *GLQ: A Journal of Lesbian and Gay Studies* 13 (2–3): 177–95.

Doan, Laura. 1994. *The Lesbian Postmodern*. New York: Columbia University Press.

Dolan, Jill. 1987. "The Dynamics of Desire: Sexuality and Gender in Pornography and Performance." *Theatre Journal* 39 (2): 157–74.

Dollerup, Cay, Iven Reventlow, and Carsten Rosenberg Hansen. 1986. "A Case Study of Editorial Filters in Folktales: A Discussion of the *Allerleirauh* Tales in Grimm." *Fabula: Zeitschrift für Erzählforschung* 27 (1–2): 12–30.

Doniger, Wendy. 1999. *Splitting the Difference: Gender and Myth in Ancient Greece and India*. Chicago: University of Chicago Press.

———. 2000. *The Bedtrick: Tales of Sex and Masquerade*. Chicago: University of Chicago Press.

Donoghue, Emma. 1993. *Passions between Women: British Lesbian Culture, 1668–1801*. New York: HarperCollins.

———. 1997. *Kissing the Witch*. London: Hamish Hamilton.

Doty, Alexander. 1993. *Making Things Perfectly Queer: Interpreting Mass Culture.* Minneapolis: University of Minnesota Press.

———. 1995. "There's Something Queer in Here." In *Out in Culture: Gay, Lesbian, and Queer Essays in Popular Culture,* edited by Corey Creekmur and Alexander Doty, 71–90. Durham, NC: Duke University Press.

———. 2000. *Flaming Classics: Queering the Film Canon.* New York: Routledge.

Douglas, Mary. 1966. *Purity and Danger: An Analysis of Concepts of Pollution and Taboo.* London: Routledge/Kegan Paul.

———. 1973. *Natural Symbols.* New York: Vintage Books.

DuBois, Page. 1995. *Sappho Is Burning.* Chicago: University of Chicago Press.

Dugaw, Dianne. (1989) 1996. *Warrior Women and Popular Balladry, 1650–1850.* Chicago: University of Chicago Press.

Dundes, Alan. 1971. "The Making and Breaking of Friendship as a Structural Frame in African Folktales." In *The Structural Analysis of Oral Tradition,* edited by Pierre Maranda and Elli Köngäs Maranda, 171–85. Philadelphia: University of Pennsylvania Press.

———, ed. 1982. *Cinderella: A Casebook.* Madison: University of Wisconsin Press.

———, ed. 1989. *Little Red Riding Hood: A Casebook.* Madison: University of Wisconsin Press.

———. 1993. *Folklore Matters.* Knoxville: University of Tennessee Press.

———. 1997. *From Game to War, and Other Psychoanalytical Essays on Folklore.* Lexington: University Press of Kentucky.

———. 2007. "The Symbolic Equivalence of Allomotifs: Towards a Method of Analyzing Folktales." In *The Meaning of Folklore: The Analytical Essays of Alan Dundes,* edited by Simon Bronner, 319–24. Logan: Utah State University Press.

Durrant, Jonathan. 2007. *Witchcraft, Gender and Society in Early Modern Germany.* Boston: Brill.

Dutheil de la Rochère, Martine Hennard. 2009. "Queering the Fairy Tale Canon: Emma Donoghue's Kissing the Witch." In *Fairy Tales Reimagined: Essays on New Retellings,* edited by Susan Redington Bobby, 13–30. Jefferson, NC: McFarland.

Edelman, Lee. 2004. *No Future: Queer Theory and the Death Drive.* Durham, NC: Duke University Press.

Eisler, Riane. 1995. *Sacred Pleasure.* San Francisco: HarperCollins.

Elliott, Mary. 1998. "When Girls Will Be Boys: 'Bad' Endings and Subversive Middles in Nineteenth-Century Tomboy Narratives and Twentieth-Century Lesbian Pulp Novels." *Legacy* 15 (1): 92–97.

Ellis, Bill. 2004. *Lucifer Ascending: The Occult in Folklore and Popular Culture.* Lexington: University Press of Kentucky.

El-Shamy, Hasan. 1979. *Brother and Sister, Type 872*: A Cognitive Behavioral Analysis of a Middle Eastern Oikotype*. Bloomington, IN: Folklore.

Eng, David. 2010. *The Feeling of Kinship: Queer Liberalism and the Racialization of Intimacy*. Durham, NC: Duke University Press.

Eng, David L., and David Kazanjian, eds. 2003. *Loss: The Politics of Mourning*. Berkeley: University of California Press.

Evans, Richard J., and W. R. Lee, eds. 1981. *The German Family: Essays on the Social History of the Family in Nineteenth-and Twentieth-Century Germany*. London: Croom Helm.

Everett, Holly. 2009. "Foodways." In *The Encyclopedia of Women's Folklore and Folklife*, edited by Liz Locke, Theresa A. Vaughan, and Pauline Greenhill, 256–63. Vol. 1. Westport, CT: Greenwood Press.

Faderman, Lillian. 1981. *Surpassing the Love of Men: Romantic Friendships and Love between Women from the Renaissance to the Present*. New York: William Morrow.

Fajardo, Kale Bantigue. 2008. "Transportation: Translating Filipino and Filipino American Tomboy Masculinities through Global Migration and Seafaring." *GLQ: A Journal of Lesbian and Gay Studies* 14 (2/3): 403–24.

Falassi, Alessandro. 1980. *Folklore by the Fireside: Text and Context of the Tuscan Veglia*. Austin: University of Texas Press.

Felman, Shoshana. 1975. "Women and Madness: The Critical Phallacy." *Diacritics* 5 (4): 2–10.

Flanagan, Victoria. 2008. *Into the Closet: Cross-Dressing and the Gendered Body in Children's Literature and Film*. New York: Routledge.

Foley, John Miles. 1999. *Homer's Traditional Art*. University Park: Pennsylvania State University Press.

Forbes, Thomas. 1966. *The Midwife and the Witch*. New York: AMS Press.

Foucault, Michel. 1977. "A Preface to Transgression." In *Language, Counter-Memory, Practice: Selected Essays and Interviews*, edited by Donald F. Bouchard, 29–52. Ithaca, NY: Cornell University Press.

———. 1985. *The History of Sexuality*. Vol. 2. Translated by Robert Hurley. New York: Pantheon Books.

Frankfurter, David. 2006. *Evil Incarnate: Rumors of Demonic Conspiracy and Satanic Abuse in History*. Princeton: Princeton University Press.

Franklin, Sarah. 2006. "The Cyborg Embryo: Our Path to Transbiology." *Theory, Culture & Society* 23 (7–8): 167–87.

Freccero, Carla. 2006. *Queer/Early/Modern*. Durham, NC: Duke University Press.

Freeman, Elizabeth. 2007. "Introduction." In "Queer Temporalities," edited by Elizabeth Freeman. Special issue, *GLQ: A Journal of Lesbian and Gay Studies* 13

(2–3): 159–76.

———. 2010. *Time Binds: Queer Temporalities, Queer Histories.* Durham, NC: Duke University Press.

Friedman, Susan Stanford. 1987. "Creativity and the Childbirth Metaphor: Gender Difference in Literary Discourse." *Feminist Studies* 13 (1): 49–82.

Garber, Marjorie. 1992. *Vested Interests: Cross-Dressing and Cultural Anxiety.* New York: Routledge.

Giffney, Noreen. 2008. "Queer Apocal(o)ptic/ism: The Death Drive and the Human." In *Queering the Non/Human,* edited by Noreen Giffney and Myra J. Hird, 55–78. Hampshire: Ashgate.

Gilbert, Sandra. 1985. "Life's Empty Pack: Notes Towards a Literary Daughteronomy." *Critical Inquiry* 11 (3): 355–84.

Gilbert, Sandra, and Susan Gubar. 1984. *The Madwoman in the Attic: The Woman Writer and the Nineteenth-Century Imagination.* New Haven, CT: Yale University Press.

Girardot, N. J. 1977. "Initiation and Meaning in the Tale of Snow White and the Seven Dwarfs." *Journal of American Folklore* 90 (357): 274–300.

Glasgow, Joanne. 1997. "Rethinking the Mythic Mannish Radclyffe Hall." In *Queer Representations: Reading Lives, Reading Culture,* edited by Martin Duberman, 197–208. New York: New York University Press.

Goldberg, Christine. 1996. "The Blind Girl, a Misplaced Folktale." *Western Folklore* 55 (3): 187–212.

———. 1997. "The Donkey Skin Folktale Cycle (AT 510B)." *Journal of American Folklore* 110 (435): 28–46.

Goldberg, Jonathan, and Madhavi Menon. 2005. "Queering History." *PMLA* 120 (5): 1608–17.

Goldman, Jane. 1999. "Introduction: Works on the Wild(e) Side—Performing, Transgressing, Queering." In *Literary Theories,* edited by Julian Wolfreys, 525–36. New York: New York University Press.

Grahn, Judy. 1985. *The Highest Apple: Sappho and the Lesbian Poetic Tradition.* San Francisco: Spinsters Ink.

Graves, Rolande J. 2001. *Born to Procreate: Women and Childbirth in France from the Middle Ages to the Eighteenth Century.* New York: Peter Lang.

Greaney, Marishka. 1999. "A Proposal for Doing Transgender Theory in the Academy." In *Reclaiming Genders: Transsexual Grammars at the Fin de Siècle,* edited by Kate More and Stephen Whittle, 159–70. London: Cassell.

Green, Joyce. 2000. "Public/Private." In *Encyclopedia of Feminist Theories,* edited by Lorraine Code, 412. New York: Routledge.

Greenhill, Pauline. 1995. "'Neither a Man Nor a Maid': Sexualities and Gendered

Meanings in Cross-Dressing Ballads." *Journal of American Folklore* 108 (428): 156–77.

———. 1997. "'Who's Gonna Kiss Your Ruby Red Lips': Sexual Scripts in Floating Verses." In *Ballads into Books: The Legacies of Francis James Child,* edited by Tom Cheesman and Sigrid Rieuwerts, 225–35. Bern: Peter Lang.

———. 1998. "Lesbian Mess(ages): Decoding Shawna Dempsey's Cake Squish at the Festival Du Voyeur." *Atlantis* 23 (1): 91–99.

———. 2008. "Fitcher's (Queer) Bird: A Fairy-Tale Heroine and Her Avatars." *Marvels & Tales: Journal of Fairy-Tale Studies* 22 (1): 143–67.

———. Forthcoming. "'If I Was a Woman as I Am a Man': Transgender Imagination in Newfoundland Ballads," in *Changing Places: Feminist Essays in Empathy and Relocation,* edited by Valerie Burton and Jean Guthrie. Toronto: Inanna Press

Greenhill, Pauline, and Emilie Anderson-Grégoire. Forthcoming. "'The Shift of Sex': ATU 514 as Transsexual Imagination." In *Unsettling Assumptions: Tradition, Gender, Drag,* edited by Pauline Greenhill and Diane Tye.

Greenhill, Pauline, and Anne Brydon. 2010. "Mourning Mothers and Seeing Siblings: Feminism and Place in The Juniper Tree." In *Fairy Tale Films: Visions of Ambiguity,* edited by Pauline Greenhill and Sidney Eve Matrix, 116–36. Logan: Utah State University Press.

Greenhill, Pauline, and Steven Kohm. 2009. "Little Red Riding Hood and Pedophile in Film: *Freeway, Hard Candy,* and *The Woodsman.*" *Jeunesse: Young People, Texts, Cultures* 1 (2): 35–65.

Greenhill, Pauline, and Sidney Eve Matrix, eds. 2010. *Fairy Tale Films: Visions of Ambiguity.* Logan: Utah State University Press.

Greenhill, Pauline, and Diane Tye, eds. 1997. *Undisciplined Women: Tradition and Culture in Canada.* Kingston, ON: McGill-Queen's University Press

Grimm, Jacob. (1835) 1854. *Deutsche Mythologie.* 3rd ed. Göttingen: Dieterich.

Grimm, Jacob, and Wilhelm Grimm. 1837. *Kinder- und Hausmärchen.* 3rd ed. 2 Vols. Göttingen: Verlag der Dieterichschen Buchhandlung.

———. 1854–1960. *Deutsches Wörterbuch.* Leipzig: S. Hirzel. http://germazope .uni-rier.de/Projects/DWB.

———. 1971. *Kinder- und Hausmärchen.* Munich: Winkler-Verlag.

———. 1975. *Die älteste Märchensammlung der Brüder Grimm: Synopse der Handschriftlichen Urfassung von 1810 und der Erstdrucke von 1812.* Edited by Heinz Rölleke. Cologny-Genève: Fondation Martin Bodmer.

———. (1982) 1993. *Märchen der Brüder Grimm: Nach der zweiten vermehrten und verbesserten Auflage von 1819, textkritisch revidiert und mit einer Biographie der Grimmschen Märchen versehen.* Edited by Heinz Rölleke. 2 vols. Vol. 1, *Diederichs*

Märchen der Weltliteratur. Reinbek bei Hamburg: Rowolt Taschenbuch Verlag.

———. 1984. *Brüder Grimm: Kinder- und Hausmärchen. Ausgabe Letzter Hand. Mit den Originalanmerkungen der Brüder Grimm. Mit einem Anhang sämtlicher nicht in allen Auflagen veröffentlichter Märchen und Herkunftsnachweisen.* Edited by Heinz Rölleke. Jubiläumsaugabe zum 200. Geburtstag der Brüder Grimm 1985/86 ed. 3 vols. Stuttgart: Philipp Reclam jun.

———. (1985) 2007. *Kinder- und Hausmärchen gesammelt durch die Brüder Grimm. Vollständige Ausgabe auf der Grundlage der dritten Auflage (1837).* Edited by Heinz Rölleke. Frankfurt am Main: Deutscher Klassiker Verlag.

Grobbelaar, P. W. 1981. "Die Volksvertelling as Kultuuruiting: Met besondere Verwysing na Afrikaans." DLitt. diss., Stellenbosch University, Stellenbosch.

Grosz, Elizabeth. 1994. *Volatile Bodies: Toward a Corporeal Feminism.* Bloomington: Indiana University Press.

Haase, Donald. 1993. "Response and Responsibility in Reading Grimms' Fairy Tales." In *The Reception of the Grimms' Fairy Tales,* edited by Donald Haase, 230–49. Detroit: Wayne State University Press.

———. 2004a. "Feminist Fairy-Tale Scholarship." In *Fairy Tales and Feminism: New Approaches,* edited by Donald Haase, 1–36. Detroit: Wayne State University Press.

———, ed. 2004b. *Fairy Tales and Feminism: New Approaches.* Detroit: Wayne State University Press.

Hagopian, Katherine A. 2007. "Apuleius and Gothic Narrative in Carter's 'The Lady of the House of Love.'" *Explicator* 66 (1): 52–55.

Halberstam, Judith. 1995. *Skin Shows: Gothic Horror and the Technologies of Monsters.* Durham, NC: Duke University Press.

———. 1998. *Female Masculinity.* Durham, NC: Duke University Press.

———. 1999. "Oh Bondage Up Yours! Female Masculinity and the Tomboy." In *Sissies and Tomboys: Gender Nonconformity and Homosexual Childhood,* edited by Matthew Rottnek, 153–79. New York: New York University Press.

———. 2005. *In a Queer Time and Place: Transgender Bodies, Subcultural Lives.* New York: New York University Press.

———. 2008. "Animating Revolt/Revolting Animation: Penguin Love, Doll Sex and the Spectacle of the Queer Nonhuman." In *Queering the Non/Human,* edited by Myra J. Hird and Noreen Giffney, 265–82. London: Ashgate.

Hall, James. 1979. *Dictionary of Subjects and Symbols in Art.* 2nd rev. ed. New York: Harper and Row.

Hallett, Martin, and Barbara Karasek, eds. 2002. *Folk and Fairy Tales.* 3rd ed. Orchard Park, NY: Broadview Press.

Halpert, Herbert, and J. D. A. Widdowson. 1996. *Folktales of Newfoundland: The*

Resilience of the Oral Tradition. Vol. 1. St. John's, NL: Breakwater.

Haney, Jack V., ed. 2001. *Russian Wondertales*. 7 vols. Vol. 2, *Tales of Magic and the Supernatural*. Aramonk, NY: M. E. Sharpe.

Hanlon, Tina L. 2000. "Strong Women in Appalachian Folktales." *Lion and the Unicorn* 24:225–46.

———. 2008. "'Mutsmag' and Other Girls Who Outwit Giants." AppLit. http://www.ferrum.edu/applit/bibs/tales/mutsmag.htm.

Haraway, Donna. 1991. *Simians, Cyborgs, and Women*. New York: Routledge.

———. 1997. *Modest_Witness@Second_Millenium: FemaleMan©_Meets_Onco-Mouse™*. New York: Routledge.

———. 2003. *The Companion Species Manifesto: Dogs, People, and Significant Otherness*. Chicago: Prickly Paradigm.

Harley, David. 1990. "Historians as Demonologists: The Myth of the Midwife-Witch." *Social History of Medicine* 3:1–26.

Harper, Douglas. 2001–2010. *Online Etymology Dictionary*. http://www.etymonline.com

Harper, Phillip Brian. 2000. "The Evidence of Felt Intuition: Minority Experience, Everyday Life, and Critical Speculative Knowledge." *GLQ: A Journal of Lesbian and Gay Studies* 6 (4): 641–57.

Harries, Elizabeth Wanning. 2001. *Twice upon a Time: Women Writers and the History of the Fairy Tale*. Princeton: Princeton University Press.

Hartland, E. Sidney. 1885. "The Forbidden Chamber." *Folk-Lore Journal* 3 (3): 193–242.

Harvey, Clodagh Brennan. 1989. "Some Irish Women Storytellers and Reflections on the Role of Women in the Storytelling Tradition." *Western Folklore* 48 (2): 109–28.

Hausen, Karin. 1981. "Family and Role-Division: The Polarisation of Sexual Stereotypes in the Nineteenth Century—an Aspect of the Dissociation of Work and Family Life." In *The German Family: Essays on the Social History of the Family in Nineteenth-and Twentieth-Century Germany*, edited by Richard J. Evans and W. R. Lee, 51–83. London: Croom Helm.

Heather, P. J. 1948. "Colour Symbolism: Part I." *Folklore* 59 (4): 165–83.

Heiner, Heidi Anne. 1998–2011. *SurLaLune Fairy Tales*. http://www.surlalune-fairytales.com.

Henein, Eglal. 1989. "Male and Female Ugliness through the Ages." *Merveilles & Contes* 3:45–56.

Heyes, Cressida. 2000. "Reading Transgender, Rethinking Women's Studies." *NWSA Journal* 12:170–80.

Hird, Myra J. 2000. "Gender's Nature: Intersexuality, Transsexualism and the 'Sex'/'Gender' Binary." *Feminist Theory* 1 (3): 347–64.

———. 2002a. "For a Sociology of Transsexualism." *Sociology* 36 (3): 577–95.

———. 2002b. "Unidentified Pleasures: Gender Identity and Its Failure." *Body &* *Society* 8 (2): 39–54.

———. 2004. "Chimerism, Mosaicism and the Cultural Construction of Kinship." *Sexualities* 7 (2): 217–32.

———. 2006. "Animal Transex." *Australian Feminist Studies* 21 (49): 35–50.

Hird, Myra J., and Noreen Giffney, eds. 2008. *Queering the Non/Human*. London: Ashgate.

Hirsch, Marianne. 1986. "Ideology, Form, and 'Allerleirauh': Reflections on *Reading for the Plot*." *Children's Literature* 14:163–68.

Hixon, Martha P. 2004. "Tam Lin, Fair Janet, and the Sexual Revolution: Traditional Ballads, Fairy Tales, and Twentieth-Century Children's Literature." *Marvels &* *Tales: Journal of Fairy-Tale Studies* 18 (1): 67–92.

Hodne, Ørnulf. 1984. *The Types of the Norwegian Folktale*. Oslo: Universitetsforlaget.

Holbek, Bengt. 1987. *Interpretation of Fairy Tales*. Helsinki: Academia Scientiarum Fennica.

Hollis, Susan Tower, Linda Pershing, and M. Jane Young, eds. 1993. *Feminist Theory and the Study of Folklore*. Urbana: University of Illinois Press.

Hopkinson, Nalo. 2001. *Skin Folk*. New York: Aspect-Warner.

Horsley, Richard. 1979. "Who Were the Witches? The Social Roles of the Accused in the European Witch Trials." *Journal of Interdisciplinary History* 9 (4): 689–715.

Hrdy, Sarah Blaffer. 2009. *Mothers and Others: The Evolutionary Origins of Mutual Understanding*. Cambridge: Belknap Press of Harvard University Press.

Hunt, Margaret, trans. 1884. *Household Tales by Jacob and Wilhelm Grimm, with the Authors' Notes*. London: George Bell.

Hurreiz, Sayyid H. 1977. *Ja'aliyyin Folktales: An Interplay of African, Arabian and Islamic Elements*. Vol. 8, *African Series*. Bloomington: Indiana University Press.

Hyde, Lewis. 1998. *Trickster Makes This World: Mischief, Myth, and Art*. New York: Farrar, Straus, and Giroux.

Ian, Marcia. 1993. *Remembering the Phallic Mother: Psychoanalysis, Modernism and the Fetish*. Ithaca: Cornell University Press.

Ikeda, Hiroko. 1971. *A Type and Motif Index of Japanese Folk-Literature*. FF Communications 209. Helsinki: Suomalainen Tiedeakatemia.

Irigaray, Luce. 1985. *This Sex Which Is Not One*. Translated by Catherine Porter with Carolyn Burke. Ithaca, NY: Cornell University Press.

Jacobs, Joseph. (1898) 1967. *English Fairy Tales*. Reprint, New York: Dover.

Jagose, Annamarie. 1996. *Queer Theory: An Introduction*. New York: New York University Press.

———. 2002. *Inconsequence: Lesbian Representation and the Logic of Sexual Sequence*. New York: Cornell University Press.

Jarvis, Shawn. 1993. "Trivial Pursuit? Women Deconstructing the Grimmian Model in the *Kaffeterkreis*." In *The Reception of Grimms' Fairy Tales: Responses, Reactions, Revisions*, edited by Donald Haase, 102–26. Detroit, MI: Wayne State University Press.

Jones, Andy, and Philip Dinn. n.d. *Jack-Five-Oh*. Unpublished manuscript.

Jones, Christine A., and Jennifer Schacker. 2012. *Marvelous Transformations: An Anthology of Fairy Tales and Contemporary Critical Perspectives*. Calgary, AB: Broadview Press.

Jones, Libby Falk, and Sarah Webster Goodwin. 1990. *Feminism, Utopia, and Narrative*. Knoxville: University of Tennessee Press.

Jones, Steven Swann. 1993. "The Innocent Persecuted Heroine Genre: An Analysis of Its Structure and Themes. *Western Folklore* 52:13–41.

———. (1995) 2002. *The Fairy Tale: The Magic Mirror of Imagination*. Reprint, New York: Routledge.

Joosen, Vanessa. 2011. *Critical and Creative Perspectives on Fairy Tales: An Intertextual Dialogue between Fairy-Tale Scholarship and Postmodern Retellings*. Detroit: Wayne State University Press.

Jordan, Elaine. 1992. "The Dangers of Angela Carter." In *Critical Essays on Angela Carter*, edited by Lindsey Tucker, 33–45. New York: G. K. Hall.

Jorgensen, Jeana. 2008. "Innocent Initiations: Female Agency in Eroticized Fairy Tales." *Marvels & Tales: Journal of Fairy-Tale Studies* 22:27–37.

Jurich, Marilyn. 1998. *Scheherazade's Sisters: Trickster Heroines and Their Stories in World Literature*. Westport, CT: Greenwood Press.

Kane, Stephanie. 1988. "Omission in Emberá (Chocó) Mythography." *Journal of Folklore Research* 25 (3): 155–86.

Karlinger, Felix. 1981. "Verwandlung auf der Flucht vor drohendem Inzest." *Schweizerisches Archiv für Volkskunde* 77 (3/4): 178–84.

Karlinger, Felix, and Erentrudis Laserer, eds. 1980. *Baskische Märchen*. Düsseldorf: Eugen Diederichs Verlag.

Katz, Steven T. 1994. *The Holocaust in Historical Context*. Vol. 1, *The Holocaust and Mass Death before the Modern Age*. Oxford: Oxford Univerity Press.

Kennedy, Elizabeth Lapovsky, and Madeline D. Davis. 1994. *Boots of Leather, Slippers of Gold: The History of a Lesbian Community*. New York: Penguin Books.

Kirsch, Max H. 2000. *Queer Theory and Social Change*. London: Routledge.

Kluge, Friedrich. (1883) 1960. *Etymologisches Wörterbuch der Deutschen Sprache: Bearbeitet von Walter Mitzka*. 18th ed. Berlin: Walter de Gruyter.

Kramer, Heinrich, and James Sprenger. 1486. *The Malleus Maleficarum of Heinrich Kramer and James Sprenger.* Translated by Montague Summers. Mineola, NY: Dover.

Kurlansky, Mark. 2002. *Salt: A World History.* New York: Penguin Books.

Kvideland, Reimund, and Henning K. Sehmsdorf, eds. 1988. *Scandinavian Folk Belief and Legend.* Minneapolis: University of Minnesota Press.

Labrie, Vivian. 2009. "Twelve Märchen and Their Maps Go as Theories in the Real World." Paper presented at the International Society for Folk Narrative Research, Athens, Greece, June 22.

Lacan, Jacques. 1977. *Ecrits: A Selection.* Translated by Alan Sheridan. New York: W. W. Norton.

———. 1993. *The Seminar of Jacques Lacan.* Edited by Jacques-Alain Miller. Translated by Russell Grigg. Bk. 3, *The Psychoses: 1955–1956.* New York: Norton.

Lamos, Colleen. 1995. "Taking on the Phallus." In *Lesbian Erotics,* edited by Karla Jay, 101–24. New York: New York University Press.

Lang, Andrew. 1890. *The Red Fairy Book.* Mineola, NY: Dover.

Langlois, Janet L. 1993. "Mothers' Double Talk." In *Feminist Messages: Coding in Women's Folklore Culture,* edited by Joan Newlon Radner, 80–97. Urbana: University of Illinois Press.

Lanser, Susan S. 1986. "Toward a Feminist Narratology." *Style* 20 (3): 341–63.

———. 1995. "Sexing the Narrative: Propriety, Desire and the Engendering of Narratology." *Narrative* 3:85–94.

Lawrence, Elizabeth A. 1990. "Rodeo Horses: The Wild and the Tame." In *Signifying Animals: Human Meaning in the Natural World,* edited by Roy Willis, 222–35. London: Routledge.

Leach, Edmund. 2000. "Animal Categories and Verbal Abuse (1964)." In *The Essential Edmund Leach,* edited by Stephen Hugh-Jones and James Laidlaw, 322–43. Vol. 1. New Haven: Yale University Press.

Lemieux, Germain. 1978. *Les vieux m'ont conté.* Vol. 2. Montreal: Les Edition Bellarmin.

Leonard, Rodney. 2009. "Dueling Performances in 'The Grave Mound'—a Queer Investigation for the Twenty-First Century." Unpublished term paper, Performance Studies Department, New York University.

Lévi-Strauss, Claude. 1966. "The Structural Study of Myth." *Journal of American Folklore* 68 (270): 428–44.

———. 1969. *The Elementary Structures of Kinship.* Edited by Rodney Needham. Translated by James Harle Bell. Boston: Beacon Press.

Lieberman, Marcia R. 1972. "'Some Day My Prince Will Come': Female Acculturation through the Fairy Tale." *College English* 34 (3): 383–95.

Liebs, Elke. 1993. "'Spieglein, Spieglein an der Wand': Mutter-Mythen, Märchen-

Mütter, Tochter-Märchen." In *Mütter-Töchter-Frauen: Weiblichkeitsbilder in der Literatur*, edited by H. Kraft and E. Liebs, 115–47. Stuttgart: J. B. Metzler.

Lorber, Judith. 1995. *Paradoxes of Gender*. New Haven: Yale University Press.

Lorber, Judith, and Lisa Jean Moore. 2006. *Gendered Bodies: Feminist Perspectives*. New York: Oxford University Press.

Lorde, Audre. (1981) 1993. "The Uses of the Erotic: The Erotic as Power." In *The Gay and Lesbian Studies Reader*, edited by Henry Abelove, Michèle Aina Barale, and David M. Halperin, 339–43. New York: Routledge.

Lundell, Torborg. 1983. "Folktale Heroines and the Type and Motif Indexes." *Folklore* 94 (2): 240–46.

———. 1989. "Gender-Related Biases in the Type and Motif Indexes of Aarne and Thompson." In *Fairy Tales and Society: Illusion, Allusion and Paradigm*, edited by Ruth B. Bottigheimer, 146–63. Philadelphia: University of Pennsylvania Press.

Lurie, Alison. 1980. *Clever Gretchen, and Other Forgotten Folktales*. New York: Crowell.

Lüthi, Max. 1982. *The European Folktale: Form and Nature*. Bloomington: Indiana University Press.

Lyons, Paul. 2006. *American Pacificism: Oceania in the U.S. Imagination*. New York: Routledge.

MacCormack, Carol, and Marilyn Strathern, eds. 1980. *Nature, Culture and Gender*. New York: Cambridge University Press.

MacKay, Christopher S., ed. and trans. 2006. *Malleus Maleficarum*, by Henricus Institoris (Heinrich Kramer) and Jacobus Sprenger. London: Cambridge University Press.

Mackensen, Lutz. 1934/1940. *Handwörterbuch des Deutschen Märchens*. Vol. 2. Berlin: Walter de Gruyter.

Magoun, Francis P., Jr., and Alexander H. Krappe. 1960. *The Grimms' German Folk Tales*. Carbondale: Southern Illinois University Press.

Makinen, Merja. 2008. "Theorizing Fairy-Tale Fiction, Reading Jeanette Winterson." In *Contemporary Fiction and the Fairy Tale*, edited by Stephen Benson, 144–77. Detroit: Wayne State University Press.

Manguel, Alberto. 2009. "A Fairy Tale for Our Time." *Geist* 72 (Spring), www.geist .com/opinion.

Manheim, Ralph. 1977. *Grimms' Tales for Young and Old: The Complete Stories*. New York: Doubleday.

Martin, Biddy. 1996. *Femininity Played Straight: The Significance of Being Lesbian*. New York: Routledge.

Marzolph, Ulrich. 1984. *Typologie des persischen Volksmärchens*. Beirut: Franz Steiner Verlag.

———. 1992. *Arabia Ridens: Die humoristische Kurzprosa der fruühen adab-Literatur im internationalen Traditionsgeflecht*. 2 vols. Frankfurt: Vittorio Klostermann.

———. 2006. *Ex Oriente Fabula*. Vol. 2, *Exploring the Narrative Culture of the Islamic Near and Middle East*. Dortmund: Verlag für Orientkunde.

Marzolph, Ulrich, and Richard van Leeuwen. 2004. *The Arabian Nights Encyclopedia*. Vol 1. Santa Barbara, CA: ABC-CLIO.

Matrix, Sidney Eve. 2010. "A Secret Midnight Ball, a Magic Cloak of Invisibility: Voyeurism and Violence in the Cinematic Folklore of Stanley Kubrick's *Eyes Wide Shut*." In *Fairy Tale Films: Visions of Ambiguity*, edited by Pauline Greenhill and Sidney Eve Matrix, 178–97. Logan: Utah State University Press.

Matthews, Boris, trans. 1986. *The Herder Symbol Dictionary: Symbols from Art, Archaeology, Mythology, Literature, and Religion*. Wilmette, IL: Chiron.

McBain, Ed. 1985. *Snow White and Rose Red*. New York: Holt, Rinehart, and Winston.

McEwen, Christian, ed. 1997. *Jo's Girls: Tomboy Tales of High Adventure, True Grit, and Real Life*. Boston: Beacon Press.

McGann, PJ. 1999. "Skirting the Gender Divide: A Tomboy Life Story." In *Women's Untold Stories: Breaking Silence, Talking Back, Voicing Complexity*, edited by Mary Romero and Abigail J. Stewart, 105–24. New York: Routledge.

McGillis, Roderick. 2003. "'A Fairytale Is Just a Fairytale': George MacDonald and the Queering of Fairy." *Marvels & Tales: Journal of Fairy-Tale Studies* 17 (1): 86–99.

McGlathery, James M. 1991. *Fairy Tale Romance: The Grimms, Basile, Perrault*. Urbana: University of Illinois Press.

McRuer, Robert. 1997. *The Queer Renaissance: Contemporary American Literature and the Reinvention of Lesbian and Gay Identities*. New York: New York University Press.

McWilliams, G. H. 1995. *The Decameron/Giovanni Boccaccio*. London: Penguin Books.

Mendelson, Michael. 1997. "Forever Acting Alone: The Absence of Female Collaboration in Grimms' Fairy Tales." *Children's Literature in Education* 28 (3): 111–25.

Mikkonen, Kai. 2001. "The Hoffman(n) Effect and the Sleeping Prince: Fairy Tales in Angela Carter's *The Infernal Desire Machines of Doctor Hoffman*." In *Angela Carter and the Fairy Tale*, edited by Danielle M. Roemer and Cristina Bacchilega, 167–86. Detroit: Wayne State University Press.

Mills, Margaret. 1985. "Sex Role Reversals, Sex Changes, and Transvestite Disguise in the Oral Tradition of a Conservative Muslim Community in Afghanistan." In *Women's Folklore, Women's Culture*, edited by Rosan A. Jordan and Susan J. Kalcik, 187–213. Philadelphia: University of Pennsylvania Press.

———. 1999. "Whose Best Tricks? *Makr—i Zan* as a Topos in Persian Oral Literature." *Iranian Studies* 32 (2): 261–70.

———. 2000a. "Seven Steps Ahead of the Devil: A Misogynist Proverb in Context."

In *Telling, Remembering, Interpreting, Guessing: A Festschrift for Prof. Anniki Kaivola-Bregenhøj on Her 60th Birthday*, edited by Pasi Enges, 449–58. Joensuu: Suomen Kansatietouden Tutkijain Seura.

———. 2000b. "Women's Tricks: Subordination and Subversion in Afghan Folk-tales." In *Thick Corpus, Organic Variation and Textuality in Oral Tradition*, edited by Lauri Honko, 453–87. Studia Fennica Folkloristica 7. Helsinki: Finnish Literature Society.

———. 2001. "The Gender of the Trick: Female Tricksters and Male Narrators." *Asian Folklore Studies* 60 (2): 238–58.

Minard, Rosemary. 1975. *Womenfolk and Fairy Tales*. Boston: Houghton Mifflin.

Moore, Lisa L. 1997. *Dangerous Intimacies: Towards a Sapphic History of the British Novel*. Durham, NC: Duke University Press.

Morrison, Jago. 2003. *Contemporary Fiction*. London: Routledge.

———. 2006. "'Who Cares about Gender at a Time like This?' Love, Sex and the Problem of Jeanette Winterson." *Journal of Gender Studies* 15 (2): 169–80.

Muhawi, Ibrahim. 2001. "Gender and Disguise in the Arabic Cinderella: A Study in the Cultural Dynamics of Representation." *Fabula* 42 (3–4): 263–83.

Muhawi, Ibrahim, and Sharif Kanaana. 1989. *Speak, Bird, Speak Again: Palestinian Arab Folktales*. Berkeley: University of California Press.

Muller, Robin. 1984. *Tatterhood*. Richmond Hill, ON: North Winds Press.

Muñoz, José Esteban. 1996. "Ephemera as Evidence: Introductory Notes to Queer Acts." *Women and Performance: A Journal of Feminist Theory* 8 (2): 5–16.

———. 1999. *Disidentifications: Queers of Color and the Performance of Politics*. Minneapolis: University of Minnesota Press.

———. 2009. *Cruising Utopia: The Then and There of Queer Futurity*. New York: New York University Press.

Munt, Sally R. ed. 1998. *butch/femme: Inside Lesbian Gender*. London: Cassell.

Najmabadi, Afsaneh. 1999. "Reading—and Enjoying—'Wiles of Women' Stories as a Feminist." *Iranian Studies* 32:203–22.

Namaste, Viviane. 2005. *Sex Change, Social Change: Reflections on Identity, Institutions, and Imperialism*. Toronto: Women's Press

Nealon, Christopher. 2001. *Foundlings: Lesbian and Gay Historical Emotion before Stonewall*. Durham, NC: Duke University Press.

Némirovsky, Irène. 2008. *Fire in the Blood*. London: Vintage Books.

Nestle, Joan. 1992. *The Persistent Desire: A Femme-Butch Reader*. Boston: Alyson Press.

Nicholson, Reynold A. 1933/1934. *The Mathnawí of Jaláluddiín Rúmí*. Bk. 5–6. London: Luzac.

Nikolajeva, Maria. 2008. "Food." In *The Greenwood Encyclopedia of Folktales and Fairy*

Tales, edited by Donald Haase, 367–70. Vol. 1. Westport, CT: Greenwood Press.

Nitschke, August. 1988. "The Importance of Fairy Tales in German Families before the Grimms." In *The Brothers Grimm and Folktale,* ed. James M. McGlathery, 164–77. Urbana: University of Illinois Press.

Noble, Jean Bobby. 2006. *Sons of the Movement: FtMs Risking Incoherence on a Post-Queer Cultural Landscape.* Toronto: Women's Press.

Norse, Harold. 2003. *In the Hub of the Fiery Force, Collected Poems, 1934–2003.* New York: Thunder's Mouth Press.

O'Brien, Sharon. 1979. "Tomboyism and Adolescent Conflict: Three Nineteenth-Century Case Studies." In *Women's Being, Women's Place: Female Identity and Vocation in American History,* edited by Mary Kelley, 351–72. Boston: G. K. Hall.

Odber de Baubeta, Patricia Anne. 2004. "The Fairy-Tale Intertext in Iberian and Latin American Women's Writing." In *Fairy Tales and Feminism: New Approaches,* edited by Donald Haase, 129–47. Detroit: Wayne State University.

Okpewho, Isidore. 1998. *Once upon a Kingdom: Myth, Hegemony, and Identity.* Bloomington: Indiana University Press.

Orme, Jennifer. 2010. "Mouth to Mouth: Queer Desires in Emma Donoghue's *Kissing the Witch.*" *Marvels & Tales: Journal of Fairy-Tale Studies* 24 (1): 116–30.

Page, Ruth. 2007. "Gender." In *The Cambridge Companion to Narrative,* edited by David Herman, 189–202. Cambridge: Cambridge University Press.

Palmer, Paulina. 1999. *Lesbian Gothic: Transgressive Fictions.* London: Cassell.

———. 2004. "Lesbian Transformation of Gothic and Fairy Tale." In *Contemporary British Women Writers,* edited by Emma Parker, 139–53. Cambridge: S. S. Brewer.

Pedroso, Consiglieri, Henriquetta Monteiro, and William Ralston Sheddon Ralston. 1882. *Portuguese Folk-Tales.* Translated by H. Monteiro. Vol. 9, *Publications of the Folk-Lore Society (Great Britain).* London: Folk-Lore Society.

Pemberton, Marilyn, ed. 2010. *Enchanted Ideologies: A Collection of Rediscovered Nineteenth-Century Moral Fairy Tales.* Lambertville, NJ: True Bill Press.

Penelope, Julia, and Susan J. Wolfe. (1980) 1989. *The Original Coming Out Stories.* Exp. 2nd ed. Freedom, CA: Crossing Press.

Peng, Emma Pi-tai. 2004. "Angela Carter's Postmodern Feminism and the Gothic Uncanny." *NTU Studies in Language and Literature* 13:99–134.

Perco, Daniela. 1993. "Female Initiation in Northern Italian Versions of 'Cinderella.'" Translated by Cristina Bacchilega. *Western Folklore* 52 (1): 73–84.

Phelps, Ethel Johnston. 1978. *Tatterhood, and Other Tales.* Old Westbury, NY: Feminist Press.

Pino-Saavedra, Yolando, ed. 1967. *Folktales of Chile.* Chicago: University of Chicago Press.

Plummer, Ken. 1995. *Telling Sexual Stories: Power, Change and Social Worlds*. London: Routledge.

Preston, Cathy Lynn, ed. 1995. *Folklore, Literature, and Cultural Theory: Collected Essays*. New York: Garland.

———. 2004. "Disrupting the Boundaries of Genre and Gender: Postmodernism and the Fairy Tale." In *Fairy Tales and Feminism: New Approaches*, edited by Donald Haase, 197–212. Detroit: Wayne State University Press.

Preves, Sharon E. 2003. *Intersex and Identity: The Contested Self*. New Brunswick, NJ: Rutgers University Press.

Probyn, Elspeth. 1995. "Queer Belongings: The Politics of Departure." In *Sexy Bodies: The Strange Carnalities of Feminism*, edited by Elizabeth Grosz and Elspeth Probyn, 1–18. London: Routledge.

———. 1999. "An Ethos with a Bite: Queer Appetites from Sex to Food." *Sexualities* 2 (4): 421–31.

Propp, Vladimir. 1968. *Morphology of the Folktale*. Translated by Laurence Scott. Austin: University of Texas Press.

Prosser, Jay. 1998. *Second Skins: The Body Narratives of Transsexuality*. New York: Columbia University Press.

Pugh, Tison. 2008. "'There Lived in the Land of Oz Two Queerly Made Men': Queer Utopianism and Antisocial Eroticism in L. Frank Baum's Oz Series." *Marvels & Tales: Journal of Fairy-Tale Studies* 22 (2): 217–39.

Purkiss, Diane. 1996. *The Witch in History: Early Modern and Twentieth-Century Representations*. London: Routledge.

Quimby, Karin. 2003. "The Story of Jo: Literary Tomboys, *Little Women*, and the Sexual-Textual Politics of Narrative Desire." *GLQ: A Journal of Lesbian and Gay Studies* 10 (1): 1–22.

Radner, Joan N., ed. 1993. *Feminist Messages: Coding in Women's Folk Culture*. Urbana: University of Chicago Press.

Radner, Joan N., and Susan S. Lanser. 1993. "Strategies of Coding in Women's Cultures." In *Feminist Messages: Coding in Women's Folklore Culture*, edited by Joan Newlon Radner, 1–29. Urbana: University of Illinois Press.

Rahmoni, Ravshan. 1995. *Afsánaháyi Darí*. Tehran: Sorush.

Ramanujan, A. K. 1997. *A Flowering Tree, and Other Oral Tales from India*. Edited by Stuart Blackburn and Alan Dundes. Berkeley: University of California Press.

Ranke, Kurt. 1978. *Die Welt der Einfachen Formen*. Berlin: Walter de Gruyter.

———, ed. 1990. *Enzyklopädie des Märchens*. Vol. 6. Berlin: Walter de Gruyter.

Renfroe, Cheryl. 2001. "Initiation and Disobedience: Liminal Experience in Angela Carter's 'The Bloody Chamber.'" In *Angela Carter and the Fairy Tale*, edited by

Danielle M. Roemer and Cristina Bacchilega, 94–106. Detroit: Wayne State University Press.

Rich, Adrienne. (1980) 1993. "Compulsory Heterosexuality and Lesbian Existence." Reprinted in *The Lesbian and Gay Studies Reader,* ed. Henry Abelove, Michèle Aina Barale, and David Halperin, 227–54. New York: Routledge.

Ritvo, Harriet. 1997. *The Platypus and the Mermaid and Other Figments of the Classifying Imagination.* Cambridge, MA: Harvard University Press.

———. 2004. "Our Animal Cousins." *differences: A Journal of Feminist Cultural Studies* 15 (1): 48–68.

Rivière, Joan. 1929. "Womanliness as a Masquerade." *International Journal of Psychoanalysis* 9:303–13.

Roberts, Leonard W. (1955) 1988. *South from Hell-fer-Sartin: Kentucky Mountain Folk Tales.* Lexington: University Press of Kentucky.

———. 1974. *Sang Branch Settlers: Folksongs and Tales of a Kentucky Mountain Family.* Austin: University of Texas Press.

Robertson, D. J. 1890. "The Story of Kate Crackernuts." *Folklore* 1 (3): 299–301.

Robinson, Orrin W. 2007. "Does Sex Breed Gender? Pronominal Reference in the Grimms' Fairy Tales." *Marvels & Tales: Journal of Fairy-Tale Studies* 21 (1): 107–23.

Roemer, Danielle M., and Cristina Bacchilega, eds. 2001. *Angela Carter and the Fairy Tale.* Detroit: Wayne State University Press.

Roessner, Jeffrey. 2002. "Writing a History of Difference: Jeanette Winterson's *Sexing the Cherry* and Angela Carter's *Wise Children.*" *College Literature* 29 (1): 103–22.

Rölleke, Heinz. 1972. "Allerleirauh: Eine bisher unbekannte Fassung vor Grimm." *Fabula: Zeitschrift für Erzählforschung* 13:153–59.

———, ed. 1980. *Kinder- und Hausmärchen,* by Jacob and Wilhelm Grimm. 7th ed. Vol. 1–3. Göttingen 1857. Stuttgart: Philipp Reclam Jun.

Roper, Lyndal. 1994. *Oedipus and the Devil: Witchcraft, Sexuality, and Religion in Early Modern Europe.* New York: Routledge.

———. 2004. *Witch Craze: Terror and Fantasy in Baroque Germany.* New Haven, CT: Yale University Press.

Roscoe, Will. 1991. *The Zuni Man-Woman.* Albuquerque: University of New Mexico Press.

Rowland, Beryl. 1973. *Animals with Human Faces.* Knoxville: University of Tennessee Press.

Rowlands, Alison. 2003. *Witchcraft Narratives in Germany, Rothenberg, 1561–1652.* Manchester: Manchester University Press.

Rubin, Gayle. 1975. "The Traffic in Women: Notes on the Political Economy of Sex." In *Toward an Anthropology of Women,* edited by Rayna R. Reiter, 157–210. New

York: Monthly Review Press.

Ruddick, Nicholas. 2004. "'Not So Very Blue, After All': Resisting the Temptation to Correct Charles Perrault's 'Bluebeard.'" *Journal of the Fantastic in the Arts* 15 (4): 346–57.

Rupp, Leila. 1996. "Finding the Lesbians in Lesbian History." In *The New Lesbian Studies: Into the Twenty-First Century,* edited by Bonnie Zimmerman and Toni A. H. McNaron, 153–59. New York: Feminist Press.

Russo, Mary. 1994. *The Female Grotesque: Risk, Excess, and Modernity.* New York: Routledge.

Sage, Lorna. 2001. "Angela Carter: The Fairy Tale." In *Angela Carter and the Fairy Tale,* edited by Danielle M. Roemer and Cristina Bacchilega, 65–82. Detroit: Wayne State University Press.

Sanday, Peggy Reeves. 1981. *Female Power and Male Dominance: On the Origins of Sexual Inequality.* Cambridge: Cambridge University Press.

Sceats, Sarah. 2001. "Oral Sex: Vampiric Transgression and the Writing of Angela Carter." *Tulsa Studies in Women's Literature* 20 (1): 107–21.

Schechner, Richard. 1985. *Between Theatre and Anthropology.* Philadelphia: University of Pennsylvania Press.

Scherf, Walter. 1987. *Die Herausforderung des Dämons: Form und Funktion grausiger Kindermärchen.* Munich: K. G. Saur.

Schmidt, Sigrid. 1991. *Aschenputtel und Eulenspiegel in Afrika: Entlehntes Erzählgut der Nama und Damara in Namibia.* Vol. 1, *Afrika erzählt.* Cologne: Rüdiger Köppe.

———. 1999. *Hänsel und Gretel in Afrika: Märchentexte aus Namibia im internationalen Vergleich.* Vol. 7, *Afrika erzählt.* Cologne: Rüdiger Köppe.

Schneider, Rebecca. 1997. *The Explicit Body in Performance.* New York: Routledge.

Scot, Reginald. 1584. *The Discoverie of Witchcraft.* Carbondale: Southern Illinois University Press.

Scott, James. 1985. *Weapons of the Weak.* New Haven: Yale University Press.

Sedgwick, Eve Kosofsky. 1985. *Between Men: English Literature and Male Homosocial Desire.* New York: Columbia University Press.

———. 1990. *Epistemology of the Closet.* Berkeley: University of California Press.

———. 1993. *Tendencies.* Durham, NC: Duke University Press.

———. 1997. *Novel Gazing: Queer Readings in Fiction.* Durham, NC: Duke University Press.

———. 2003. *Touching Feeling: Affect, Pedagogy, Performativity.* Durham, NC: Duke University Press.

Seifert, Lewis. 2008. "Gay and Lesbian Tales." In *The Greenwood Encyclopedia of Folktales and Fairy Tales,* edited by Donald Haase, 400–402. Westport, CT: Greenwood Press.

Shakespeare, William. 1988. *William Shakespeare: The Complete Works*, edited by Stanley Wells and Gary Taylor. Oxford: Clarendon Press.

Shelley, Christopher. 2008. *Transpeople: Repudiation, Trauma, Healing*. Toronto: University of Toronto Press.

Shotwell, Alexis. 2009. "A Knowing That Resided in My Bones: Sensuous Embodiment and Trans Social Movement." In *Embodiment and Agency*, edited by Sue Campbell, Letitia Meynell, and Susan Sherwin, 58–75. University Park: Pennsylvania State University Press.

Smith, Kevin Paul. 2007. *The Postmodern Fairytale: Folkloric Intertexts in Contemporary Fiction*. New York: Palgrave Macmillan.

Smith-Rosenberg, Carroll. 1985. *Disorderly Conduct: Visions of Gender in Victorian America*. New York: Alfred A. Knopf.

Solis, Santiago. 2007. "Snow White and the Seven 'Dwarfs' Queercripped." *Hypatia* 22 (1): 114–31.

Steig, William. 1990. *Shrek!* New York: Farrar, Straus, and Giroux.

Stein, Gertrude. (1925) 1968. *The Making of Americans*. Reprint, London: Peter Owen.

Stephens, Walter. 2002. *Demon Lovers: Witchcraft, Sex, and the Crisis of Belief*. Chicago: University of Chicago Press.

Stockton, Kathryn Bond. 1994. *God between Their Lips: Desire between Women in Irigaray, Brontë, and Eliot*. Stanford: Stanford University Press.

———. 2004. "Growing Sideways, or, Versions of the Queer Child: The Ghost, the Homosexual, the Freudian, the Innocent, and the Interval of Animal." In *Curiouser: On the Queerness of Children*, edited by Steven Bruhm and Natasha Hurley. 277–315. Minneapolis: University of Minnesota Press.

———. 2009. *The Queer Child, or, Growing Sideways in the Twentieth Century*. Durham, NC: Duke University Press.

Stokes, Maeve. 1879. *Indian Fairy Tales*. Calcutta: privately printed.

Stone, Kay. 1986. "Feminist Approaches to the Interpretation of Fairy Tales." In *Fairy Tales and Society: Illusion, Allusion, and Paradigm*, edited by Ruth B. Bottigheimer, 229–36. Philadelphia: University of Pennsylvania Press.

———. 1993. "Burning Brightly: New Light from an Old Tale." In *Feminist Messages: Coding in Women's Folklore*, edited by Joan Newlon Radner, 289–305. Urbana: University of Illinois Press.

———. 2004. *The Golden Woman: Dreaming as Art*. Winnipeg, MB: J. Gordon Shillingford.

———. 2008. *Someday Your Witch Will Come*. Detroit: Wayne State University Press.

Stryker, Susan. 2004. "Transgender Studies: Queer Theory's Evil Twin." *GLQ: A*

Journal of Lesbian and Gay Studies 10 (2): 212–15.

Stryker, Susan, and Stephen Whittle, eds. 2006. *The Transgender Studies Reader.* New York: Routledge.

Sullivan, Nikki. 2003. *A Critical Introduction to Queer Theory.* New York: New York University Press, 2003.

Symons, Michael. 1998. *A History of Cooks and Cooking.* Champaign: University of Illinois Press.

Synnott, Anthony. 1987. "Shame and Glory: A Sociology of Hair." *British Journal of Sociology* 38 (3): 381–413.

Taggart, James M. 1990. *Enchanted Maidens: Gender Relations in Spanish Folktales of Courtship and Marriage.* Princeton: Princeton University Press.

Tatar, Maria. 1987. *The Hard Facts of the Grimms' Fairy Tales.* Princeton: Princeton University Press.

———. 1992. *Off with Their Heads: Fairy Tales and the Culture of Childhood.* Princeton: Princeton University Press.

———, ed. 1999. *The Classic Fairy Tales: Texts, Criticism.* New York: W. W. Norton.

———, ed. 2002. *The Annotated Classic Fairy Tales.* New York: W. W. Norton.

———. 2003. *The Hard Facts of the Grimms' Fairy Tales.* 2nd exp. ed. Princeton: Princeton University Press.

———. 2004a. *The Annotated Brothers Grimm.* New York: W. W. Norton.

———. 2004b. *Secrets beyond the Door: The Story of Bluebeard and His Wives.* Princeton: Princeton University Press.

Tawney, C. J. 1928. *The Ocean of Story.* London: C. J. Sawyer.

Thomas, Hayley S. 1999. "Undermining a Grimm Tale: A Feminist Reading of 'The Worn-Out Dancing Shoes' (KHM 133)." *Marvels & Tales: Journal of Fairy-Tale Studies* 13 (2): 170–83.

Thompson, Stith. 1946. *The Folktale.* New York: Holt, Rinehart and Winston.

———. 1966. *Motif-Index of Folk Literature.* Vol. 1, *A–C.* Bloomington: Indiana University Press.

Tiffin, Jessica. 2009. *Marvelous Geometry: Narrative and Metafiction in Modern Fairy Tale.* Detroit: Wayne State University Press.

Toivo, Raisa. 2008. *Witchcraft and Gender in Early Modern Society: Finland and the Wider European Experience.* Burlington, VT: Ashgate.

Torgovnick, Marianna. 1990. *Gone Primitive: Savage Intellects, Modern Lives.* Chicago: University of Chicago Press.

Traub, Valerie. 2002. *The Renaissance of Lesbianism in Early Modern England.* Cambridge: Cambridge University Press.

Tuana, Nancy. 2004. "Coming to Understand: Orgasm and the Epistemology of

Ignorance." *Hypatia* 19 (1): 194–232.

Tucker, Holly. 2003. *Pregnant Fictions: Childbirth and the Fairy Tale in Early Modern France*. Detroit: Wayne State University Press.

Tucker, Lindsey. 1998. Introduction to *Critical Essays on Angela Carter*, edited by Lindsey Tucker, 1–23. New York: G. K. Hall.

Turner, Kay. 2009. "Queering Structuralism." Paper presented at the annual meeting of the American Folklore Society, Boise Idaho, October 21–24.

———. 2010. "Rethinking the Phallic Mother with 'Frau Trude.'" Paper presented at the annual meeting of the American Folklore Society, Nashville, TN, October 13–17.

Turner, Victor W. (1964) 1972. "Betwixt and Between: The Liminal Passage in *Rites de Passage*." In *Reader in Comparative Religion*, edited by William A. Lessa and Evon Z. Vogt, 338–47. 3rd ed. New York: Harper and Row.

Uther, Hans-Jörg, ed. 1996. *Kinder- und Hausmärchen: nach der grossen Ausgabe von 1857, textkritisch revideiert, kommentiert und durch Register geschlossen*. 4 vols. Munich: Diederichs.

———. 2004. *The Types of International Folktales: A Classification and Bibliography*. 3 vols. Helsinki: Academia Scientiarum Fennica.

———. 2008. *Handbuch zu den "Kinder- und Hausmärchen" der Brüder Grimm: Entstehung—Wirkung—Interpretation*. Berlin: Walter de Gruyter.

Vance, Carole S., ed. 1984. *Pleasure and Danger: Exploring Female Sexuality*. New York: Routledge/Kegan Paul.

Van der Kooi, Jurjen. 2002. "Priesters Gäste." In *Enzyklopädie des Märchens*, 10:1308–11. Berlin: Walter de Gruyter.

Vanita, Ruth. 2005. *Gandhi's Tiger and Sita's Smile: Essays on Gender, Sexuality, and Culture*. New Delhi: Yoda Press.

Vaz da Silva, Francisco. 2002. *Metamorphosis: The Dynamics of Symbolism in European Fairy Tales*. New York: Peter Lang.

———. 2008. "Colors." In *The Greenwood Encyclopedia of Folktales and Fairy Tales*, edited by Donald Haase, 226–227. Westport, CT: Greenwood Press.

Velay-Vallantin, Catherine. 1998. "From 'Little Red Riding Hood' to the 'Beast of Gévaudan': The Tale in the Long Term Continuum." Translated by Binita Mehta. In *Telling Tales: Medieval Narratives and the Folk Tradition*, edited by Francesca Canadé Sautman, Diana Conchado, and Giuseppe Carlo di Scipio, 269–95. New York: St. Martin's Press.

Verdier, Yvonne. 1980. "Le petit chaperon rouge dans la tradition orale." *Le debat* 3:31–56.

Vicinus, Martha. 1993. "'They Wonder to Which Sex I Belong': The Historical Roots of the Modern Lesbian Identity." In *The Lesbian and Gay Studies Reader*, edited by Henry Abelove, Michèle Aina Barale, and David M. Halperin, 432–52. New York: Routledge.

———. 2004. *Intimate Friends: Women Who Loved Women, 1778–1928*. Chicago: University of Chicago Press.

Von Franz, Marie-Louise. 1995. *Shadow and Evil in Fairy Tales, Revised Edition*. Boston: Shambhala.

———. 1996. *The Interpretation of Fairy Tales*. Rev. ed. Boston: Shambhala.

Von Löwis of Menar, August, and Reinhold Olesch, eds. 1959. *Russische Volksmärchen*. Düsseldorf-Cologne: Eugen Diederichs Verlag.

Waddell, Terry. 2003. "The Female/Feline Morph: Myth, Media, Sex and the Bestial." In *Cultural Expressions of Evil and Wickedness: Wrath, Sex, Crime*, edited by Terrie Waddell, 75–96. Amsterdam: Rodolpi.

Walker, Virginia, and Mary E. Lunz. 1976. "Symbols, Fairy Tales, and School-Age Children." *Elementary School Journal* 77 (2): 94–100.

Wander, Karl Friedrich Wilhelm. (1867–80) 1964. *Deutsches Sprichwörterlexicon: Ein Hausschatz für das deutsche Volk*. 5 vols. Darmstadt: Wissenschaftliche Buchgesellschaft.

Warner, Marina. 1994. *From the Beast to the Blonde: On Fairy Tales and Their Tellers*. London: Chatto and Windus.

Warner, Michael, ed. 1993. *Fear of a Queer Planet: Queer Politics and Social Theory*. Minneapolis: University of Minnesota Press.

Watts, Linda S. 1993. "Twice upon a Time: Back Talk, Spinsters, and Re-Verse-Als in Gertrude Stein's *The World Is Round* (1939)." *Women and Language* 16 (1): 53–57.

Weed, Elizabeth, and Naomi Schor, eds. 1997. *Feminism Meets Queer Theory*. Bloomington: Indiana University Press.

Weldon, Fay. 1977. *Words of Advice*. New York: Random House.

Welty, Eudora. 1942. *The Robber Bridegroom*. New York: Harcourt Brace.

Westling, Louise. 1996. "Tomboys and Revolting Femininity." In *Critical Essays on Carson McCullers*, edited by Beverly Lyon Clark and Melvin J. Friedman, 155–65. New York: G. K. Hall.

Weston, Kath. 1991. *Families We Choose: Lesbians, Gays, Kinship*. New York: Columbia University Press.

White, Patricia. 1999. *Uninvited: Classical Hollywood Cinema and Lesbian Representability*. Bloomington: Indiana University Press.

Wiesner, Merry E. 1993. "The Midwives of South Germany and the Public/Private Dichotomy." In *The Art of Midwifery: Early Modern Midwives in Europe*, edited by Hilary Marland, 77–94. London: Routledge.

Wilchins, Riki Anne. 2004. *Queer Theory, Gender Theory: An Instant Primer*. Los

Angeles, CA: Alyson Books.

Williams, Linda. 1989. *Hard Core: Power, Pleasure and the "Frenzy of the Visible."* Berkeley: University of California Press.

Williams, Raymond. 1977. *Marxism and Literature.* Oxford: Oxford University Press.

Willingham, Bill. 2002a. *Fables,* issue 1. New York: DC Comics.

———. 2002b. *Fables,* issue 6. New York: DC Comics.

———. 2002c. *Fables,* issue 9. New York: DC Comics.

Willis, Deborah. 1995. *Malevolent Nurture: Witch-Hunting and Maternal Power in Early Modern England.* Ithaca: Cornell University Press.

Willis, Roy. 1974. *Man and Beast.* London: Hart-Davis, McGibbon.

Wilson, Adrian. 1995. *The Making of Man-Midwifery: Childbirth in England, 1660-1770.* Cambridge, MA: Harvard University Press.

Winterson, Jeanette. 1985. *Oranges Are Not the Only Fruit.* London: Pandora Press.

———. 1989. *Sexing the Cherry.* London: Bloomsbury Publishing.

———. 1994. *Written on the Body.* New York: Vintage.

———. 2008. "Books: Sexing the Cherry." Jeannette Winterson.com. http://www.jeanettewinterson.com/pages/content/index.asp?PageID=14.

Wisker, Gina. 1997. "Revenge of the Living Doll: Angela Carter's Horror Writing." In *The Infernal Desires of Angela Carter: Fiction, Femininity, Feminism,* edited by Joseph Bristow and Trev Lynn Broughton, 116–31. London: Longman.

Woodman, Marian. 1992. *Leaving My Father's House: A Journey to Conscious Femininity.* Boston: Shambala Press.

Wyatt, Susan. 2005. "Awakening the Trickster." Paper presented at the first international congress of Qualitative Inquiry, May 5–7, University of Illinois at Urbana-Champaign, http://www.iiqi.org/C4QI/httpdocs/qi2005/papers/wyatt3.pdf.

Young, Katharine Galloway. 1987. *Taleworlds and Storyrealms: The Phenomenology of Narrative.* Boston: Nijhoff.

Zimmerman, Bonnie. 1993. "Perverse Reading: The Lesbian Appropriate of Literature." In *Sexual Practice, Textual Theory: Lesbian Cultural Criticism,* edited by Susan J. Wolfe and Julia Penelope, 135–49. Cambridge: Blackwell.

Zipes, Jack. 1979. *Breaking the Magic Spell: Radical Theories of Folk and Fairy Tales.* Austin: University of Texas Press.

———. 1983a. *Fairy Tales and the Art of Subversion: The Classical Genre for Children and the Process of Civilization.* New York: Wildman.

———. 1983b. *The Trials and Tribulations of Little Red Riding Hood: Versions of the Tale in Sociocultural Context.* South Hadley: Bergin and Garvey.

———, trans. 1987. *The Complete Fairy Tales of the Brothers Grimm.* New York: Bantam Books.

———. 1988a. *The Brothers Grimm: From Enchanted Forests to the Modern World.* New York: Routledge.

———. 1988b. "Dreams of a Better Bourgeois Life: The Psychosocial Origins of the Grimms' Tales." In *The Brothers Grimm and Folktale,* edited by James M. McGlathery, 205–19. Urbana: University of Illinois Press.

———. 1989. *Beauties, Beasts and Enchantment: Classic French Fairy Tales.* Markham, ON: Penguin.

———, trans. 1992. *The Complete Fairy Tales of the Brothers Grimm.* 2nd ed. New York: Bantam Books.

———. 1995a. *Creative Storytelling: Building Community, Changing Lives.* London: Routledge.

———. 1995b. "Once upon a Time beyond Disney: Contemporary Fairy-Tale Films for Children." In *In Front of the Children: Screen Entertainment and Young Audiences,* edited by Cary Bazalgette and David Buckingham, 109–26. London: British Film Institute.

———. 2001. *The Great Fairy Tale Tradition: From Straparola and Basile to the Brothers Grimm: Texts, Criticism.* New York: W. W. Norton.

———. 2002a. *Breaking the Magic Spell: Radical Theories of Folk and Fairy Tales.* Rev. and exp. ed. Lexington: University of Kentucky Press.

———, trans. 2002b. *The Complete Fairy Tales of the Brothers Grimm.* 3rd ed. New York: Bantam Books.

———. 2006a. *Fairy Tales and the Art of Subversion.* 2nd ed. New York: Routledge.

———. 2006b. *Why Fairy Tales Stick: The Evolution and Relevance of a Genre.* New York: Routledge.

Zipes, Jack, and Joseph Russo, trans. and eds. 2009. *The Collected Sicilian Folk and Fairy Tales of Giuseppe Pitrè.* 2 vols. New York: Routledge.

Zita, Jacquelyn N. 1992. "Male Lesbians and the Postmodernist Body." *Hypatia* 7 (4): 106–27.

INDEX

Note: ATU numbers refer to Hans-Jörg Uther, *The Types of International Folktales*; wherever possible the ATU entry is most comprehensive. KHM numbers refer to Jacob & Wilhelm Grimm, *Kinder- und Hausmärchen*.

223–43 passim; incest in, 243n4

ATU 510B*, 93–101, 116n3

ATU 514, "The Shift of Sex," 16, 102

ATU 533, "The Goosegirl," 53, 215

ATU 545B, "Puss in Boots," 181, 205n26

ATU 565, "The Sweet Porridge," 246, 269n3

ATU 706, "The Maiden Without Hands," 54

ATU 708, "The Wonder Child," 192

ATU 709, "Snow White," 152, 161–78 passim

ATU 710 (KHM 3), "Mary's Child," 209–10

ATU 711, "The Beautiful and Ugly Twinsisters" or "Tatterhood," 182, 183, 192–94, 196–97, 199, 202n1. *See also* "Peg Bearskin" and "La Poiluse," 181–205 passim.

ATU 720 (KHM 47), "The Juniper Tree," 9, 44n7, 155

ATU 815, "The Grave Mound," 21, 250, 295–302; compared with ATU 1130, 21

ATU 872*, "Brother and Sister," 81

ATU 884, "The Twelve Huntsmen" or "The Forsaken Fiancée: Service as Menial," 227

ATU 923, "Love Like Salt," 53, 116n12, 223–25, 230

ATU 955, "The Robber Bridegroom," 15, 220n4, 246

ATU 1130, compared with "The Grave Mound," 21

ATU 1353, "The Old Woman as Trouble Maker," 46n21

ATU 1383, "The Woman Does Not Know Herself," 45n17

ATU 1384, "The Husband Hunts Three Persons as Stupid as His Wife," 45n17

ATU 1387, "The Woman Goes to Get Beer," 45n17

ATU 1430, "The Man and His Wife Build Air Castles," 47n26

ATU 1430–1439, "The Foolish Couple" (tale type category), 47n26

ATU 1449*, "The Stingy Hostess and the Inn," 204n20

ATU 1450, "Clever Else," 18, 27–47; misogyny in, 46n21; typology of, 45n17

ATU 1565*, "The Big Cake," 204n20

ATU 1725–1724 "Clergyman is Tricked" (tale type category), 28

ATU 1741, "Clever Gretel" or "The Priest's Guest and the Eaten Chickens," 18, 27–47

ATU 1842C*, "The Clergyman's Nights," 204n20

Atwood, Margaret, 2

audience, 8, 52, 70, 81, 91, 116n2, 186, 202, 278ff., 290n2, 296

authenticity, 1

authority figures, 32, 84, 208–12, 215–19, 242, 261, 268, 280, 282–84, 285, 290nn8–9, 291n22

autoeroticism, 30, 33. *See also* eroticism

avatars, 213, 216, 217

Bakhtin, Mikhail, 235–36

ballads, 12, 23n8, 200, 203n3, 205n24, 270n5, 271n13

baptism, 58, 62, 67n9, 72; satanic, 57

Barthes, Roland, 7, 259, 272n21

bears, 161–78 passim
"Bearskin," 103, 243n7
beautification, 182
"Beautiful and Ugly Twinsisters, The."
 See ATU 711
beauty, 161–78 passim; disguised,
 91–118 passim, 207–21 passim,
 223–43 passim; maiden, 75–85
 passim; somnambulist, 121–39,
 transformation from ugliness to,
 51–64 passim, 181–205 passim. See
 also ugliness, unattractiveness
"Beauty and the Beast," 205n26
becoming- (Deleuze and Guattari),
 223–43; becoming-animal, 228,
 235, 238; definition, 228
bedtrick plots, 216–18
Belmont, Nicole, 215
Bettelheim, Bruno, 2, 209, 273
Biebuyck, Brunhilde, 215
"Big Cake, The" (ATU 1565*), 204n20
binaries and polarities, 5, 11, 15, 51, 58,
 186, 247–49, 260, 261, 264, 268,
 274; male/female, 202, 205n29;
 sex/gender, 115, 199–200, 237. See
 also dichotomies
biology, 5, 16, 24n11, 70
Block, Francesca Lia, 145
blood, 72, 76, 125, 129, 130, 165, 207,
 208, 211, 236, 247, 251, 264, 266,
 267. See also menses, menstruation
Bloody Chamber, The (Carter), 131ff.,
 151, 272
"Bluebeard." See ATU 312
body, the, 12, 17, 30, 77, 85, 230, 232,
 235
boundaries (social/cultural), 12, 16, 18,
 85, 198, 219, 226ff., 273n31

Brewer, Elizabeth, 182, 184, 188
bridegrooms, 87, 116n1, 134, 205; true
 and false, 20, 207–21
brides, 87, 137, 194, 203, 205, 224,
 226, 227
brides, false, 20, 207–21, esp. 213ff.; as
 villains, 215–16
brides, true, 20, 207–21; tests of, 212
"Brier Rose," or "Little Brier Rose." See
 ATU 410
brothels, 130
brother-sister relationships, 69–89,
 209. See also siblings
burning, 10, 21, 32, 263; of a person,
 71–72, 86, 155, 190–91, 247, 261,
 263, 272n24; of witches, 214. See
 also fire and flames
butch (trait), 194
Butler, Judith, 38, 39, 42, 45n20,
 46n22, 76–77, 84, 88n5, 89n12,
 146, 238
Byatt, A. S., 2

Canadian fairy tales, 20, 192
cannibalism, 8–9, 18, 34, 44n7, 44n9,
 44n11, 72, 77, 128, 185–86, 203n6,
 246, 251, 272n24
canon, fairy-tale, 1, 124, 278
"Cap O' Rushes." See ATU 510B
Carter, Angela, 2, 3, 19, 29, 30, 43n3,
 121–39, 145, 151, 272n19
Case, Sue Ellen, 124–25, 133, 137, 266
Castle, Terry, 256
castration, 34, 75, 88n5
categories, 11, 17, 102, 172, 231; cultural, 13, 102; genre, 29; normative,
 11; sex/gender, 5, 102, 149, 187, 238,
 265

chastity, 125, 139n7, 173, 214, 261, 282

childbirth, 49–67 passim, 122–23, 264

children, childhood, 121, 164, 165, 296–97; beautiful and ugly, 57, 167–68; intersex, 199; misbehaving, 292n27; mothers and, 76–77; parents and, 72–75, 88n5, 89n12, 138n1; play, 89n7; queer and transgender, 188–205 passim, 223–43 passim; rearing of, 156; socialization of, 79–80; stolen, 76, 84; transition to adulthood, 122; unbaptized, 54; Wilhelm Grimm's, 81, 89n10; wish for, 185, 189–205 passim

Children's and Household Tales (Grimm). *See Kinder- und Hausmärchen*

children's literature, 2, 8, 22n2; 145, 173–74, 176, 207, 227, 252, 253

chimeras, 264

Christianity, 31, 32, 148–49, 214, 215, 232, 260, 272n24, 274n33, 295–96, 297, 302n1

"Cinderella." *See* ATU 510A; KHM 21

cinema. *See* film

Cixous, Hélène, 45n14

class (social), 2, 28, 29, 31, 32, 56, 133, 164, 182, 186, 195, 197, 201, 202, 204n18, 226–27, 237, 282–83

"Clergyman's Nights, The" (ATU 1842C*), 204n20

"Clever Else." *See* ATU 1450

"Clever Gretel." *See* ATU 1741

cleverness. *See* tricksters, trickery

codes, coding, and decoding, 7, 14, 23, 33, 41, 42, 44n7, 47n25, 73, 76, 89n7, 203n11, 149, 262, 266; defi-

nition of, 88n6

coming out, 250, 255, 267, 270n12, 271n16

coming-out stories, 250, 255, 270n11

competition, 34, 44, 83, 99, 256

constative utterance, 52, 65, 66n4

contingency, contingent, 22, 248, 255, 259

contradiction, 22, 149, 154, 254, 265, 266

convents. *See* nuns

cooking and kitchens, 20, 29–30, 44n7, 67n12, 98, 100, 108–12, 116n13, 168, 186, 190, 201, 204n20, 285

cooks, 28–35, 42, 49, 54, 92ff., 98, 100, 116n13

corpses, 53, 122, 130, 132, 137, 138n4, 138n7, 208, 267

costume and disguise, 9, 16, 17, 20, 53, 63–64, 67n13, 91–118, esp. 117n15, 170, 207–21, 220, 223–43

counterhegemony. *See* hegemony and counterhegemony

counternormativity, 2, 33, 146, 147, 248ff., 257, 258, 274n34, 295, 297. *See also* normativity, homonormativity

courtship, 79; rituals, 60

crones, 126, 187. *See also* hags

cross-dressers, cross-dressing, 2, 5, 16, 99, 188, 227, 239; female to male, 227

cross-generational relationships. *See* intergenerational relationships

culture, Victorian, 172–73

curiosity, 3, 20, 40, 97, 121, 209, 211, 224, 245ff., 271n18, 271n19; sexual,

curiosity (*continued*)
268
curses, 73, 74, 75, 121, 143, 164, 228, 286, 287

daddy stories, 225
Daly, Mary, 272n23
dance, 2, 23n2, 30, 98, 99, 110, 112, 114, 141ff., 159n3, 196, 299
"Danced Out Shoes, The." *See* ATU 306
daughters, 37–38, 50ff., 72ff., 91–118, 143ff., 159n3, 166, 169, 173, 175, 189, 190, 191, 194, 223ff., 253, 256–57, 263, 300; of Eve, 277; ugly, 50
death, 6, 54, 75, 85, 159n2, 163–64, 204n14, 224, 236, 247, 251, 252, 264–68 passim, 281, 287, 289, 292n26, 296; by burning, 272n24; by dancing, 30, 155; desire for, 121–39 passim; -drive, 77–78, 252; fear of, 292n26; gruesome, 19; -likeness, 168; near-death, 281; of mother, 83; patriarchal power and, 211–21 passim; sentences, 76, 77, 233
debasement (social), 226, 230
deception, 219
decoding. *See* codes, coding, and decoding
defiance, 65, 157, 258, 271n16
Deleuze, Gilles, 227ff., 235ff.
Derrida, Jacques, 44n9
desire, 3ff., 30, 33, 34, 44n12, 78, 81, 86, 88n5, 103, 123ff., 144, 154, 158, 188, 217, 228, 237, 241, 242, 243n2, 246ff., 273n28, 274n34; aggressive, 240; autonomous, 259; carnal, erotic, or sexual, 91, 104, 124ff., 138n7, 139n8, 139n9, 165ff., 172, 248ff., 280; female or women's, 84, 158, 160n5, 185; fire or flames as metaphor for, 20, 260–64, 266, 268; forbidden, 197; heterosexual, 88n5, 165; homicidal, 73; inappropriate, 233; incestuous, 103, 110, 225, 233; infantile, 281; lesbian, 149, 262ff.; male, 213; narrative, 199; necrophiliac, 122; non-normative, 147ff., 265ff.; queer, 125, 249ff.; romantic, 74, 167; same-sex, 145; transgressive, 23n4, 31, 144ff., 258ff.
devil, the, 20, 46, 54, 57, 95, 103, 203n9, 210, 247ff., 272n25, 273n26, 277, 286, 288, 296–97, 301
devourer tales, 251
Diagnostic and Statistical Manual of Mental Disorders (American Psychiatric Association), 199
diaries, 172
dichotomies, 57, 169, 174, 198, 283; manifest/latent, 15; public/private, 186, 197; sex/gender, 16–17, 188; virgin/whore, 173. *See also* binaries and polarities
Dinshaw, Carolyn, 248, 255
direct speech, 89, 121, 221, 253, 254
disempowerment. *See* empowerment and disempowerment
disenchantment. *See* enchantment and disenchantment
disguise. *See* costume and disguise
disidentification, 14, 137; definition of, 139n10

disobedience. *See* obedience and disobedience

divine: figures, 210; intervention, 295, 297

diviners, 67

division of labor, by sex, 187

Doan, Laura, 145–47

dolls, 96, 124

domestic: arrangements, 296; art, 32; authority, 282; comfort, 260; competence, 75; duty, 40; femininity, 199; labor, 32, 194; partners, 297; peace, 267; servants, 98, 186; setting, space, or sphere, 116, 186, 194, 196, 283; tasks, 98; tool, 35

domesticity, 33, 42, 160, 163, 168, 187, 194; lack of, 174

Doniger, Wendy, 216, 217

"Donkeyskin." *See* ATU 510B

Donoghue, Emma, 3, 10, 27, 145, 151, 249, 271n13

Doty, Alexander, 10, 149, 150

Douglas, Mary, 273n31

drag, 142, 218, 238

drag queens, 297–302

dreams, 22, 122, 128, 133–34, 159, 235; logic, 231

dwarfs, 161, 163–65, 168, 169–70, 171, 174. *See also* ATU 709

"East of the Sun and West of the Moon" (ATU 425A), 182, 186

economic: freedom of women, 158; roles, 34; use of women, 39

economy, 33–34, 261; socio-, 295; world crisis, 47n27

emotion, 82, 254, 259, 266

emotional: demands, 255; disclosure, 51; experiences, 240; forces, 259; impressions, 88n2; intricacies and contradictions, 266; life, 61; longing, 268; love, 75, 172; punch, 207; reactions, 220; resources, 74; states, 254; status, 257; strength, 81; tensions, 249; ties, 78; vulnerability, 266

empowerment and disempowerment, 71, 75, 83, 223; female, 161–78; gender, 227; social, 226.

enchantment and disenchantment, 6, 72, 73, 84, 87, 196, 202, 248, 259

endings, happy. *See* happy endings

eroticism, 7, 8, 17, 64, 122, 123, 137, 200, 211, 262, 268; homo-, 263, 272n25; lesbian, 161–78. *See also* autoeroticism

escape, 19, 92, 95–96, 103, 105, 123, 130, 135ff., 143, 144, 149ff., 168, 170, 176, 186, 189, 195, 207ff., 225, 236, 251ff., 262, 266

ethnographers, 290n4

ethnography, 79, 290n4; xeno-, 284

exaggeration, of gender traits, 208, 211

excess, 4–5, 32, 33, 35, 126; of consumption, 233; of devotion, 77; of emotion, 78; of fatherly love, 86; of love, 86; of meaning, 148; of salt, 233; of transgression, 263

exchange and use of women, 39, 44n8, 83, 169, 187

exile, 52, 59, 61, 66n3, 73, 130, 224, 225, 233, 237, 242, 258

experience and inexperience, 7, 13, 55, 93, 102, 165, 167, 172, 200, 250, 268, 282, 297; affective, 240; authentic, 237; embodied, 66, 224,

femme fatale, 177

fertility and infertility, 57, 58, 167, 213, 237, 273

film, fairy-tale, 2, 22n2, 23n3, 145, 159, 160n5, 161, 170–71, 178n2, 182, 195, 204n23, 260; lesbian, 271n13

fire and flames, 21, 33, 109, 111, 163, 167, 201, 209, 245–74; as metaphor for desire or sexual ripening, 20, 260–64, 266, 268. See also burning

"Fitcher's Bird" (KHM 46). See ATU 311

flames. See fire and flames

flaming, in gay culture, 263; definition, 273n27

folktale types. See under ATU numbers

folktales, 16, 21, 33, 44, 70, 73, 80–81, 108, 175, 176, 181, 195, 197, 202, 203n3, 203n7, 205n25, 278, 282. See also fairy tales

food, 27–47, 185, 223–43, 268, 296; relationship to sex, 8, 17, 18

"Foolish Couple, The" (ATU 1430–1439), 47n26

Foucault, Michel, 257–58

Franklin, Sarah, 5

"Frau Trude" (KHM 43), 245–74. See also ATU 334

Freeman, Elizabeth, 6, 7

Freud, Sigmund, 22, 88n5, 185, 264, 273n30. See also Oedipus complex

friendships, 44; intimate, 19, 171–73

frogs, 2, 142, 151, 181, 184–85

frogskin, 96

fur, 91–118, 223–43

gaze, male, 20, 207, 217, 221n8; patriarchal, 219

gender; of pronouns in Grimm, 104–18 passim; benders and bending, 23, 92, 186; fluidity of, 238, 245. See also gender roles; performance, performativity

genderfuck, 5, 16, 187, 194; definition, 23n6, 203n11

gender identity, 5, 11, 194, 205n27, 237, 239, 283

gender identity disorder/dysphoria (GID), 199, 243n6

gender roles, 69, 79–80, 83, 187, 205n33, 214; normative, 208, 220; parody or subversion of, 146, 208, 211, 214, 218. See also performance, performativity

gender trouble, 238, 265

genitalia, 187, 205; male, 185, 240

genre. See fairy tales

giants, 128, 183, 190, 191, 194–96, 200, 202, 204n22, 210

girls, 233–43. See also tomboys

gluttony, 32–33

"Goosegirl, The" (ATU 533), 53, 215

"Goose Girl at the Spring, The," 18, 49–67

gossip, 15, 55, 66n7, 245, 256

gothic, the, 123, 132

grandfathers, 150

grandmothers, 2, 8, 9, 51, 52, 63, 95, 197, 246, 251; devil's, 253

"Grave Mound, The" (Mercer), 21, 250, 295–302. See also ATU 815 and ATU 1130

Grimm, Jacob and Wilhelm, 22, 79, 81, 83, 91, 93, 203n6; children (of Wilhelm), 81, 89n10; editorial practices of, 104, 252–53, 278–79. See also

indirect speech, 254

inexperience. *See* experience and inexperience

infanticide, 8, 76, 203n6

infantilization, 281

infertility. *See* fertility and infertility

ingenue characters, 16, 166, 186, 193

inheritance, 71, 74, 125, 133, 194, 198, 242; disinheritance, 224, 260; patriarchal, 124

initiations, 204n16, 211, 258, 270n12, 272n19; narratives of, 192

innocence, 9, 105, 125, 127, 129, 136, 165, 170, 175, 221n5, 256, 260–61, 268, 271n14, 272n25. *See also* experience and inexperience; innocent persecuted heroines

innocent persecuted heroines, 19, 53–54, 165, 177

interdictions, 20, 72, 183, 189, 190, 193, 200, 247, 257. *See also* prohibitions

intergenerational relationships, 21, 49–67, 246–47, 255ff., 271n14. *See also* parental authority and control

interpellation, 36, 37, 38, 41, 42, 45n20, 50, 139n10

interrogations, 252, 267

intersex, intersexuals, 5, 16, 93, 102, 199; definition, 205n29

intersubjectivity, 239

intertexts, intertextuality, 123, 132, 133, 135, 137, 152, 159n1, 246; definition, 138n3; tales, 124–31

intimate friendships, 19, 171–73

inversions: of fortune, plot, 51–52; of gender, 125

Irigaray, Luce, 34, 45n12

"Iron Stove, The," 182

irony, 27, 35ff., 160n7, 76, 278, 283

"Jack and the Beanstalk," 128, 205n26

Jack-Five-Oh (drama), 182

Jagose, Annamarie, 4, 10, 148, 271n15

jealousy, 6, 73, 269n2, 170, 200, 205n31, 230, 263, 273n28; of fathers, 142; rages of, 83; sexual, 269n2; of stepmother, 168, 196

jokes, 27–47

"Jorinda and Joringle" (ATU 405), 246, 269n3

jouissance, 9, 30, 254

"Juniper Tree, The" (ATU 720, KHM 47), 9, 44n7, 155

Kaffeter [literary salon], 270n10

Kaplan, David, 23

"Kate Crackernuts" 159n2, 182ff., 196–97, 200, 204n17, 205n25. *See also* ATU 306; ATU 709

KHM 3 (ATU 710), "Mary's Child," 209–10

KHM 9, "The Twelve Brothers," 70

KHM 21 (ATU 510A) "Cinderella," 33, 155

KHM 25, "The Seven Ravens," 70

KHM 43 (ATU 334), "Frau Trude"

KHM 46 (ATU 311), "Fitcher's Bird"

KHM 47 (ATU 720), "The Juniper Tree" 9, 44n7, 155

KHM 49, "The Six Swans," 70

KHM 53 (ATU 426), "Snow White and Rose Red," 30, 155, 161–78

KHM 133 (ATU 306), "The Worn-Out Dancing Shoes," 142, 243n7

killing. *See* murder

man-eating: monster, 264, sociopath, 267

marginality, marginalization, 4, 11, 18, 52, 173, 246, 255, 256, 265; men, 296; old women, 56, 173n31; women, 57

marriage, 6, 20, 51, 72ff., 92ff., 131, 134, 139n9, 141–60 passim, 161–78 passim, 184, 190, 193, 195, 201, 205n34, 208, 227–29, 248, 274n34; bad, 185; episode, 77; gay, 89n12; heterosexual, 70, 158, 208, 220; as measure of success, 63; same-sex, 297; women, 38–40, 42

Mary (the Virgin), 114, 210, 257, 272n19

Mary Magdalene, 264

"Mary's Child" (ATU 710, KHM 3), 209–10

Marzolph, Ulrich, 46n21, 278

masculinity, 34, 70, 164, 167, 198, 239; female, 188; hegemonic, 16; unnatural, 210

masochism, 125, 136; sadomasochism, 146

masquerade, 2, 6, 11, 181, 200, 216, 292n29

matriarchy, 158

Matrix, Sidney Eve, 23, 160n5

McBain, Ed, 174–75

McGann, PJ, 199

McGillis, Roderick, 4

memorials, 64

memory, 51, 52, 53, 65, 85, 115, 142, 153, 156, 230

Memory (song), 300

Mendelson, Michael, 156

menses, menstruation, 18, 127, 129, 165–66

mermaids, 142, 157

metanarrative, 123, 132–36, 153

metaphor, the metaphorical, 16–17, 50, 74, 108, 126, 133, 137, 164, 172, 174, 214, 220, 226ff., 248, 261, 267

metonymy, 9, 50, 58, 62, 248

midwifery, midwives, 18, 49–67 passim; etymology of word, 55; and wise women, 56–57

mimesis, 153

mirror images, 215

mirrors, 9, 200, 212, 213, 242

misdirection, 74, 219

misogyny, 46n21, 209, 217, 279, 283

modernity, 34, 260. *See also* postmodernity

"Molly Whuppie." *See* ATU 327B/328

monsters, 16, 128, 194, 210, 212, 264

Moore, Lisa, 172–73

Morrison, Jago, 146, 148–49

"Mother Holle" (ATU 480), 15, 67n12, 269n3

motherhood, 49–67 passim, 76, 139. *See also* stepmothers

mothers-in-law, 44n7

movies. *See* film

murder, 8, 9, 84, 128, 142, 175, 176, 186, 266, 203n6, 221n9, 252, 253, 266, 267; serial, 209, 218

murderousness, 87, 128, 220, 252, 272n24

muteness, 75, 85, 123, 126, 210, 217, 254. *See also* speech; voice (speaking)

mutilation, 8, 54, 75, 203n6, 212

"Mutsmag" or "Mutzmag." *See* ATU 327B/328

myth, mythology, demythologizing, 5, 15, 124, 215, 237, 251, 264

narratology, feminist, 150–51
"Necessity of Salt, The," 53–54
necromancy, 57
necrophilia, 19, 121–39 passim, 186, 217
negotiation, 34, 44n9, 169, 225
non-normativity. *See* counternormativity
normative categories, 11; femininity, 208, 211, 215; roles, 122
normativity, 2ff., 27, 41, 42, 122, 144, 146, 149, 208, 211, 215, 220, 234, 243n2, 248ff.; hetero-, 249. *See also* counternormativity, homonormativity
norms, 33, 42; behavioral, 263; gender and sexuality, 205, 258; heterosexist, 184; heterosexual, 13; kinship, 76; patriarchal, 279; social, 83, 227
nuns (and convents), 141, 156–59

obedience and disobedience, 10, 19, 31, 200, 208, 209–11, 253, 254, 258; Eve's 271n19. *See also* parental authority and control
oedipal: drama, 205n28; rivalry, 269n2
Oedipus complex, 88n5, 273n28
"Old Woman as Trouble Maker, The" (ATU 1353), 46n21
old women, 15, 18, 49–67 passim; 84, 93, 96, 98, 100, 102, 121, 189–91, 226, 246, 248, 255, 256, 265, 267, 273n26, 273n28, 273n31; queer, 246–47, 255ff., 271n14
1001 Nights, 44n11, 278, 281, 282

outcasts, outlaws, 52, 56, 246

Page, Ruth, 150
Palmer, Paulina, 145–47
parables, 29
paradigmatic, 15, 21
paradigms, 177; heteronormative, 234; social, 158
paradox, 84, 148–49
parental authority and control, 10, 20, 73, 75, 86, 144, 224–25, 229–32, 246–47, 253, 255, 256–58, 260–61, 268–69. *See also* obedience and disobedience
parody, 146, 208, 214, 218
passing (as another sex), 188, 224, 238, 241
passivity, 9, 16, 19, 21, 49, 51, 60, 62, 87, 104, 121–39, 168, 171, 186, 193, 195, 201, 271n14
patriarchs, patriarchy, 3, 9, 18, 22n2, 27–47 passim, 70, 83, 125, 128, 132ff., 143, 144, 155–58, 163, 165, 171, 177, 182, 187, 207–21 passim, 225, 227, 232, 236, 237, 264, 265, 277–93; authority and power, 208, 209, 212, 215, 236; family, 32; heteronormative, 35; heterosexual, 31; inheritance, 124; institutions, 76; tricking of, 220. *See also* heteropatriarchy
patrilocality, 63, 83; defined, 267n14
"Peau d'Asne" ["Donkeyskin"]. *See* ATU 510B
pedophilia, 22n2, 129
"Peg Bearskin," 181–205. *See also* ATU 327B/328; ATU 711; "La Poiluse"
penis, 166, 214, 264

stereotypes, 38, 41, 201, 204n20, 280, 283

"Stingy Hostess and the Inn, The" (ATU 1449*), 204n20

Stockton, Kathryn Bond, 228–29, 231–35

Stone, Kay F., 3, 83, 250, 255, 257

storytellers, 32, 45n19, 51, 54, 55, 148–50, 153, 160n6, 278, 279, 282, 290n1, 291n20, 293

"Strange Feast, The," 252–53

subalterns, 30, 33, 290n4

subservience, 76, 193, 208

succubus, 217

supernatural, the, 3, 95, 170, 205n24, 212, 259. See also wonder

survivors, 32, 208; of incest, 91, 93, 160n2

"Sweet Porridge, The" (ATU 565), 246, 269n3

symbolic, the, 243n2

symbolic order, 35, 42, 230

taboos, 7, 8, 16, 21, 86, 163, 172, 187, 211; against incest, 77, 91

tales: devourer, 251; feminine, 71; secular vs. religious sources, 261

tale types, 41. For specific tale types see under ATU numbers

tall tales, 29

tar-and-feathering, 219

tasks, impossible, 183, 191, 195–96

taste, tasting, 18, 30–32, 33, 190, 230, 231, 236, 266

Tatar, Maria, 2, 3, 8, 49, 83, 93, 196, 203n6, 209–10, 218, 225, 262, 270n7, 271n19, 273n28

"Tatterhood." See ATU 711

tears, 31, 36, 51, 61, 135, 230; changed into pearls, 50–51, 54. See also weeping

temporality, 7, 62–64, 132, 259, 268; definition, 6; and queerness, 6, 233–34. See also enchantment; magic

thieves, 208, 241

Thomas, Hayley, 155

Thompson, Stith, 70, 192, 211

Thousand and One Nights, A. See 1001 Nights

"Three Spinners, The" (ATU 501), 250, 269n3

Tiffin, Jessica, 6

time. See temporality; magic; enchantment

tomboys, 23n4, 171, 188, 194, 195, 197–99. See also girls

touch, touching, 210, 240, 248, 255, 262, 267

transbiology, 2, 3, 5–6, 11, 16–18, 70, 84–85, 213

transformation, 10, 22, 49–67 passim, 69–89 passim, 91–118, 161–78 passim, 181–205, 207–21, 223–43, 245–74 passim

transgender, 2, 3, 5, 11, 12, 16, 93, 94, 101–4, 149, 194, 199, 202, 237–39, 243n6; child, 227; defined, 188–89; imagination, 200; studies, 5; theory, 11, 16, 224

transgression, 10, 155, 165, 208, 209, 245–74; boundary, 226; sexual, 44n11

transsex, transsexuals, transsexuality, 5, 11, 16, 20, 93–94, 103, 149, 188–89, 192, 199–202, 205n30;